protects against climate-related disasters and hence against global warming—or cooling.'

"Perhaps the most intriguing part of the book is the description with examples of the corruption of the scientific method meant to silence anyone and everyone who questions the orthodoxy of the climate industrial complex. These authors are willing to question orthodoxy and follow the science where it leads."

—**Douglas W. Domenech,** former assistant secretary, U.S. Department of the Interior

"Between the extremes of hysterical alarmism and knee-jerk denial lie reasonable perspectives that rest on science, fact, and optimism. Those views are well represented in this accessible and much-needed anthology, superbly edited by Beisner and Legates. It deserves to be the indispensable handbook for anyone who is serious about the climate debate."

—**Lawrence W. Reed,** president emeritus, Foundation for Economic Education

"Characterized by an unprecedented degree of scientific dishonesty, bureaucratic empire-building, corporate pursuit of government favors, and media ignorance and biases, the public debate over climate policy has been dismal even by the shameful standards of Beltway discourse. This tidal wave of disinformation carries with it severely adverse implications not only for environmental and energy policies, but more broadly for the preservation of free speech, the pursuit of scientific understanding, the free enterprise system, and the constitutional institutions of American governance. That is why this book is supremely important. It offers clarity, rigor, and adherence to facts. It is a one-stop shop for those interested in cutting through the massive misinformation, malarkey, and mindlessness that are the essentials of the climate debate. Read it."

—**Benjamin Zycher,** senior fellow, American Enterprise Institute

"*Climate and Energy: The Case for Realism* presents a thorough and carefully documented assessment of critical issues related to the problem of human-induced climate change. It discusses scientific debate about the subject, proposed responses, and the likely impact of transforming the global energy infrastructure of continued reliance on traditional energy sources on human flourishing, especially on the poor. Written primarily for the layperson, it also includes in-depth treatment to satisfy subject experts. Although the authors are skeptical of the conventional wisdom about climate change, the book is balanced in its presentation of competing theoretical assertions and empirical estimates."

—**Tracy Miller,** senior research editor, Mercatus Center at George Mason University

"The aptly titled *Climate and Energy: The Case for Realism* is authored by exceptionally well-qualified climate scientists, economists, and professionals immersed in climate and energy analysis and policy. The intelligent perspective delivered in this book is sorely needed to clear today's climate change atmosphere polluted with too much scientism. *Climate and Energy* proposes a return to hard science and solid reasoning when addressing one of the defining issues of our time."

—**Anthony J. Sadar,** certified consulting meteorologist and adjunct associate professor of science at Geneva College, Beaver Falls, Pennsylvania

"I highly recommend this remarkable book. It could change the entire debate over climate change and energy policy. In these pages, scientific experts explain in nontechnical language why we need not fear man-made catastrophic global warming. I find this position consistent with a Judeo-Christian worldview which understands that God created a "very good" earth (Genesis 1:31), and that the Earth's abundant supplies of coal, oil, and natural gas are God's blessings to be used with thanksgiving and joy, not with guilt and fear."

—**Wayne Grudem,** Ph.D., Distinguished Research Professor of Theology and Biblical Studies, Phoenix Seminary

"In their compelling book, *Climate and Energy: The Case for Realism*, Beisner and Legates offer a comprehensive introduction to the multifaceted science of climate change. Their approach is both scholarly and accessible, providing an updated review of the literature and overflowing with relevant citations. Exceptionally readable for the intelligent layperson, this book is a beacon of clarity in an area that is often hopelessly politicized, empowering readers to engage constructively and knowledgeably with one of the most contentious issues of our time."

—**Jeffrey Haymond,** dean and professor of economics, Robert W. Plaster School of Business, Cedarville University

"*Climate and Energy: The Case for Realism* is a terrific book. The highly qualified authors of the chapters provide clear, factual information and expert analysis on the whole range of issues in the climate and energy debate. It is especially fitting that the editors have dedicated their book to one of the authors, the late Pat Michaels, my highly valued and much-missed former colleague at CEI."

—**Myron Ebell,** senior fellow, Center for Energy and Environment, Competitive Enterprise Institute

"*Climate and Energy* is a powerful book that should be considered mandatory reading for anybody in these fields. It sheds urgently needed light on important but little-known truths that, if more widely known, could save humanity from a great deal of pain. Mankind is being dangerously misled, and this book proves it masterfully. It is past time for the voices of common sense in this extraordinary book to be elevated above the propaganda being peddled by special interests."

—**Alex Newman,** president, Liberty Sentinel Media

"Lately, I have been lectured to 'follow the science.' So far a lot of doomsday catastrophes, without the doom burger or the side order of catastrophe. Editors Cal Beisner and David Legates and the thirteen other contributors to this volume have brought wisdom, common sense, and a reasoned understanding of the scientific models to help us understand the emotionally charged climate change science and agenda. They are clear and calm, helping me to remain clear and calm. The book is important, the authors are brilliant, and the writing is smart and accessible even for a solid C student like me. This is science I will follow."

—**Bill Arnold,** host, *Afternoons with Bill Arnold,* MyFaithRadio.com

"Dr. Cal Beisner is a long-time friend and my go-to source for sanity when it comes to 'climate change' and the radical environmentalism that is essentially becoming a national religion in America. His latest resource, *Climate and Energy: The Case for Realism* (edited alongside David Legates), will doubtless prove to be of great value for thoughtful, Bible-believing Christ-followers who desire to be well armed for debate on these critical issues."

—**Tony Perkins,** president, Family Research Council

"This book, featuring eminent scientists, provides extraordinary evidence that proposed attempts to eliminate global warming will be much more harmful to our liberty and prosperity than reasonably working through it and adapting. These are not science deniers. They are expert realists using excellent research, fair analysis, and scientific inquiry to come to truth. They will be shunned by the cottage industry of climate apocalypse, too often funded by foreign elements with an agenda. Anyone seeking truth over narrative should read this book. Science that cannot be questioned is not true science. It was Dr. Einstein who taught us to never stop asking questions. The authors of this book asked, and the true answers they found may surprise you."

—**Kevin D. Freeman,** host, *Economic War Room*, specialist in economic warfare and financial terrorism

"Few would disagree that climate change, its causes, and our policy responses to it are dominant issues of our times, and that trillions of dollars and the welfare of billions of people around the world are at stake. This book of essays, by experts for lay persons, discusses the science of greenhouse gases; the science and art of climate modeling; the climate change scenarios to the year 2100, reported since its inception by the Intergovernmental Panel on Climate Change; the different forms of energy that propelled economic development; and the critical role of rising energy density in economic development. All this lays the groundwork for policy recommendations. Adaptation, not mitigation, is the efficient and ethical public policy response to climate change. It is also the only realistic response in a world where two-thirds of the population have very different values and priorities from the rich, developed West. This book makes a strong case for the middle ground between denying climate change and catastrophizing it, the two options that sadly seem to be the only two available today. I highly recommend it."

—**Joseph Schaafsma**, professor emeritus, Department of Economics, University of Victoria, Victoria, British Columbia

"Is climate change an existential threat or a hoax? 'Code red for humanity' or a plot by the commies to overturn the global economic order? It's often hard to tell given the postmodern deconstruction of language through the use of drama-laden vocabulary that characterizes everyday meteorological phenomena as apocalyptic threats to civilization. Winter storms are now named similarly to hurricanes, and the large ones are no longer called blizzards but bomb cyclones. Cold air masses during the winter months in the northern tier of the U.S. are now the result of the polar vortex. Al Gore, the producer of *An Inconvenient Truth*, recently went on an unhinged rant at the World Economic Forum in Davos, Switzerland, warning about 'atmospheric rivers,' 'rain bombs,' 'boiling oceans,' and increasing atmospheric carbon dioxide trapping as much heat in the Earth's troposphere as '600,000 Hiroshima class bombs every day.'

"*Climate and Energy: The Case for Realism* provides a much-needed calm in this storm of hyperbolic rhetoric from the CAGW crowd. The authors—over a dozen experts in their respective fields—provide 'solid scientific, engineering, and economic reasons to think that human-induced climate change, while real, is extremely unlikely to become catastrophic and that adaptation rather than mitigation...will have better results for humanity and the rest of life on Earth.'

"Sixteen well-researched chapters, covering such topics as the history and politics of climate change, the science of climate, climate models, the role of the Sun, the oceans, greenhouse gases and the effects of human-induced warming, demonstrate that 'anthropogenic (human-induced) global warming/climate change, while real, is not now and will not become a crisis, a catastrophe, or—despite ill-informed claims to the contrary—an "existential threat" to human or planetary well-being; that its benefits to humanity and the rest of life on Earth could very well outweigh its costs; and that attempting to curb it by mandatory transition from fossil fuels to wind, solar, and other so-called green or renewable energy sources would do far more harm than good, not only to humanity but also to the ecosphere.'"

—**Gregory Rummo,** lecturer in chemistry, Palm Beach Atlantic University

"Timely and factual, *Climate and Energy* shows a way out of the quagmire of pseudoscience, excessive subsidies, regressive energy policies, et cetera that harm human flourishing due to the false narrative that climate change is an 'existential threat.'"

—**David E. Shormann,** Ph.D., owner, Digital Interactive Video Education, Kohola Flow Tech

"*Climate and Energy: The Case for Realism* is a treatise on the dominant issue of our time, efforts by wealthy nations to force a global transition from hydrocarbon to renewable energy, driven by the fear of human-caused global warming. Calvin Beisner and David Legates compiled sixteen chapters from world-leading scholars and scientists. The book thoroughly covers the IPCC and climate alarm, climate science, including solar, atmospheric, and oceanic factors, and climate modeling. Hydrocarbons and renewables are assessed, along with misguided directives from rich nations, as well as the energy needs of developing countries. *Climate and Energy* is essential reading for all who use energy in modern society."

—**Steve Goreham,** speaker, author, and executive director, Climate Science Coalition of America

"*Climate and Energy: The Case for Realism* is an excellent book. It provides real scientific information about the climate, energy, climate models, and the role of the Sun, oceans, and clouds in the Earth's climate, and how climate alarmism impacts economic factors at home and around the globe. If you want to understand these important issues, this is the book for you! It is well-written, informative, and fact-based."

—**George Landrith**, president, Frontiers of Freedom

"Beisner and Legates have put together an impressive set of essays about various questions related to the important public issue of climate change. Now more than ever we need wise and sound education and counsel on this issue, and *Climate and Energy* fits the bill. Everyone of all opinions needs to seriously consider the cogent arguments advanced in this book."

—**Shawn Ritenour**, professor of economics, Grove City College

"My mother in South Africa has no electricity for many hours every day; she experiences life in a low-energy state. Unfortunately, much of the ruling caste in the West has decided that energy poverty is necessary to 'save the planet.' I'm not sanguine about our prospects, because energy poverty means inevitable destruction of infrastructure essential to a successful modern civilization. This book presents a case for clear-eyed realism, a necessary antidote to the delusional green juggernaut driving current policy on climate and energy—driving us to oblivion. The war on reliable energy, and hence the pursuit of energy poverty for the masses, means that plebs in the West may soon begin to experience what is a normal day for my mother."

—**James A. Wanliss**, professor of engineering, Anderson University

"The last quarter century has made it clear that the public can't afford to assume that experts will arrive at the best solutions without any warping influence of institutions, prestige, and power. That has been true in international affairs, public health, and other areas. This book can help citizens understand the potential impact of various approaches to climate change without emotional displays, hysteria, and mockery. The stakes are high both for how we live and how we are governed. It is essential that we take the time to learn more about what climate change means, the extent to which it is happening, and how realists should approach it."

—**Hunter Baker,** J.D., Ph.D., provost, North Greenville University

"Two-handed experts tend to say '*on the one hand* x; *on the other hand* y.' Thinking through *x* and *y* requires homework of policy-makers. It's easier to follow the dictates of one-handed experts. Forsaking scientific integrity, one-handed experts often proclaim *x* and dismiss *y* in deference to a political agenda. Written by two-handed experts, *Climate and Energy* is a tour de force of why climate forecasting is anything but certain. Uncertainty among these authors isn't a function of ignorance; rather it is a function of great knowledge and humility. A must-read if you have the latter."

—**Gordon Wilson,** senior fellow of natural history, New Saint Andrews College

"This is a much-needed book at a time when only one side of the debate on energy and climate gets to make its case in nearly all sectors of the public square. Beisner and Legates have assembled an impressive array of experts in the relevant domains, including climate science, energy, economics, and policy. I highly recommend this timely book for anyone trying to make sense of these issues."

—**Guillermo Gonzalez,** Ph.D., astronomer, Tellus1 Scientific, LLC, co-author of *The Privileged Planet: How Our Place in the Cosmos Is Designed for Discovery*

Climate and Energy

Climate and Energy

The Case for Realism

EDITED BY

E. Calvin Beisner and David R. Legates

Regnery Publishing
WASHINGTON, D.C.

Cataloging-in-Publication data on file with the Library of Congress

ISBN: 978-1-68451-267-6
eISBN: 978-1-68451-395-6

Published in the United States by
Regnery Publishing
A Division of Salem Media Group
Washington, D.C.
www.Regnery.com

Manufactured in the United States of America

10 9 8 7 6 5 4 3 2 1

To Dr. Patrick Michaels,

a true climate warrior to the end, from whom we have learned much about climate and climate change… and about life in general.

"The spotless purity of truth must always be at war with the blackness of heresy and lies."

—Charles Spurgeon

ONTENTS

Contents

PREFACE

How Did This Book on Climate Change Come About?

BY E. CALVIN BEISNER

Over thirty years ago, while writing a book on the economics of population, resources, and the environment (Beisner 1990), I developed an interest in the science and economics of climate change and climate and energy policy. That interest grew as I served as managing editor of Julian L. Simon's monumental *The State of Humanity* (Simon 1995), a book of fifty-eight chapters by sixty authors (including eight Nobel Prize winners) examining long-term historical data on all kinds of measures of human and ecological well-being, including global climate change.

In the early 2000s, seeking to understand scientists' conflicting views of climate change, I read *Global Warming: The Complete Briefing* (Houghton 2004), by Sir John Houghton, who had long chaired the United Nations Intergovernmental Panel on Climate Change (IPCC), and major parts of the IPCC's first, second, and third Assessment Reports, as an able proponent of a view that came to be called catastrophic anthropogenic global warming. Seeking also to understand why some scientists rejected that view, I read several books written or edited by Patrick J. Michaels (Michaels 1992, 2000, 2004, 2005), a veteran meteorologist, highly published in the refereed literature. The last of these, *Shattered Consensus: The True State of Global Warming*, included contributions by ten other climate scientists or environmental economists specializing in climate policy, some of whom—along with Michaels himself—have become my friends and two of whom (David Legates and Willie Soon) contributed to this book, as did Michaels, who, to our sorrow, died shortly after writing his chapter.

In 2005, I started a think tank on environmental stewardship, of which I became president. It being the dominant environmental issue of our time, climate change naturally became a major focus. In the intervening years, I've read over sixty books and thousands of articles on the science of climate change and over thirty books and thousands of articles on the economics and engineering of climate and energy policy. My studies persuade me that

- anthropogenic global warming is real but unlikely to become catastrophic;
- it could, but won't necessarily, be moderated, prevented, or even reversed by a new natural cycle of global cooling, or augmented by a new warming cycle;
- the cost/benefit ratio of adapting to whatever future climate we face is better than that of mitigation, that is, trying to control global temperature by substituting wind, solar, and other renewable energy sources for the hydrocarbon fuels (also known as "fossil" fuels—coal, oil, and natural gas), whose abundance, affordability, and

reliability lifted much of mankind out of poverty and short lifespans over the past two centuries and are needed to lift the rest; and

- if we choose adaptation over mitigation, life after climate change will most likely be better than it is today or ever has been.

That is the perspective of this book, and it is reflected in a number of studies the think tank has published (Spencer, Driessen, and Beisner 2005; Beisner et al. 2006; Mitchell et al. 2009; Terrell 2011; Legates and van Kooten 2014).

The experts who wrote the chapters that follow did so with lay readers in mind—citizens just like you. And members of Congress, the president, governors and state legislators, mayors and city council members, high-ranking federal, state, and local agency regulators, and business leaders. Very few of these decision-makers are experts in the science of climate change or the science, engineering, and economics of climate and energy policy. Yet they must make decisions affecting how trillions—indeed, hundreds of trillions—of dollars will be spent on climate and energy policy, with profound effects on the lives of billions of people worldwide. This book is intended to help them, and you, come to well-informed, wise decisions.

Acknowledgments

Many people—far too many to name, including donors to our think tank (which receives no major support from corporations or foundations)—have encouraged us in this project. Thomas Spence, president and publisher of Regnery Publishing, embraced the idea and, with its wonderful production staff, including especially assistant editor Joshua Monnington and senior editor Elizabeth Kantor, shepherded the book through to publication. John R. Christy, Distinguished Professor of Atmospheric Science and director of the Earth System Science Center at the University of Alabama in Huntsville, deserves special thanks for updating some data and graphs for chapter 4 following author Patrick J. Michaels's death shortly after he submitted the chapter. All of the authors of course deserve thanks for taking time out of their academic and professional schedules to write for this book. David R. Legates, retired professor of climatology at the University of Delaware, was indispensable as co-editor. He also wrote two chapters. Kevin Murphy wrote the chapter summaries, which will help many non-specialists grasp the issues better. My wife, Deborah, deserves thanks for her patience for more than eighteen months when this project has dominated my attention; her support and encouragement have been invaluable.

References

Beisner, E. C. (1988). *Prosperity and Poverty: The Compassionate Use of Resources in a World of Scarcity*. Wheaton, Illinois: Crossway Books.

———. (1990). *Prospects for Growth: A Biblical View of Population, Resources, and the Future*. Wheaton, Illinois: Crossway Books.

Beisner, E. C., et al. (2006). *A Call to Truth, Prudence, and Protection of the Poor: An Evangelical Response to Global Warming*. Collierville, Tennessee: Cornwall Alliance for the Stewardship of Creation. Online at https://www.cornwallalliance.org/docs/a-call-to-truth-prudence-and-protection-of-the-poor.pdf.

Legates, D. R., and G. C. van Kooten (2014). *A Call to Truth, Prudence, and Protection of the Poor 2014: The Case against Harmful Climate Change Policies Gets Stronger*. Collierville, Tennessee: Cornwall Alliance for the Stewardship of Creation. Online at https://cornwallalliance.org/wp-content/uploads/2019/07/2014-Call-to-Truth-full.pdf.

Mitchell, C. V., et al. (2009). *A Renewed Call to Truth, Prudence, and Protection of the Poor: An Evangelical Examination of the Theology, Science, and Economics of Global Warming.* Collierville, Tennessee: Cornwall Alliance for the Stewardship of Creation. Online at https://www.cornwallalliance.org/docs/a-renewed-call-to-truth-prudence-and-protection-of-the-poor.pdf.

Simon, J., ed. (1995). *The State of Humanity.* Cambridge, Massachusetts: Blackwell.

Spencer, R. W., P. K. Driessen, and E. C. Beisner (2005). *An Examination of the Scientific, Ethical, and Theological Implications of Climate Change Policy.* Collierville, Tennessee: Cornwall Alliance for the Stewardship of Creation (previously named Interfaith Stewardship Alliance). Online at https://www.cornwallalliance.org/wp-content/uploads/2014/04/an-examination-of-the-scientific-ethical-and-theological-implications-of-climate-change-policy.pdf.

Terrell, T. D. (2011). *The Cost of Good Intentions: The Ethics and Economics of the War on Conventional Energy.* Collierville, Tennessee: Cornwall Alliance for the Stewardship of Creation. Online at https://cornwallalliance.org/wp-content/uploads/2019/07/Terrell-The-Cost-of-Good-Intentions.pdf.

Prologue

Why Don't You Learn of Climate Realism from Science Journals or Mainstream Media?

BY DAVID R. LEGATES

A central aim of climate alarmists is to control the narrative in published, refereed literature.

Climate and other scientific journals publish articles that adhere to what Johns Hopkins University climate scientist Patrick T. Brown calls "the mainstream narrative that climate change impacts are pervasive and catastrophic, and the primary way to deal with them is not through practical adaptation measures but through policies that reduce greenhouse gas emissions" (Brown 2023a). Then they issue press releases touting the latest science. The authors get recognition, the journal garners prestige in the popular press, and news outlets that report on it get credit for up-to-the-minute climate change news.

Conversely, most scientific journals shun articles that question the alarmist narrative. If a journal does publish one, alarmist scientists and their allies in the press often attack the paper and its authors with such vitriol that the journal retracts the paper or at least distances itself from it for fear of bad press.

The winner is the alarmist narrative—but not science.

I have seen this play out numerous times over the past twenty or more years, and it has happened to me on several occasions. Here are three examples:

Gianluca Alimonti et al. (2022) published an article in the *European Physical Journal Plus* entitled "A Critical Assessment of Extreme Events Trends in Times of Global Warming." *The Guardian* (Readfearn 2022, 2023) and Agence France-Presse (Lloyd Parry and Hood 2022) attacked the article, citing four scientists who were highly critical of the paper, including Professor Michael Mann and Stefan Rahmstorf of the Real Climate website.

Loud alarmist scientists raised their voices in protest . . . and the journal capitulated. On August 23, 2023—more than nineteen months after publication—the editors in chief retracted the article.

In 2003, we (Soon et al. 2003) published an article in *Climate Research* that argued that the Medieval Warm Period (MWP) and the Little Ice Age (LIA) had been identified in many regional studies, in contrast with Michael Mann and colleagues' famous Hockey Stick graph of global temperature that seemed to erase both the MWP and the LIA. *Climate Research* was a cutting-edge journal at the time.

After an outcry from alarmist scientists, the publisher and senior editor of *Climate Research* reviewed the process that led to the article's acceptance. The publisher stood behind the process and the article by concluding that the editor had "done a good and correct job as editor" and that the authors had addressed the reviewers' concerns appropriately (Costella 2010). He even admitted that the key assertions of the article "may be true," while citing "critics" who "point out" that some key assertions "cannot be concluded convincingly from the evidence provided in the paper" (Kinne 2003)—hardly a rebuttal or an obvious justification for saying a peer reviewed paper should not have been published. Soon and I even testified with Mann at a congressional hearing, where the process was scrutinized, our veracity was called into question, and we successfully defended ourselves (EPW 2004; EPA 2016).

In the summer of 2023, several of us (Connolly et al. 2023; Katata et al. 2023; Soon et al. 2023) published three papers related to urban heat island effect and the construction of surface air temperature time series. As before, scientists from the Real Climate website (Mann, Rahmstorf, and Gavin Schmidt) leveled complaints. They argued that the authors of the three papers were unqualified to write on climate change issues, that we had based our results on faulty assumptions and bad science, and that we were paid by fossil fuel money. The critics denigrated the authors' credentials and beliefs, and deployed ad hominem attacks on Soon. Connolly and Soon have provided an extensive rebuttal to these claims (CERES 2023a, 2023b).

But if there is an ongoing campaign to discredit research that disagrees with the alarmist narrative, does a concomitant effort exist to bias research in favor of the alarmist narrative so that the paper has a better chance of being published? Many scientists have suspected this for some time. Indeed, Stanford's John Ioannidis demonstrated, in a famous paper, "Why Most Published Research Findings Are False," that "for many current scientific fields, claimed research findings may often be simply accurate measures of the prevailing bias"; that scientists "may be prejudiced purely because of their belief in a scientific theory or commitment to their own findings"; that "[m]any otherwise seemingly independent, university-based studies may be conducted for no other reason than to give . . . researchers qualifications for promotion or tenure"; and that "[p]restigious investigators may suppress via the peer review process the appearance and dissemination of findings that refute their findings, thus condemning their field to perpetuate false dogma" (Ioannidis 2005).

These problems have troubled climate science for decades. Now, they have become more obvious.

Just before this book went to press, Brown—quoted above—and co-authors published a paper offering evidence that "Climate warming increases extreme daily wildfire growth risk in California" in the prestigious journal *Nature* (Brown et al. 2023). Several media outlets including NPR and the *Los Angeles Times* (Borunda 2023; Wigglesworth 2023) touted the findings.

Afterward, however, Brown published on his blog "The Not-so-Secret Formula for Publishing a High-Profile Climate Change Research Paper" (Brown 2023a), a version of which then appeared in the Free Press as "I Left Out the Full Truth to Get My Climate Change Paper Published" (Brown, 2023b). This ignited a firestorm. Within two weeks, a Google search for the latter title yielded ~4,900 results.

In their *Nature* paper, Brown et al. (2023) conclude, "Overall, our results indicate that anthropogenic warming . . . increases the risk of extreme daily wildfire growth in California" and "temperature is the variable . . . that is the most directly related to increasing greenhouse gas concentrations." National outlets praised the article in their daily postings, citing specific events such as "warming substantially increased the extreme growth risk of several lightning-sparked complex fires in 2020" (Wigglesworth 2023). Thus, the article melded in with the myriad of other articles that argue extreme events are directly attributable to global warming due to increasing greenhouse gas concentrations.

About a week after *Nature* published the article online, Brown published the following qualification in a blog post entitled "I Left Out the Full Truth to Get My Climate Change Paper Published" (Brown 2023b). He wrote,

> I just got published in *Nature* because I stuck to a narrative I knew the editors would like. That's not the way

> science should work. I am a climate scientist. And while climate change *is* an important factor affecting wildfires over many parts of the world, it isn't close to the only factor that deserves our sole focus. So why does the press focus so intently on climate change as the root cause? Perhaps for the same reasons I just did in an academic paper about wildfires in *Nature*, one of the world's most prestigious journals: it fits a simple storyline that rewards the person telling it. The paper . . . focuses exclusively on how climate change has affected extreme wildfire behavior. I knew *not* to try to quantify key aspects other than climate change in my research because it would dilute the story that prestigious journals like *Nature* and its rival, *Science*, want to tell. [Emphases original]

Note that Brown did not say he and his colleagues lied about what they wrote. They didn't. But he states that they made sure the conclusion of their paper fit with the alarmist narrative by limiting the focus to just climate change and ignoring all other important variables (such as poor forest management) so as not to dilute the climate change message. Brown (2023b) concludes,

> [T]he editors of these journals have made it abundantly clear, both by what they publish and what they reject, that they want climate papers that support certain preapproved narratives—even when those narratives come at the expense of broader knowledge for society. To put it bluntly, climate science has become less about understanding the complexities of the world and more about serving as a kind of Cassandra, urgently warning the public about the dangers of climate change. It distorts a great deal of climate science

> research, misinforms the public, and, most importantly, makes practical solutions more difficult to achieve.

In response to this revelation by Brown, the editor in chief of *Nature* responded that "when it comes to science, *Nature* does not have a preferred narrative" (Woolfolk 2023). As a result, she added, "[W]e are now carefully considering the implications of his stated actions" as "they reflect poor research practices and are not in line with the standards we set for our journal." She also noted that peer review concluded that Brown and his colleagues had ignored other important variables but they had "argued against including" them nonetheless. Brown has disputed this assertion on social media (Woolfolk 2023).

A number of scientists have told me over the years that they have had to include the influence of climate change in their research or to overstate its importance to obtain funding or to secure publication. However, it is impossible to prove that Brown's paper would not have been accepted had issues other than climate change been included. Although he claims the decision to slant the paper to favor publication by *Nature* was his alone, some of his colleagues have distanced themselves from Brown's actions, although they have not suggested that the paper was biased (Woolfolk 2023). They stand behind the methodology and conclusions of the paper—and they must since their names are on it—but distance themselves from Brown's criticism of journals like *Nature*. Brown's home institution, San Jose State University, summarized the situation among the seven co-authors of the paper: "[T]he study's lead author expressed his opinion about the peer review process, which has no impact on the validity of the work" (Woolfolk 2023).

As I write this (October 2, 2023), the article remains published, and no retractions or notes exist on the *Nature* website. Brown, meanwhile, left San Jose State in 2022 and now works for the Breakthrough Institute. This change of employer "gave him freedom to critique the academic system and its publish-or-perish incentives that he says undermine sound science" (Woolfolk 2023). The academic system has long been intolerant of those who express dissenting views of the climate change alarmist narrative (see Vrielink et al. 2011; Legates 2016).

It would seem that, rather than base decisions on defensible science, many journals—including some of the most prestigious—select articles based largely on their support of the alarmist narrative. As a *Wall Street Journal* editor put it in commenting on Brown's revelations, "Scientific journals and preprint servers aren't selective about research quality. They're selective about the conclusions. If experts want to know why so many Americans don't trust 'science,' they have their answer. Too many scientists no longer care about science" (Finley 2023).

Climate science is truly in a perilous situation. We hope this book will contribute to its recovery.

References

Alimonti, G., et al. (2022). "A Critical Assessment of Extreme Events Trends in Times of Global Warming." *European Physical Journal Plus* 137, no. 112 (January). Online at https://link.springer.com/article/10.1140/epjp/s13360-021-02243-9. Paper retracted on August 23, 2023.

Borunda, A. (2023). "Climate Change Makes Wildfires in California More Explosive." NPR, August 30. Online at https://www.npr.org/2023/08/30/1196637141/climate-change-makes-wildfires-in-california-more-explosive.

Brown, P. T. (2023a). "The Not-So-Secret Formula for Publishing a High-Profile Climate Change Research Paper." Patrick T. Brown, PhD (blog), September 5. Online at https://patricktbrown.org/2023/09/05/the-not-so-secret-formula-for-publishing-a-high-profile-climate-change-research-paper.

———. (2023b). "I Left Out the Full Truth to Get My Climate Change Paper Published." The Free Press, September 5. Online at https://www.thefp.com/p/i-overhyped-climate-change-to-get-published.

Brown, P. T., et al. (2023). "Climate Warming Increases Extreme Daily Wildfire Growth Risk in California." *Nature* 621 (August): 760–66. Online at https://doi.org/10.1038/s41586-023-06444-3.

CERES (Center for Environmental Research and Earth Sciences) (2023a). "Reply to Erroneous Claims by RealClimate.org on Our Research into the Sun's Role in Climate Change." CERES-Science, September 8. Online at https://www.ceres-science.com/post/reply-to-erroneous-claims-by-realclimate-org-on-our-research-into-the-sun-s-role-in-climate-change.

———. (2023b). "The Orchestrated Disinformation Campaign by RealClimate.org to Falsely Discredit and Censor Our Work." CERES-Science, September 18. Online at https://www.ceres-science.com/post/the-orchestrated-disinformation-campaign-by-realclimate-org-to-falsely-discredit-and-censor-our-work.

Connolly, R. et al. (2023a). "Challenges in the Detection and Attribution of Northern Hemisphere Surface Air Temperature Trends since 1850." *Research in Astronomy and Astrophysics* 23, no. 10 (September), in press. Online at https://iopscience.iop.org/article/10.1088/1674-4527/acf18e.

Costella, J., ed. (2010). *The Climategate Emails.* Victoria, Australia: The Lavoisier Group.

EPA (2016). *EPA's Response to the Petitions to Reconsider the Endangerment and Cause or Contribute Findings for Greenhouse Gases under Section 202(a) of the Clean Air Act.* Vol. 3. *Process Issues Raised by Petitioners* (Washington, D.C.: U.S. Environmental Protection Agency). 48–50. Online at https://www.epa.gov/sites/default/files/2016-08/documents/response-volume3.pdf.

EPW (U.S. Senate Environment and Public Works Committee) (2004). *Climate History and the Science Underlying Fate, Transport, and Health Effects of Mercury Emissions.* Washington, D.C.: U.S. Government Printing Office. Online at https://www.govinfo.gov/content/pkg/CHRG-108shrg92381/pdf/CHRG-108shrg92381.pdf.

Finley, A. (2023). "How 'Preapproved Narratives' Corrupt Science." *Wall Street Journal*, October 1. Online at https://www.wsj.com/articles/how-preapproved-narratives-corrupt-science-false-studies-covid-climate-change-5bee0844.

Ioannidis, J. P. A. (2005). "Why Most Published Research Findings Are False." *PLOS Medicine* 2, no. 8 (August): e124. Online at https://doi.org/10.1371/journal.pmed.0020124.

Katata, G., R. Connolly, and P. O'Neill (2023). "Evidence of Urban Blending in Homogenized Temperature Records in Japan and in the United States: Implications for the Reliability of Global Land Surface Air Temperature Data." *Journal of Applied Meteorology and Climatology* 62, no. 8 (August): 1095–1114. Online at https://doi.org/10.1175/JAMC-D-22-0122.1.

Kinne, O. (2003). "Climate Research: An Article Unleashed Worldwide Storms." *Climate Research* 24 (September): 197–98.

Legates, D. R. (2016). "The University vs. Academic Freedom." *Academic Questions* 29, no. 1 (February): 15–23. Online at https://www.nas.org/academic-questions/29/1/the_university_vs._academic_freedom/pdf.

Lloyd Parry, R., and Marlowe Hood (2022). "Posts Downplaying Climate 'Emergency' Cite Paper with Cherry-Picked Evidence." AFP Fact Check, September 27. Online at https://factcheck.afp.com/doc.afp.com.32K66UE-1.

Readfearn, G. (2022). "Sky and the Australian Find 'No Evidence' of a Climate Emergency—They Weren't Looking Hard Enough." *The Guardian*, September 21. Online at https://www.theguardian.com/environment/2022/sep/22/sky-and-the-australian-find-no-evidence-of-a-climate-emergency-they-werent-looking-hard-enough.

———. (2023). "Scientific Journal Retracts Article That Claimed No Evidence of Climate Crisis." *The Guardian*, August 25. Online at https://www.theguardian.com/environment/2023/aug/26/scientific-journal-retracts-article-that-claimed-no-evidence-of-climate-crisis.

Soon, W., et al. (2003). "Reconstructing Climatic and Environmental Changes of the Past 1000 Years: A Reappraisal." *Energy & Environment* 14, no. 2–3 (May): 233–96.

Soon, W., et al. (2023). "The Detection and Attribution of Northern Hemisphere Land Surface Warming (1850–2018) In Terms of Human and Natural Factors: Challenges of Inadequate Data." *Climate* 11, no. 9 (August): 179. Online at https://doi.org/10.3390/cli11090179.

Vrielink, J., et al. (2011). "Academic Freedom as a Fundamental Right." *Procedia—Social and Behavioral Sciences* 13 (December): 117–41.

Wigglesworth, A. (2023). "Climate Change Boosts Risk of Explosive Wildfire Growth in California by 25%, Study Says." *Los Angeles Times*, September 4. Online at https://www.latimes.com/california/story/2023-09-04/climate-change-boosts-california-wildfire-risk-by-25.

Woolfolk, J. (2023). "Scientist Says He 'Left Out the Full Truth' to Get Climate Change Wildfire Study Published in Journal." Phys.org, September 11. Online at https://phys.org/news/2023-09-scientist-left-full-truth-climate.html.

CHAPTER 1

Introduction
Life after Climate Change—Better Than Before

BY E. CALVIN BEISNER

CHAPTER SUMMARY

Between the extreme opinions of climate change—from viewing it as an existential threat to considering it a hoax—there is a broad spectrum of views about its causes and consequences and how to respond. This book discusses key facets of this global controversy to provide a basis on which to develop well-reasoned climate policy in the interest of human welfare in a well-stewarded natural world.

This book reviews the evidence that human-induced climate change is real but not catastrophic. Progress in human welfare is evident in the tremendous strides to conquer poverty over the last two centuries, with more remaining to be done. While climate change poses no existential threat to humanity, ill-informed climate policy does threaten economic systems and hence human welfare. Further progress will be slowed or reversed if societies are deprived of access to abundant, affordable, reliable energy sources. Instead, economic development can fund the adaptation measures that protect against climate-related effects. Those will have better results than ineffective and self-defeating efforts to suppress greenhouse gas emissions to mitigate climate change.

Climate change is an existential threat. A crisis. "Code red for humanity," to quote the United Nations secretary general (IPCC 2021). Everyone knows it. Everyone who knows anything, anyway. Some people disagree. But they needn't be engaged. They can be written off, instead, as a lunatic fringe, "global warming denialists," "climate deniers," "science deniers." After all, one of them titled a book on climate change *The Greatest Hoax*. Obviously that's nonsense.

Climate change is a hoax. Not happening. Only Commies say it is, and they're using it as a rationale to overturn the global economic order. After all, "...we redistribute de facto the world's wealth by climate policy," to quote former Intergovernmental Panel on Climate Change (IPCC) co-chair Ottmar Edenhofer (Pötter 2010), and the task of the Paris climate summit was to "transform the economic development model for the first time in human history," to quote Christiana Figueres, former executive secretary of the United Nations Framework Convention on Climate Change (Marijnissen and Zaccheo 2016).

Between those two ends of the spectrum, there are all kinds of views about the causes, pace, magnitude, and consequences of climate change, now and into the distant future, and how, if at all, people should respond to it. Danish statistician and environmentalist Bjørn Lomborg, for instance, thinks life after climate change will be "better than you think" (Lomborg 2023). That, of course, could mean it will be much worse than it is today, but not as much as you think. Or it could mean it will be much better than it is today.

This book will help you navigate the troubled waters of this global controversy to reach a well-reasoned conclusion.

It's easy to mistake where people stand, especially when caricature abounds. All who question "catastrophic anthropogenic global warming," according to RationalWiki (whose articles often fall well short of exclusively rational—and RationalWiki is not associated with Wikipedia [Wikipedia n.d.]), are "global warming denialists," and indeed the very phrase, or its initials (CAGW), is a "snarl word" (RationalWiki n.d.a), "a derogatory label that can be attached to something (or even to people), in order to dismiss their importance or worth, without guilt" (Rational Wiki n.d.b). Hmmm. Are *global warming denialism*, *denial*, *denier*, and *denialist*—terms RationalWiki uses seventy-six out of the eighty times it uses any word starting with *deni-* in its article on "Climate Change" (excluding its list of references)—"snarl words"?

I'm not picking low-hanging fruit. RationalWiki isn't alone in using such terms. Google searches on May 18, 2023, found

1. 8,220 uses of "climate change denialist";
2. 8,350 uses of "global warming denialism," including an article published by one of the world's foremost academic publishing houses, "Addressing Global Warming Denialism" (Rotman 2020);
3. 73,600 uses of "climate denialism";
4. 41,600 uses of "climate change denialism";
5. 464,000 uses of "climate change deniers"; and so on for variations on the theme.

Ironically, sometimes skeptics of CAGW who affirm both that the world has warmed significantly over the past 150 years and that human activity has contributed significantly to the warming shoot themselves in the foot. Thus U.S. Senator James Inhofe (R-OK) allowed his book to be titled *The Greatest Hoax* (Inhofe 2012), making it the perfect target for ridicule. Yet its introduction begins, "Since July 2003, when I stood alone on the Senate floor and declared that man-made *catastrophic* [emphasis mine] global warming was the greatest hoax ever perpetrated on the American people. . . ." Inhofe didn't deny that the world had warmed or was still warming. He didn't deny that human action could have contributed to it. What he denied was that it was catastrophic.

Reasonable People Do Question CAGW

Granted such epithets for those who question CAGW (but almost without exception acknowledge AGW), many people would be surprised to learn that in 1998 over one hundred scientists signed "The Leipzig Declaration on Global Climate Change" saying that "the dire predictions of a future warming have not been validated by the historic climate record, which appears to be dominated by natural fluctuations, showing both warming and cooling" and rejecting the view that "envisages climate catastrophes and calls for hasty actions" (Singer 1998). They would also be surprised to learn of the publication, a decade later, of Lawrence Solomon's *The Deniers: The World-Renowned Scientists Who Stood Up against Global Warming Hysteria, Political Persecution, and Fraud*, which told the stories of twenty-four eminent scientists who affirmed AGW but rejected CAGW (Solomon 2008). Or that over thirty-one thousand American scientists—including over nine thousand with Ph.D.s, including a former president of the U.S. National Academy of Sciences—signed a statement saying,

> There is no convincing scientific evidence that human release of carbon dioxide, methane, or other greenhouse gases is

> causing or will, in the foreseeable future, cause catastrophic heating of the Earth's atmosphere and disruption of the Earth's climate. Moreover, there is substantial scientific evidence that increases in atmospheric carbon dioxide produce many beneficial effects upon the natural plant and animal environments of the Earth. (GWPP [1998] 2007)

The chapters that follow should set aside such oversimplifications, indeed mischaracterizations, of why anyone might oppose action on climate change. Written by nine climate scientists (David R. Legates, Roy W. Spencer, Patrick J. Michaels [with final edits, after his death, by John R. Christy], Michael Connolly, Ronan Connolly, Willie Wei-Hock Soon, Anthony Lupo, Nicola Scafetta, and Vijay Jayaraj), two energy scientists/engineers (Robert A. Hefner and Bill Peacock), and two environmental and energy economists (Timothy Terrell and G. Cornelis van Kooten), these chapters offer comprehensive scientific, engineering, and economic reasons to "oppose [some] action on climate change." No honest reader can write them off as "climate change deniers," let alone "climate deniers" or "science deniers." They present powerful evidence that anthropogenic (human-induced) global warming/climate change, while real, is not now and will not become a crisis, a catastrophe, or—despite ill-informed claims to the contrary—an "existential threat" to human or planetary well-being; that its benefits to humanity and the rest of life on Earth could very well outweigh its costs; and that attempting to curb it by mandatory transition from fossil fuels to wind, solar, and other so-called "green" or "renewable" energy sources would do far more harm than good not only to humanity but also to the ecosphere.

Indeed, that transition would slow, stop, or reverse the conquest of poverty and the high rates of disease and premature death that invariably accompany it for billions of people around the world and would force back into poverty hundreds of millions to billions more who have achieved prosperity and the health and longevity that accompany it by depriving them of the abundant, affordable, reliable energy indispensable to lifting and keeping any whole society out of poverty.

Better Than Today—Really?

One more point to develop: I said above that life after climate change will be better than today (unless we largely abandon fossil fuels to pursue mitigation rather than adaptation). Why? Because poverty is a far greater risk to human health and life than anything related to climate and weather. Our ancestors before the Industrial Revolution, who lived on the purchasing power equivalent of perhaps a dollar a day, could do very little to protect themselves from severe cold, heat, drought, flooding, hurricanes, tornadoes, or any other extreme weather or its consequences—like wildfires. If the purchasing power of your income isn't many times better than that, you can't thrive in the greatest tropical paradise. No wonder, then, that average life expectancy at birth before the Industrial Revolution was about twenty-seven years, and nearly half the children born died before their fifth birthdays. But if you have purchasing power equivalent to that of the bottom quintile of Americans, you can thrive in any climate from the Arctic Circle to the Sahara Desert to the Brazilian rainforest. You can build structures to protect yourself from extreme weather, you can predict when it's coming, or, in the case of very fast-developing things like tornadoes, at least give enough warning for people to take shelter. You can build flood control channels, water-storage systems, aqueducts, canals, irrigation systems, and so on, to protect against floods and droughts. No wonder, then, that the average number of human deaths per year from extreme weather events has fallen by over 98 percent in the last hundred years (Lomborg 2021). Put simply, prosperity protects against climate-related disasters and hence against global warming—or cooling.

Now, what will climate change do to the world's economy? Will it make our descendants poorer than we are, leaving them more vulnerable to climate-related disasters?

William D. Nordhaus, who in 2018 won the Nobel Prize in economics, integrated climate and economic models to project GDP per capita under various IPCC scenarios of climate change (Nordhaus 2018). Statistician Bjørn Lomborg showed that Nordhaus's data entailed that, with no damage from climate change, global GDP per capita, in constant purchasing-power-parity dollars, would likely rise from about $15,000 in 2019 to 4.73 times as much, over $71,000, in 2100. With damage from the most likely scenario of climate change, GDP per capita would multiply 4.56 times instead of 4.73 times. The loss from climate change damage? Just 3.9 percent—and not 3.9 percent of today's GDP, but of a GDP nearly 5 times higher than today's.

Are Nordhaus and Lomborg's calculations overly optimistic? Not likely. Indeed, they're probably overly pessimistic.

G. Cornelis van Kooten documents in chapter 15 that, according to the IPCC, global per capita purchasing power in 2100 is projected to be *at least* two and a half times what it was in 2005. That's the *worst* of five GDP per capita scenarios (SSP3), according to the IPCC, and it's unlikely, because it assumes population grows to 12.8 billion (which is highly unlikely; see Kurtz 2005; Last 2014; Callegari and Stokes, 2023) and the world fails to adopt low-carbon energy technologies, leading to the second-highest carbon dioxide levels (and hence second-highest global warming and second-highest harms from the warming). In the *best* of the five GDP per capita scenarios (SSP5), global per capita purchasing power in 2100 is projected to be sixteen times what it was in 2005, but that, too, is unlikely, because while it reasonably assumes population grows to 8.6 billion in 2050 and declines to 7.4 billion in 2100 (which is fairly likely, per the sources last cited), it also unreasonably assumes, as van Kooten puts it, "absurdly large increases [in income] accompanied by high energy requirements and CO_2 emissions." IPCC's first, second, and fourth scenarios are all more likely than either the first or fifth; in them, global per capita purchasing power in 2100 is approximately nine, seven, or four times what it was in 2005.

What this means, so far, is that the average person at the end of this century will almost certainly have at least four times the purchasing power of the average person in 2005, and quite possibly seven to nine times. But that's not all. Growth in purchasing power will happen faster in less developed countries than in highly developed countries. As van Kooten continues, "[T]he poor get richer faster than the rich. In the worst scenario, SSP3, the average *real* incomes of Middle East and African countries are assumed to increase nearly fourfold by 2100; under SSP5, it rises to almost 33 times current income." One study projects that Africa will produce about 130 times as much in 2100 as it did in 2020; Asia, about 16 times; Oceania, about 10 times; North, South, and Central America, about 6 times; and Europe, about 5 times (Hooke and Alati 2022). In none of those regions is population likely even to double, but if it did, in each, the average African would still be producing 67 times as much as in 2020; the average Asian, 8 times; Oceanian, 5 times; North, South, or Central American, almost 4 times; and European, 2 times.

The implications are stark for the question "Will life be better or worse after climate change?" There is no reason to think it will be worse. Climate change might make it a *little bit less better*, but it won't make it worse. Instead, life will be better, much better, after climate change than before it.

These are bold claims. Skeptical? Read on.

What's Ahead in This Book

The following fifteen chapters will provide solid scientific, engineering, and economic reasons to think that human-induced climate change, while real, is extremely unlikely to become catastrophic and that adaptation rather than mitigation (trying to control global temperature) will have better results for humanity and the rest of life on Earth.

Chapter 2 traces the history and politics of the climate change movement. In chapters 3–10, nine climate scientists explain how Earth's climate works (chapter 3), how climate scientists seek to model Earth's climate to anticipate future climate change (chapter 4), and the roles of the Sun (chapter 5), oceans (chapter 6), evaporation, precipitation, and clouds (chapter 7), and greenhouse gases (chapter 8) in shaping Earth's climate. Chapter 9 examines the "holy grail" of climate change: how much global-average temperature is likely to rise in response to our additions of carbon dioxide and other greenhouse gases, and chapter 10 describes the likely effects of warming.

In chapters 11–16, five scholars in the engineering and economics of energy, two with expertise also in climate science, explain why and how human thriving depends on abundant, affordable, reliable energy and what are the best sources of that energy (chapters 11, 12, and 13); the costs and benefits of energy options (chapters 12 and 15); how economics can contribute to the development of sound climate and energy policy (chapter 16); and how and why the rush to transition from fossil fuels to wind, solar, and other renewable energy sources threatens to stall or reverse the conquest of poverty in the less developed world and even push hundreds of millions of people in the more developed world back into poverty—with consequences far more dire than those of climate change itself (chapter 16).

The book concludes with an appendix, "Climate Papers You Should Read," by David R. Legates, which lists and summarizes forty-four important peer reviewed papers, published from 1896 through 2023, that are crucial contributions to our understanding of climate change.

References

Alper, B. A. (2022). *How Religion Intersects with Americans' Views on the Environment*. Washington, D.C.: Pew Research Center. Online at https://www.pewresearch.org/religion/wp-content/uploads/sites/7/2022/11/PF_2022.11.17_climate-religion_REPORT.pdf.

Bean, L., and S. Teles (2015). *Spreading the Gospel of Climate Change: An Evangelical Battleground*. Washington, D.C.: New American. Online at https://static.newamerica.org/attachments/11649-spreading-the-gospel-of-climate-change/climate_care11.9.4f0142a50aa24a2ba65020f7929f6fd7.pdf.

Beisner, E. C. (2014). *Evangelical Environmentalism: Bought and Paid For by Liberal Million$$$?* Collierville, Tennessee: Cornwall Alliance for the Stewardship of Creation. Online at https://www.cornwallalliance.org/wp-content/uploads/2014/10/Beisner-Evangelical-Environmentalism-Bought-and-Paid-for-web-version-near-final.pdf.

Callegari, B., and P. E. Stokes. (2023). *People and Planet: 21st-Century Sustainable Population Scenarios and Possible Living Standards within Planetary Boundaries*. Earth4All. Version 1.0. Online at https://earth4all.life/wp-content/uploads/2023/04/E4A_People-and-Planet_Report.pdf.

Cornwall Alliance (2015). "An Open Letter to Pope Francis on Climate Change." April 27. Online at https://cornwallalliance.org/2015/04/an-open-letter-to-pope-francis-on-climate-change.

GWPP (1998, 2007). Global Warming Petition Project. Online at http://www.petitionproject.org/index.php.

Hooke, A., and L. Alati (2022). "What Will the World Economy Look Like in 2100?" *UBSS Scholarship Series*, no. 3. July 22. Online at https://www.ubss.edu.au/articles/2022/july/what-will-the-world-economy-look-like-in-2100.

Houghton, J. (2004). *Global Warming: The Complete Briefing*. 3rd ed. Cambridge, United Kingdom: Cambridge University Press.

ICES (2000). "The Cornwall Declaration on Environmental Stewardship." Interfaith Stewardship Council. Online at https://cornwallalliance.org/landmark-documents/the-cornwall-declaration-on-environmental-stewardship.

Inhofe, J. (2012). *The Greatest Hoax: How the Global Warming Conspiracy Threatens Your Future*. Washington, D.C.: WND Books.

IPCC (2021). "IPCC Report: 'Code Red' for Human Driven Global Warming, Warns UN Chief." August 9. Online at https://news.un.org/en/story/2021/08/1097362.

Kurtz, S. (2005). "Demographics and the Culture War: The Implications of Population Decline." The Hoover Institution, February 1. Online at https://www.hoover.org/research/demographics-and-culture-war.

Last, J. V. (2014). *What to Expect When No One's Expecting: America's Coming Demographic Disaster*. New York: Encounter Books.

Lomborg, B. (2019). "Here is the graph from the model of Nobel Nordhaus. . . . ," Twitter, August 3, 8:55 p.m. Online at https://twitter.com/BjornLomborg/status/1157636110618648576.

———. (2020). *False Alarm: How Climate Change Panic Costs Us Trillions, Hurts the Poor, and Fails to Fix the Planet*. New York: Basic Books.

———. (2021). "We're Safer from Climate Disasters Than Ever Before." *Wall Street Journal*, November 3. Online at https://www

.wsj.com/articles/climate-activists-disasters-fire-storms-deaths-change-cop26-glasgow-global-warming-11635973538.

———. (2023). "Life after Climate Change: Better Than You Think." *National Review*, March 30. Online at https://www.nationalreview.com/magazine/2023/04/17/life-after-climate-change.

Marijnissen, C., and F. Zaccheo (2016). "Getting Down to Business: Turning Momentum to Action in the Implementation of the Environmental Dimension of the Sustainable Development Agenda." European Commission Newsroom, December 7. Online at https://ec.europa.eu/newsroom/intpa/items/50911/en.

Michaels, P. J. (2004). *Meltdown: The Predictable Distortion of Global Warming by Scientists, Politicians, and the Media*. Washington, D.C.: Cato Institute.

———. (2005). *Meltdown: The Predictable Distortion of Global Warming by Scientists*. Lanham, Maryland: Rowman & Littlefield.

Michaels, P. J., and R. C. Balling Jr. (2000). *The Satanic Gases: Clearing the Air about Global Warming*. Washington, D.C.: Cato Institute.

Mitchell, C. V., et al. (2009). *A Renewed Call to Truth, Prudence, and Protection of the Poor: An Evangelical Examination of the Theology, Science, and Economics of Global Warming*. Collierville, Tennessee: Cornwall Alliance for the Stewardship of Creation. Online at https://www.cornwallalliance.org/docs/a-renewed-call-to-truth-prudence-and-protection-of-the-poor.pdf.

Nordhaus, W. (2018). "Projections and Uncertainties about Climate Change in an Era of Minimal Climate Policies." *American Economic Journal: Economic Policy* 10, no. 3 (August): 333–60. Online at https://pubs.aeaweb.org/doi/pdfplus/10.1257/pol.20170046.

Pötter, B. (2010). "Klimapolitik verteilt das Weltvermögen neu." *Neue Zürcher Zeitung*, November 14. German original online at https://

web.archive.org/web/20101122162022/http://www.nzz.ch/nachrichten/schweiz/klimapolitik_verteilt_das_weltvermoegen_neu_1.8373227.html. English translation online at https://www.netzerowatch.com/ipcc-official-climate-policy-is-redistributing-the-worlds-wealth.

Rational Wiki (n.d.a). "Climate Change." Online at https://rationalwiki.org/wiki/Climate_change.

———. (n.d.b). "Loaded Language." Online at https://rationalwiki.org/wiki/Loaded_language.

Rotman, J. D., T. J. Weber, and A. W. Perkins (2020). "Addressing Global Warming Denialism: The Efficacy of Mechanism-Based Explanations in Changing Global Warming Beliefs." *Public Opinion Quarterly* 84, no. 1 (February): 74–103. Online at https://www.researchgate.net/publication/339365861_addressing_global_warming_denialism_the_efficacy_of_mechanism-based_explanations_in_changing_global_warming_beliefs.

Singer, S. F. (1998). *The Leipzig Declaration on Global Climate Change.* Washington, D.C.: Science and Environmental Policy Project. Text online at https://heartland.org/opinion/the-leipzig-declaration-on-global-climate-change. Original signers listed online at https://web.archive.org/web/19980629120420/http://www.sepp.org/LDsigs.html.

Solomon, L. (2008). *The Deniers: The World-Renowned Scientists Who Stood Up against Global Warming Hysteria, Political Persecution, and Fraud.* Minneapolis: Richard Vigilante Books.

Wikipedia (n.d.). "RationalWiki." Online at https://en.wikipedia.org/wiki/RationalWiki.

Chapter 2

The History and Politics of "Climate Change"

by David R. Legates

"People with a sense of fulfillment think it a good world and would like to conserve it as it is, while the frustrated favor radical change."
—*Eric Hoffer*

Chapter Summary

More than thirty years ago, climate research employed classical scientific inquiry using deductive and inductive reasoning with observations to test hypotheses. Then post-normal and relativistic post-modern science emerged that incorporated subjective interpretations and the proposition that results are only valid in the context of belief systems. The existence of scientific truth could thereby be denied, and facts would no longer matter. These approaches were embraced to support the activism of concerned scientists and environmental groups since they negate rigorous scientific refutations of their agendas. Influence and funding opportunities flourished, accessing the political arena through assertions of "science experts."

In the mid-1970s, fears over global cooling gave way to concerns about global warming. Activist scientists pushed for greater international attention, culminating in the creation of the United Nations Intergovernmental Panel on Climate Change (IPCC). IPCC participants are appointed by government regulators, nongovernmental organizations, activist scientists, and international organizations. Coincidentally, perhaps, in the late 1980s significant political pressure and increasing media attention were emerging from events such as alarmist U.S. congressional testimonies in June 1988.

Debate among dissenting voices once characterized scientific advancement, but insistence upon a consensus is now accompanied by groupthink, emotionalism, intimidation, ad hominem attacks, suppression of dissent, and gross oversimplifications that cheapened science. Climate change is now a well-funded and orchestrated ecosocialist campaign to transform global society through wealth redistribution. Climate summits have become economic summits, and environmental policy has become social engineering, as evidenced by initiatives from the World Economic Forum's "Great Reset." True scientific inquiry has been relegated to obscurity.

"Climate change" has become as much of a political debate as it is a scientific argument. Billions of dollars are spent each year on attempts to mitigate and to adapt to a changing climate—and yes, some of it is spent on the science. But more than half a century ago, climatology was a poor stepchild in the study of atmospheric science, and, when scientists began to realize that our climate did indeed change, it was global cooling that changed the paradigm. How did "climate change" become the most important scientific challenge of our lifetime?

Greenhouse Gases as Agents of Climate Change

Svante August Arrhenius (1859–1927) is largely viewed as the father of our understanding of the "greenhouse effect." After studying electrolytes and discovering the concept of ions—for which he narrowly received a Ph.D. degree but was awarded a Nobel Prize in 1903—he turned his attention to how carbon dioxide in the atmosphere absorbs electromagnetic radiation and its impact on the climate of the Earth (Baliunas and Soon 1999). However, Arrhenius was not the first to suggest the warming potential of greenhouse gases.

As early as 1807, Joseph Fourier (1768–1830) studied the Earth's temperature and observed that the surface of the Earth should be much colder if solar radiation were the only factor considered. He ultimately concluded in 1822 that the radiative importance of greenhouse gases was less than other variables—he suggested that the temperature of space itself might contribute to a warmer Earth—but that the greenhouse effect exists, which is the first instance of a scientist noting the importance of the radiative impact of trace gases (Fleming 1999). In 1859, John Tyndall (1820–1893) performed the first reliable experiments on the ability of some gases (notably water vapor and carbon dioxide) to absorb infrared radiation and concluded that water vapor was the most important greenhouse gas. Tyndall further speculated that changes in greenhouse gas concentrations might have been responsible for the geological record (Baliunas and Soon 1999).

Arrhenius calculated a figure for climate sensitivity (that is, the change in temperature for a doubling or halving) due to atmospheric carbon dioxide concentration—4°C (7.2°F). While this value matches well with the range of consensus values suggested by the Intergovernmental Panel on Climate Change (IPCC) (Baliunas and Soon 1999), this number was pure speculation since Arrhenius could only rely on measurements of the electromagnetic spectrum between 0.3 and 3 microns; indeed, major absorbing bands of carbon dioxide exist at about 15 microns, which could not be measured in Arrhenius's time, due to the lack of equipment necessary to measure infrared radiation longer than 9.5 microns (Baliunas and Soon 1999; Fleming 1999; Rogalski 2012). Indeed, as Arrhenius (1896, 248) noted, "...[at this time,] we possess no direct observations of the emission or absorption of [water vapor or carbon dioxide]." Nevertheless, Arrhenius concluded,

> We often hear lamentations that the coal stored up in the earth is wasted by the present generation without any thought of the future, and we are terrified by the awful destruction of life and property which has followed the volcanic eruptions of our days. We may find a kind of consolation in the consideration that here, as in every other case, there is good mixed with the evil. By the influence of the increasing percentage of carbonic acid [carbon dioxide] in the atmosphere, we may hope to enjoy ages with more equable and better climates, especially as regards the colder regions of the earth, ages when the earth will bring forth much more abundant crops than at present, for the benefit of rapidly propagating mankind. (1908, 63)

Before the Storm—When Climate Did Not Change

The Second World War led to a renaissance in meteorology. Military campaigns needed real-time meteorological observations and short-term forecasts to facilitate bombing raids and aerial reconnaissance, parachute drops, surface tractionability for troops and mechanized vehicles, and ship movement for naval operations (Laboratory of Climatology 1954; Durschmied 2012, 333; Galvin 2020). Developments in meteorological concepts also arose from the war efforts, most notably, the jet stream (Maksel 2018). Pilots of B-29 flights discovered that westward flights (in mid-latitudes) encountered strong headwinds while eastward flights experienced equally strong tailwinds. The strong winds at higher altitudes made bomb drops less accurate and often caused planes to run out of fuel and crash before returning to base.

Consequently, atmospheric science departments experienced a considerable increase in interest and enrollment. The need to train a new cadre of meteorologists to support not just the military, but all aspects of life, including air travel and emergency preparedness, led many to go into meteorology. Meteorology was a very science- and math-oriented discipline, and all the "action" in the atmosphere was believed to occur on shorter (meteorological) timescales. Climate, however, was little more than an actuarial science with a basic course in statistics providing the only math needed by a climatologist. The Dust Bowl, for example, was identified as a human-induced change in the local climate, but the belief was that these changes were local and did not have global meteorological significance. These beliefs are elucidated in the quintessential work *Man's Role in Changing the Face of the Earth* (Thomas 1956).

While meteorology developed as a discipline, climatology fell behind. As an actuarial science, climatology was simply the study of the average state of the atmosphere, its variability, and its extremes. Adding to this stigma was the use of phrases such as "climate is average weather" and "climate is what you expect; weather is what you get." These further underscored the belief that climate was not dynamic—all the atmospheric energy and variability was contained in the weather, and climate was simply descriptive. This led to the misunderstanding that climate does not change (except, of course, on glacial or astronomic timescales), and therefore one could erroneously expect the Earth's climate to be constant.

A Change to the Status Quo

Some climatologists, however, did not accept their lot in atmospheric science and saw that climate could indeed be affected by human activity.

Pioneering scientists such as Helmut Landsberg (Landsberg 1981) and Stanley A. Changnon Jr. (Changnon et al. 1971) investigated the urban heat island around Washington, D.C., and St. Louis, Missouri (called the METROMEX experiment), respectively. Other pioneers, such as C. Warren Thornthwaite, studied the impact of land-use changes on the climate, or *topoclimatology*, as he defined it (Thornthwaite 1954; 1957), and Jerome Namias focused on the interface between meteorology and climatology through long-range forecasting as it manifests itself within ocean-atmosphere interactions (Roads 1998). What resulted from these studies was the realization that local effects could alter meteorological observations and affect our understanding of climate. Moreover, local climates can and do change because of human activities so that, indeed, climate is more than simply an actuarial science.

That the atmosphere itself could be changed by human activity was also a novel concept. Reid Bryson, founder of the University of Wisconsin–Madison's meteorology department and its Center for Climatic Research, observed on a flight over India that dust obscured the view of the ground, which made him a strong proponent of atmospheric dust as an agent for climate change (Bryson 1974; Bryson and Goodman 1980). Hubert H. Lamb, founder of the Climatic Research Unit at the University of East Anglia, also felt that aerosols were increasing, due to both human and volcanic activity (Lamb 1970). These and similar observations led to a concern during the 1970s that global cooling might be the pattern of human-induced climate change, a concern reflected in books like *The Cooling* (Ponte 1976) and *The Genesis Strategy* (Schneider 1976). Indeed, an evaluation of the trend in global air temperatures indicated that the planet seemed to be cooling. As Stephen Schneider noted,

> The last 200 years have been unusually warm when compared to the last 1,000. But there is considerable evidence

> that this warm period is passing and that temperatures on the whole will get colder. For example, in the last 100 years mid-latitude air temperatures peaked at an all-time warm point in the 1940's and have been cooling ever since. (Shapely 1976)

The consensus of scientists of the day indicated that the planet was headed toward a new ice age, and the posited solutions were necessarily draconian. Ponte (1976), for example, noted efforts toward mitigation of global cooling that included damming the Mediterranean Sea to restrict the flow of warm, saline water into the Atlantic Ocean or covering Arctic ice with coal dust to change the albedo and absorb more solar radiation. Climate was now changing, and, if unchecked, these colder temperatures would lead to global-scale famine and political instability. Noting the extreme weather of the early 1970s, Schneider (1976, 4) concluded that "there is growing evidence that such damaging weather may occur more frequently in the next decade than in the last one." Indeed, as Hecht and Tirpak (1995, 377) note, "[I]t is ironic that the propelling concern for climate research in the 1970s was the possibility of climate *cooling*, rather than climate warming" [emphasis original].

The "Sign" of Climate Change Turns

As the 1980s unfolded, several major changes occurred in both the observational networks and the observations themselves that caused "global cooling" to turn around and become "global warming." Prior to 1980, our observational network was station-based. Data on air temperature, precipitation, and other meteorological variables were recorded at individual stations located around the terrestrial landscape. Observations were made near the surface at a height comfortable to an average person, or about 1.5 m (~5 ft.). These data were spatially biased; that is, they tended to be in mid-latitudes, in developed countries, near the coasts, and at lower altitudes. Measurements were sparse in both the tropics and polar regions, at high altitudes, in deserts and rainforests, and—most notably—over the oceans, which cover about 71 percent of the Earth's surface. Moreover, these data also were temporally biased in that entire networks were begun and ended because of political upheaval or funding issues. For example, the extensive weather network in Japan ended abruptly in 1945 because of Japan's surrender to the Allies.

Following the launch of the TIROS series (Television InfraRed Observational Series) of weather satellites in the 1960s and the Nimbus series of weather satellites launched in the 1960s and 1970s, satellite observations of weather began in earnest with polar-orbiting satellites in 1979 (Smith et al. 1986). The advantage that satellite measurements have over surface-station observations is their near complete temporal and spatial coverage. In addition, they are far less affected by local impacts (for example, the urban heat island or urban pollution), station moves, and instrumentation changes (Groisman and Legates 1994). And after a decade of observations, satellite estimates of air temperature were beginning to indicate that global air temperatures were rising, not falling.

At the same time, several major political and environmental changes were occurring around the globe. Many groups, such as Greenpeace and the Union of Concerned Scientists (UCS), had been founded on concerns over nuclear weapons testing and military/nuclear proliferation (Greenpeace: Biagini and Sagar 2004; Santese 2020; UCS: Moore 2009; UCS 2023). But in the late 1980s, the Soviet Bloc nations began to collapse, and the risk of nuclear war seemed less likely. Rather than claim a victory and move on, however, these organizations chose to turn their efforts toward another cause, and the emerging *cause célèbre* in the late 1980s and early 1990s was global warming.

The History of "Climate Change"

To understand how climate change came to be perceived as an existential social and political issue (or threat), as it is today, one must first understand how science has changed. "Normal" science is usually described by the *scientific method*, which relies upon accurate observations to verify or falsify scientific theories. It focuses on theory and model development using observational data to prove, or disprove, our view of the real world. Formalized by Karl Popper (1934), the scientific method—or *deductive reasoning*—begins with observations of the real world. These observations allow scientists to posit questions about how the world works, from which formal hypotheses can be drawn. To test these hypotheses, experiments are devised from which results either confirm the validity of the hypothesis or reject it. In either case, the results provide new insights into how the observations are to be interpreted, or maybe even suggest other observations that might be beneficial, or possibly yield new questions to ponder.

Aristotle proposed an alternative view of the scientific method that combines deductive reasoning with an alternative path of scientific inquiry—called *inductive reasoning*. While deductive reasoning proceeds by proposing and validating hypotheses, inductive reasoning generalizes observations to provide new theories. So, while deductive reasoning proceeds by using a general concept (a hypothesis), tested by specifics (observations), inductive reasoning uses the specifics to derive general concepts (Losee 2001). Historically, science has advanced through both means of inquiry.

The scientific method, as it is specifically practiced, has long been criticized as being, among other things, too naïve, too simplistic, too restrictive, and a myth (Woodcock 2014). A particularly common complaint is that Popper's view can only be used to falsify hypotheses, not validate them, because the standard statistical test can only reject the null hypothesis (that is, the hypothesis that the observed difference between two possibilities is due to chance alone). Woodcock (2014) goes so far as to proffer that the entire concept of the scientific method should be discarded. Indeed, with respect to global warming, Mercer (2018, 139) concluded that "studies of the science of [the] Anthropogenic Global Warming debate would benefit from taking greater interest in questions raised by un-reflexive and politically expedient public understanding(s) of the philosophy of science of both critics and supporters...." Alternatives have been proposed, including probabilistic induction (theories have only a certain probability of being correct) or methodological anarchism (good scientific methods do not follow any prescribed formulae), but none of these has gained much attention.

More recently, an alternative to the scientific method—*Post-Normal Science*—has risen to present a challenge. Post-normal science is defined by its founders, Silvio O. Funtowicz and Jerome R. Ravetz, as applicable when "facts are uncertain, values in dispute, stakes high, and decisions urgent" (cited by Carrozza 2015, 111). It is a "reaction against long-term trends of 'scientization' of politics—the tendency towards assigning to experts a critical role in policymaking while marginalizing laypeople" (Carrozza 2015, 110). In the mid-1980s, a demand for policy-oriented climate science arose that is based on complexity, uncertainty of issues, and risks for humanity and ecosystems and is widely applicable when answers to difficult questions are needed immediately. Thus, proponents believe post-normal science can cut through the delay created by the scientific method and arrive at viable solutions. And climate science was a perfect application for this new method of conducting science.

Just what is post-normal science? Buschke et al. (2019) outline several differences between the scientific method and post-normal science. Most notably, the scientific method relies on the proficiency of experts who can interpret data, formulate hypotheses, and provide an appropriate explanation. By contrast, post-normal science goes far beyond expert knowledge by incorporating "an extended community of peers with diverse backgrounds, experience and expertise" (Buschke et al. 2019, 2). Unlike the scientific method, which is fact-based, post-normal science utilizes what it refers to as *extended facts*—facts supplemented by individual experiences and interpretations. While the scientific method is a problem-solving exercise that is best suited for simple questions with clear-cut solutions, post-normal science is designed for complex problems with multiple causes that may not have simple, or even attainable, solutions. Thus, post-normal science relaxes the strict definitions of facts and expertise by including subjective perceptions, interpretations, and feelings.

As previously discussed, proponents of post-normal science suggest it is best suited for problems where the stakes associated with the decision-making process are high or the uncertainties are extreme (Figure 2.1, Ravetz 1999).

This leaves the scientific method to problems where the impact of the outcome is low or when the problem is well-defined. Clearly, a highly complex problem such as climate change with lots of uncertainties that (at least allegedly) poses an existential threat to the survival of the planet (as posited by proponents) is a classic application for post-normal science. Many researchers have reached this conclusion (Saloranta 2001; Ravetz 2011; Turnpenny et al. 2011; Turnpenny 2012; Barwell 2013; Carrozza 2015; Hauge and Barwell 2017; Saltelli and Funtowicz 2017; Karpinska 2018; Bruggemann et al. 2020). Indeed, post-normal science was designed to be an "emerging science" to address "the environmental crises of this century" (Ravetz 2006, 275). As Wesselink and Hoppe (2011, 390) noted, the arrogance of post-normal science "can be traced back to [its] origin in concerned scientists' activism, which in effect accessed the political arena through the scientific entrance."

Unfortunately, the descent into anti-science through the rejection of the scientific method does not end with post-normal science. Climate science now lies on the edge of *Post-Modern Science*—the

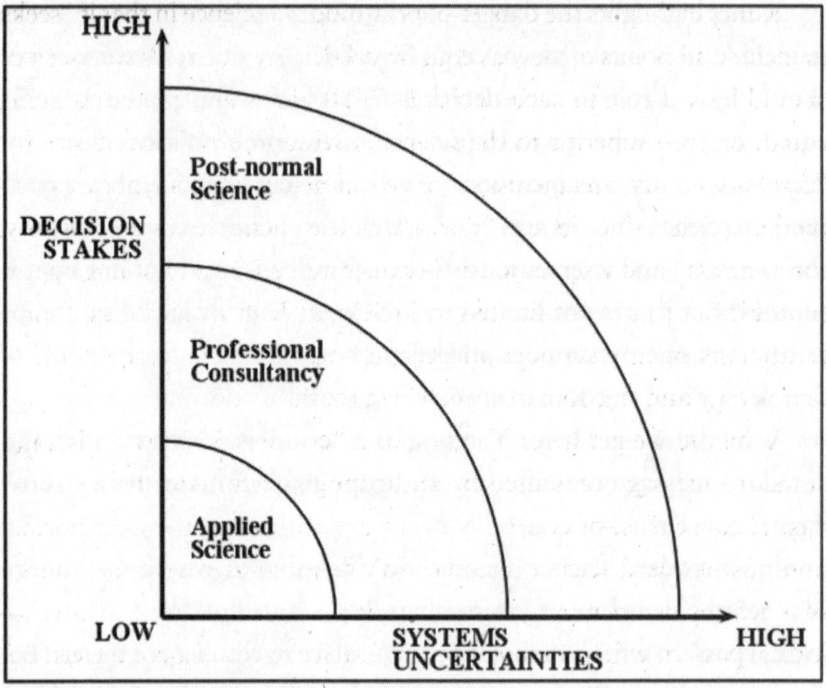

Figure 2.1. The sphere of influence for the application of post-normal science. *Source: Ravetz (1999). Courtesy of Jerome Ravetz.*

scientific equivalent of the relativist world of post-modern art and design (Paltridge 2018). This is a dangerous development "…where results are valid only in the context of society's beliefs, and where the very existence of scientific truth can be denied" (Paltridge 2018, 6). Paltridge continues:

> Post-modern science envisages a sort of political nirvana in which scientific theory and results can be consciously and legitimately manipulated to suit either the dictates of political correctness or the policies of the government of the day. (Paltridge 2018, 6)

Kuntz highlights the danger of post-modern science in that it "seeks to include all points of view as equally valid...even denying that science should have a role in such decisions." All views are treated as being equal, or even superior to the science, owing to a political desire for "diversity, equity, and inclusion." Environmental groups embrace post-modern science since its aim "is to attack the science that stands against their agenda" and it serves to further their influence and funding opportunities. But this is not limited to NGOs; as Kuntz concludes, "some politicians openly support anti-technology activists in the name of democracy and freedom of speech" (2012, 888).

Why did we get here? Yielding to a "consensus" of scientists is a standard message presented by anthropogenic climate change activists. A consensus, of course, is necessary to further the post-normal and post-modern science agenda. Isn't developing a consensus a sign of a healthy democracy? Janis (1972) defined *groupthink* as a psychological pattern where a group of people strive to reach a consensus. But attempts to force a consensus often result in silencing dissenting views, particularly in stressful situations and when the stakes are potentially very high. Groupthink tends to thrive in high-stakes situations—but these are exactly the conditions where proponents of post-normal and post-modern science believe they are most well-suited (Booker 2018).

The Goal of the Last Forty Years—Decarbonization

With the demise of global cooling in the late 1970s, to be replaced by global warming in the 1990s, carbon dioxide became an evil gas, threatening our very existence. Since then, the central aim of climate change alarmists has been to "decarbonize" the world's economy. Their goal is to eliminate the use of fossil fuels, on which mankind's material progress has been based for at least two hundred years, and to rely instead on "carbon-free" sources of energy, most notably wind and solar.

Such efforts, it is argued by alarmists, will bring about a reduction in human emissions of carbon dioxide sufficient to have a significant influence on the Earth's climate. Consequently, the global warming narrative is poised to fundamentally transform our civilization by undermining the energy sources that have led to our modern industrial society (Booker 2018). But why?

For years, the redistribution of wealth has focused on *the collective* over the individual—emphasizing the *greater good* over the needs and wants of a single person. This requires everyone to be *equal*; not just equal in opportunity but equal in outcome—or as the word is now defined, *equity* (though the word originally meant fairness or impartiality, not equality). In wealth redistribution, the struggle lies between "the haves" and "the have-nots"—those who "have" acquired what they have by exploiting those who now "have not." This posits a class struggle, which activists seek to eliminate through a guarantee of equality of outcome, or the redefined term, "equity."

But how can "equity" be enacted on a global scale? Clearly, there are countries that "have" and countries that "have not." Unlike the traditional Marxist state that invokes "equity" among individuals, it is not possible to engineer a society where equality of outcomes is legislated across countries. A solution is needed to punish the rich states and give to the poor states. Thus, redistribution of wealth requires both an agent and a mechanism to punish the "haves" by taking away what they have and giving it to those who have not, much like the story of Robin Hood, who robbed from the rich and gave to the poor.

Indeed, many in positions of power see climate change as merely a means to an end. The oft-cited quote by Saikat Chakrabarti, former chief of staff to Representative Alexandria Ocasio-Cortez (D-NY), is "the interesting thing about the Green New Deal is it wasn't originally a climate thing at all...because we really think of it as a how-do-you-change-the economy thing" (Montgomery 2019). He was speaking with Sam Ricketts, climate director for Governor Jay Inslee (D-WA), who added, "[The Green New Deal] is both rising to the challenge that is existential around climate *and* it is building an economy that contains more prosperity...and more broadly shared prosperity, equitability and justice throughout" [emphasis added]. Maurice Newman, who formerly served as chair of the Australian Broadcasting Corporation, chancellor of Macquarie University, and chair of the board of the Australian Stock Exchange, has stated, "But then climate change is not about credible scientific evidence...it has its roots in Marxism" (Chan 2015). Morano (2021, 127) demonstrates clearly that the "ideological battle between capitalism and socialism is at the heart of climate alarmism and of proposed *solutions* like the Green New Deal" [emphasis original].

Ecosocialism, the nexus between environmentalists and socialists (see Barkdull and Harris 2015; Harvey 1993; Heron 2021; Löwy 2005; Reitan and Gibson 2012; Trein 2018), has been active and developing for some time. While ecosocialists believe the capitalist system is responsible for virtually all the environmental maladies that humans have inflicted on the planet, they also recognize that socialism and environmentalism "share objective goals that imply a questioning of this economic automatism" (Löwy 2005, 15). Löwy (2005, 24) concludes that "radical political ecology has become one of the most important ingredients of the vast movement against capitalist neoliberal globalization." Barkdull and Harris sum it up best:

> A global society premised on eco-socialism, on a Hospice Earth, where the future is bleak but where people are nurtured to maximize their welfare, may enable humanity to minimize and cope with climate change in the best ways possible. The beauty of creating Hospice Earth is that it

> offers a more humane and peaceful future regardless of what happens to the global climate.... To live, and indeed to die, in a hospice is better than to starve (or worse) in a lifeboat. We have nothing to lose. (2015, 243)

In their view, humanity is too preoccupied with material growth and responds only when crises present themselves. Consequently, eco-socialism must ensure that all receive basic human needs, and economic responses should focus solely on production and distribution of these necessities. They liken it to being in hospice, where terminally ill patients are provided only with the resources needed to keep them alive, which they see as preferable to perishing by self-isolation.

The Role of the United Nations

The United Nations (UN) was designed as a forum for nations to communicate—which is a requisite opportunity. The UN also provides a way to combat injustice. It can sanction, penalize, and/or with force go after dictators and rogue nations that are not living within the agreed consensus framework specified by civilized societies. The UN can also coordinate international relief efforts to save and/or protect populations at risk. All these efforts help provide much-needed global solutions.

But the UN can become the agent to accomplish social change among nations by becoming the modern-day Robin Hood. The UN could demand money from rich nations and give it to poor nations—that is, provide global wealth redistribution. But in addition to an agent for this change, wealth redistributionists also need a mechanism, a *cause célèbre*, to justify such actions and move nations to join in them.

Indeed, the UN has taken up this mantle. In 2018, the UN Committee for Development Policy (CDP) wrote to support "international action to enable global wealth redistribution and support countries' capacity to enact and finance their development strategies" through their "Leaving No One Behind" initiative, of which climate change is a driving issue (CDP 2018).

In parallel with Marxism, the nature of climate change politics is that the poor are those most harmed by the impact of global warming (Chikulo 2014; Diffenbaugh and Burke 2019). To allow poor countries to become *industrialized,* the alarmists argue, is to hurt them even more, despite wealthy nations' historically overcoming poverty in this way (Szirmai, Naudé, and Alcorte 2013). It is a Catch-22 in that to become like a developed nation, they must adopt self-harming policies as well as policies that harm other nations. Thus, alarmists usually demand that undeveloped countries remain undeveloped to ensure that they are "protected" from the evils of climate change. Alarmists believe we must keep underdeveloped and undeveloped nations as they have existed for centuries—at one with nature and living within the *noble savage* stereotype: that primitive humans were uncorrupted by civilization and thus symbolize innate goodness and harmony with nature. Of course, such policies are not "at one with nature," as environmental degradation and childhood mortality plague such societies (Ellingson 2001). Only after such pressing needs as food, clothing, shelter, and safety have been met can environmental issues rise to the level of being important enough to consider.

Although it predates the climate change issue, the first UN Conference on the Human Environment, held in Stockholm in 1972, focused on environmental issues raised by growing industrial and nuclear societies and a rapidly growing global economy. It featured a clash between conservationists (who see the Earth as resources to be managed) and "preservationists" (who espoused eco-centric views of a "wild" nature that must be preserved, irrespective of human needs). The winner, as Reitan and Gibson (2012, 397) note, was the "reformist wing of environmental thought and action that has been widely recognized as among the most successful movements of the twentieth century." But this conference set the stage for the forthcoming climate change emphasis that would permeate the UN. Indeed, "it is the social, political, and cultural upheavals wrought by [climate] changes that are [of] central concern to social movement activists and policymakers alike" (Reitan and Gibson 2012, 398).

Founding the IPCC and Its *First Assessment Report*

If the UN is the agent to address societal change, then climate change is the mechanism by which it can be accomplished. And within the UN, the Intergovernmental Panel on Climate Change (IPCC) is the agency that specifically addresses climate change. Although the IPCC was founded in 1988, its origins go back more than a decade earlier—to a time when global cooling and its associated fears were beginning to give way to global warming and its associated fears.

After about three decades of declining air temperatures, the 1970s saw the resumption of the rise in air temperature that had been observed as far back as the mid-1800s, bringing to its close a period known as the *Little Ice Age* (~1650–1850). Despite the global cooling arguments of the early 1970s, several scientists had become convinced—owing to work going back to Fourier and Arrhenius—that increasing atmospheric carbon dioxide concentrations must necessarily lead to a warming of the globe. Leading this group was Swedish scientist Bert Bolin, who had noted that the cooling since the 1940s had seemingly ended and had been replaced by a modest warming (Booker 2018).

In 1979, Bolin attended the first World Climate Conference (WCC), held in Geneva, Switzerland, and organized by the World Meteorological Organization (WMO) of the UN (WMO 1979). Bolin's arguments were very persuasive, particularly to members of the conference organizing committee, Robert M. White and James Dooge.

Future conferences were scheduled to further discuss the possibility of global warming (Agrawala 1998a; Booker 2018). Moreover, the World Climate Programme (WCP) of the UN subsequently was founded through the WMO, the UN Environmental Programme (UNEP), the UN Educational, Scientific and Cultural Organization (UNESCO), and the International Council of Scientific Unions (ICSU—now the International Council for Science).

Subsequent workshops were held in Villach, Austria, in 1980, 1983, and 1985 (Agrawala 1998a). At the third Villach workshop (WMO 1985), Bolin argued that anthropogenic increases in greenhouse gases called for immediate action, and the conference attendees were summarily impressed (Booker 2018). As noted by Agrawala (1998a, 608), "[A] consensus was reached by an international group of scientists (participating in their personal capacities) that 'in the first half of the next century a rise of global mean temperature would occur which is greater than any in man's history.'" It was subsequently recommended that scientists and policymakers should work together to examine policies that would effectively address the problem. Sir John T. Houghton, then head of the United Kingdom (UK) Meteorological Office (UKMO), was significantly impressed with Bolin's arguments and joined him as Bolin's most influential ally (Booker 2018).

Following the third Villach workshop, global warming had become a major topic of discussion both in the media and with respect to international policymaking. Four important players were responsible for elevating global warming to this status—two were part of the UN (UNEP and WMO), one was a non-governmental organization (ICSU), and the fourth was the United States government (Agrawala 1998a). In the United States, efforts by the National Research Council (NRC), the Environmental Protection Agency (USEPA), and the Department of Energy (USDOE) had focused on climate impacts and mitigation and shaped policies in other countries (Agrawala 1998a).

But more importantly, the United States had the biggest carbon footprint, was home to many fossil fuel companies, and was the biggest financier of the UN.

Of the four actors, the UNEP was the most proactive. Its head, Mostafa Tolba (a plant pathologist), saw success through the Vienna Convention on Ozone and felt that this achievement could be recreated on a much wider scale with respect to climate change (Agrawala 1998a; Booker 2018). Tolba brought the ICSU and the WMO together with the UNEP to collaborate on climate change. He also lobbied U.S. secretary of state George Shultz to enlist U.S. involvement. Two subsequent conferences were held, but it became clear that two significant problems existed. The new governing body established by UNEP, ICSU, and the WMO—the Advisory Group on Greenhouse Gases (AGGG)—had neither a budget nor power nor authority. Moreover, the AGGG set "acceptable" rates of air temperature increases and sea level rise that not all participants felt were reasonable; indeed, some members felt that "all" climate change needed to cease. In particular, it was argued that "...whether climate change under any particular (arbitrary) threshold should be defined as socially tolerable, and exceeding it as dangerous, was clearly a value judgment scientists were not qualified to make" (Agrawala 1998a, 610).

However, this group needed a political ally with lots of influence within the UN. Enter Maurice Strong, a Canadian businessman with ties to oil fields in Alberta. Strong, a self-professed "socialist in ideology" and "capitalist in methodology" (cited in Bailey 1997), had long believed that the UN must be transformed into a world government (Booker 2018). After leading a World Conference on the Environment, Strong was appointed as the first head of UNEP, where he organized expert meetings on climate change. He had been connected to the UN since 1970, when he was called upon to rejuvenate a faltering UN Conference on the Human Environment. Strong became the Secretary General of the

Conference in his new title, Undersecretary General of the UN responsible for environmental affairs (from http://MauriceStrong.net). He became the champion of the developing world when he headquartered UNEP in Nairobi, rather than New York, Geneva, or Vienna. By the mid-1980s, Strong had left UNEP and become the head of the Canadian national oil company, PetroCanada. He would return to the UN in the early 1990s, just when he was needed again.

Considering the AGGG was failing in its mission, Tolba's letter to George Shultz had led the United States to discuss a different tack. The government concluded that the myriad of views of various U.S. agencies had to be unified, and the same was required for the countries of the world. Thus, the United States recommended an *intergovernmental* framework be established to present the scientific evidence for both natural and anthropogenic climate change, which became Resolution 9 of the Tenth WMO Congress in May 1987 (Agrawala 1998a). As Agrawala (1998a, 612) argues, "[T]he trigger for the IPCC was the activism by Mostafa Tolba, the dissatisfaction in the US about the AGGG, and sharply differing views on climate change amongst various US government agencies and the White House administration."

Unifying the various agencies in the United States proved to be a difficult task. The Republican White House under George H. W. Bush was reluctant to justify expensive climate change policy, while the USEPA and the U.S. Department of State wanted a government-sponsored international assessment (Hecht and Tirpak 1995; Agrawala 1998a). The United States finally agreed to a group of "official" experts to assess the science of climate change but precluded assessment of global policy actions, in part because the WMO was not proficient in policy matters. And while the UNEP had the requisite expertise, the United States had reservations about Mostafa Tolba, who had made enemies in Latin America during the ozone discussions (Agrawala 1998a). Thus, the proposal from the United States was for an intergovernmental panel administered jointly by UNEP and the WMO. At this point, ICSU became superfluous—it was an NGO and interested more in global change research and not in global policy implications (Agrawala 1998a, 1998b).

The UNEP, and Strong in particular, had envisioned using the UN as a mechanism to promote a socialist agenda (Booker 2018). Anthropogenic global warming was thought to be the ultimate exploitation of "the have-nots" by "the haves." Rich Western countries had benefited by abusing the Earth's natural resources at the expense of the poor. The UN must be allowed to play the modern-day Robin Hood by forcing the West to fund poorer countries to help their economies, thereby providing the ultimate redistribution of wealth on a global scale. In 1987, Strong and the UNEP were able to further their goals through the Brundtland Commission (named for commission chair and Norwegian prime minister Gro Harlem Brundtland), which introduced the concept of "sustainable development" (Booker 2018). The commission's report proclaimed that the science was "settled" and that anthropogenic climate change "could raise global temperatures to such a level that it would have serious effects on agriculture, raise sea levels, flood coastal cities, and disrupt national economies" (Booker 2018, 8). The takeaway message from the report was that a major global effort was required to stop the emission of "all" greenhouse gases.

In the late 1980s, the Montreal Protocol—where Strong had played a key organizing role—became the first global treaty to phase out, in order to protect the Earth's ozone layer, the use of chlorofluorocarbons (Booker 2018). Strong saw this as just a warm-up act and believed that global warming could be a much more powerful agent by which global wealth redistribution would be achieved. On March 25, 1988, the secretary general of the WMO, Godwin Olu Patrick Obasi from Nigeria, sent a letter to member governments of the WMO to determine whether representation on a then proposed Intergovernmental Panel on Climate Change (IPCC) would be something in which each nation would be interested (Agrawala 1998a). A draft resolution introduced at the subsequent UN General Assembly (in Malta and immediately prior to the first plenary of the IPCC) called on the new IPCC to provide a comprehensive evaluation of climate change science and social/environmental impacts, and to make recommendations for policy responses by participating governments to "delay, limit or mitigate the impact of adverse climate change" and to recommend "relevant treaties and other legal instruments dealing with climate" (Agrawala 1998a, 616). Although some were lobbying for five working groups, Tolba insisted on a division into three groups, which led to the development of the IPCC working group (WG) framework—the physical science basis (WG1), impacts, adaptation, and vulnerability (WG2), and mitigation of climate change (WG3).

Climate Theater Comes to Congress

Concomitant with the IPCC meeting in Malta, political theater in the summer of 1988 was about to bring the United States on board with the global climate change narrative. Senator Timothy Wirth (D-CO) chaired a hearing of the Senate Committee on Energy and Natural Resources on a hot and humid day in June. The media were told that this hearing would result in something Earth-shattering, and they turned out in force. Six experts testified at the hearing—James E. Hansen, head of the Goddard Institute for Space Studies of the National Aeronautics and Space Administration (NASA); Syukuro Manabe of the Geophysical Fluid Dynamics Laboratory of the National Oceanic and Atmospheric Administration (NOAA); George Woodwell, director of the Woods Hole Research Center in Woods Hole, Massachusetts; Michael Oppenheimer, an atmospheric physicist with the Environmental Defense Fund (a national environmental NGO); Dan Dudek, senior economist of the Environmental Defense Fund; and Bill Moomaw, senior associate of the World Resources Institute (also a national environmental NGO).

Hansen was unequivocally the star of the hearing, so much so that many retellings refer to the event as the "Hansen Hearing of 1988." His extremely alarmist prognostications for a hellishly hot future world headlined newspapers and magazines for weeks. His declaration that he was "99 percent certain" that a global warming trend had resulted from anthropogenic increases in carbon dioxide is an oft-cited quote (Shabecoff 1988). Wirth, who was not the chair of the committee but was granted control of the hearing by Chairman J. Bennett Johnson (D-LA), asserted in an interview with PBS Frontline in 2007 that the entire event was "staged":

> Believe it or not, we called the Weather Bureau and found out what historically was the hottest day of the summer. Well, it was June 6 or June 9 or whatever it was, so we scheduled the hearing that day, and bingo: It was the hottest day on record in Washington, or close to it. It was stiflingly hot that summer. [At] the same time you had this drought all across the country, so the linkage between the Hansen hearing and the drought became very intense.... What we did it was [sic] went in the night before and opened all the windows, I will admit, right? So that the air conditioning wasn't working inside the room and so when the, when the hearing occurred there was not only bliss, which is television cameras in double figures, but it was really hot.... So Hansen's giving this testimony, you've got these television cameras back there heating up the room, and the air conditioning in the room didn't appear to work. So it was sort of a perfect collection of events that happened that day, with the wonderful Jim Hansen, who was wiping his brow at the

witness table and giving this remarkable testimony. (retold by Kessler 2015b)

However, Wirth's confession has raised significant questions. First, the U.S. Weather Bureau had been renamed the U.S. National Weather Service and moved from the Department of Agriculture to the NOAA within the Department of Commerce in 1970. Second, the warmest day of the year in Washington, D.C., does not typically come in early June but in late July. Third, June 23 was the third of three hot days in June (98°F or 36.7°C), and June 22 was warmer (101°F or 38.3°C). Nevertheless, the day of the hearing, June 23, was and is still the hottest June 23 on record in Washington, D.C. (at Reagan National Airport), although eleven days that year were as warm or warmer than June 23, with July 16 reaching the annual high of 104°F (40°C). Despite conditions outside the hearing room, there is no reference to excessive heat within the hearing room or picture of Hansen wiping his brow, although the numerous cameras and a nonfunctioning air-conditioning system may have led to elevated air temperatures (Kessler 2015b). Wirth's principal staff aide for climate change, David Harwood, told the *Washington Post* that the windows were not open and were not left open overnight. "I have no idea where that came from," he said (Kessler 2015b). Moreover, Secretary of State John F. Kerry (who later became Special Presidential Envoy for Climate under President Joe Biden) has repeatedly claimed that he organized this hearing, but he did not, nor was he even a member of the Senate committee (Kessler 2015a).

Whether the "Hansen Hearing of 1988" was staged or not, it successfully raised media concern over anthropogenic global warming. Following the hearing, several notable and influential scientists were highly critical of Hansen's testimony. For example, S. Fred Singer, with a long and distinguished career as an academic, scientist, and government bureaucrat in the field of climatology, published a particularly pointed op-ed in the *Wall Street Journal* (Singer 1988). Singer noted that although human actions had caused the atmospheric concentration of several greenhouse gases to increase, the real question is whether the Earth's climate system would compensate. Singer (1988) noted that "a cottage industry has sprung up on *climate policy*—not climate science—populated by professional regulators, environmental activists and assorted scientists—all heavily supported before important congressional committees—all about a problem that may or may not be real—and which in any case may defy any easy solution" [emphasis original]. A similar article was published by Singer, Roger Revelle, and Chauncey Starr (1992) in *Cosmos*. That article resulted in a lawsuit by Singer against former Revelle associate Justin Lancaster, who—Singer argues elsewhere (Singer 2003)—had been persuaded by then senator Al Gore (D-TN, who had taken a course from Revelle while Gore was at Harvard) to assert that Singer only added Revelle's name over Revelle's objections. Singer sued for libel and won, earning a retraction and an apology from Lancaster (Singer, Legates, and Lupo 2021).

The IPCC Begins—the *First Assessment Report*

All this media coverage came at a perfect time, because in November of 1988, the IPCC held its inaugural meeting with thirty-four nations in attendance (Booker 2018). IPCC was, and has since been, touted as an impartial group of scientists issuing authoritative reports on the state of climate science. It was not and is not, as its composition and the history of its founding show. Bolin was appointed as the first chair of the IPCC, and Houghton became chair of the science-based WG1 (Booker 2018). As discussed earlier, both were already anthropogenic climate change alarmists, as were nearly all other scientists on the IPCC. The meeting concluded with a goal of producing a series of Assessment Reports (AR) every five years, first in 1990, just two years hence.

Selection of which country would head the various working groups was a highly charged affair (Agrawala 1998a; Hecht and Tirpak 1995). Various U.S. agencies were at odds over which working group the U.S. would chair—and the U.S. could not chair more than one. NASA and NOAA wanted WG1, while the Department of State and the EPA wanted WG3. Eventually, the United States was awarded WG3 (with co-chairs Canada, China, Malta, the Netherlands, and Zimbabwe), while WG1 went to the United Kingdom (with co-chairs Senegal and Brazil). Chair of WG2 went to the USSR (with co-chairs Australia and Japan). Thus, much to the delight of Senator Wirth and his colleagues, the United States was put in control of climate change policy, not science.

The creation of the IPCC caused most environmentally oriented NGOs to focus primarily or exclusively on global warming. It also spawned several entry-level NGOs that participated in the rapidly developing financial gravy train. For example, Greenpeace and the Union of Concerned Scientists turned their efforts from nuclear proliferation campaigns to global warming, now perceived as the greatest danger faced by mankind (Booker 2018). Umbrella organizations were created to organize smaller environmental groups to have a larger voice. The Climate Action Network, for example—a global network of over 1,300 NGOs in more than 130 countries—was founded by Oppenheimer (who testified at the Senate hearing with Hansen in 1988) to facilitate action by governments and individuals to minimize the effect of anthropogenic climate change.

Although the IPCC's *First Assessment Report* (*FAR*) was still two years away, global warming alarmists could not wait. Noel Brown, then director of the New York Office of UNEP, was quoted as saying,

> Entire nations could be wiped off the face of the Earth by rising sea levels if the global warming trend is not reversed

> by the year 2000. Coastal flooding and crop failures would create an exodus of "eco-refugees," threatening political chaos. (Mayraz 2019)

Brown went on to state that "governments have a 10-year window of opportunity to solve the greenhouse effect before it goes beyond human control" (Mayraz 2019). Although that deadline for disaster passed more than twenty years ago, UNEP, a sponsor of the IPCC, had weighed in on the science before the *FAR* was even written (Booker 2018).

Protocol for the development of the IPCC ARs is quite extensive and was codified only after *FAR* was completed (Agrawala 1998b; Moss 1994). A plenary session is first organized (which formally ends the previous assessment cycle) to review the previous AR and set the agenda for the upcoming cycle. Following the plenary, participants of the three working groups are established from experts nominated not so much by other experts in their fields as by governments, NGOs, and international organizations, and timelines are proposed for writing the AR. Writers retreat home to write their chapters, usually taking up to two years. A review is then conducted by expert scientists, government bureaucrats, and interested third parties, although the lead author of each chapter has final say on the content. These finalized documents then are presented at an IPCC plenary session for approval and ratification by all member states (Agrawala 1998b; Moss 1994). Note that the summaries are prepared independently from the working group reports and approved line-by-line by governments in the final plenary. By contrast, the expert report is not subject to government approval, and although expert review is sought (Agrawala 1998b), lead authors of each chapter have the final say on what is or is not included.

The line-by-line consensus for approval of the *Summary for Policymakers* is a highly politically charged process (Agrawala 1998b). States jockey to guarantee that their agendas are represented within the document, with those states guaranteed a possible financial gain (that is, developing and underdeveloped states) pitted against those who are likely to have to pay (namely, developed nations). As Agrawala notes, "[T]his makes the IPCC process particularly susceptible to political pressure in terms of which aspects its summaries should emphasize more." Indeed, Agrawala goes on to cite a British diplomat who characterized a 1990 meeting as "having started in a very organized fashion with songs about the future from children's choirs ... [but] finished at four o'clock in the morning, one day late, with most of the delegates having abandoned their chairs in the conference hall to gather on the front podium and shout at each other" (1998b, 627). Such a consensus document is merely an effort to make the summary credible among the member states and to make tradeoffs between scientific accuracy and enhancing policymaking opportunities (Agrawala 1998b), rather than to accurately present the science.

As promised, the *FAR* was published in 1990, and, in keeping with Brown's proclamation, climate trends were portrayed as portending dire conditions because of anthropogenic warming. The *FAR* used climate models to argue that twenty-first-century warming would be as much as 0.9°F (0.5°C) per decade, as much as eight times the calculated decadal rate for the entire twentieth century (0.05–0.11°F, 0.03–0.06°C), and "greater than those which have occured [sic] naturally on Earth over the past 10,000 years" (Houghton, Jenkins, and Ephraums 1990, xxviii). According to Booker, the *FAR Summary for Policymakers*, far from being the "CliffsNotes" of the larger tome, was drafted solely by Houghton, much to the dismay of other scientists (Booker 2018). As Booker explains, Houghton made sure that despite the caveats, concerns, and contradictions raised in the actual text, the *Summary* put an alarmist spin on the results, asserting that climate change was indeed what it would later be called—an existential threat—and this biased presentation produced exactly what

Strong, Tolba, and others wanted: attention and a positive response from media and politicians (Booker 2018). As expected, leaders of most countries were quick to signal that their countries would do their part to stop anthropogenic global warming. Prime Minister Margaret Thatcher pledged that the United Kingdom would stabilize its emissions at 1990 levels by 2005, while West Germany's environment minister, Klaus Töpfer, proposed a decrease of 25 percent from present emissions for Europe.

Setting 1990 as a baseline favored Western Europe and Russia at the expense of the United States. In 1990, Britain was switching from coal to natural gas, while the collapse of the Soviet Union allowed Russia and Germany (after it had reacquired East Germany) to benefit from the temporary collapse of communism (Singer, Legates, and Lupo 2021). The Kyoto Protocol of 1997 provided for emission-trading permits with the European Union (EU), whereby European countries could buy unused credits from other Kyoto-participating nations or by sponsoring emission-reducing projects in developing and underdeveloped nations. It also led to proliferation of wind, solar, and ethanol energy subsidies designed to provide a transfer of wealth from consumers to a variety of special interests. Nevertheless, ethanol does not reduce carbon dioxide emissions and has detrimental environmental effects (Singer, Legates, and Lupo 2021).

Following the release of the *FAR* and its impact in 1990, Strong organized an Earth Summit in 1992, which became the largest conference ever held (Booker 2018). Approximately twenty thousand official delegates and more than one hundred world leaders attended the meeting in Rio de Janeiro. They were joined by as many climate activists and environmental NGOs, who had been recruited and sponsored by Strong himself, through Oppenheimer's Climate Action Network, using UN funds. The entire Earth Summit was conceived and overseen by Strong, which led to the establishment of the UN Framework Convention on Climate

Change (UNFCCC) to oversee global climate policy (Booker 2018). Several NGOs benefited considerably from the funding and visibility afforded by the UNFCCC, including Friends of the Earth, Greenpeace, and the World Wide Fund for Nature (known as the World Wildlife Fund in the United States and Canada). President George H. W. Bush committed the United States to the results of the summit by signing the UNFCCC, which was ratified by the U.S. Senate in October 1992 (Hecht and Tirpak 1995; Singer, Legates, and Lupo 2021). President Clinton, on Earth Day in 1993, went further by committing the United States to emission stabilization at 1990 levels by 2000 and establishing a trend of emission reductions every year that followed (Hecht and Tirpak 1995).

In its founding document, the objective of the UNFCCC is to "achieve stabilization of greenhouse gas concentrations in the atmosphere at a level that would prevent dangerous anthropogenic interference with the climate system" by creating an "economic system that would lead to sustainable economic growth and development" (cited by Singer, Legates, and Lupo 2021). The presuppositions upon which the UNFCCC was established are flawed: the UNFCCC assumes that (1) an unequivocal anthropogenic global warming signal exists in the observational climate record; (2) a substantial future warming will be catastrophic, leading to a collapse of agriculture and spread of tropical diseases; (3) this impending disaster can be avoided simply by the reduction of atmospheric greenhouse gases to a to-be-defined "safe" level, which is known and achievable; and (4) that such reductions of greenhouse gases must be accomplished regardless of any negative consequences, as the catastrophe of climate change must be avoided at all cost (Singer, Legates, and Lupo 2021).

Not all scientists were pleased with the newfound attention provided to climate science and the immense funding that was beginning to accompany it. Richard Lindzen documented the extreme pressure placed upon scientists to argue that a scientific consensus supported the anthropogenic global warming hypothesis and how NGOs, particularly in the United States, were profiting from it:

> In Europe the movement centered on the formation of Green parties; in the United States the movement centered on the development of large public interest advocacy groups. Those lobbying groups have budgets of several hundred million dollars and employ about 50,000 people; their support is highly valued by many political figures. As with any large groups [sic], self-perpetuation becomes a crucial concern. "Global warming" has become one of the major battle cries in their fundraising efforts. At the same time, the media unquestioningly accept the pronouncements of those groups as objective truth. (Lindzen 1992, 91)

Lindzen discussed how results supportive of the alarmist narrative were emphasized while those that detracted from it were ignored. Scientists involved in the writing of the *FAR* were put under extreme pressure to follow the narrative, and dissenters were treated rather rudely (Lindzen 1992). Fifteen years later, Trimble lamented the same problem, illustrating that nothing had changed. Instead, it had become worse:

> If we learned nothing else from authoritarian regimes of the past, it is that ideology and science do not mix. Group-think, emotionalism, ad hominem attacks, and suppression of dissent are unthinkable in both a free society and certainly in a productive scientific atmosphere. We must insist that exaggeration or distortion of scientific findings to support public opinion or a policy position is always illegitimate.... [A]dvocacy based on twisted science and intimidation not only discredits the scientists who practice it and the scientific community in

general, but more importantly it risks significant diversion of public resources from the resolution of real problems. (Trimble 2007, 22)

IPCC Redux—the *Second Assessment Report*

Five years later, in 1995, the *Second Assessment Report* of the IPCC (SAR) was scheduled for release. Its *Summary for Policymakers* was released on time before the full report came out in the next calendar year. As it happened, the *SAR* was far more controversial than its predecessor. The agreed-upon IPCC process was such that various nations approve the *Summary* line-by-line. That process had been followed in the final discussions in Madrid, but it became clear after the *Summary* was published that fifteen key statements had been deleted from the final text—and they all expressed doubts about identifying increasing carbon dioxide concentrations as the cause of climate change. For example, the statement "None of the studies cited above has shown clear evidence that we can attribute the observed changes to the specific cause of increases in greenhouse gases" had been approved but omitted from the final document (Seitz 1996). Several more statements were added after the *Summary* had been approved in Madrid. One sentence stood out, which cited chapter 8 of the yet unpublished Working Group I: "The balance of evidence suggests that there is a discernible human influence on global climate" (Houghton et al. 1996). Frederick Seitz, president emeritus of Rockefeller University, wrote, "In my more than sixty years as a member of the American scientific community, including service as president of both the National Academy of Sciences and the American Physical Society, I have never witnessed a more disturbing corruption of the peer-review process than the events that led to this IPCC report" (Seitz 1996, 16).

According to Booker, the culprit of the added sentence was one of the lead authors on this portion of the report—Ben Santer of the Lawrence Livermore National Laboratory. When questioned, neither Santer nor anyone else was willing to admit that any rules had been violated (Booker 2018). But what really happened was revealed two years later via a congressional committee request for evidence. The changes were made after the Madrid meeting by the chapter authors at the request of a U.S. Department of State communique sent to Houghton during the UNFCCC meeting. The communique read,

> It is essential that the chapters not be finalized prior to the completion of the discussions at the IPCC Working Group 1 Plenary in Madrid, and that chapter authors be prevailed upon to modify their text in an appropriate manner following the discussion in Madrid. (cited by Booker 2018)

Clearly, this *was* a violation of IPCC protocol. The communique was sent by then U.S. Under Secretary of State for Global Affairs Timothy Wirth. At an upcoming global climate conference to be held in Kyoto in 1997 and sponsored by the UNFCCC, Wirth and others planned to realize Strong's long-term agenda. The Kyoto Protocol (as it would come to be known) would commit the Western nations to reducing their carbon dioxide emissions (since they were the "oppressors") and paying out exorbitant sums of money to still-developing nations (the "oppressed"), including China and India (Booker 2018). This would provide funds to the developing nations (and to the UN and assorted NGOs) while putting the brakes on the economies of the West.

Wirth was the head of the U.S. delegation and had proposed legally binding targets to which greenhouse gas emissions must be reduced and time frames for the reductions (Singer, Legates, and Lupo 2021).

Declaring that the science was settled and that it demanded urgent action, Wirth was furious that several countries did not accept his proposal. Consequently, he issued a declaration on July 18, 1996, signed by several sympathetic nations, calling for a protocol to control carbon dioxide emissions and thus limit energy generation (Singer, Legates, and Lupo 2021). The UNFCCC meeting in Kyoto—through the Kyoto Protocol—would become the modern-day Robin Hood.

To guarantee a successful outcome to the upcoming conference in Kyoto, the White House under President Bill Clinton felt that the *SAR* must forcefully state that anthropogenic global warming was both a scientific and consensus-supported fact and that any doubts about this theory had now been alleviated (Booker 2018). As Booker (2018, 22) noted, "[T]his might have led observers to question whether the IPCC was quite the impartial, non-political body it was purported to be.... But such was the power of the groupthink... that the dust soon settled."

At the UNFCCC in Kyoto, Vice President Al Gore delivered the opening speech. By the end of the conference on December 11, Strong and Wirth had received their wish—the West was obliged to reduce emissions of greenhouse gases by an average of 5.2 percent (from 1990 levels) by 2012 (Singer, Legates, and Lupo 2021). But Kyoto was only to be the beginning as another, more stringent treaty was planned down the road. As for the U.S. Senate, without whose two-thirds majority consent the United States cannot enter a treaty, the Kyoto Protocol was a bridge too far. It had voted 95–0 the previous summer in the Byrd-Hagel Resolution of July 1997 that the United States would not ratify any treaty emanating from Kyoto that hindered the U.S. economy and freed developing countries from constraints imposed on the West. That put Gore in a difficult situation as he had emerged as a major player in international environmental politics. Nevertheless, Gore signed the treaty to unanimous applause in the hall in Kyoto (Booker 2018). The lack of Senate approval made Gore's act purely symbolic, without legal force.

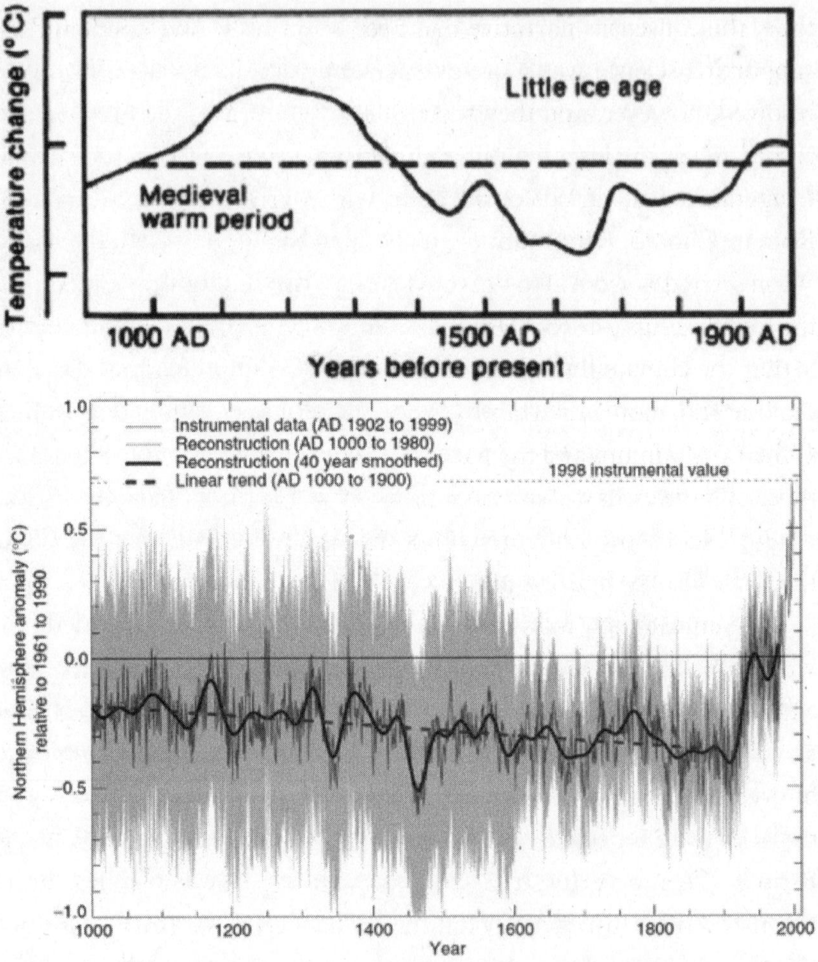

Figure 2.2. Air temperature for the last millennium as represented in the report of Working Group 1 of the IPCC *First Assessment Report* (top) and in Figure 2.20 of the report of Working Group 1 of the IPCC *Third Assessment Report* (bottom). *Courtesy of IPCC.*

Third Time Is a Charm: The IPCC *Third Assessment Report*

The *Third Assessment Report* of the IPCC (*TAR*) was released in 2001, one year behind schedule (Houghton et al. 2001). In the intervening time, the consensus narrative had been more fully developed, and the supporting science was more extensive. Several issues remained to be resolved, however, and they focused on the historical air temperature record. Over the last two millennia, it was widely recognized that air temperature had varied considerably, with warm conditions during the Roman Climatic Optimum (~250 BC to ~400 AD) and the Medieval Warm Period (~950 AD to ~1250 AD) and a decidedly cold period during the Little Ice Age (~1650 AD to ~1850 AD). The problem with this picture is that the climate fluctuated naturally and without forcing by carbon dioxide and, more importantly, that air temperatures during the Roman Climatic Optimum and the Medieval Warm Period rivaled or exceeded those of the present without a concomitant rise in carbon dioxide. Indeed, the *FAR* had shown a figure with both the Medieval Warm Period and the Little Ice Age figuring prominently (Figure 2.2, top).

But immediately following the release of the *SAR*, an IPCC scientist wrote an e-mail to several colleagues lamenting that it was difficult to explain why air temperatures during the Medieval Warm Period were as warm as they are today, particularly when anthropogenic releases of greenhouse gases could not possibly be responsible. In that e-mail, the scientist concluded, "[W]e have to get rid of the Medieval Warm Period" (Deming 2005, 248–49). A variety of global air temperature reconstructions (using proxy data) were posited by several researchers, but the one selected for eventual inclusion in *TAR* was developed by Michael Mann (Mann, Bradley, and Hughes 1998; 1999). At the time, Mann was a young scientist. Nevertheless, he was selected to head the important chapter from WG1 that focused on historical air temperature reconstructions and paleoclimate studies—which explains how Mann's graph, later dubbed the "Hockey Stick," came to be included in the *TAR* (Figure 2.2, bottom).

And with that, the Medieval Warm Period and the Little Ice Age were no more. Relegating these periods merely to "regional patterns," the caricature of average global air temperature now slowly decreased over the entire millennium until human activity and greenhouse gas emissions caused it to shoot upward. This made the case that climate changes only very slowly, except when human activity interrupts, as during the twentieth century. Media reports buzzed over the Hockey Stick; but it was even more important that it allowed 1998 to be labeled the warmest year and the 1990s the warmest decade of the last millennium (Booker 2018). The Hockey Stick provided cover for the IPCC to state that human activity is the most important component of climate change over the past millennium. Mann was only a post-doctoral researcher, one year removed from his Ph.D.; nevertheless, he was promoted to IPCC lead author and became editor of a major professional journal—the *Journal of Climate* (Singer, Legates, and Lupo 2021).

To develop the Hockey Stick, Mann and colleagues utilized air temperature proxies (primarily tree rings) to reconstruct the temperature record from 1000 AD to 1980. They then grafted the surface record from 1980 to 1999 onto the end of the proxy reconstruction (Singer, Legates, and Lupo 2021). This created a visually striking graph with air temperatures in the late twentieth century increasing radically, thereby providing a hockey stick shape from which the curve gets its name. Unsurprisingly, the reconstructed air temperature record (up to 1980) showed no perceptible rise or fall that corresponded to either the Medieval Warm Period or the Little Ice Age; that was the import of the Hockey Stick. Reconstructions by others imply that the proxy data do not reflect the surface record (McIntyre and McKitrick 2005; Singer, Legates, and Lupo 2021).

Several researchers subsequently demonstrated that the Hockey Stick was indeed flawed; that is, the relative flatness of the "shaft" and the rise of the "blade" accorded nicely with the IPCC climate narrative but not with the data. Stephen McIntyre and Ross McKitrick requested the original data from Mann and wrote that they could not reproduce

Mann's Hockey Stick "due to collation errors, unjustifiable truncation or extrapolation of source data, obsolete data, geographical location errors, incorrect calculation of principal components and other quality control defects" (McIntyre and McKitrick 2003, 751). Correcting errors that they had identified and updating the source data, McIntyre and McKitrick (2003) used the Mann methodology to recreate the period from 1400 AD to 1980 and found that the early fifteenth century was warmer than values from the twentieth century. Yes, there was a Medieval Warm Period, and it was warmer than the 1990s.

Diagnosing why Mann's Hockey Stick methodology failed to reproduce the Medieval Warm Period, McIntyre and McKitrick (2003) found that Mann's code contained an algorithm not reported in the journal article that always produced hockey-stick-shaped trends, even from random data. McIntyre and McKitrick (2003) also found that Mann had relied on tree rings from ancient bristlecone pines from the western United States. Growth rates of these trees are determined more by carbon dioxide levels than air temperature, and Mann cited a source that specifically noted this tendency; nonetheless, he used them as proxies for temperature. Thus, the proxy data Mann used yielded the hockey-stick-shaped trend presented as proof of the climate alarmist narrative (Singer, Legates, and Lupo 2021). Six years later, Mann and his colleagues published a correction (Mann, Bradley, and Hughes 2004, 105) acknowledging errors in their previous work, but they claimed, "none of these errors affect our previously published results." Subsequent analyses by McIntyre and McKitrick (2005), a report commissioned by a U.S. House committee (Wegman, Scott, and Said 2006), and the National Academy of Sciences (NAS 2006) all concluded, to varying degrees, that the Hockey Stick created by Mann and his colleagues was flawed. But it has been used as absolute proof that humans are causing rising temperatures again and again to varying degrees of certainty.

Statistical logic aside, proving the Hockey Stick did not accurately represent the global trend of air temperatures over the past millennium was not a difficult task. First, 1816 has been called the "Year Without a Summer" (Soon and Yaskell 2003) because annual global air temperatures were 0.4–0.7°C (0.7–1.0°F) below normal, and air temperatures during the summer were the coldest on record. This occurred because of three factors that came together: (1) 1816 occurred during the middle of an extended period of low magnetic activity of the Sun, called the Dalton Minimum, which decreased the incoming solar radiation during the Little Ice Age; (2) significant eruptions of several volcanoes between 1812 and 1814 (La Soufrière, Mount Awu, Suwanosejima Volcano, and Mayon Volcano), culminating in the major eruption of Mount Tamboro in the Philippines in 1815, led to significant amounts of volcanic debris in the stratosphere, reflecting solar energy back into space before it could warm the Earth; and (3) a shift of the Sun in the solar system, *inertial solar motion*, which occurs approximately every 180 years, occurred (Soon and Yaskell 2003). Data from the Hockey Stick, however, shows that for the eleven years between 1811 and 1821, 1816 ranked sixth; that is, for the eleven years surrounding the "Year Without a Summer," the Hockey-Stick-reconstructed value for 1816 was the median value. This illustrates that, at the very least, the Hockey Stick is unable to reproduce either annual- or decadal-scale variability that is highly significant, thereby undermining the claim made by proponents of the Hockey Stick that the 1990s were the warmest decade of the previous millennium, with 1998 being the warmest year.

Willie Soon, Sallie Baliunas, and their colleagues (Soon and Baliunas 2003; Soon et al. 2003) also easily confirmed the presence of a global Medieval Warm Period (and the Little Ice Age) by evaluating locally reconstructed trends presented in the published literature at more than 125 geographically diverse places. They examined local and regional studies of climate reconstructions from documentary and cultural sources, ice cores, glaciers, boreholes, speleothems, tree/forest-growth limits, lake fossils, mammalian fauna, coral and tree-ring growth, peat cellulose, pollen, phenological data, and seafloor sediments from all over the globe. Based on the results of the authors of the various articles, Soon and colleagues (Soon and Baliunas 2003; Soon et al. 2003) sought the answers to the question "Is there an objectively discernible climate anomaly during the Medieval Warm Period?" Their requirement was to determine if the proxy record showed a period of fifty years or longer of warming, dryness, or wetness during the period identified as the Medieval Warm Period. They concluded that "many records reveal that the 20th century is likely not the warmest nor a uniquely extreme climatic period of the last millennium, although it is clear that human activity has significantly impacted some local environments" (Soon et al. 2003, 233). Later, Craig Idso of the Center for the Study of Carbon Dioxide and Global Change analyzed more than two hundred papers and concurred from this myriad of independent results covering a variety of diverse locales that the Medieval Warm Period did indeed occur on a global scale and that global air temperatures were likely at least as great as present-day conditions, although the degree of warming varied considerably (Bezdek et al. 2019).

However, the biggest argument that the Hockey Stick is misleading was provided by Soon et al. (2004). Soon and his colleagues demonstrated that in subsequent drafts of the Hockey Stick, the observed 1999 air temperature for the Northern Hemisphere was different. An early, unpublished draft of Figure 2.21 of the IPCC *TAR* WG1 showed that the observational data for 1999 (see the red line in the top part of Figure 2.3 in the color figures section between pages 240 and 241) reached a value near 0.3°C (0.54°F). However, the published version (Figure 2.3, bottom, red line) exhibits a value of more than 0.4°C (0.72°F)—an adjustment of nearly 0.15°C (0.27°F). Note that the uncertainty region (shaded area in both figures) reached as high as 0.4°C (0.72°F) just prior to 1200 AD. In the early draft, the uncertainty would not have allowed the claim that 1999 was the warmest year in the past millennium; increasing the value to more than 0.4°C (0.72°F) affected the unsmoothed series (see *TAR* WG1 Figure 2.20, shown in Figure 2.3, bottom) and permitted the claim to be made.

After publication of the IPCC *TAR*, Mann, alone and with colleagues, published at least three other representations of his Hockey Stick (see Figure 2.4 in the color figures section between pages 240 and 241). Mann (2002) was presumably submitted and was accepted at about the same time as the draft version of IPCC *TAR* was submitted since its value for 1999 was 0.3°C (0.54°F—Figure 4a). Similarly, Mann et al. (2003) is commensurate with the published version of the IPCC *TAR*, with a value for 1999 of more than 0.4°C (0.72°F—Figure 4b). However, a subsequent publication (Mann and Jones 2003) exhibits an even higher value for 1999 than the IPCC TAR—nearly 0.6°C (1.08°F—Figure 4c). This latter paper suggests a warming of almost 1.0°C (1.8°F) over the last century, a figure that is considerably higher than suggested by any observational dataset and even the IPCC *TAR* itself, even though the curve purports to represent the observations (Soon et al. 2004).

Although Mann's Hockey Stick has been described as a "fictitious construct" (Singer, Legates, and Lupo 2021), its influence is pervasive. It allowed the IPCC *TAR* to make the Medieval Warm Period disappear so that the inconvenient question of "Why did air temperatures rise during the Medieval Warm Period when they could not possibly be forced by atmospheric greenhouse gases?" could be avoided. And with the Hockey Stick, the public was provided with misleading evidence suggesting that humans are the only real agent of climate change on millennium scales or shorter. The Hockey Stick fit the narrative perfectly. As Singer, Legates, and Lupo (2021, 76) note, "[I]ts prominence in the climate change debate even today, some twenty years after it entered the literature and was thoroughly debunked, is testimony to the influence of politics on science and the failure of the science community to police itself."

Beyond the *Third Assessment Report*

Agrawala (1998b, 621) noted that the IPCC "has attempted to walk the tightrope of being scientifically sound *and* politically acceptable" [emphasis in the original] with an overwhelming emphasis on the "science" documents (that is, WG1). The four players in the original IPCC in 1988—WMO, UNEP, ICSU, and the United States—morphed into leadership by a cast of characters, led by Bolin (chairman of the IPCC) and other international political figures and by the United States, which was highly represented by its scientists and governmental bureaucrats who chaired key positions within the IPCC (Agrawala 1998b). But as the IPCC began to wield more global influence, power, and financial status, the member states of the UNFCCC began to exert demands on it. After all, member nations were both sources and recipients of its funding, which not only kept the IPCC in power (Agrawala 1998b) but also constituted a major conflict of interest.

Subsequent IPPC reports have been produced, with the *Fourth Assessment Report* (AR4) in 2007, the *Fifth Assessment Report* (AR5) in 2013, and the WG1 of the *Sixth Assessment Report* (AR6) in 2021 followed by WG2 in 2022. Each report has proclaimed the condition of Earth's climate being more dire, and called for a more draconian response, than the previous. The Copenhagen Summit, held in mid-December of 2009 (two years after the release of AR4) ended in disarray, largely due to international legal issues, a lack of consensus regarding air temperature targets, and rejection by developing countries (most notably, Brazil, China, India, and South Africa), which "have not got[ten] the deal they wanted" (BBC News 2009; Reitan and Gibson 2012; Singer, Legates, and Lupo 2021).

The Paris Agreement in 2015 followed the release of AR5, and supporters hoped the agreement would replace Kyoto and set targets through 2030. This round of negotiations produced a largely toothless treaty: each nation proposed to reduce its emissions with a self-imposed voluntary emissions target for carbon dioxide (no target was set for global reduction) and to self-report its emissions with no outside supervision. No sanctions would be levied on any country that failed to meet its self-imposed restrictions (Gao 2016; Singer, Legates, and Luop 2021). Although the Paris Agreement was accepted by the Obama administration, the Trump administration withdrew the United States, and the Biden administration restored the United States into the agreement. Nevertheless, Gao (2016, 374) suggests that the Paris

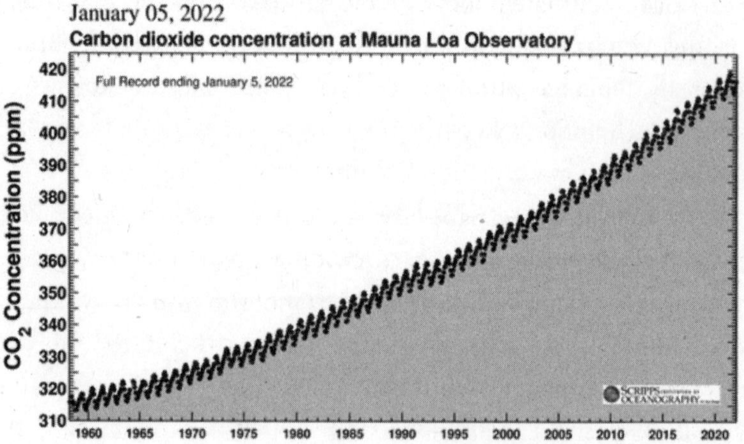

Figure 2.5. Atmospheric carbon dioxide concentrations measured at Mauna Loa Observatory in Hawaii. *Courtesy of the Scripps Institution of Oceanography (https://scripps.ucsd.edu/bluemoon/co2_400/mlo_full_record.png, downloaded August 24, 2023).*

Agreement provided "a clear, strong, positive and long-term signal for the sustainable transformation of the world economy."

Thirty years of climate treaties, wrangling at the UNFCCC meetings (Conferences of the Parties, or COPs), and virtue-signaling by virtually every country regarding how much it cares about "saving the planet" have had no measurable effect on the global rate of increases of atmospheric carbon dioxide (Figure 2.5).

Why? At the UNFCCC meeting in Paris in 2015, its executive secretary Christiana Figueres (with degrees in anthropology) admitted that the meeting was "the first time in the history of mankind that we are setting ourselves the task of intentionally, within a defined period of time, changing the economic development model that has been reigning for at least 150 years, since the Industrial Revolution" (Booker 2018, 70). Ottmar Edenhofer, chair of IPCC WG3, said,

> One must say clearly that we redistribute de facto the world's wealth by climate policy.... One has to free oneself from the illusion that international climate policy is environmental policy. This has almost nothing to do with environmental policy anymore. (Morano 2021, 14).

As the German newspaper *Neue Zürcher Zeitung* would summarize, "[T]he next world climate summit in Cancun is actually an economy summit during which [re]distribution of the world's resources will be negotiated" (cited by Hayward 2010). Note that carbon dioxide is merely the mechanism by which wealth can be redistributed—whether carbon dioxide concentrations actually decrease is immaterial.

The "Great Reset" sprang from the fiftieth annual meeting of the World Economic Forum held in June of 2020 in Davos, Switzerland. It involves dramatically increasing the power of government through expansive new social programs, like the Green New Deal, and using vast regulatory schemes and government programs to coerce corporations into supporting socialist causes. Proponents argue that the "four horsemen of the apocalypse"—climate change, loss of biodiversity, overpopulation, and a consumer economy—require us to change to a government-controlled society. Currently, climate change legislation has the biggest traction. The Great Reset has already been backed by influential leaders, activists, academics, and institutions. In addition to the World Economic Forum and the United Nations, the Great Reset movement counts among its supporters the International Monetary Fund, heads of state, Greenpeace, and CEOs and presidents of large corporations and financial institutions.

Today, the science of climate change is a well-funded and well-orchestrated campaign "to fundamentally transform global societies" (Hermwille 2016, 19). At some point, more than thirty years ago and before the IPCC, the science mattered. Legitimate questions were raised, and the science of climate was truly a science that spurred on many to study the Earth's systems and to marvel at its beauty and complexity. The money and fame that followed the transformation of climate science to a mechanism for societal and economic reforms for wealth redistribution have corrupted it, turning it into a consensus-driven deception that has cheapened and grossly oversimplified the science (for example, "carbon dioxide heats the surface like a blanket covering the Earth"). Facts no longer really matter to the "true believers." As Trimble (2007, 22) noted, "[I]deology and science do not mix. Groupthink, emotionalism, ad hominem attacks, and suppression of dissent" are characteristics of global warming alarmists, and these traits are still prevalent today. As Hoffer (1951, 107) concluded, "The quality of ideas seems to play a minor role in mass movement leadership. What counts is the arrogant gesture, the complete disregard of the opinion of others, the singlehanded defiance of the world."

Climate change is not about the science. Since it morphed into climate change policy activism, it has not been.

References

Agrawala, S. (1998a). "Context and Early Origins of the Intergovernmental Panel on Climate Change." *Climatic Change* 39, no. 4 (August): 605–20. Online at https://link.springer.com/article/10.1023/A:1005315532386.

———. (1998b). "Structural and Process History of the Intergovernmental Panel on Climate Change." *Climatic Change* 39, no. 4 (August): 621–42. Online at https://link.springer.com/article/10.1023/A:1005312331477.

Arrhenius, S. (1896). "On the Influence of Carbonic Acid in the Air upon the Temperature of the Ground." *London, Edinburgh, and Dublin Philosophical Magazine and Journal of Science*, 5th ser., 5, no. 251 (April): 237–76.

———.(1908). *Worlds in the Making: The Evolution of the Universe.* Translated by H. Borns. New York: Harper.

Bailey, R. (1997). "Who Is Maurice Strong?" *National Review* 49, no. 16. September 1.

Baliunas, S., and W. Soon (1999). "Pioneers in the Greenhouse Effect." *World Climate Report* 4 (19): 6. Online at https://lweb.cfa.harvard.edu/~wsoon/myownPapers-d/BaliunasSoon99-WCR-onArrhenius+GHGeffect.pdf.

Barkdull, J., and P. G. Harris (2015). "Climate-Induced Conflict or Hospice Earth: The Increasing Importance of Eco-Socialism." *Global Change, Peace & Security* 27 (2): 237–43. Online at https://www.tandfonline.com/doi/abs/10.1080/14781158.2015.1019442?journalCode=cpar20.

Barwell, R. (2013). "The Mathematical Formatting of Climate Change: Critical Mathematics Education and Post-Normal Science." *Research in Mathematics Education* 15 (1): 1–16. Online at https://www.tandfonline.com/doi/abs/10.1080/14794802.2012.756633.

BBC News (2009). "Key Powers Reach Compromise at Climate Summit." December 19. Online at http://news.bbc.co.uk/2/hi/europe/8421935.stm.

Bezdek, R., C. D. Idso, D. R. Legates, and S. F. Singer, eds. (2019). *Climate Change Reconsidered II: Fossil Fuels*. Arlington Heights, Illinois: Nongovernmental International Panel on Climate Change (NIPCC), The Heartland Institute. Online at http://climatechangereconsidered.org/wp-content/uploads/2019/01/Full-Book.pdf.

Biagini, B., and A. Sagar (2004). "Non-Governmental Organizations (NGOs) and Energy." In *Encyclopedia of Energy*. Vol. 4, edited by C. J. Cleveland. Amsterdam: Elsevier Science. 301–14.

Booker, C. (2018). *Global Warming: A Case Study in Groupthink*. GWPF Report 28. London: Global Warming Policy Foundation. Online at https://www.thegwpf.org/content/uploads/2018/02/Groupthink.pdf.

Brüggemann, M., I. Lörcher, and S. Walter (2020). "Post-Normal Science Communication: Exploring the Blurring Boundaries of Science and Journalism." *Journal of Science Communication* 19 (22): 1–22. Online at https://jcom.sissa.it/article/pubid/JCOM_1903_2020_A02.

Bryson, R. A. (1974). "A Perspective on Climate Change." *Science* 184, no. 4138 (May): 753–60. Online at https://www.science.org/doi/10.1126/science.184.4138.753.

Bryson, R. A., and B. M. Goodman (1980). "Volcanic Activity and Climatic Changes." *Science* 207, no. 4435 (March): 1041–44. Online at https://www.science.org/doi/10.1126/science.207.4435.1041.

Buschke, F. T., E. A. Botts, and S. P. Sinclair (2019). "Post-Normal Conservation Science Fills the Space between Research, Policy, and Implementation." *Conservation Science and Practice* 1, no. 8

(August): e73. Online at https://conbio.onlinelibrary.wiley.com/doi/full/10.1111/csp2.73.

Carrozza, C. (2015). "Democratizing Expertise and Environmental Governance: Different Approaches to the Politics of Science and Their Relevance for Policy Analysis." *Journal of Environmental Policy & Planning* 17 (1): 108–26. Online at https://www.tandfonline.com/doi/abs/10.1080/1523908X.2014.914894.

CDP (2018). "Leaving No One Behind." In *Report on the Twentieth Session (12–16 March 2018)*, Official Records of the Economic and Social Council, Supplement No. 13 (E/2018/33), by United Nations Committee for Development Policy. New York: United Nations. Online at https://www.un.org/development/desa/dpad/wp-content/uploads/sites/45/CDP-excerpt-2018-1.pdf.

Chan, G. (2015). "Climate Sceptic Maurice Newman Says World Leaders Embracing Junk Science." *The Guardian*, December 27. Online at https://www.theguardian.com/australia-news/2015/dec/28/climate-sceptic-maurice-newman-says-world-leaders-embracing-junk-science.

Changnon, S. A., Jr., F. A. Huff, and R. G. Semonin (1971). "METROMEX: An Investigation of Inadvertent Weather Modification." *Bulletin of the American Meteorological Society* 51, no. 10 (October): 958–67.

Chikulo, B. C. (2014). "An Analysis of Climate Change, Poverty and Human Security in South Africa," *Journal of Human Ecology* 47, no. 3 (September): 295–303. Online at https://www.researchgate.net/publication/321207777_An_Analysis_of_Climate_Change_Poverty_and_Human_Security_in_South_Africa.

Deming, D. (2005). "Global Warming, the Politicization of Science, and Michael Crichton's *State of Fear*," *Journal of Scientific Exploration* 19, no. 2 (October): 247–56. Online at https://www.scientificexploration.org/docs/19/jse_19_2_deming.pdf.

Diffenbaugh, N. S., and M. B. Burke (2019). "Global Warming Has Increased Global Economic Inequality." *Proceedings, National*

Academies of Science, 116, no. 20 (April): 9808–13. Online at https://www.pnas.org/doi/10.1073/pnas.1816020116.

Durschmied, E. (2012). *The Weather Factor: How Nature Has Changed History*. New York: Arcade Publishing.

Ellingson, T. (2001). *The Myth of the Noble Savage*. Berkeley: University of California Press.

Fleming, J. R. (1999). "Joseph Fourier, the 'Greenhouse Effect', and the Quest for a Universal Theory of Terrestrial Temperatures." *Endeavour* 23 (2): 72–75. Online at https://www.sciencedirect.com/science/article/abs/pii/S0160932799012107.

Galvin, J. (2020). "Meteorology and the Second World War." *Weather* 75, no. 10 (October): 325–28. Online at https://rmets.onlinelibrary.wiley.com/doi/abs/10.1002/wea.3687.

Gao, X. (2016). "The *Paris Agreement* and Global Climate Governance: China's Role and Contribution." *China Quarterly of International Strategic Studies* 2, no. 3 (Fall): 365–81. Online at https://www.worldscientific.com/doi/abs/10.1142/S2377740016500226.

Groisman, P. Y., and D. R. Legates (1994). "The Accuracy of United States Precipitation Data." *Bulletin of the American Meteorological Society* 75, no. 3 (February): 215–27. Online at https://journals.ametsoc.org/view/journals/bams/75/2/1520-0477_1994_075_0215_taousp_2_0_co_2.xml.

Harvey, D. (1993). "The Nature of Environment: The Dialectics of Social and Environmental Change," *The Socialist Register* 29. Online at https://socialistregister.com/index.php/srv/article/download/5621/2519/0.

Hauge, K. H., and R. Barwell (2017). "Post-Normal Science and Mathematics Education in Uncertain Times: Educating Future Citizens for Extended Peer Communities." *Futures* 91 (August): 25–34. Online at https://www.sciencedirect.com/science/article/pii/S0016328717300484.

Hayward, S. F. (2010). "From Cancun to Kyoto." *National Review*, December 8. Online at https://www.nationalreview.com/2010/12/cancun-kyoto-steven-f-hayward.

Hecht, A. D., and D. Tirpak (1995). "Framework Agreement on Climate Change: A Scientific and Policy History." *Climatic Change* 29, no. 4 (April): 371–402. Online at https://link.springer.com/article/10.1007/BF01092424.

Hermwille, L. (2016). "Climate Change as a Transformation Challenge: A New Climate Policy Paradigm?" *Gaia* 25, no. 1 (January): 19–22. Online at https://www.researchgate.net/publication/299400291_Climate_Change_as_a_Transformation_Challenge_A_New_Climate_Policy_Paradigm.

Heron, K. (2021). "Dialectical Materialisms, Metabolic Rifts and the Climate Crisis: A Lacanian/Hegelian Perspective." *Science & Society* 85, no. 4 (October): 501–26. Online at https://guilfordjournals.com/doi/10.1521/siso.2021.85.4.501.

Hoffer, E. (1951). *The True Believer: Thoughts on the Nature of Mass Movements*. New York: Harper and Row.

Houghton, J. T., G. J. Jenkins, and J. J. Ephraums, eds. (1990). *Climate Change: The IPCC Scientific Assessment.* (*IPCC First Assessment Report*) Cambridge, United Kingdom: Cambridge University Press. Online at https://www.ipcc.ch/site/assets/uploads/2018/03/ipcc_far_wg_I_full_report.pdf.

Houghton, J. T., et al. (1996). *Climate Change 1995: The Science of Climate Change, Contribution of Working Group I to the Second Assessment Report of the Intergovernmental Panel on Climate Change.* (*IPCC Second Assessment Report*) Cambridge, United Kingdom: Cambridge University Press. Online at https://www.ipcc.ch/site/assets/uploads/2018/02/ipcc_sar_wg_I_full_report.pdf.

Houghton, J. T., et al. (2001). *Climate Change 2001: The Scientific Basis, Contribution of Working Group I to the Third Assessment*

Report of the Intergovernmental Panel on Climate Change (IPCC Third Assessment Report). Cambridge, United Kingdom: Cambridge University Press. Online at https://www.ipcc.ch/site/assets/uploads/2018/03/WGI_TAR_full_report.pdf.

Janis, I. L. (1972). *Victims of Groupthink: A Psychological Study of Foreign-Policy Decisions and Fiascoes*. Boston: Houghton Mifflin Company.

Karpinska, A. (2018). "Post-Normal Science. The Escape of Science: From Truth to Quality?" *Social Epistemology* 32 (5): 338–50. Online at https://www.tandfonline.com/doi/abs/10.1080/02691728.2018.1531157.

Kessler, G. (2015a). "Kerry's Claim that He Organized the 'Very First' Hearings on Climate Change." *Washington Post*. March 18. Online at https://www.washingtonpost.com/news/fact-checker/wp/2015/03/18/kerrys-claim-that-he-organized-the-very-first-hearings-on-climate-change.

———. (2015b). "Setting the Record Straight: The Real Story of a Pivotal Climate-Change Hearing." *Washington Post*, March 30. Online at https://www.washingtonpost.com/news/fact-checker/wp/2015/03/30/setting-the-record-straight-the-real-story-of-a-pivotal-climate-change-hearing.

Kuntz, M. (2012). "The Postmodern Assault on Science." *EMBO Reports* 13, no. 10 (October): 885–89. Online at https://www.ncbi.nlm.nih.gov/pmc/articles/PMC3463968.

Laboratory of Climatology (1954). "Estimating Soil Tractionability from Climatic Data." *Publications in Climatology* 7, no. 3. Online at https://www.google.com/books/edition/Estimating_Soil_Tractionability_from_Cli/Ip3mUw2qLXYC?hl=en.

Lamb, H. H. (1970). "Volcanic Dust in the Atmosphere; with a Chronology and Assessment of Its Meteorological Significance." *Philosophical Transactions of the Royal Society of London* 266, no. 1178 (January): 425–533. Online at https://royalsocietypublishing.org/doi/10.1098/rsta.1970.0010.

Landsberg, H. (1981). *The Urban Climate*. International Geophysics Series. Vol. 28. New York: Academic Press.

Lindzen, R. S. (1992). "Global Warming: The Origin and Nature of the Alleged Scientific Consensus." *Regulation* (Spring): 87–98. Online at https://www.cato.org/sites/cato.org/files/serials/files/regulation/1992/4/v15n2-9.pdf.

Losee, J. (2001). *A Historical Introduction to the Philosophy of Science*. 4th ed. Oxford, United Kingdom: Oxford University Press.

Löwy, M. (2005). "What Is Ecosocialism?" *Capitalism Nature Socialism* 16, no. 2 (June): 15–24. Online at https://www.tandfonline.com/doi/abs/10.1080/10455750500108237.

Maksel, R. (2018). "Why Was the Discovery of the Jet Stream Mostly Ignored?" *Air & Space Magazine*, April. Online at https://www.smithsonianmag.com/air-space-magazine/as-next-may-unbelievablebuttrue-180968355.

Mann, M. E. (2002). "Climate Reconstruction: The Value of Multiple Proxies." *Science* 297, no. 5586 (September): 1481–82. Online at https://www.researchgate.net/publication/11185417_Climate_reconstruction_The_value_of_multiple_proxies.

Mann, M. E., R. S. Bradley, and M. K. Hughes (1998). "Global-Scale Temperature Patterns and Climate Forcing over the Past Six Centuries." *Nature* 392, no. 6678 (April): 779–87. Online at https://www.nature.com/articles/33859.

———. (1999). "Northern Hemisphere Temperatures during the Past Millennium: Inferences, Uncertainties, and Limitations." *Geophysical Research Letters* 26, no. 6 (March): 759–62. Online at https://agupubs.onlinelibrary.wiley.com/doi/10.1029/1999GL900070.

———. (2004). "Correction: Corrigendum: Global-Scale Temperature Patterns and Climate Forcing over the Past Six Centuries." *Nature*

430, no. 6678 (April): 105. Online at https://www.nature.com/articles/nature02478.

Mann, M. E., and P. D. Jones (2003). "Global Surface Temperatures over the Past Two Millennia." *Geophysical Research Letters* 30, no. 15 (August): 1820. Online at https://agupubs.onlinelibrary.wiley.com/doi/full/10.1029/2003GL017814.

Mann, M. E., et al. (2003). "On Past Temperatures and Anomalous Late-20th Century Warmth." *EOS* 84, no. 27 (July): 256–57. Online at https://agupubs.onlinelibrary.wiley.com/doi/abs/10.1029/2003EO270003.

Mayraz, N. (2019). "U.N. Predicts Disaster If Global Warming Not Checked, Peter James Spielmann, June 29, 1989." Associated Press, June 29. Online at https://energycentral.com/c/cp/un-predicts-disaster-if-global-warming-not-checked-peter-james-spielmann-june-29; original AP article, untitled, at https://apnews.com/article/bd45c372caf118ec99964ea547880cd0.

McIntyre, S., and R. R. McKitrick (2003). "Corrections to the Mann et. al. (1998) Proxy Data Base and Northern Hemispheric Average Temperature Series." *Energy & Environment* 14, no. 6 (November): 751–71. Online at https://journals.sagepub.com/doi/10.1260/095830503322793632.

———. (2005). "Hockey Sticks, Principal Components, and Spurious Significance." *Geophysical Research Letters* 32, no. 3 (February): L03710. Online at https://agupubs.onlinelibrary.wiley.com/doi/full/10.1029/2004GL021750.

Mercer, D. (2018). "Why Popper Can't Resolve the Debate over Global Warming: Problems with the Uses of Philosophy of Science in the Media and Public Framing of the Science of Global Warming." *Public Understanding of Science* 27, no. 2 (May): 139–52. Online at https://pubmed.ncbi.nlm.nih.gov/27150265.

Montgomery, D. (2019). "AOC's Chief of Change." *Washington Post Magazine*, July 10. Online at https://www.washingtonpost.com/news/magazine/wp/2019/07/10/feature/how-saikat-chakrabarti-became-aocs-chief-of-change.

Moore, M. P. (2009). "The Union of Concerned Scientists on the Uncertainty of Climate Change: A Study of Synecdochic Form." *Environmental Communication* 3, no. 2 (June): 191–205.

Morano, M. (2021). *Green Fraud: Why the Green New Deal Is Even Worse Than You Think*. Washington, D.C.: Regnery Publishing.

Moss, R. (1994). "Intergovernmental Panel on Climate Change." *Human Dimensions Quarterly*, 1 (2).

NAS (National Academy of Sciences) (2006). *Surface Temperature Reconstructions for the Last 2,000 Years*. Washington, D.C.: The National Academies Press. Online at https://nap.nationalacademies.org/download/11676.

Paltridge, G. W. (2018). "Four Questions on Climate Change." GWPF Essay 6. London: The Global Warming Policy Foundation. Online at https://www.thegwpf.org/content/uploads/2018/05/Paltridge2018.pdf.

Ponte, L. (1976). *The Cooling*. Ann Arbor, Michigan: Prentice-Hall.

Popper, K. (1934). *Logik der Forschung: zur Erkenntnistheorie der modernen Naturwissenschaft*. Wien, Österreich: Verlag von Julius Springer. Published in English as *The Logic of Scientific Discovery*. London: Hutchinson, 1959.

Ravetz, J. R. (1999). "What Is Post-Normal Science?" *Futures* 31, no. 7 (February): 647–53. Online at http://www.andreasaltelli.eu/file/repository/Editorials2.pdf.

———. (2006). "Post-Normal Science and the Complexity of Transitions towards Sustainability." *Ecological Complexity* 3, no. 4 (December): 275–84. Online at https://www.sciencedirect.com/science/article/abs/pii/S1476945X07000037.

———. (2011). "'Climategate' and the Maturing of Post-Normal Science." *Futures* 43, no. 2 (March): 149–57. Online at https://www.sciencedirect.com/science/article/abs/pii/S0016328710002302.

Reitan, R., and S. Gibson (2012). "Climate Change or Social Change? Environmental and Leftist Praxis and Participatory Action Research." *Globalizations* 9, no. 3 (June): 395–410. Online at https://www.tandfonline.com/doi/abs/10.1080/14747731.2012.680735.

Roads, J. O. (1998). "Jerome Namias 1910–199[7]: A Biographical Memoir." *Biographical Memoirs* 76, Washington, D.C.: National Academy Press. Online at http://www.nasonline.org/publications/biographical-memoirs/memoir-pdfs/namias-jerome.pdf.

Rogalski, A. (2012). "History of Infrared Detectors." *Opto-Electronics Review* 20, no. 3 (July): 279–308. Online at https://link.springer.com/article/10.2478/s11772-012-0037-7.

Saloranta, T. M. (2001). "Post-Normal Science and the Global Climate Change Issue." *Climatic Change* 50, no. 4 (September): 395–404. Online at https://link.springer.com/article/10.1023/A:1010636822581.

Saltelli, A., and S. O. Funtowicz (2017). "What Is Science's Crisis Really About?" *Futures* 91 (August): 5–11.

Santese, A. (2020). "Between Pacifism and Environmentalism: The History of Greenpeace." *USAbroad—Journal of American History and Politics* 3, no. 1S (November): 107–15.

Schneider, S. H., and L. E. Mesirow (1976). *The Genesis Strategy: Climate and Global Survival.* New York: Springer.

Seitz, F. (1996). "A Major Deception on Global Warming." *Wall Street Journal*, June 12. Online at https://www.wsj.com/articles/SB834512411338954000.

Shapely, D. (1976). "The Genesis Strategy." *New York Times*, July 18.

Shabecoff, P. (1988). "Sharp Cut in Burning of Fossil Fuels Is Urged to Battle Shift in Climate." *New York Times*, June 24. Online at https://www.nytimes.com/1988/06/24/us/global-warming-has-begun-expert-tells-senate.html.

Singer, S. F. (1988). "Fact and Fantasy on Greenhouse Earth." *Wall Street Journal*, August 30.

———. (2003). "The Revelle-Gore Story: Attempted Political Suppression of Science." In *Politicizing Science: The Alchemy of Policymaking*, edited by Michael Gough. Stanford: Hoover Institution Press. 283–97.

Singer, S. F., D. R. Legates, and A. R. Lupo (2021). *Hot Talk, Cold Science: Global Warming's Unfinished Debate*. 3rd ed. Oakland, California: Independent Institute.

Singer, S. F., R. Revelle, and C. Starr (1992). "What to Do about Greenhouse Warming: Look before You Leap." *Cosmos: A Journal of Emerging Issues* 5, no. 2 (Summer). Online at http://ruby.fgcu.edu/courses/twimberley/envirophilo/lookbeforeyouleap.pdf.

Smith, W. L., et al. (1986). "The Meteorological Satellite: Overview of 25 Years of Operation." *Science* 231, no. 4737 (January): 455–62. Online at https://www.science.org/doi/10.1126/science.231.4737.455.

Soon, W., and S. L. Baliunas (2003). "Proxy Climatic and Environmental Changes of the Past 1000 Years." *Climate Research* 23, no. 2 (January): 89–110. Online at https://www.int-res.com/abstracts/cr/v23/n2/p89-110.

Soon, W., D. R. Legates, and S. L. Baliunas (2004). "Estimation and Representation of Long-Term (>40 Year) Trends of Northern-Hemisphere-Gridded Surface Temperature: A Note of Caution." *Geophysical Research Letters* 31, no. 3 (February): L03209. Online at https://agupubs.onlinelibrary.wiley.com/doi/full/10.1029/2003GL019141.

Soon, W., and S. H. Yaskell (2003). "Year without a Summer," *Mercury* 32 (May–June): 13–22. Online at https://lweb.cfa.harvard.edu/~wsoon/myownPapers-d/Summer_of_1816.pdf.

Soon, W., et al. (2003). "Reconstructing Climatic and Environmental Changes of the Past 1000 Years: A Reappraisal." *Energy &*

Environment 14, no. 2–3 (May): 233–96. Online at https://journals.sagepub.com/doi/10.1260/0958305037651846 19.

Szirmai, A., W. Naudé, and L. Alcorta (2013). *Pathways to Industrialization in the Twenty-First Century: New Challenges and Emerging Paradigms*. Oxford, United Kingdom: Oxford University Press.

Thomas, W. L., ed. (1956). *Man's Role in Changing the Face of the Earth*. Chicago: University of Chicago Press.

Thornthwaite, C. W. (1954). "Topoclimatology." In *Proceedings of the Toronto Meteorological Conference, 1953: Held from 9 to 15 September 1953*. London: Royal Meteorological Society. 227–32.

———. (1957). "The Task Ahead in Climatology." *WMO Bulletin* 6, no. 1 (January): 2–7.

Trein, E. S. (2018). "An Argument for Vindicating a Marxist Ontology in Environmental Education Research." *Environmental Education Research* 24, no. 10 (January): 1464–75. Online at https://www.tandfonline.com/doi/abs/10.1080/13504622.2018.1545153?journalCode=ceer20.

Trimble, S. W. (2007). "The Double Standard in Environmental Science." *Regulation* 30, no. 2 (Summer): 16–22. Online at https://papers.ssrn.com/sol3/papers.cfm?abstract_id=1001452.

Turnpenny, J. R. (2012). "Lessons from Post-Normal Science for Climate Science-Sceptic Debates." *WIREs Climate Change* 3, no. 5 (September): 397–407. Online at https://www.researchgate.net/publication/260415516_Lessons_from_post-normal_science_for_climate_science-sceptic_debates.

Turnpenny, J. R., M. Jones, and I. Lorenzoni (2011). "Where Now for Post-Normal Science? A Critical Review of Its Development, Definitions, and Uses." *Science, Technology, & Human Values* 36, no. 3 (May): 287–306. Online at https://www.jstor.org/stable/41149056.

UCS (2023). "History." Union of Concerned Scientists. Accessed August 25, 2023. Online at https://www.ucsusa.org/about/history.

Wegman, E., D. W. Scott, and Y. Said (2006). *Ad Hoc Committee Report on the "Hockey Stick"; Global Climate Reconstruction.* Washington, D.C.: U.S. House of Representatives. Online at https://web.archive.org/web/20060716210311/http://energycommerce.house.gov/108/home/07142006_Wegman_Report.pdf.

Wesselink, A., and R. Hoppe (2011). "If Post-Normal Science Is the Solution, What Is the Problem? The Politics of Activist Environmental Science." *Science, Technology, & Human Values* 36, no. 3 (November): 389–412. Online at https://journals.sagepub.com/doi/10.1177/0162243910385786.

Woodcock, B. A. (2014). "'The Scientific Method' as Myth and Ideal." *Science & Education* 23, no. 10 (October): 2069–93. Online at https://www.researchgate.net/publication/271919313_The_Scientific_Method_as_Myth_and_Ideal.

WMO (1979). *Proceedings of the World Climate Conference: A Conference of Experts on Climate and Mankind.* Geneva: World Meteorological Organization. WMO No. 537. February 12–13. Online at https://library.wmo.int/doc_num.php?explnum_id=8346.

———. (1985). *Report of the International Conference on the Assessment of the Role of Carbon Dioxide and Other Greenhouse Gases in Climate Variations and Associated Impacts.* Villach, Austria: World Meteorological Organization. WMO No. 661. October 9–15. Online at https://library.wmo.int/doc_num.php?explnum_id=8512.

CHAPTER 3

The Science of Climate

BY ROY W. SPENCER

CHAPTER SUMMARY

The word "climate" is understood in science to mean the thirty-year average of a meteorological variable such as temperature, precipitation, humidity, and so forth, taken at a location over a seasonal time window. Therefore "climate normals" serving as the basis for weather comparisons are thirty-year averages (recently from 1991–2020). There can be significant weather variability within a thirty-year statistic, but any particular event does not constitute a change in climate. Weather is not climate.

The study of climate change necessitates an understanding of all controlling processes. Only then is there hope of predicting future changes. The Sun is the radiative energy source for Earth's climate system, driving weather processes and thereby the climate state over time. It is accepted that a differential in incoming radiation, which warms, versus outgoing radiation, which cools, will create an average temperature to achieve an energy rebalance. Greenhouse gas changes modify this effect, warming or cooling the Earth.

But there are other immensely complex energy exchange processes such as clouds, precipitation, evapotranspiration, oceanic exchanges, snow and ice, volcanoes, and so forth. Natural energy flows through these systems are immense but not yet well understood, and their contributions can be attributed mistakenly to greenhouse gas effects. That variabilities can be chaotic challenges the assumption that, without human influence, nature is in long-term balance. Climate change should therefore not be treated as a single-variable greenhouse gas system.

To understand the chapters later in this book dealing with climate change and its prediction, it is useful first to understand the basic processes controlling the average state of today's climate system. Much of what follows represents mainstream, consensus understanding of the processes controlling the climate system. Not all processes are well understood. We will put special emphasis on those that lead to considerable uncertainty in predictions of climate change in response to human greenhouse gas emissions. We will also examine the reasons why the climate can vary naturally, without any human influence.

While there is no formal definition, "climate" is generally understood to mean time-averaged weather, by season, for a location, a region, or the whole Earth (for example, the global area-averaged surface temperature, or the average January precipitation in Podunk, Michigan). It has been traditional to average over a recent thirty-year period (for example, 1991–2020) for determining "normal" weather. These so-called climate "normals" include all elements of weather, including temperature, humidity, precipitation, clouds, air pressure, and wind.

Until the 1970s, little interest was given to climate research because climate did not change enough on a human timescale to warrant much attention. This all changed in the 1970s–80s when global warming theory began to address the possibility that increasing CO_2 from fossil fuel burning and cement production might cause changes to weather that depart significantly from the average weather—that is, changes to climate—experienced in previous decades. The study of climate change necessitated an understanding of all the processes controlling average climate so that we might have some hope of predicting changes in the climate system of the future.

The climate change issue generated great interest among scientists, environmental activists, politicians, and world governments. As a result, many of us who were trained as research meteorologists went into climate research instead of weather research. The use of computerized forecast models has been central to that effort. In the last forty years, weather-forecast models have improved steadily and have had immense socio-economic benefits for the global population.

The advent of global warming theory required that our weather-forecast models be modified to produce forecasts of how the average weather (climate) might change in coming decades and centuries. The outputs of these climate models, discussed in chapter 4, are the basis for proposed energy policy changes to reduce the threat of climate change.

So, to study climate change, we must first understand the processes that control climate in the absence of change. It is easier to explain the operation of the current climate system in an average sense (this chapter) than to explain the processes involved in climate change (the next chapter). Anyone can attempt to explain the current climate using even incorrect physical reasoning, but accurately predicting the future is much more difficult. As evidence of this, about two dozen different computerized climate models developed at research centers around the world all produce about the same average global climate but produce quite different kinds of climate change in the years to come. While much research has been done by these groups, the model-produced range of global warming estimates by 2100 actually broadened from 1990 to 2020 (Zelinka et al. 2020).

Earth's Energy Budget and Temperature

The energy source for Earth's climate system is the Sun, which provides a yearly and globally averaged energy input at the rate of about 240 watts per square meter (W/m^2). Locally, that value can exceed 1,000 W/m^2 at noon in the tropics under cloud-free conditions. It drops to zero at high latitudes in the winter when the Sun does not shine at all. Geothermal energy input into the climate system is much less than 1 W/m^2 and so is generally ignored in climate research. The solar energy input drives all weather processes, and thus the average state of the climate system.

As shown in Figure 3.1, at the top of the atmosphere all the solar energy absorbed by the climate system is approximately balanced by the loss of an equal amount of infrared (longwave, or heat) radiation to outer space.

To the extent that these rates of energy gain and loss at the top of the atmosphere are equal, the climate system remains at about the same average temperature. All weather processes, in one way or another, affect energy flows within the system, and thus the global energy balance.

Importantly, the top-of-atmosphere energy flows of ~240 W/m^2 are not known exactly. We have satellites that estimate it, but their

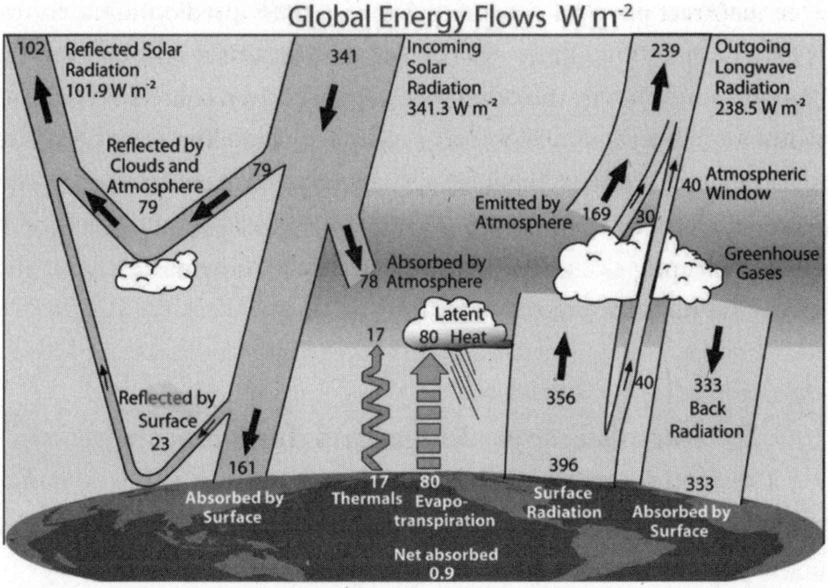

Figure 3.1. Globally averaged energy flows (W/m²) during 2000–2004 as estimated from satellites and other data sources (Trenberth et al. 2009). Processes affecting sunlight are on the left, while those affecting infrared radiation are on the right. In the middle are the processes by which heat is lost by the Earth's surface, which includes dry convection (thermals) and moist convection (evapotranspiration). © *American Meteorological Society. Used with permission.*

calibration is not good enough to know whether it's 235, 240, or 245. Significantly, that 10-watt range of uncertainty is bigger than the estimated radiative forcing (energy imbalance) of the climate system, shown at the bottom of Figure 3.1 to be 0.9 W/m^2. This small net energy input (energy left over after deducting outflow from inflow) into the climate system is based upon the average slight warming trend of the global oceans in recent decades as observed by thousands of drifting and diving instrumented buoys called Argo floats (Feder 2000).

It is worth repeating that the approximate global-average energy balance is what keeps globally averaged temperatures almost constant from one decade to the next. Any imbalance in those energy flows will cause either warming (more energy gained than lost if inflows exceed outflows) or cooling (more energy lost than gained if outflows exceed inflows). Importantly, any source of warming that causes temperatures to rise results in enhanced infrared radiation (heat) loss to outer space, which then restores global energy balance. This is the same process as a fire in a fireplace emitting radiant heat, which your skin perceives as intensifying as the fire gets hotter. This increased emission of IR energy with increasing temperature is what stabilizes the climates of all planetary bodies and similarly limits the warming produced by all computerized climate models.

Of course, talking about global-average energy flows and temperatures misses the huge variations in these processes on a global basis. For example, the tropics gain more radiant energy than they lose (which is why they are so warm), and high latitudes lose more radiant energy than they gain (which is why they are so cold). Consistent with this, there is a net transport of energy from the warmer tropics to the cooler high latitudes. The energy flows through the climate system and the induced weather we experience (for example, warm fronts and cold fronts) involve processes that are often related to temperature, and especially to temperature differences horizontally and between layers of the atmosphere vertically. If the climate system had the same temperature everywhere, weather (for example, wind, clouds, and precipitation) as we know it would not exist.

It is a common misconception that temperature is determined by the rate of energy absorbed from sunlight. It's easy to see why people might think this since the tropics have intense sunlight and are hot, while the Arctic and Antarctic have little sunlight and are cold. But, like all physical systems having temperature (your body, a car engine, the interior of a house in winter, a pot of water on the stove), the temperature of the climate system is a function of *both* the rate of absorbed energy *and* the rate at which energy is lost to cooler surroundings.

In the case of the human body, you lose heat to the air around you through conduction to cooler air, infrared (heat) radiation, and evaporation of water from your skin. That energy loss is balanced by energy gain from metabolism, and the rates of energy gain and energy loss become equal at an average body temperature around 98.6°F. This concept of energy balance controlling temperature is fundamental to an understanding of both average climate and climate change.

A fascinating demonstration of the importance of energy loss to temperature is a comparison between the human body and the interior of the Sun. It is surprising that, for equal amounts of mass, the Sun generates energy at a lesser rate through nuclear fusion than the human body does through metabolism. But the Sun reaches much higher temperatures (millions of degrees) because the energy generated in the interior of the Sun must travel as much as 430,000 miles to reach the surface before it can escape to the cold depths of outer space. For the human body, the energy only needs to travel several inches to reach the skin's surface and escape to cooler surroundings. In a sense, the Sun is very well insulated against heat loss, while the human body is not.

Global temperatures are therefore influenced by not only the processes controlling the rate of *gain* of solar energy (say, the reflectivity of clouds or the land surface), but also those processes affecting the rate of energy *loss* (say, the infrared absorption and emission properties of water vapor, carbon dioxide, and clouds). These latter processes constitute what is called Earth's "greenhouse effect" (GE). Globally averaged, the GE has about a 50 percent contribution from water vapor, 25 percent from clouds, 20 percent from carbon dioxide, and 5 percent from minor greenhouse gases such as methane (Kiehl and Trenberth 1997). In later chapters of this book (especially 5, 6, 7, and 8), these processes will be explored in greater detail, particularly how they affect our estimates of global warming from increasing carbon dioxide, which slightly reduces the rate at which the Earth cools to outer space.

Clouds

Clouds reflect some incoming sunlight back to outer space, which is a cooling effect, but they also reduce infrared emission to space (a warming effect), because they are typically at a colder temperature than the Earth's surface. Averaged over the Earth, the solar reflection cooling effect dominates, but this varies with cloud type—low-altitude clouds have a net cooling effect on climate, while high-altitude clouds (especially if they are thin) have a net warming effect. So, you can see that any changes in clouds with a warming climate have the potential either to amplify or to reduce the warming depending upon what kinds of clouds are changing. This remains a source of large uncertainty in global warming projections.

As you might expect, the microphysical processes involved in cloud production are very complex. Generally speaking, clouds cannot be included explicitly in computerized climate models because computers are nowhere near fast enough to resolve their fine structure. Instead, clouds are mostly "parameterized," which means that they are statistically estimated from other model variables such as atmospheric temperature and water vapor content. We will examine this issue in more detail in chapter 7 in the context of climate change prediction.

Evaporation and Precipitation

At any given time, most surface areas of the Earth are losing water through evaporation (and from snow or ice through sublimation). This change of phase from liquid (or solid) water to water vapor requires energy (called the latent heat of evaporation), and so it cools the surface of the Earth.

So, why does this continuous flow of water vapor into the atmosphere not lead to a super humid climate with ever-increasing humidity? The answer is that all evaporated water flowing into the atmosphere from the surface must be balanced, in the global average, by precipitation removing water vapor from the atmosphere. Precipitation thus limits how much water vapor (the main greenhouse gas) is allowed to build up in the atmosphere, and so provides a natural limiting effect on global temperatures. Since water vapor is a greenhouse gas, the processes controlling precipitation must be well known to explain the current climate from physical principles, and how they might change with warming is especially important for forecasting climate change. A study of this issue (Renno, Emmanuel, and Stone 1994) showed that a climate having highly efficient precipitation systems (water vapor efficiently converted to precipitation) will be drier and cooler, while low precipitation efficiency leads to a warm, moist climate.

Furthermore, when precipitation occurs, the heat required to evaporate the water is released into the atmosphere. The most dramatic example of this is the warm core (eye) of hurricanes and typhoons, where the air through a great depth of the atmosphere is warmed by latent heat release from precipitation occurring in the eyewall surrounding the eye.

The Oceans

The world's oceans have a large moderating effect on surface climate, with little variation in temperature throughout the seasons. This is called a maritime climate. It is due to the vertical mixing of heat in the ocean, which rapidly spreads any surface warming or cooling influence over a much larger mass than the land surface can accomplish. At the other extreme is a continental climate, such as in Siberia, where lack of a moderating influence from the ocean causes summer temperatures to be hot and winter temperatures to be exceedingly cold.

Through a network of thousands of instrumented Argo floats, the oceans' temperature structure from the surface down to 2,000-meter depth has provided important insight into how much of an energy imbalance in the climate system has occurred during the warming of recent decades. If we are to believe the Argo measurements of slight warming (hundredths to tenths of a degree Celsius), it equates to a global-average energy imbalance of only ~1 W/m^2 (the number at the bottom of Figure 3.1). As mentioned above, this is very small compared to the average natural energy flows into and out of the climate system (~240 W/m^2), and it is only about a tenth of the range of uncertainty in those natural energy flows (~10 W/m^2). This has important consequences for how much faith we can have that humans are responsible for 100 percent of recent warming, a position widely held by mainstream climate researchers.

The oceans also play an important role by transporting excess heat from the tropics toward the poles (high latitudes) and the return flow of cold water to the tropics (low latitudes). The atmosphere also carries out some of that heat transfer. As a result, the tropics are kept cooler—and the high latitudes warmer—than if this heat transport did not occur.

A vertical circulation exists in the ocean (the thermohaline circulation), which is driven by surface cooling and salinity-increasing evaporation at high latitudes. The resulting cold, dense water sinks to the ocean bottom and spreads equatorward. These water flows, over centuries to millennia, have filled the global oceans with cold water over most of their depth, even in the tropics.

All of that sinking cold water must be exactly matched by an equal volume of rising (upwelling) water elsewhere at the same depths. For example, in the tropics on average, there is a very slow upwelling of cold water from below, which is constantly eroding the bottom of the warm surface layers. That influx of cold water from below is matched by the warming influence of the Sun. Thus, the warm ocean waters we associate with tropical tourist destinations are a feature of only the tropical oceans near the surface. Most of the total volume of global oceans is exceedingly cold, below 5°C (41°F).

This large reservoir of cold ocean water plays an important role in year-to-year climate variations. El Niño and La Niña climate events cause warming and cooling, respectively, of the global-average atmosphere by changing the rate at which the cold water in the deep tropical oceans upwells to the surface. The existence of the huge reservoir of cold water also has important—and seldom considered—implications for climate change. If the thermohaline overturning circulation of the ocean were to change on centennial to millennial timescales, it could cause long-term cooling or warming trends.

What could cause such a change? The climate system, including the ocean, is an example of a chaotic system. This means it can change for no apparent reason, just due to the complex nonlinearities within the system. This fact, important to keep in mind when searching for causes of climate change, has two important consequences. First, in a chaotic system, change doesn't require a cause, per se. Change might be a fundamental feature of Earth's "average" climate, making the attempt to identify causes of climate change and the magnitudes of their contributions a fool's errand. Second, as the Intergovernmental Panel on Climate Change itself put it, "The climate system is a coupled non-linear chaotic system, and therefore the long-term prediction of future climate states is not possible. Rather the focus must be upon the prediction of the probability distribution of the system's future possible states by the generation of ensembles of model solutions" (Houghton et al. 2001, 771).

Snow and Ice Cover

Wherever surface ice is present, whether sea ice, glaciers, or snow cover, more sunlight is reflected to outer space than from bare rock or soil, vegetation, or open water, causing less energy input into the climate system and thus cooler temperatures. Ice is often considered a climate change positive-feedback mechanism, because if warming causes a melting of ice, the resulting increase in absorbed sunlight of the resulting darker surface will enhance the warming. Conversely, if cooling causes more ice to form, the cooling will be amplified as the ice reflects more sunlight to outer space, reducing the rate of absorbed sunlight.

Glaciers (especially Greenland and Antarctica) deserve special consideration. First, they represent large storehouses of water. If they were to melt completely, the global oceans would rise by 60 meters from the Antarctic melt, and 7 meters from the Greenland melt. Conversely, the last ice age had much greater coverage of land by glaciers, and sea levels were about 120 meters lower twenty thousand years ago than today—which implies that the amount of ice then on land was about twice that currently on Greenland and Antarctica.

While video documentaries of global warming often highlight dramatic calving of ice from Greenland, it should be noted that this is what glaciers do naturally and always have done. As long as snow accumulates on Greenland and Antarctica, there is a gravity-driven flow of these ice sheets toward the oceans. In Greenland, this leads to calving of icebergs around the periphery of the ice sheet. In Antarctica, the shedding of ice is through the occasional breaking off of ice shelves ringing the continent. It remains uncertain whether Antarctica is gaining or losing ice in recent decades, while Greenland has been losing about two hundred gigatons of ice per year in recent decades, a rate at which it would take 6,500 years to lose half of Greenland's ice, or enough to raise sea level by 3.5 meters.

Volcanoes

Explosively erupting volcanoes, called stratovolcanoes, which loft sulfur dioxide into the stratosphere, can cause temporary global cooling as sulfuric-acid aerosol produced by them acts as a near-global Sun shield. The 1982 eruption of El Chichón in Mexico and the larger 1991 eruption of Mount Pinatubo in the Philippines produced two to three years of cooling, after which the aerosols were naturally cleaned from the atmosphere and the climate system returned to normal.

A common misconception about volcanoes is that they are significant sources of atmospheric CO_2, which is not the case. In fact, after the 1991 Pinatubo eruption, atmospheric CO_2 levels counterintuitively dropped below what they should have been based upon known rates of global CO_2 emissions and the average rate at which nature has been observed to remove CO_2 from the atmosphere. The reason appears to be the increase in indirect sunlight (scattered by the aerosols) from the atmosphere penetrating more deeply into vegetation canopies, promoting enhanced growth (Gu et al. 2003).

Finally, despite the intense heat produced by volcanoes (including those on the ocean floor), their estimated heat input into the climate system is very small, much less than 1 W/m^2 (Pollack et al. 1993). This level of energy input into the climate system is much smaller than other processes, and so is largely ignored in climate change research.

Summary

From this brief introduction it should be clear that the climate system is immensely complex. The estimated natural energy flows through the system are huge, and even the uncertainties in the magnitudes of those flows are larger than the theoretically calculated effect of increasing carbon dioxide in the atmosphere. This means that there could be natural influences causing some, or even all, of our recent global warming, and we would not even know it. Chaotic changes in clouds, evaporation, water vapor, precipitation processes, and ocean circulation (to name a few) are all potential contributors to past, current, and future changes in climate. As we will see, the computerized climate models the world's governments now rely upon for energy policy make myriad assumptions regarding these natural processes. The most central and critical of these assumptions is that, without human influence, nature is in a long-term state of balance. But this is more of a religious position than a scientific one, and that should be kept in mind when climate experts talk with great certainty about the negative impacts humans have on the climate system.

References

Feder, T. (2000). "Argo Begins Systematic Probing of the Upper Oceans." *Physics Today* 53, no. 7 (July): 50–51. Online at https://doi.org/10.1063/1.1292477.

Gu, L., et al, (2003). "Response of a Deciduous Forest to the Mount Pinatubo Eruption: Enhanced Photosynthesis." *Science* 299, no. 2999 (March): 2035–38. Online at https://doi.org/10.1126/science.1078366.

Houghton, J. T., et al. (2001). *Climate Change 2001: The Scientific Basis, Contribution of Working Group I to the Third Assessment Report of the Intergovernmental Panel on Climate Change* (*IPCC Third Assessment Report*). Cambridge, United Kingdom: Cambridge University Press. Online at https://www.ipcc.ch/site/assets/uploads/2018/03/WGI_TAR_full_report.pdf.

Kiehl, J. T., and K. E. Trenberth (1997). "Earth's Annual Global Mean Energy Budget." *Bulletin of the American Meteorological Society* 78, no. 2 (February): 197–208. Online at http://www.geo.utexas.edu/courses/387H/PAPERS/kiehl.pdf.

Pollack, H. N., S. Hurter, and J. R. Johnson (1993) "Heat Flow from the Earth's Interior: Analysis of the Global Data Set." *Reviews of Geophysics* 31, no. 3 (August): 267–80. Online at https://doi.org/10.1029/93RG01249.

Rennó, N. O., K. A. Emmanuel, and P. H. Stone (1994). "Radiative-Convective Model with an Explicit Hydrological Cycle: 1. Formulation and Sensitivity to Model Parameters." *Journal of Geophysical Research: Atmospheres* 99, no. 7 (July), 14429–41. Online at https://agupubs.onlinelibrary.wiley.com/doi/abs/10.1029/94jd00020.

Trenberth, K. E., J. T. Fasullo, and J. Kiehl (2009). "Earth's Global Energy Budget." *Bulletin of the American Meteorological Society* 90, no. 3 (March): 311–23. Online at https://journals.ametsoc.org/view/journals/bams/90/3/2008bams2634_1.xml.

Vinas, M.-J. (2017). "NASA Study: Mass Gains of Antarctic Ice Sheet Greater Than Losses." NASA, August 6. Online at https://www.nasa.gov/feature/goddard/nasa-study-mass-gains-of-antarctic-ice-sheet-greater-than-losses.

Zelinka, M. D., et al. (2020). "Causes of Higher Climate Sensitivity in CMIP6 Models." *Geophysical Research Letters* 47, no. 1 (January): e2019GL085782. Online at https://doi.org/10.1029/2019GL085782.

CHAPTER 4

Climate Models and Scientific Method

BY PATRICK J. MICHAELS
(FINAL EDITING BY JOHN R. CHRISTY)

CHAPTER SUMMARY

IPCC predictions of future climate are essentially based upon modified weather models run for century-long simulations—far longer than the ten days over which weather-forecasting capability has been demonstrated. The computing time, memory, and disk storage required to run them are vast as they try to emulate very complex atmospheric processes. They are therefore variously simplified with coarse approximations to estimate important factors that cannot be generated from first principles.

Reviews of the models' predictive capability consistently show they simulate warming in excess of historical observations. Weather forecasting uses the accepted scientific practice of identifying models with the best track record. Climate forecasting does not. Instead, it uses a wide range of predictions, together with an average, deferring to all models rather than the most realistic. Parameterizations (mathematical representations of physical processes) can ensure that model results fall within a predetermined "acceptable" range. Then science becomes subservient to policy.

There are investigative alternatives using historical records of observed atmospheric change in response to rising carbon dioxide (CO_2) levels. These methods find that climate sensitivity is half the IPCC's mid-range climate model value and lower than the lowest warming. This indicates a very different future, one with only modest warming.

One of the wonders of this planet is our ever-changing weather and climate, driven by the very essence of our special Earth. It is a rotating body with an extremely heterogenous upper layer, where a gaseous atmosphere interacts with water and land. The land is itself very uneven, extending from sea level to over five miles up. Massive global wind systems, such as the midlatitude westerlies or the tropical trade winds, are influenced hourly by this complexity.

There is nothing in our solar system like Earth, and we have no evidence whatsoever for communicating life elsewhere in the vast universe. If that seems remarkable because of the uncountable number of planets out there, well, it is.

Being in such a special place requires us to care for and understand our home, and that is complicated. Simply calculating the state of weather for two to three days in advance is such a daunting problem that it required a revolution in computing. While most weather forecasts fall apart around ten days ahead, how can we possibly forecast the climate of the next one hundred years? Especially since we are changing the atmosphere with our civilization? It should not be ignored that surface temperature has warmed around one degree (C) since 1900, that fossil fuel combustion has something to do with this (not everything), while our life expectancies have doubled and per-capita wealth increased twelvefold (in the developed world). In my mind, these changes are astonishingly salubrious.

There is no doubt that we live short lives breathing a changing atmosphere and that the warming that has occurred is *ipso facto* a net benefit. Compare the current climate to the geologically recent past. *We are in a brief interglacial period within an ice age*, since an ice age is defined as any cold period where permanent ice sheets exist (see chapter 5). Twenty thousand years ago, a blink of a geologist's eye, ice up to ten thousand feet thick covered much of North America, with at least a mile over where the Chicago Cubs now fitfully attempt to play baseball. Today, there are still ten thousand feet of ice over Greenland, slightly over two hours away by jet from Boston. If we weren't flirting with another glaciation (since we are still within an ice age), Greenland's ice wouldn't be there.

Voltaire's Pangloss was wrong: Before the Industrial Revolution and the emissions that change our atmosphere, we were hardly living in his "best of all possible worlds." There's no doubt that our planet is greener than it was, producing more food and plant matter. Even the tropical rainforests are growing luxuriantly, despite what you may hear on legacy media (Zhu et al. 2016). Food production continues to increase exponentially, while population growth is leveling off. Malthus was more wrong than Pangloss. But how can we estimate the future?

Our future climate is estimated by many "models" of Earth's climate.

In the context of science, "model" is often misunderstood. People may think of one as a miniature reality, like a model plane that might only superficially resemble a Boeing 737. Unlike this conception, a "model" of Earth's three-dimensional atmosphere is far more complicated, attempting to reproduce very complex processes. Because of their substantial policy implications, inadequate climate models will lead to inadvisable policies.

Let's begin with models that everyone benefits from: those for the daily weather forecast. There are about a dozen worldwide, and the scientific practices used to turn them into good forecasts illustrate the correct way to determine tomorrow's weather. Each forecast—because tomorrow hasn't happened yet—is a hypothesis whose validity or invalidity is only known when the future arrives.

Why do we have so many weather models? After all, the behavior of Earth's atmosphere shouldn't be a mystery, and *theoretically*, accurate assessment of all the input parameters should result in a stable, long-duration forecast. As stated by Collins et al. (2013), "Due to the amount of computer processor time, memory, and disk storage required to run numerical [weather-forecasting] models, the atmosphere cannot be represented perfectly by the model and thereby is approximated by a finite data set" (Zhang and Ray 2013, chapter 4).

This requires breaking the atmosphere into discrete grid points in the horizontal and vertical. In forecasting, the three-dimensional input data largely come from vertically launched weather balloons released simultaneously in the globe's atmosphere. The standard times are midnight Greenwich Mean Time (GMT; think London) and noon GMT. These three-dimensional measurements are of air pressure, temperature, and humidity. Wind is inferred with GPS (or radio) tracking.

Below, we compare a forecasting process that uses accepted scientific best practice (the daily weather forecast) to one that does not (the forecast for twenty-first-century global temperature).

How to Craft a Long-Range Forecast: 2012's Hurricane Sandy as a Case Study

There are striking similarities between making a very long-range weather forecast for the next ten days and a climate forecast for the next one hundred years. Consider that

- accurate forecasts may be highly beneficial, while inaccurate ones can be very costly;
- there are a large number of forecast models for both weather and climate; and
- some models can be demonstrated to be more reliable than others, depending upon the forecast problem at hand. For example, some weather models have demonstrated superiority for U.S. West Coast cyclones associated with El Niño events, while others may be better for cyclones along the U.S. East Coast, including hurricanes and tropical storms.

All long-range weather-forecast models require some subjective interpretation. For example, with Sandy, there were generally two week-in-advance solutions, and operational forecasters had to choose which to employ.

One solution was a general expectation consistent with the long-term climatology of tropical cyclones. Sandy's initial position in the Atlantic between Cuba and the Bahamas and its time of year (late October—Sandy's landfall was October 30) would normally be associated with a northward trajectory along the U.S. Atlantic Coast, ultimately moving out to sea as the cyclone encounters increasing midlatitude westerly winds. This was the general consensus of various runs of the Global Forecast System (GFS) model, beginning on October 22, from the United States' National Centers for Environmental Prediction (NCEP), the federal agency responsible for civilian weather models.

The alternative solution similarly moved Sandy northward, but on days seven through eight of the forecast issued on October 22, the solution turned the cyclone westward—in the opposite direction compared to the NCEP models—and strengthened it before landfall as it interacted with a strong (but not unusual) dip in the midlatitude westerlies. This was the solution from the European Centre for Medium-Range Weather Forecasts (ECMWF) model, and it had much more severe implications than the GFS, because it forecast a direct hit on the densely populated northern New Jersey shore.

Public forecasters had a clear range of choices between the GFS and ECMWF models, or some blend of the two. But soon both governmental (U.S. National Weather Service and National Hurricane Center) forecasts—as well as prominent private ones, such as AccuWeather and WeatherBELL Analytics—converged upon the ECMWF forecast.

The ECMWF models had better horizontal and vertical resolution than the GFS, which turned out to be very important with regard to tropical cyclones (tropical storms and hurricanes), which are generally smaller than common midlatitude cyclones.

Indeed, to examine what caused their superior forecast, ECMWF researchers replaced their grid with that of the coarser GFS, and the result was the same wrong forecast, turning Sandy out to sea instead of running it into the northern Mid-Atlantic Coast as a huge, intensifying cyclone (Bassill 2014).

The reasons forecasters—both governmental and private—quickly adopted the ECMWF solution were its higher resolution and better track record with storms near the U.S. East Coast. This is rational scientific behavior and can, in many ways, be considered a "scientific best practice" when there are multiple models to choose from.

Weather Models and Climate Models

The first comprehensive climate models (for example, Manabe and Wetherald 1975) were modified versions of then nascent operational weather-forecasting models, with slight but important differences (Manabe and Wetherald 1975). Instead of having the objective of simulating surface weather several days ahead, the climate models were run with much longer time steps with gradual changes in the distribution of radiation within the atmosphere resulting from slowly increasing concentrations of atmospheric carbon dioxide. The early Manabe model, produced at the Department of Commerce's Geophysical Fluid Dynamics Laboratory (GFDL), was recently recognized as such a pioneering effort that it was awarded the 2021 Nobel Prize for physics, the first one ever awarded in atmospheric science. (Close inspection of Figure 4.2a reveals that its direct descendent, model "GFDL-CM3," has the largest errors among the dozens of extant climate models.)

As such, some of the same general scientific practices extended to the daily weather-forecast problem should also apply to the climate sphere. Some models will work better than others when applied to certain aspects of climate.

But solutions to the climate-forecast problem don't appear to be analogous to those applied to the weather problem.

How NOT to Craft the Twenty-First-Century Forecast: The CMIP5 and CMIP6 Model Suites

The potential costs of a rapid global warming could be severe—"rapid," meaning a 5°C (9°F) surface average warming, or greater, in this century.

As shown with Sandy, daily forecasts are generated by multiple computer models, and professional forecasters pick and choose judiciously from what is available based upon what today's weather situation might be. How do climate forecasters handle the fact that they have an even larger number of models to choose from?

They don't choose based on any rational consideration.

There are two periodic summaries of climate science that are extremely important in the formulation of global climate policies. These are the scientific "Assessment Reports" from the United Nations' Intergovernmental Panel on Climate Change (IPCC) and the "National Climate Assessments" of climate change and its effects on the United States produced by the U.S. Global Change Research Program (USGCRP). The IPCC *Assessments* come out every six or seven years. There have been five, and the sixth was released in various stages, for example, the Working Group I report in August 2021, Working Groups II and III in February and April 2022 respectively, and the grand "Synthesis Report" in March 2023. To the interested observer, this orchestration is clearly designed to feed the media a relatively continuous stream of attention-getting pronouncements.

It is important, when assessing the credibility of these reports, to understand that the IPCC authors are chosen only by governments, governments that have clear agendas concerning climate change and associated policies. Likewise, the USGCRP, source of the U.S. National Climate Assessments, is a consortium of every federal entity that consumes or disburses climate-science (and policy) funding, and all participants in it have an interest in keeping funds flowing to their institutions.

Getting back to the forecast problem, because the time horizon of climate is so long compared to the situation with a hurricane, there's no obvious "wrong" forecast. Similarly, there's no professional onus extracted for a mistake because the detection of error is also far into the future.

Periodically, largely coinciding with the schedule for IPCC Assessments, the U.S. Department of Energy collects definitive models from each modeling center, such as the U.S. National Center for Atmospheric Research (NCAR), the Meteorological Research Institute (MRI) of the Japan Meteorological Agency, or Russia's Institute for Numerical Mathematics (INM).

These collections are called "Coupled Model Intercomparison Projects," and the generation in use at the time of this writing was the fifth such exercise, or CMIP5, which consisted of (usually) multiple runs of models from about 35 modeling centers, with the output from 105 model/run combinations used for the 2014 IPCC Scientific Assessment, also known as IPCC's *Fifth Assessment Report* and often abbreviated as AR5. (The model output can be accessed at a Netherlands website, KNMI Climate Explorer at https://climexp.knmi.nl/start.cgi.)

The KNMI site allows one to use the models in "hindcast" mode, where a given date (in the past, present, or future) starts the model in a simulated forecast. Plotting them all out is laborious, but John Christy at the University of Alabama in Huntsville did it and presented the results both as sworn congressional testimony and in articles in the peer reviewed scientific literature (for example, Christy and McNider 2017).

Two illustrations in particular summarize the CMIP5 models versus observations in three dimensions over the Earth's vast tropics (20°N to 20°S).

Figures 4.1a and 4.1b (in the color figures section between pages 240 and 241) compare predicted and observed average tropospheric temperature over the tropics starting when orbiting satellites began to return consistently instrumented global temperature data. The observations come from satellites, weather balloons, and reanalyses, the last of which produce synthetic histories of recent climate and weather using all available observations, a consistent data assimilation system, and mathematical modeling to fill in data gaps (NCAR n.d.; ECMWF n.d.). A careful look at the figure reveals that only one of the thirty-two model groups' runs correctly simulates what has been observed. This is the Russian climate model INM-CM4, which also has the least prospective warming. (See Figure 4.1a.)

A Note on Quantitative Intercomparison of Climate Models

One of the principal "intercomparison-metrics" in CMIP5 (or other CMIPs) is something called the "equilibrium climate sensitivity," or ECS. It is a somewhat theoretical calculation of the average amount of surface warming that will result from a doubling of the atmospheric carbon dioxide content over its "pre-industrial" baseline.

Flynn and Mauritsen (2020) give the average ECS of the CMIP5 models as 3.2°C, the same value given in AR5 (2014).

The ECS for the one model group that appears to "work," the Russian INM-CM4, is 2.05°C, the lowest ECS of all the thirty-two model groups used in Christy's chart. (See Figure 4.1a)

We might have hoped that with the passing of nearly another decade and the expenditure of millions more dollars attempting to improve the models, the results would be better. They weren't. As Christy demonstrated in Figure 4.1b, the mismatch between model predictions and actual observations remains as bad as ever.

A further expansion of Figure 4.1a to cover different levels in the troposphere (the lowest layer of the atmosphere) was published by Christy and McNider (2017) and updated by Christy in 2023 (Figure 4.1b). This further expansion is worth examining because the CMIP5 models predict what is often called an "upper tropospheric hot spot" in the tropics with a substantially enhanced warming rate compared to layers above and beneath. The striking differences in recent decadal warming rates between the climate models and observations are obvious in Figure 4.2a (in the color figures section between pages 240 and 241). Again, only one model correctly calculates the temperature changes with altitude: the Russian model INM-CM4 (Volodin, Dianskii, and Gusev 2010).

Best forecasting practice should rely heavily upon this model. Instead, influential documents, such as the *Fourth National Assessment*, do otherwise: "In this report, future projections are based on CMIP5 alone" (Wuebbles et al. 2017). However, the 2017 *Assessment* did "weight" the individual CMIP5 models based upon their ability to reproduce aspects of North American climate. Unfortunately, the large number of available models (compared to the *one* that actually worked) swamped any weighting effects.

In an appendix relating to the weighting technique, Sanderson and Wehner (2017) noted that "[a]s such, mean projections using the CMIP5 ensemble are not strongly influenced by the weighting." Therefore, the *Fourth Assessment* essentially used the average of all of the models rather than concentrating on the one (or very few) that realistically reproduced three-dimensional climate over the lower forty-eight states. This is like saying, "We know only INM-CM4 got it right, but we're going with the majority because—they're the majority." That's not science, it's politics.

Again, one might have hoped that with time and expense the models might have improved. Again, they did not, as Figure 4.2b (in the color figures section between pages 240 and 241) reveals.

Figures 4.2a and 4.2b may initially appear confusing. While the scale on the horizontal axis is rather clear, indicating the warming rate in °C/decade, the Y-axis scale seems arcane. In it, altitude, measured by barometric pressure, declines with height rather than increasing. In this representation, the surface pressure (at the origin of the plot) is given as 100000 Pascals. That is 1000 millibars. In English/mercury units, the average surface barometric pressure reading is 29.92 inches of mercury. Therefore, 50000 Pascals is roughly halfway up through the atmosphere (one-half of 100000) by volume. This is around 18,000 feet, and it is at this level that the *predicted* warming rates begin to escalate rapidly. (Note that Figure 4.2a uses the vertical axis in linear pressure [Pa] units and Figure 4.2b in linear distance [ft.] units.)

The *observations* (in Figure 4.2a, the circles and squares to the left of most of the lines representing the model data) consist of three different assemblages of upper-air data as well as their average. Only one of the twenty-five different model assemblages is consistent with this data, and once more this is the Russian INM-CM4, plotted as the dotted line that is the farthest to the left. Ironically, the direct descendent of Manabe's original Nobel Prize–winning model, GFDL-CM3, plotted as the solid line farthest to the right, is by far the worst model. Its errors are actually off the chart. Why would policymakers use something so obviously wrong?

The next-generation collection of models (CMIP6) is essentially complete. According to Hausfather (2020), they show an even larger range of ECS values compared to CMIP5, from 1.8°C (not surprisingly, generated by the updated Russian model INM-CM4.8), all the way up to 5.6°C, as shown in Figure 4.3. (This means the modelers' misunderstanding of climate processes is actually increasing.) Hausfather further demonstrates that the larger the ECS is in CMIP6 models, the more they overpredict warming in recent decades. Again, best scientific practice would eliminate these models from an operational forecast ensemble.

McKitrick and Christy examined the available CMIP6 models and concluded that the errors the CMIP5 models were making in the three-dimensional tropical atmosphere have now extended to the globe:

> The literature drawing attention to an upward bias in climate model warming responses in the tropical troposphere extends back at least 15 years (Karl et al. 2006) Rather than

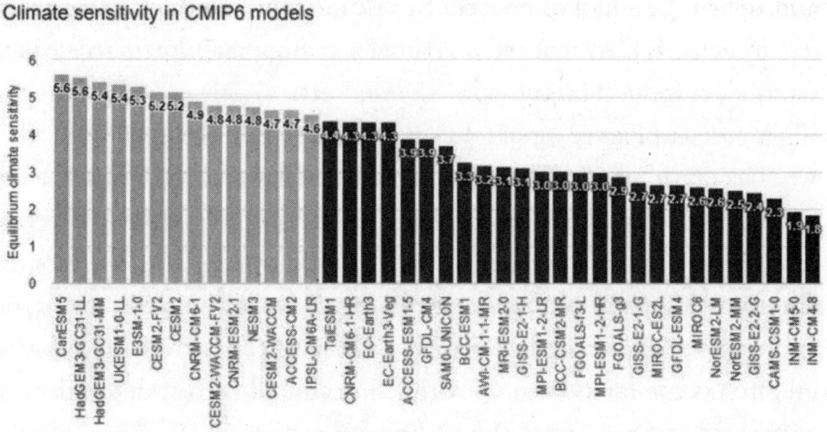

Figure 4.3. The CMIP6 model suite (Hausfather 2020). Models warmer than the warmest CMIP5 versions are in light gray. As shown below, they are also the least reliable. The models with the lowest ECS are the Russian INM-CM4.8 (1.8°C) and INM-CM5.0 (1.9°). In CMIP5, the INM-CM4 ECS was 2.05°C, and all these conform to observed temperatures better than the others. *Courtesy of The Breakthrough Institute.*

> being resolved, the problem has become worse, since now every member of the CMIP6 generation of climate models exhibits an upward bias in the entire global troposphere as well as in the tropics. (McKitrick and Christy 2020)

We add here that Christy and McNider (1994), almost thirty years ago, demonstrated the excessive warming of climate models when attempting to replicate the rates of warming at that time.

Are the Climate Models Systematically Flawed?

The CMIPs are collections of General Circulation Climate Models and Earth System Models, which attempt to reproduce all important atmospheric processes in an interactive whole. But, as shown by Voosen (2016), a large number of factors, including heat transfer into the oceans and the formation and effects of clouds, have to be "parameterized" (or "tuned") with quantitative estimates of important processes whose true values remain unknown.

Voosen's *Science* report was in response to an accepted paper that was circulating heavily over the internet and was titled "The Art and Science of Climate Model Tuning," by Frédéric Hourdin, a director of research at the French National Centre for Scientific Research. The paper was published in print in 2017 in the *Bulletin of the American Meteorological Society* and included fourteen co-authors, all of whom were associated with leadership of various international climate modeling efforts (Hourdin et al. 2017).

Hourdin et al. made several insightful observations about the tuning process:

> With the increasing diversity in the applications of climate models, the number of potential targets for tuning increases. There are a variety of goals for specific problems, and different models may be optimized to perform better on a particular metric, related to *specific goals, expertise or cultural identity of a given modelling center.* [Emphasis added]

They speculated on why so little was known about the "black box" (Voosen's words) nature of climate model tuning:

> In fact, the tuning strategy was not even part of the required documentation in the CMIP5 simulations.... Why such a lack of transparency? Maybe because tuning is often seen as an unavoidable but dirty part of climate modelling. Some may be concerned that explaining that models are tuned could strengthen the arguments of those who question the validity of climate change projections. (Hourdin et al. 2017)

The unfortunate (but true) translation of this landmark statement by the cream of the world's climate modeling community is that they agreed not to transparently describe the degree and mechanisms of climate model tuning because it would provide logical ammunition for those who opposed climate policies that the modelers espoused.

Finally, Hourdin et al. (2017) delivered the *coup de grâce*:

> One can imagine changing a parameter which is known to affect the sensitivity, keeping both this parameter and the ECS in the *anticipated acceptable range*. [Emphasis added]

The inescapable (and striking) conclusion is that scientists predetermine the "acceptable range"; scientists parameterize the models to generate that "acceptable range"; and so scientists, not the science—not even the subjectively "tuned" model code—determine the sensitivity of the manifold climate models. This is science changing into a subjective process unavoidably subservient to rogue actors in the service of a desired policy objective. (An expanded version of the Voosen article and its implications is given in chapter 10 of Michaels and Kealey [2019].)

It is reasonable to conclude that Hourdin et al. provide serious reasons not to trust either the CMIP models' objectivity or their results.

The root cause is simple: the atmosphere is simply too complicated to model from a first-principle approach if the desire is to understand the four-dimensional evolution of climate at the scales of the CMIP models.

Judith Curry, retired head of the School of Earth and Atmospheric Sciences at Georgia Tech, has perhaps the most insightful scientific blog (www.judithcurry.com) on climate change on this planet. In it she wrote,

> If ever in your life you are to read one paper on climate modeling, this [Hourdin et al.] is the paper that you should read. (Curry 2016)

I concur. She concluded,

> But most profoundly, after reading this paper regarding the "uncertainty monster hiding" that is going on regarding climate models, not to mention their structural uncertainties, how is it possible to defend highly confident conclusions regarding attribution of 20th century warming, large values of ECS, and alarming projections of 20th century warming? (Curry 2016)

Clearly, the bases for profound and disruptive energy policies are *not* normative science. Is there a better way to project the future than with these complicated models?

Alternatives to the CMIP Models

There are alternative approaches to the problem of forecasting future climate—using historical records rather than bottom-up modeling. Generally, there are two historic inputs: greenhouse gas changes, usually expressed as carbon dioxide concentrations, and atmospheric aerosols, which are particulates resulting from the combustion of fossil fuels (mainly coal) and the burning of vegetation.

The aerosols were first invoked as significant in the second (1995) IPCC *Assessment Report*, which noted that climate models driven only by greenhouse gases were producing too much warming and that the likely cause was either that they simply had too high a sensitivity or that the aerosols (mainly sulfate particulates) were counteracting the warming (IPCC 1996). However, the IPCC, in all subsequent reports, indicated very wide estimates of the sulfate effects, ranging from a slight warming to a substantial cooling (of well over 1°C) during their historical record, which begins in the mid-nineteenth century.

After the 2014 IPCC report, one of the most important papers on atmospheric aerosols, "Rethinking the Lower Bound on Aerosol Radiative Forcing," by Bjorn Stevens (2015), who heads a prestigious research group at the Max Planck Institute in Hamburg, was published in the *Journal of Climate*, a centrist publication of the American Meteorological Society. Stevens noted that tuning the climate models to attribute the early twentieth-century warming to human influence indeed produces unreliable results in recent decades. That is because there had been only a minimal change in carbon dioxide when this half-degree (C) warming began around 1910. This tuning required that the effect of the cooling aerosols, mainly from the combustion of coal, had to be minimized in the 1910–1945 warming, but then maximized to account for the aforementioned overprediction of warming in recent decades by carbon dioxide–only models. This is absurd, as the world's industry and transportation (think steam engine–powered freight and passenger trains) were almost exclusively powered by aerosol-belching coal until the mid-twentieth century, a fuel progressively replaced afterward by diesel, which produces far fewer aerosols. Stevens ultimately reduced the estimate of recent aerosol cooling to around half of the IPCC's mean estimate.

Nic Lewis, an independent researcher in the United Kingdom (along with Curry, when she was still at Georgia Tech), ultimately incorporated Stevens's estimates (along with observed surface temperature changes), estimated the equilibrium climate sensitivity to be 1.5°C, and published the result in *Journal of Climate* (Lewis and Curry 2018). This is the value that is most consistent with observed surface temperature changes.

Christy and McNider (2017) employed another empirical approach, filtering their satellite-sensed temperatures to remove volcanic and El Niño cycles, as well as some other internal climate oscillations, and derived a sensitivity very similar to that of Lewis and Curry (Sanderson and Wehner 2017). It is worth noting that the decadal trend in their satellite data, of 0.14°C, is approximately two-thirds of that in land-based records, and that the consistent (multi-decadal) differences in these trends have never been explained adequately, nor have any prospective differences between satellite-sensed and surface-measured future temperatures been definitively explained.

The important fact remains that empirically derived twenty-first-century temperature forecasts, using the methods of Lewis and Curry or Christy and McNider, produce a temperature sensitivity that is slightly lower than that of the Russian INM-CM4, CM4.8 and CM5 models, which are themselves lower than all other CMIP5 and CMIP6 simulations.

The lowest limit given for the ECS in the text of the last complete (2014) IPCC assessment was 1.5°C, which has been raised to 2.0°C in the newer version, but with a best-guess low limit of 2.5°C. It appears that the IPCC has conferred credibility on the newer CMIP6 model suite, despite the fact that its warmer models clearly overpredict warming in recent decades. Nonetheless, it would appear that the more "scientific" (that is, data-based) estimates for sensitivity are consistent with Lewis and Curry, Christy and McNider, and the models from the Russian Institute for Numerical Mathematics, and that these results should be most heavily weighted for planning purposes—that is, that policies designed in light of projections of future global warming, whether intended to mitigate that warming or adapt to it, should be devised in light of lower, not higher, estimates of equilibrium climate sensitivity.

Summary and Conclusions

There is no doubt that continuing advances in *weather*-forecasting models have resulted in a product whose utility has grown in both accuracy and the length of time in which a forecast can be extended. In producing increasingly accurate forecasts, operational meteorologists select which models are more reliable given current conditions, or a specific forecast problem.

Do scientists do the same with climate models? No, and for multiple reasons. Except for one recent rudimentary attempt to scale models for reliability (which, noted above, had little detectable effect), the climate modeling community, as expressed in the summaries of the IPCC, or in the "National Assessments" from the USGCRP, does not employ best scientific practice of selective model usage. Rather than heavily relying upon models that properly forecast recent decades (for example, the Russian INM-CM4 and CM4.8), these summary documents still revert largely (but not completely) to the mean and the spread of all the forecast models—consequently skewing ECS upward.

Further, it is now known that (unlike *weather*-forecasting models) the *climate* models are "parameterized" to quantitatively estimate important factors that the models cannot reliably generate from scientific first principles. The word *parameterized* has many meanings. Hourdin et al. (2017) believe these are mathematically designed to keep the model results within an "anticipated acceptable range" subjectively determined by those supervising the operation of individual climate models. Another meaning would be "fudged," analogous to changing the inputs in a failed pre-med chemistry lab to achieve an expected outcome.

In contrast, the best scientific practice would be to use models that appear to work best in the real world. For whatever reason, these are also simulations that produce far less prospective warming than the larger CMIP suites. Why the climate science community has been so reluctant to use these is not known at this time, but Hourdin et al. (2017) have made it abundantly clear that the CMIP modelers target what they call an "anticipated acceptable range" of results. What makes the range "acceptable" is not scientific evidence or logic. This is not best scientific practice. It is not even science. As it stands today, most "climate science," with regard to future projections, is unreliable.

That is the only conclusion one can draw if evaluating the community of climate models that the UN and our government rely upon. The revealed data paint a much different picture, one with modest warming for the foreseeable future. Given past behavior, this would imply a global increase of wealth and, hopefully, life expectancy.

I make no claim, and neither should anyone else, that we can possibly see the technological world of 2100. Therefore we only have a very narrow climate-forecast window. That forecast for coming decades would be "fair and slightly warmer."

References

Bassill, N. P. (2014). "Accuracy of Early GFS and ECMWF Sandy (2012) Track Forecasts: Evidence for a Dependence on Cumulus Parameterization." *Geophysical Research Letters* 41, no. 9 (May): 3274–81. Online at https://agupubs.onlinelibrary.wiley.com/doi/full/10.1002/2014GL059839.

Christy, J. R., and R. T. McNider (1994). "Satellite Greenhouse Signal." *Nature* 367 (January): 325. Online at https://www.nature.com/articles/367325a0.

———. (2017). "Satellite Bulk Tropospheric Temperatures as a Metric for Climate Sensitivity." *Asia-Pacific Journal of Atmospheric Science* 53, no. 4 (November): 511–18. Online at https://link.springer.com/article/10.1007/s13143-017-0070-z.

Christy, J.R., S. Po-Chedley, and C. Mears (2018). "Tropospheric Temperature." In Hartfield, G., J. Blunden, and D. S. Arndt (2018), *State of the Climate in 2017*. Special Supplement to *Bulletin of the American Meteorological Society* 99, no. 8 (August). S16–S18. Online at https://doi.org/10.1175/2018BAMSStateoftheClimate.1.

Christy, J. R., S. Po-Chedley, C. Mears, and L. Haimberger (2020). "Tropospheric Temperature." In Blunden, J. and D. S. Arndt, eds. (2020). *State of the Climate in 2019. Bulletin of the American Meteorological Society* 101, no. 8 (August): S30–S32, S108–S110. Online at https://doi.org/10.1175/2020BAMSStateoftheClimate.1.

Collins, S. N., et al. (2013). "Grids in Numerical Weather and Climate Models." In *Climate Change and Regional/Local Responses*, edited by Ray, P. and Y. Zhang, chapter 4. Rijeka, Croatia: IntechOpen. Online at https://cdn.intechopen.com/pdfs/43438/InTech-Grids_in_numerical_weather_and_climate_models.pdf.

Curry, J. (2016). "The Art and Science of Climate Model Tuning." Climate Etc., August 1. Online at https://judithcurry.com/2016/08/01/the-art-and-science-of-climate-model-tuning.

ECMWF (n.d.). "Climate Reanalysis." European Center for Medium-Range Weather Forecasts. Online at https://www.ecmwf.int/en/research/climate-reanalysis.

Flynn, C. M. and T. Mauritsen. (2020). "On the Climate Sensitivity and Historical Warming Evolution in Recent Coupled Model

Ensembles." *Atmospheric Chemistry and Physics* 20, no. 13 (July): 7829–42. Online at https://doi.org/10.5194/acp-20-7829-2020.

Hartfield, G., J. Blunden, and D. S. Arndt (2018), *State of the Climate in 2017*. Special Supplement to *Bulletin of the American Meteorological Society* 99, no. 8 (August). Online at https://doi.org/10.1175/2018BAMSStateoftheClimate.1.

Hausfather, Z. (2020). "Cold Water on Hot Models." The Breakthrough Institute, February 11. Online at https://thebreakthrough.org/issues/energy/cold-water-hot-models.

Hourdin, F., et al. (2017). "The Art and Science of Climate Model Tuning." *Bulletin of the American Meteorological Society* 98, no. 3 (March): 589–602. Online at https://journals.ametsoc.org/view/journals/bams/98/3/bams-d-15-00135.1.xml.

IPCC (1996). *Climate Change 1995: The Science of Climate Change: Contribution of Working Group I to the Second Assessment Report of the Intergovernmental Panel on Climate Change*. Cambridge, United Kingdom: Cambridge University Press for Intergovernmental Panel on Climate Change. Online at https://www.ipcc.ch/site/assets/uploads/2018/02/ipcc_sar_wg_I_full_report.pdf.

Lewis, N., and J. Curry (2018). "The Impact of Recent Forcing and Ocean Heat Uptake Data on Estimates of Climate Sensitivity." *Journal of Climate* 31, no. 15 (August): 6051–71. Online at https://journals.ametsoc.org/view/journals/clim/31/15/jcli-d-17-0667.1.xml.

Manabe, S. and R. T. Wetherald (1975). "The Effects of Doubling the CO_2 Concentration on the Climate of a General Circulation Model." *Journal of the Atmospheric Sciences* 32, no. 1 (January): 3–15. Online at https://journals.ametsoc.org/view/journals/atsc/32/1/1520-0469_1975_032_0003_teodtc_2_0_co_2.xml.

McKitrick, R., and J. Christy (2020). "Pervasive Warming Bias in CMIP6 Tropospheric Layers." *AGU Earth and Space Science* 7, no. 9 (July): e2020EA001281. Online at https://agupubs.onlinelibrary.wiley.com/doi/epdf/10.1029/2020EA001281.

Michaels, P. J. (2019). "Endangered Science and the EPA's Finding of Endangerment from Carbon Dioxide." In *Scientocracy: The Tangled Web of Public Science and Public Policy*, edited by Michaels, P. J., and T. Kealey, 239–56. Washington, D.C.: Cato Institute.

NCAR (n.d.). "Atmospheric Reanalysis: Overview & Comparison." National Center for Atmospheric Research. Online at https://climatedataguide.ucar.edu/climate-data/atmospheric-reanalysis-overview-comparison-tables.

Sanderson, B. M., and M. F. Wehner (2017). "Appendix B: Model Weight Strategy." In Wuebbles, D. J., et al. (2017). *Climate Science Special Report: Fourth National Climate Assessment: Volume 1*. Washington, D.C.: U.S. Global Change Research Program. Online at https://science2017.globalchange.gov/downloads/CSSR2017_FullReport.pdf.

Stevens, B. (2015). "Rethinking the Lower Bound on Aerosol Radiative Forcing." *Journal of Climate* 28, no. 12 (June): 4794–4819. Online at https://journals.ametsoc.org/view/journals/clim/28/12/jcli-d-14-00656.1.xml.

Volodin, E. M., N. A. Dianskii, and A. V. Gusev (2010). "Simulating Present-Day Climate with the INMCM4.0 Coupled Model of the Atmospheric and Oceanic General Circulations." *Izvestiya, Atmospheric and Oceanic Physics* 46, no. 4 (September): 414–31. Online at https://link.springer.com/article/10.1134/S0001433810040002X.

Voosen, P. (2016). "Climate Scientists Open Up Their Black Boxes to Scrutiny." *Science* 354, no. 6311 (October): 401–2. Online at https://www.researchgate.net/publication/309539289_Climate_scientists_open_up_their_black_boxes_to_scrutiny.

Wuebbles, D. J., et al., eds. (2017). *Climate Science Special Report: Fourth National Climate Assessment: Volume 1*. Washington, D.C.: U.S. Global Change Research Program. Online at https://science2017.globalchange.gov/downloads/CSSR2017_FullReport.pdf.

Zhu, Z., et al. (2016). "Greening of the Earth and Its Drivers." *Nature Climate Change* 6, no. 8 (April): 791–95. Online at https://www.nature.com/articles/nclimate3004.

Chapter 5

The Role of the Sun

by Michael Connolly, Ronan Connolly, and Willie Soon

Chapter Summary

Two general explanations for ice ages of thousands of years ago are changes in the sunlight reaching the Earth and atmospheric changes. Two mechanisms are offered for the first—orbital changes and changes in solar emissions. Scientists have concluded ice ages were likely caused by variations in the planet's elliptical orbit, axial tilt, and precession, resulting in variations on multi-thousand-year timescales. Whether there are contributions on shorter timescales remains a subject of ongoing research.

Sunspot cycles of eleven-year typical duration are hypothesized to moderate solar radiation; but enhanced bright areas called faculae also follow similar cyclicality. Both positive and negative trends as well as high and low variability for incoming solar radiation over recent decades are revealed by different composite analyses of their effects, leaving the significance of the Sun's climate change role an ongoing scientific challenge.

Surface temperature measurement biases are acknowledged to exist between rural areas and urban heat islands. While extensive efforts are made to eliminate these to arrive at reliable data for research, debate continues about what remains. Interestingly, combined urban-rural data displays near continuous warming, while rural records, when examined alone, reveal cyclical behavior, suggesting alternative warming contributions (see the chapter on oceans). The IPCC minimizes urban bias trends, and its climate models do not render natural cyclicality. Warming contributions of these alternative effects are sufficient to question the declaration of a single human cause of global warming.

Geological evidence shows that for billions of years the world has gone through cycles of global warming and cooling. Any cold period when permanent ice sheets exist in both of the world's polar regions is defined as an "ice age." According to this definition, because there are ice sheets in both Greenland and Antarctica, the Earth is currently in an ice age, although it is in a relatively mild "interglacial period," less extreme than the "glacial periods" that typically come to mind when we think of "ice ages."

Geological records indicate that five major ice ages occurred during the last 2.5 billion years, starting with the Huronian Ice Age (from 2.4 until 2.1 billion years ago) and ending with the present Quaternary (from 2.6 million years ago until the present). Intervening warm periods, when there were no large areas of permanent ice on the Earth, are sometimes called "greenhouse (or hothouse) periods." From geological evidence, the Earth has been in a "greenhouse period" about 80–85 percent of the time.

Since the evidence for ice ages was discovered nearly two hundred years ago, various theories have been put forward to explain these cycles in the Earth's surface temperature. Most consist of various combinations of two main hypotheses—changes in the amount of sunlight reaching the top of the Earth's atmosphere or changes in the atmosphere that alter the balance between the amount of sunlight that reaches the Earth's surface and the amount of heat energy that radiates out to space (Budyko 1969; Sellers 1969).

Hypothesis 1: Changes in the Amount of Sunlight Reaching the Top of the Earth's Atmosphere

Most of the energy that heats the Earth's surface comes directly or indirectly from the sunlight that arrives at the top of the atmosphere. Only a relatively small amount of the energy that heats the Earth's surface comes from inside the Earth. The total amount of energy arriving at the top of the atmosphere from the Sun is called the *Total Solar Irradiance* (TSI). As you would expect, changes in TSI will affect the temperature at the Earth's surface. Two main mechanisms have been offered as to how changes in TSI might occur—changes to the Earth's orbit around the Sun, and changes to the luminosity, that is, the amount of light emitted by the Sun itself (Gough 1990; Soon 2014).

The Orbital Change Mechanism

In 1824, the Danish-Norwegian geologist Jens Esmark examined geological evidence for the ebb and flow of glaciers and proposed a series of worldwide ice ages to explain his observations. He suggested these ice ages were due to changes in climate caused by changes in the Earth's orbit. Similarly, in 1842, the French mathematician Joseph Adhémar suggested that the ice ages were due to the already established changes in the elliptical nature of the Earth's orbit (Berger 2012). Various other nineteenth-century scientists (for example, James Croll) proposed similar orbital change explanations for the ice ages (Edwards 2022).

Every year the Earth completes one orbit around the Sun. However, this orbit is elliptical and not circular. The Earth is currently closest to the Sun about two weeks after the December solstice (during the Northern Hemisphere winter) and farthest away about two weeks after the June solstice (during the Northern Hemisphere summer). This two-week difference is not constant. It drifts about a day every fifty-eight years and can vary by up to two days from one year to another. Today, TSI is 6.7 percent greater in January when the Earth is closest to the Sun than in July when it is farthest away. Because the seasons are reversed between the Northern and Southern Hemispheres, this means that the Northern Hemisphere winters and summers are a bit milder than their Southern Hemisphere equivalents.

However, the shape of the Earth's elliptical orbit is not constant. Due to the gravitational effects of the moon and planets, it can vary approximately every one hundred thousand years from being nearly circular to being more elliptical. Other long, millennial-period changes also occur in the axial tilt and precession of the Earth itself (the change in the orientation of the Earth's axis), which could also give rise to changes in the amount of TSI reaching the Earth throughout the year. Thus, it may not be entirely coincidental that the word "climate" has its roots in the Greek word *klima*, which, according to *Merriam-Webster*, "means 'inclination,' 'slope,' or 'latitude.'"

In 1920, the Serbian mathematician and engineer Milutin Milankovitch explained how the full set of cyclic variations in Earth's elliptical eccentricity, axial tilt, and precession caused distinct variations in incoming solar radiation at different latitudes and changes on multi-thousand-year timescales. His mathematical solutions are known as the Milankovitch Cycles (Berger 1988).

In the 1960s and 1970s, researchers began calculating the timing of past glacial and interglacial periods by "coring," that is, drilling, several meters of mud from the ocean floor. The composition of the mud at each layer in these "ocean sediment cores" provides estimates of past climate information that can go back hundreds of thousands of years. They discovered that the intervals between glacial periods seemed to be roughly one hundred thousand years (Hays et al. 1976). This coincided with one of the Milankovitch Cycles, and many scientists decided that Milankovitch had probably been right. More recently, in the 1980s and 1990s, researchers drilling ice cores in Greenland and Antarctica have found that the same roughly one-hundred-thousand-year cycle has been occurring for at least the last eight hundred thousand years.

Szarka et al. (2021) have provided an overview of current views on the role of Milankovitch's orbitals in terms of long-term climate change (that is, on timescales of tens to hundreds of thousands of years). Currently, some scientists are building on Milankovitch's ideas to try to see if subtle orbital changes might also play a role in climate change on interannual, decadal, centennial, and millennial timescales (Cionco and Soon 2017; Fedorov 2019; Cionco, Soon, and Quaranta 2020; Cionco Kurdyavtsev, and Soon 2021).

Changes in the Solar Luminosity Mechanism

Besides the effects on TSI due to orbital changes, we also must consider that the Sun is not a constant star—that is, the amount of sunlight the Sun produces every year is not constant. Every so often, dark areas, called sunspots, occur on the Sun's surface. Sunspots have been recognized by Chinese astrologers/astronomers as early as the fourth century BC, and a sunspot observation dating from 165 BC has been recognized as the earliest precisely dated sunspot. With the invention of telescopes at the time of Galileo in the sixteenth century AD, astronomers (including Galileo) began to systematically record these sunspots. Velasco Herrera et al. (2022) recently provided a comprehensive update and review of the reconstruction of sunspots and group sunspot activity since Galileo's first observations.

We now know that the occurrence of these sunspots is quasi-periodic (or quasi-cyclical) with periods of about eleven years between the two maxima or between the two minima number of sunspots on the surface. We say these "sunspot cycles" are quasi-periodic because although the average length of a cycle is about eleven years, the exact length of each cycle can vary from as few as eight to as many as fourteen years. However, from around 1645 to 1715 CE (known as the Maunder Minimum), virtually no sunspots occurred on the Sun's surface.

Since the discovery of sunspots, there has been much debate over what effect, if any, they have on the Earth. Some people have maintained that since sunspots are dark, an increase in their number would reduce the amount of light given off by the Sun, and this would reduce the amount of TSI coming to Earth. This would make the Earth colder. But as E. Walter Maunder and Annie Maunder pointed out in the early 1900s, just as the dark sunspots went through a roughly eleven-year cycle, brighter areas called faculae (Latin for "little torch" or "bright spot") and plages also follow the same roughly eleven-year cycle. The increase in the energy from faculae could equal or exceed the reduction caused by sunspots depending on the ratio of sunspots to faculae. Astronomers and astrophysicists who study other "Sun-like" stars have shown that this ratio varies from star to star. Whether this is because the ratio is constant for each star and varies from star to star, or is not constant but varies over time, has not been fully established quantitatively.

Until the start of the satellite era, it was not possible, due to atmospheric interference, to directly measure the TSI reaching the top of the atmosphere. This is because ground-based measurements of the incoming TSI can vary based on how the atmosphere, which is always changing, interacts with the incoming TSI. However, starting in the late 1970s, satellites orbiting the Earth have been able to make TSI measurements. Unfortunately, due to the short orbital life of these satellites, records from each satellite must be stitched together with records from other satellites to get a continuous record of TSI for the satellite era. This is not as easy as it sounds. Satellite orbits change over their lifetimes, their instruments degrade, and different satellites have different instruments. For the TSI records from the different satellites to be stitched together, they need to be calibrated relative to each other. There are several plausible TSI composites in the peer review literature, some of which imply quite different trends in TSI over the satellite era (see Soon 2014; Soon, Connelly, and Connelly 2015; Connolly et al. 2021). Of the two main rival TSI composites, the ACRIM group finds a positive trend in TSI during the 1980s and 1990s, while the PMOD group finds a negative trend over the entire satellite era from the 1970s to the present.

By comparing each of these satellite-era composites to various proxies for TSI such as sunspot numbers, sunspot sizes, faculae numbers and sizes, 10.7 cm microwave emissions, and variations in the Earth's magnetic field, it is possible to extend our estimates of past TSI back over at least the last 150 years.

Many plausible TSI reconstructions currently exist in the scientific literature. For instance, eight different estimates are plotted in Figure 5.1, which is based on Soon, Connelly, and Connelly (2015). Of them, four imply little solar variability since the seventeenth century. If any of these "low variability" estimates are correct, then it is unlikely that changes in TSI have played a major role in the climate changes seen

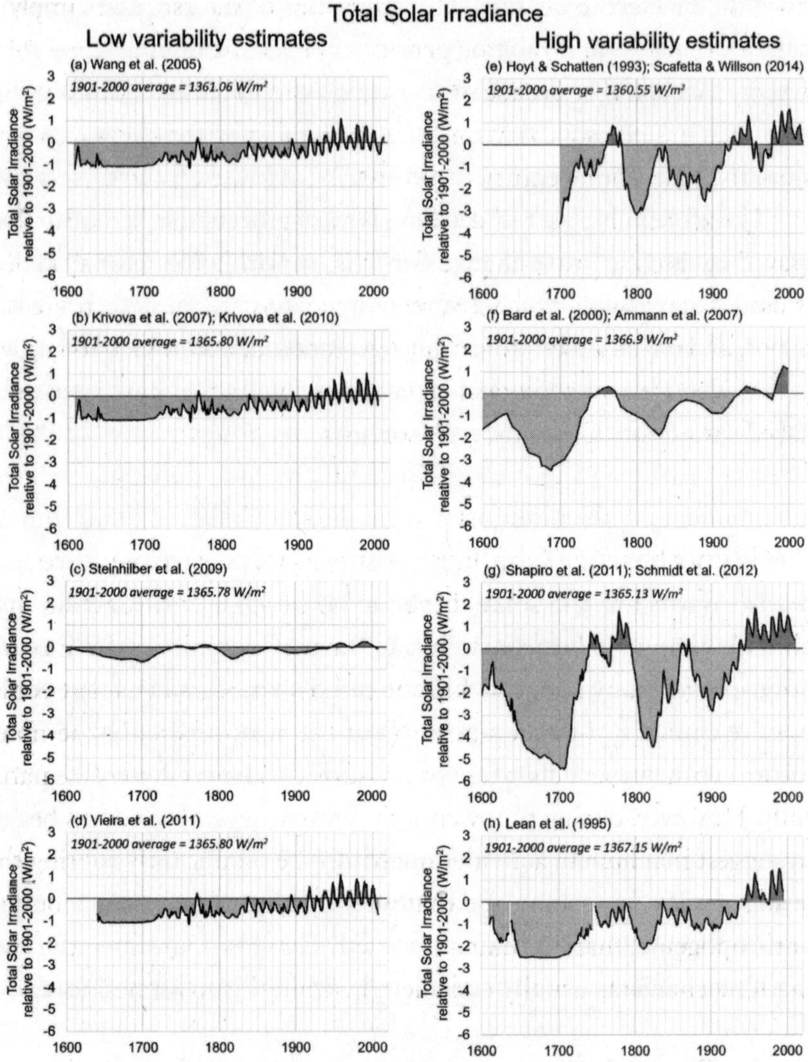

Figure 5.1. Eight different estimates of how TSI has changed since the seventeenth century relative to the twentieth-century average (1901–2000). All estimates are calibrated to match with one of the satellite-based TSI composites over the satellite era, and then each uses different "solar proxies" to describe the trends before the satellite era. *Source: Adapted from Soon, Connolly, and Connolly (2015). Used by permission.*

since the nineteenth century. However, four of the estimates imply a highly variable Sun, exhibiting periods of increasing or decreasing solar activity over multiple decades. If these high variability estimates are correct, then it is plausible that much (or even most) of the climate change since the nineteenth century could have been caused by solar activity.

Therefore, a big part of deciding how significant a role the Sun has played in recent climate change depends on which TSI reconstruction is used. Establishing which TSI reconstructions are most accurate is a major, and ongoing, scientific challenge. Indeed, recently Connolly et al. (2021) identified an additional eight TSI estimates that have been published since Soon, Connolly, and Connolly (2015).

Hypothesis 2: Changes in the Earth's Atmosphere

In contrast to the solar-driven hypothesis, which suggests that climate change is largely driven by factors outside of the Earth's atmosphere, many scientists have focused on mechanisms that could involve changes in the composition of the atmosphere. In the nineteenth century, these changes were assumed to have taken place naturally. However, during the twentieth century, several scientists began to suggest that human activities might also be significantly altering the atmospheric composition and that we might therefore be contributing anthropogenic, that is, "human-caused" changes. Currently, the two main mechanisms usually considered within this hypothesis are:

1. Changes in the atmospheric concentration of the so-called "greenhouse gases"—chiefly water vapor (H_2O), carbon dioxide (CO_2), methane (CH_4), ozone (O_3), and nitrous oxide (N_2O). These changes could occur either naturally or as an effect of human activities. Increased greenhouse

gas concentrations are believed to lead to a long-term warming trend.

2. Changes in the concentration of tiny particles called aerosols. These changes could also occur either naturally (for example, from volcanic eruptions), or from human activities (such as industrial emissions). Increased aerosols are believed to lead to a temporary cooling effect that can last for one to two years.

Because the second mechanism is mostly just a short-term one, here we will focus instead on the historical development of the first mechanism.

The Greenhouse Effect Mechanism

In 1767, the Swiss scientist Horace Bénédict de Saussure used a cork-insulated box with a triple-glazed roof to show that sunlight, coming in through the glass, heated the inside of the box to the same temperature whether at the top of Mont Crammont in the Swiss Alps or in the plains below. This was remarkable, because the air temperature at the lower altitude was 34°F (19°C) warmer than that at the higher altitude. In 1822, the French scientist Joseph Fourier suggested the explanation for this result might be that the air trapped the energy given off by the Sun heating the ground, much like the glass in Saussure's solar oven.

Then in 1862, an Irish scientist, John Tyndall, discovered in his laboratory that although oxygen and nitrogen were transparent to terrestrial rays (heat rays/infrared rays), some gases, such as water vapor and carbon dioxide, were not. He concluded, "As a dam built across a river causes a local deepening of the stream, so our atmosphere, thrown as a barrier across the terrestrial rays, produces a local heightening of the temperature at the Earth's surface." Svante Arrhenius (who subsequently won a Nobel prize for chemistry) accepted Tyndall's conclusions and used arguments by Luigi De Marchi to reject changes in the Earth's orbit and the Sun's luminosity as contributing to the occurrence of the ice ages. Instead, Arrhenius proposed that changes in the levels of carbon dioxide in the air would change the amount of "sky radiation" (infrared radiation given off by warm air) incident on the Earth's surface, which would change the climate. In 1896, he calculated that halving the concentration of carbon dioxide in the atmosphere would be enough to cause an ice age.

It is now recognized that the data available at the time were inadequate for the task, and even at the time, his fellow Swedish scientist Knut Ångström, who published an infrared spectrum for carbon dioxide, rejected his conclusions, claiming that the effects of water vapor would overwhelm any effect due to carbon dioxide, because the concentration of water vapor is much higher in the atmosphere and water vapor absorbs over a much wider range of infrared wavelengths. Indeed, it appears that by the time Arrhenius wrote his analysis building on Tyndall's 1860s work, Tyndall himself had shifted towards favoring the orbital change mechanism (Edwards 2022).

Measuring Global Air Temperatures

Following the invention of a reliable thermometer by the Dutch scientist Daniel Gabriel Fahrenheit in 1714 and his later development of the temperature scale that bears his name, people and institutions started to keep records of local daily temperatures. However, it was not until roughly 1880 that enough observations became available to make reliable estimates of the average temperature of the planet.

In 1938, Guy Stewart Callendar revived Arrhenius's theory that changes in atmospheric carbon dioxide could make a significant contribution to the world's temperature, but not enough to cause ice ages. Using temperature records from two hundred locations around the world that were available from the Smithsonian Institution,

Callendar calculated an annual global temperature series dating back to the mid-1800s (based on the temperature anomalies for each station). This temperature series suggested that global temperatures had increased by roughly 0.45°F (0.25°C) over the preceding fifty years. He also estimated the contribution that the burning of fossil fuels made to the concentration of carbon dioxide in the atmosphere over the same period. By comparing these two calculations, he estimated that, when the concentration of carbon dioxide reached 360 ppm, the world temperature would increase by 0.9°F (0.5°C)—see Table 5.1.

While praising the courage and work of Callendar, several of the reviewers of his paper (G. Simpson, F. J. W. Whipple, and C. E. P. Brooks) criticized his arguments on scientific grounds. These criticisms are listed at the end of Callendar (1938), along with Callendar's responses. Although Callendar's (1938) work is widely cited, many of those original criticisms remain valid. Included among them was the observation that the Earth's atmosphere is not in a state of radiative equilibrium and that much of the observed rise in the air temperature noted by Callendar, especially those in Arctic regions, could also be explained by changes in atmospheric circulation.

Most notably, carbon dioxide concentrations reached 360 ppm much more quickly than Callendar predicted (that is, in 1990 and not 2200). Yet the global temperature was roughly the same in 1990 as it was in 1938, and the current best estimate of the airborne fraction of carbon dioxide remaining in the atmosphere due to the burning of fossil fuels is closer to 50 percent than his estimate of 75 percent.

Nonetheless, Callendar's work has had considerable influence. In 1955, Roger Revelle was inspired by Callendar's idea that increasing carbon dioxide in the atmosphere could cause an enhanced greenhouse effect. Revelle promoted what he referred to as the "Callendar Effect" and said publicly that considerable harmful effects could be realized by

Table 5.1. Increase of Mean Temperature from Artificial Production of Carbon Dioxide

Annual excess of carbon dioxide to the air is 4,300 million tons. The partial pressure of carbon dioxide [P(CO_2)] is expressed in units of a ten-thousandth of an atmosphere. DT is the increase from the mean temperature of the nineteenth century. Sea water equilibrium time is 2,000 years.

Period	1910–1930	20th Century	21st Century	22nd Century
Mean P(CO_2)	2.82	2.92	3.30	3.60
Mean DT	+0.07°C	+0.16°C	+0.39°C	+0.57°C
Polar Displacement of Climate Zones	15 km	36 km	87 km	127 km

Adapted from Callendar (1938).

the end of the twentieth century. Nevertheless, the twentieth century ended without these dire warnings taking effect.

Revelle, along with Charles Keeling and Harry Wexler, established the Mauna Loa Observatory measurements program (in consultation with Callendar and others) in 1958 to monitor atmospheric changes in carbon dioxide. The results of this program, which continues to this day, are now referred to as the "Keeling Curve."

The Keeling Curve has shown that the concentration of carbon dioxide has increased from 0.031 percent of the atmosphere in 1958 to 0.041 percent in 2022. According to current computer models, based on the work of Callendar and others, this should have led to a noticeable long-term anthropogenic (human-caused) global warming from the enhanced greenhouse-effect mechanism. Therefore, scientists relying on these models believe that most of the climate changes since the nineteenth century have been human-caused. Meanwhile, other scientists argue that the models are unreliable; that the mechanisms of

Hypothesis 1 are probably more important; and that most of the climate changes since the nineteenth century have been natural.

Where Are We Today?

Most scientists now agree that changes in carbon dioxide did not actually cause the ice ages. They were rather caused by the Milankovitch Cycles. However, with respect to climate change over the last 150 years, the effects of Milankovitch Cycles are generally assumed to be relatively slow and gradual; therefore most scientists look elsewhere for an explanation of changes over the past two centuries.

Since Callendar's time, thousands more station records have become available, more than half a century of carbon dioxide concentrations have been measured, and satellite estimates of TSI have been established. But despite these advances, many of the problems that were considered by Callendar and his peers remain unresolved in assembling a global temperature time series. Moreover, a suite of additional problems has revealed more scientific difficulties.

Consider, for example, one such bias—the urban heat island (UHI) effect. Urban areas are known to be warmer than the surrounding countryside. As areas become more urbanized, the associated UHI becomes larger. Therefore, if a weather station lies in an area with urban growth, there is a risk that the weather station's record might become biased by this localized urban warming. Callendar had suspected an urban bias might exist, but he calculated that it was quite modest. A comparison of the rural air temperature time series for the Northern Hemisphere with the combined rural and urban air temperature series (Figure 5.2), however, indicates that the conclusion reached by Callendar that an urban bias did not exist was indeed erroneous. That is, the rural temperature time series (top right) shows much less warming and is also more cyclical in nature than the combined urban-rural temperature record (top left).

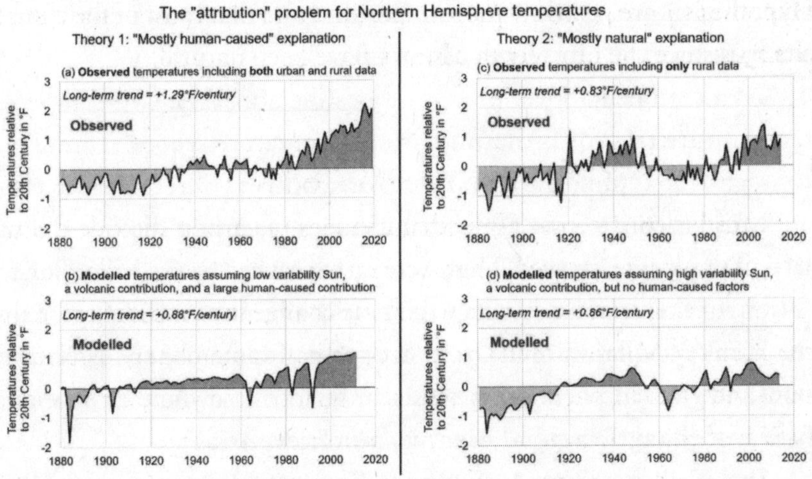

Figure 5.2. Comparison of two competing "attribution" explanations for Northern Hemisphere temperature trends since the late nineteenth century. The two graphs on the left present an explanation that suggests the trends are mostly human caused with a very small role for the Sun, while the two graphs on the right suggest that the trends are mostly natural with a very large role for the Sun. The "long-term trend" values correspond to the linear temperature trend over the same common period, 1881–2011, for each time series. *Source: Adapted from Connolly, Connolly, Carter, and Soon, (2020). Used by permission.*

To this day, there is an ongoing debate in the scientific community over whether urban biases are substantial or relatively minor. For instance, the Intergovernmental Panel on Climate Change (IPCC) has argued that the net effects of UHI biases are much smaller than the long-term global warming since the late nineteenth century. The latest report of the UN IPCC—AR6 (2021)—has claimed that "it is unlikely that any uncorrected effects from urbanization . . . or from changes in land use or land cover . . . have raised global Land Surface Air Temperature (LSAT) trends by more than 10%" (IPCC 2021, chapter 2, pp. 43–44). However, several recent papers have concluded the opposite, that is, that urbanization bias is responsible for a substantial fraction of the apparent global warming (Soon, Connolly, and Connolly 2015; Zhang et al. 2021; Scafetta 2021; Connolly et al. 2021).

As mentioned above, what is interesting about the two competing temperature records is that the rural temperature record (Figure 5.2, top right) looks almost cyclical in nature, whereas the combined urban and rural record shows almost continuous warming (Figure 5.2, top left). As an aside, in the United States, which has the best and largest set of rural station records in the world, opinion polls suggest that the rural population tends to believe that climate change is natural, while the urban population tends to believe that climate change is human-caused (Diamond, Bonnie, and Rowe 2020).

In its most recent *Assessment Report*, AR6, 2021, the IPCC decided to consider only the low solar variability estimates of TSI. For this reason, they assumed that the Sun had only played a minor role in recent climate change. Therefore, they argued that most of the observed warming since the nineteenth century was probably human-caused, chiefly due to increasing carbon dioxide from the burning of fossil fuels. This perspective can be summarized by the bottom left panel of Figure 5.2. Alternatively, as can be seen from the right side of Figure 5.2, if you use the rural-only estimates and consider one of the high solar variability TSI estimates, then you can explain most of the trends since at least 1881 in terms of natural climate change.

Which of the two competing explanations is correct, or are they both wrong?

Many nonscientists assume that the scientific process is linear and is always moving forward. That is, once scientists come up with an answer, their research is complete, and they can move on to the next problem. The reality is much messier. Unlike common sense, science is nonintuitive. Scientists analyzing the same data can often come up with different conclusions. New data and insights are constantly revising our previous understanding. Rather than declaring which explanation we believe is correct, we encourage inquiry, digging deeper, and asking questions. If you are curious and want to learn more, we hope this discussion will help you on your journey.

References

Berger, A. (1988). "Milankovitch Theory and Climate." *Reviews of Geophysics* 26, no. 4 (November): 624–57. Online at https://ebme.marine.rutgers.edu/HistoryEarthSystems/HistEarthSystems_Fall2008/Week12a/Berger_Reviews_Geophysics_1988.pdf.

———. (2012). "A Brief History of the Astronomical Theories of Paleoclimates." In *Climate Change: Inferences from Paleoclimate and Regional Aspects*, edited by Berger, A., F. Mesinger, and D. Šijački (2012). Vienna: Springer, 107–29.

Budyko, M. I. (1969). "The Effect of Solar Radiation Variations on the Climate of the Earth." *Tellus*, 21, no. 5 (October): 611–19. Online at https://onlinelibrary.wiley.com/doi/10.1111/j.2153-3490.1969.tb00466.x.

Callendar, G. S. (1938). "The Artificial Production of Carbon Dioxide and Its Influence on Temperature." *Quarterly Journal of the Royal Meteorological Society* 64, no. 275 (April): 223–40. Online at https://rmets.onlinelibrary.wiley.com/doi/abs/10.1002/qj.49706427503.

Cionco, R. G., and W. W.-H. Soon (2017). "Short-Term Orbital Forcing: A Quasi-Review and a Reappraisal of Realistic Boundary Conditions for Climate Modeling." *Earth-Science Reviews* 166 (March): 206–22. Online at https://www.sciencedirect.com/science/article/abs/pii/S0012825216303865.

Cionco, R. G., W. W.-H. Soon, and N. E. Quaranta (2020). "On the Calculation of Latitudinal Insolation Gradients throughout the Holocene." *Advances in Space Research* 66, no. 3 (August): 720–42. Online at https://www.sciencedirect.com/science/article/abs/pii/S0273117720302684.

Cionco, R. G., S. M. Kudryavtsev, and W. W.-H. Soon (2021). "Possible Origin of Some Periodicities Detected in Solar-Terrestrial Studies: Earth's Orbital Movements." *Earth and Space Science* 8, no. 8 (July): e2021EA001805. Online at https://agupubs.onlinelibrary.wiley.com/doi/full/10.1029/2021EA001805.

Connolly, R., et al. (2020). "How Much Human-Caused Global Warming Should We Expect with Business-As-Usual (BAU) Climate Policies? A Semi-Empirical Assessment." *Energies* 13, no. 6 (March): 1365. Online at https://www.mdpi.com/1996-1073/13/6/1365.

Connolly, R., et al. (2021). "How Much Has the Sun Influenced Northern Hemisphere Temperature Trends? An Ongoing Debate." *Research in Astronomy and Astrophysics* 21, no. 6 (April): 131. Online at https://iopscience.iop.org/article/10.1088/1674-4527/21/6/131.

Diamond, E. P., R. Bonnie, and E. Rowe (2020). *Rural Attitudes on Climate Change: Lessons from National and Midwest Polling and Focus Groups*. Durham, North Carolina: Nicholas Institute, Duke University.

Edwards, K. J. (2022). "'The Most Remarkable Man': James Croll, Quaternary Scientist." *Journal of Quaternary Science* 37, no. 3 (April): 400–419. Online at https://onlinelibrary.wiley.com/doi/full/10.1002/jqs.3420.

Fedorov, V. M. (2019). "Earth's Insolation Variation and Its Incorporation into Physical and Mathematical Climate Models." *Physics-Uspekhi, Russian Academy of Sciences* 62, no. 1 (2019): 32–45. Online at https://iopscience.iop.org/article/10.3367/UFNe.2017.12.038267.

Gough, D. O. (1990). "On Possible Origins of Relatively Short-Term Variations in the Solar Structure." *Philosophical Transactions of the Royal Society of London, Series A* 330 (April): 627–40. Online at https://royalsocietypublishing.org/doi/10.1098/rsta.1990.0043.

Hay, J. D., J. Imbrie, and N. J. Shackleton (1976). "Variations in the Earth's Orbit: Pacemaker of the Ice Ages." *Science* 194, no. 4270 (December): 1121–32. Online at https://www.science.org/doi/10.1126/science.194.4270.1121.

Hoyt, D. V., and K. H. Schatten (1997). *The Role of the Sun in Climate Change.* 1st ed. Oxford, United Kingdom: Oxford University Press.

IPCC (2021). *Climate Change 2021: The Physical Science Basis; Working Group I Contribution to the Sixth Assessment Report of the Intergovernmental Panel on Climate Change* (*Sixth Assessment Report*). Cambridge, United Kingdom, and New York: Cambridge University Press. Online at https://report.ipcc.ch/ar6/wg1/IPCC_AR6_WGI_FullReport.pdf.

Scafetta, N. (2021). "Detection of Non-Climatic Biases in Land Surface Temperature Records by Comparing Climatic Data and Their Model Simulations." *Climate Dynamics* 56, no. 9–10 (May): 2959–82. Online at https://ui.adsabs.harvard.edu/abs/2021ClDy...56.2959S/abstract.

Scafetta, N., et al. (2019). "Modeling Quiet Solar Luminosity Variability from TSI Satellite Measurements and Proxy Models during 1980–2018." *Remote Sensing* 11, no. 21 (November): 2569. Online at https://www.mdpi.com/2072-4292/11/21/2569.

Sellers, W. D. (1969). "A Global Climatic Model Based on the Energy Balance of the Earth-Atmosphere System." *Journal of Applied Meteorology and Climatology* 8, no. 3 (June): 392–400. Online at https://journals.ametsoc.org/view/journals/apme/8/3/1520-0450_1969_008_0392_agcmbo_2_0_co_2.xml.

Soon, W. W.-H. (2014). "Sun Shunned." In *Climate Change: The Facts 2014*, edited by A. Moran, 57–66 Melbourne, Victoria, Australia: Institute of Public Affairs.

Soon, W. W.-H., R. Connolly, and M. Connolly (2015). "Re-Evaluating the Role of Solar Variability on Northern Hemisphere Temperature

Trends since the 19th Century." *Earth-Science Reviews* 150 (November): 409–52. Online at https://www.sciencedirect.com/science/article/abs/pii/S0012825215300349.

Soon, W. W.-H., and S. H. Yaskell (2003). *The Maunder Minimum and the Variable Sun-Earth Connection*. River Edge, New Jersey: World Scientific Publication Company, Inc.

Szarka, L., W. W.-H. Soon, and R. G. Cionco (2021). "How the Astronomical Aspects of Climate Science Were Settled? On the Milankovitch and Bacsák Anniversaries, with Lessons for Today." *Advances in Space Research* 67, no. 1 (January): 700–707. Online at https://www.sciencedirect.com/science/article/pii/S0273117720306499.

Velasco Herrera, V. M., et al. (2022). "Group Sunspot Numbers: A New Reconstruction of Sunspot Activity Variations from Historical Sunspot Records Using Algorithms from Machine Learning." *Solar Physics* 297, no. 1 (January). Online at https://ui.adsabs.harvard.edu/abs/2022SoPh..297....8V/abstract.

Zhang, P., et al. (2021). "Urbanization Effects on Estimates of Global Trends in Mean and Extreme Air Temperature." *Journal of Climate* 34, no. 5 (March): 1923–45. Online at https://journals.ametsoc.org/view/journals/clim/34/5/JCLI-D-20-0389.1.xml.

Chapter 6

The Role of the Oceans

by Anthony R. Lupo

Chapter Summary

Of the various components of the Earth, oceans have the largest ability to absorb heat per unit mass for a temperature change, and they are a thousand times more massive than the atmosphere, covering 71 percent of Earth's surface at depths from tens to thousands of meters. They are therefore certain to affect global temperature.

Various ocean dynamics induce natural oscillations that exert influence on each other and on weather and climate, resulting in cyclical temperature effects superimposed on longer-term trends. Their net effects can therefore disguise underlying trends, enhancing or suppressing them and leading to mischaracterizations. The most well-known is El

Niño, which recurs in three-to-eight-year cycles and causes brief temperature spikes. But climate records of the last thousand years reveal longer fifty-to-eighty-year cycles, such as the Pacific Decadal Oscillation, the Atlantic Multidecadal Oscillation, and the Atlantic Meridional Mode. These cycles are missing from the IPCC climate models, which don't know how to represent them alone or in natural combinations, leading to inaccurate temperature attribution as well as poor estimation of climate sensitivity to greenhouse gases.

Introduction

Chapter 3 discussed the various components of the climate system and their interactions via the exchange of heat and mass. What is clear is that the combined heat capacity and mass of the atmosphere are the smallest among the components of the climate system (for example, Peixoto and Oort 1992). As such, the time needed for the atmosphere to adjust to external forcing is quite short (one to three weeks) compared to that of the other parts of the climate system. The oceans, in contrast, have the highest heat capacity of the parts of the climate system as well as being three orders of magnitude (one thousand times) more massive than the atmosphere. Since water covers 71 percent of the Earth's surface, the oceans are bound to exert a very strong influence on global atmospheric temperatures. Given the fact that the atmosphere is generally transparent to solar radiation, as a first approximation, the atmosphere receives its energy from the underlying surface. In other words, in general, the atmosphere is considered a servant to the Earth's surface.

The behaviors of geophysical fluids such as the oceans and atmosphere are governed by very basic physical conservation laws such as conservation of mass, momentum, and energy, and they are described in many atmospheric science (for example, Ahrens and Henson 2022) and climate textbooks (for example, Rohli and Vega 2017). These basic principles are represented by a highly nonlinear set of differential equations called the "primitive equations." These principles and equations, when solved in a general way, can represent the naturally occurring wavelike motions that are observed when a geophysical fluid is forced. These motions are named in accord with the force that restores the initial balance, and these waves can be generated internally or at the interface between fluid layers of differing densities (for example, Pedlosky 1987, chapter 3). The simplest or most relatable example is something many of us have done: throw a stone into a tranquil water body. The stone disturbs the water's surface, and gravity attempts to restore equilibrium to the water's surface. These wave motions will have various characteristic timescales depending on the forcing and the composition and density of the fluid. The goal here is not to discuss the physics and mathematics of these motions, but to give the basic background regarding the principles that describe some well-known natural oscillations in the ocean and atmosphere, together with a description of how these oscillations impact weather and climate, especially global temperatures.

Some of these oceanic oscillations or cycles are germane to the oceans, which then exert strong influence on the atmosphere and are relatively recently described but not necessarily well understood (for example, Pacific Decadal Oscillation—PDO). Others have been known for a long time and represent the complex relationships between the oceans and atmosphere, such as El Niño and Southern Oscillation (ENSO) and North Atlantic Oscillation (NAO). What is common among them is that these oscillations will exert their influence on each other as well as on weather and climate regardless of any longer-term trends that have been observed. The rest of this chapter will explore the connection between these atmospheric and oceanic phenomena and global temperature.

Ocean-Atmosphere Interactions

El Niño and Southern Oscillation

The phenomenon referred to as El Niño and Southern Oscillation (abbreviated as ENSO) became common knowledge in the public domain during the strong El Niño event of 1982–1983. El Niño refers to the irregular warming (approximately every two to eight years) of the upper part of the ocean in the Eastern Tropical Pacific (see, for example, Philander 1990; Diaz and Markgraf 2000, and Figure 6.1 in the color figures section between pages 240 and 241). El Niño is not new but was finally recognized in the scientific literature during the 1960s (for example, Bjerknes 1966, 1969) and connected with the Southern Oscillation. The Southern Oscillation describes the mean sea level pressure difference between Tahiti and the city of Darwin, Australia. This difference is typically positive but becomes negative during an El Niño. The opposite or cold phase of what is now viewed as an irregular cycle is called the La Niña, and anomalously cold waters would be observed where, in Figure 6.1, the anomalously warm waters are located.

The typical El Niño cycle begins with subtle changes in the atmosphere and ocean circulations during the spring of a particular year, and the dynamics involve waves discussed in the introduction. The surface water of the Eastern Tropical Pacific begins to warm throughout the summer and fall, resulting in maximum sea surface temperature (SST) anomaly during December and January (for example, Diaz and Markgraf 2000). Figure 6.1 shows one type of El Niño pattern, which occurred during December 2015 close to the maximum of the 2015–2016 event. These SST anomalies change the surface heat distribution on Earth, often over an area larger than the United States. This heating has a profound impact on the path of the jet stream and consequently the weather worldwide, as shown by many peer reviewed studies, but especially over North America. The jet stream is responsible for the poleward transfer of excess energy, momentum, and moisture, which characterizes the tropics, to the polar regions, which have relative deficits of the aforementioned quantities.

From Figure 6.1 we can also infer that the El Niño is responsible for depositing heat energy into the tropical atmosphere from the ocean surface. This energy will be distributed eventually worldwide by the jet stream. Within a fluid this happens by contact (conduction) and transfer in bulk fluid elements (convection). If the underlying surface is warmer than the atmosphere, energy will be transferred into the atmosphere by conduction and evaporation of water from the surface into the atmosphere. This heat will be distributed into the atmosphere by convection and condensation during the formation of clouds and precipitation.

We can estimate the potential of El Niño to warm the global atmosphere simply through the process of conduction. If we consider a unit volume of water (one meter cubed), its mass is about 1,000 kg. The SST anomalies in the area bounded by 170° W to 120° W longitude and from 5° S to 5° N latitude are used to determine whether the Pacific is in the El Niño, La Niña, or neutral state (see Shi, L'Heureux, and LaJoie 2022). If the mean SSTs are 1.0°C above normal within this area over a depth of 150 m, we can calculate how much energy could be deposited into the atmosphere from the oceans, provided all this warm anomaly in the volume described above was dispersed in this direction. This calculation is based on the heat capacity and density of the ocean included in well-known formulations (for example, Tilly et al. 2008). If we consider that the heat capacity of a given volume of the atmosphere is roughly one-quarter that of the same volume of water, and its density is roughly 0.001, distributing this energy over the entire volume of the atmosphere results in the atmosphere being warmed by approximately 0.75°C (1.4°F).

During the El Niño event of 2015–2016, the global atmospheric temperature as estimated by satellites (Figure 6.2) warmed by

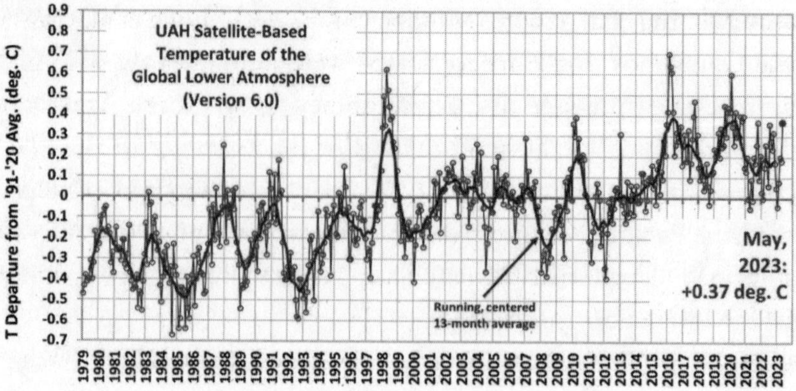

Figure 6.2. The monthly temperature anomaly (measured relative to the 1991–2020 global mean) of the global lower atmosphere (1979–2023) based on satellite measurements and provided by the University of Alabama-Huntsville. *Source: Roy W. Spencer, https://www.drroyspencer.com/wp-content/uploads/UAH_LT_1979_thru_May_2023_v6_20x9.jpg. Used by permission.*

approximately 0.6°C. This El Niño was associated with SSTs that were 2–3°C warmer than normal in the Eastern Tropical Pacific within the box outlined above, which is far more than enough to account for the temperature spike in Figure 6.2. The calculation above assumes an ideal scenario, and not all of the energy associated with the El Niño warm anomaly would be transferred exclusively from the ocean into the atmosphere. El Niño, however, provides a clear example of how a shorter-term event occurring within the ocean circulations can influence global temperatures. Other recent El Niño temperature "spikes" (Figure 6.2) are seen in 1998, 2010, 2016, and 2020, while La Niña cold "valleys" can be seen in 1999–2000, 2008–2009, 2011–2012, 2018, and 2021.

The Pacific Decadal Oscillation

The Pacific Decadal Oscillation (PDO) was not defined until relatively recently, and among the first published papers to describe it were Mantua et al. (1997), Minobe (1997), and Zhang et al. (1997), while Gershunov and Barnett (1998) were among those who first described the influence of this phenomenon on North American surface weather. The first indications of the existence of the PDO occurred earlier in the twentieth century as SSTs changed drastically within the Pacific Ocean during the late 1970s, and the event was first termed "The Great Climate Shift" or the "1976–1977 Climate Shift" (Miller et al. 1994).

The Pacific Decadal Oscillation can be described as a Pacific Ocean basin-wide ENSO-like seesaw in the SSTs over a fifty-to-seventy-year period (see Figure 6.3 in the color figures section between pages 240 and 241). The warm or positive phase of the PDO features a warm ENSO-like pattern for SSTs in the eastern tropics, but the cold phase shows cooler SSTs in the ENSO region. Dates marking the epochs of the PDO during the twentieth century can be found on the website of the Joint Institute for the Study of the Atmosphere and Ocean at the University of Washington (http://research.jisao.washington.edu/pdo). The warm phases persisted from 1924 to 1946 and from 1977 to 1998, and there is some indication that the later part of the 2010s showed the reemergence of this phase. The cool phase persisted from 1890 to 1924, from 1947 to 1976, and from 1998 to the late 2010s. Recent research using tree-ring data has traced the epochs of the PDO back to the first millennium AD (for example, MacDonald and Case 2005).

The mechanisms governing the change in phase for the PDO epochs are not well understood, and recent studies have concluded that the PDO is a result of combined physical processes such as tropical forcing and atmosphere-ocean interactions in the North Pacific (for example, Newman et al. 2016). One of these may be a feedback process between these longer-term SST changes and ENSO. It is clear from looking at Figure 6.3 that the positive or warm phase of the PDO would favor the occurrence of stronger El Niño events and weaker La Niña events, and the negative or cool phase would favor the reverse. There is also a strong interaction between the two at intermediate timescales (eight to fourteen years) when studying a time series of the tropical Pacific SSTs (for example, Mesta-Nunñez and Enfield 2001). Additionally, a time series of the PDO Index (see JISAO or a similar website) would show that the value is not uniformly negative or positive during the epochs defined above.

The PDO, like ENSO, has been shown to have an impact on climate variables worldwide, including the occurrence of droughts over North America (for example, Cook et al. 2014) or the frequency and occurrence of stationary ridging events in the jet stream called atmospheric blocking (for example, Lupo et al. 2019), on a multidecadal scale. There is a correspondence between the predominance of large-scale flow regimes in the Northern Hemisphere jet stream, a dynamic quantity called information entropy, and the phases of the PDO, as well as a rough correspondence to global temperature epochs as shown in, for example, van Geel and Ziegler (2013) and Kononova and Lupo (2020). Others, such as Wyatt and Curry (2014), suggest that relationships between oceanic and atmospheric circulation have a nearly sixty-year variability or periodicity. Their work will be discussed later. However, given the discussion thus far, it should be clear that the positive phase of the PDO would be associated with increasing global temperature, and the negative phase with decreasing global temperature, in a manner similar to that discussed with ENSO except over a longer period of time.

The Atlantic Multidecadal Oscillation

The Atlantic Multidecadal Oscillation (AMO) is somewhat similar to the PDO in that the timescale is relatively long (about sixty to eighty years in total; Trenberth and Zhang 2021), but this phenomenon is characterized by a distinct north-south SST pattern variation. During one phase (positive or warm), the tropical and far north Atlantic SSTs are anomalously warm while the central Atlantic is anomalously cool (Figure 6.4, top, in the color figures section between pages 240 and 241) and vice-versa during the opposite (negative or cool) AMO phase. The AMO index (Figure 6.4, bottom) is simply the SST anomalies averaged over the whole of the Atlantic Ocean (0–65° N and 80° W–0° E). Like the PDO, there is evidence of the AMO in proxy data (for example, tree rings, ice cores, and so forth) going back for about one thousand years or more.

A definitive mechanism for the cause of AMO has yet to be identified, but there is some evidence that changes in the Atlantic thermohaline circulation may at least partly drive the cycle (for example, O'Reilly et al. 2016). Others have postulated an ocean-atmosphere feedback mechanism for the cause of the AMO (Yuan et al. 2016). The thermohaline circulation is a global deepwater circulation driven by changes in the density of ocean water as driven by changes in salinity. Saltier water is more dense than fresher water and so sinks (for example, Knauss 1988). These denser waters are formed by surface evaporation. Surface currents such as the Gulf Stream carry this water mainly to the North Atlantic Ocean, and there the denser water sinks into the deeper ocean. The currents eventually mix waters across the entire globe via deepwater currents with upwelling waters in the Southern Hemisphere and Northern Pacific.

Since the Atlantic part of this circulation is associated with the Gulf Stream, which is responsible for the relatively moderate climate of places like Northern Europe through the transport of heat in the surface ocean, the intensity or vigor of the thermohaline circulation impacts the climate of the North Atlantic Ocean basin region. Changes in the strength of the thermohaline circulation occur on very long timescales (decades to centuries). If this circulation slows down, the climate of the North Atlantic can cool considerably, and such slowdowns were thought to cause temporary cold periods following the last ice age (for example, the Younger Dryas; Carlson 2010). In pop culture, an immediate shutdown of this circulation is the premise of the movie *The Day after Tomorrow* (2004), though such sudden change in temperature in such great mass is not physically possible. However, these topics are discussed in publications dealing with longer-term climate change and variability.

On the decadal scale, the AMO has been linked to the occurrence of weather phenomena such as tropical cyclones and their intensity in the Atlantic basin (for example, Klotzbach and Gray 2008; Camargo et al. 2010). Many researchers have shown an impact on regional temperature and precipitation patterns in the Northern Hemisphere due to AMO, especially in North America, Europe, and North Africa. The AMO can also be linked to changes in the Atlantic region's general circulation and jet stream, which will be discussed later. These changes can be quantified using the NAO index.

While it may seem intuitive that the positive (warm) phase of the AMO would be associated with an increase in global temperature and the opposite for the cool phase, Maruyama (2019) found a more complex relationship among global temperature, AMO, and PDO. Maruyama discovered that during periods when the global temperature decreased, or increased little (for example, 1950–1976 and 1998–2012), the AMO was positive/warm generally, while the PDO was negative/cool. During the increase in global temperature from the late 1970s to 1998, the PDO was positive/warm, and the AMO was generally negative/cool. These results suggest there is a relationship between longer-term oceanic cycles themselves and global temperature.

Connections between these modes of variability in the ocean and atmosphere could be linked to one another and may change in sequence. This sequential change was likened to the "stadium wave," a pop culture phenomenon observed at well-attended baseball or football games where fans stand and sit in sequence, appearing as a propagating "wave" of humanity to observers. The "stadium wave" hypothesis was proposed by Wyatt, Kravtsov, and Tsonis (2012) and is characterized as multidecadal variability in the climate signal that is associated with the propagation of a "wave" of index-phase changes across the Northern Hemisphere. The existence of this phenomenon in the Southern Hemisphere is also suspected.

Wyatt, Kravtsov, and Tsonis (2012) examined observed SSTs and sea level pressure patterns and used eight indexes or indicators of ocean and atmosphere variability including some examined here (AMO, NAO, ENSO, and PDO). They also used various bioindicators (such as fish populations) to confirm interannual and interdecadal variability. Their paper showed, for example, that if we began with a negative AMO, it would take about nine years for the NAO to become positive, then another five for the appearance of a positive ENSO. Then three years later, the positive PDO would appear, and fifteen years later a positive AMO, a total of thirty-two years. It then takes another roughly thirty-two years (sixty to eighty years total) to sequence back to the negative AMO.

As this "stadium wave" relates to surface temperatures across at least the Northern Hemisphere and likely the globe, a warm North Atlantic (warm AMO) is associated with a decades-long trend in cooling surface temperatures. Conversely, a cool North Atlantic (cool AMO) is associated with a decades-long trend of warming surface temperatures. Thus the "stadium wave" relates changes in the mode of these indexes to temperature trends, not necessarily surface or atmospheric temperature itself.

Atlantic Meridional Mode

The Atlantic Meridional Mode (AMM) is not the same as the AMO, but, occasionally, these are confused with one another. This phenomenon occurs in the tropical Atlantic and is another example of ocean and atmosphere interactions or feedbacks. The AMM (for example, Xie

2009; Foltz, McPhaden, and Lumpkin 2012) exhibits strong variability on the interannual and interdecadal timescales. The positive phase of the AMM is characterized by warmer-than-normal SSTs in the tropical north Atlantic and vice versa in the tropical south Atlantic. Surface air pressure varies in step with the SST anomalies, becoming higher than normal over the anomalously cold SSTs and lower than normal over anomalously warm SSTs. The decadal mode of the AMM can be excited by the AMO (for example, Delworth and Mann 2000).

While the AMM has an impact on Atlantic tropical cyclone variability (positive AMM leading to increased Atlantic tropical cyclone activity; for example, Vimont and Kossin 2007), any connection to Northern Hemisphere or global temperature is likely to be indirect or via the AMO.

North Atlantic Oscillation

The NAO is a teleconnection index in the atmosphere that is commonly misunderstood. The term "teleconnection" refers to weather or climate anomalies that are related over long distances on the globe. These often take the form of a series of anomalous high and low pressures, and this is demonstrated in Figure 6.5. The NAO index shows variability on interannual and interdecadal timescales as associated with the oceanic oscillations discussed above and is often errantly referred to as "forcing itself."

The NAO index is based on the difference in sea level pressure between the Azores Islands in the subtropical Atlantic and Iceland in the North Atlantic (for example, Wilby et al. 1997). The former are dominated by a subtropical high, while the latter is dominated by a subpolar low. The positive NAO is associated with lower atmospheric heights and pressure across the higher latitudes and higher heights and pressure across the lower latitudes, resulting in a more zonal (west to east or "flat") jet stream across the Atlantic and warmer temperatures

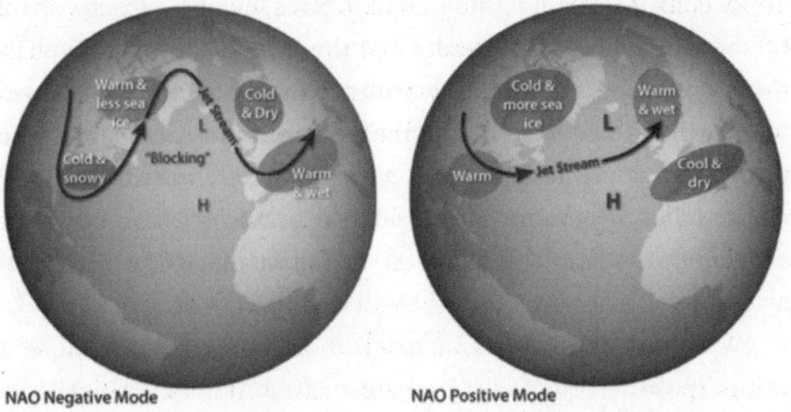

Figure 6.5. The typical jet stream and surface sensible weather conditions associated with the NAO. *Courtesy of NOAA (National Oceanic and Atmospheric Administration), online at https://www.climate.gov/news-features/understanding-climate/climate-variability-north-atlantic-oscillation.*

in Europe. The negative phase results in a more meridional (north-south or "wavy") jet stream pattern across the Atlantic (Figure 6.5).

The NAO index itself is based on daily weather patterns, and the daily value and change are related to the dynamic behavior of the Northern Hemisphere jet stream. Jensen et al. (2018) and references therein provide more detail on this behavior, which has its roots in the primitive equations discussed in the introduction. Briefly, the Northern Hemisphere atmospheric flow has two relatively stable states that could be represented as a more zonal jet stream and a more meridional jet stream. The atmosphere remains in one of these two states for about eight to twelve days at a time before transitioning to the other. However, the period between transitions is highly irregular, lasting anywhere from three to thirty-five days. The NAO can be thought of as the Atlantic Ocean basin version of the Northern Hemisphere dynamic variability as a whole, and the dynamics can be represented using a simple model (for example, Kravtsov, Robertson, and Ghil 2005; Luo, Lupo, and Wan 2007).

A daily (or monthly) time series of this index is available through the NOAA Climate Prediction Center (2022). An analysis of the index shows strong variability on the sub-seasonal (less than four months) to seasonal timescales. It is known that the time series of the daily or monthly NAO index values possesses interannual (for example, Da Costa and de Verde 2002; Mokhov and Smirnov 2006) or interdecadal (for example, Wang et al. 2012; Woollings et al. 2015) variability as well. Thus, the NAO will correlate on different timescales to midlatitude phenomena such as atmospheric blocking (Lupo et al. 2019). However, the forcing or cause of interannual or interdecadal variability in the NAO index will have its roots in the oceanic indexes examined here, such as the AMO, and even external variability, such as solar cycles (for example, Lüdecke et al. 2020). The dynamics of other atmospheric indexes such as the Pacific North American (PNA) index or the Arctic Oscillation (AO) are similar to those of the NAO, and interannual and interdecadal variability will arise for reasons similar to those that drive the NAO as well (for example, Jensen et al. 2018; Lupo et al. 2019).

Summary and Conclusions

This chapter is a review of interannual and interdecadal cycles that are driven by oceanic and atmospheric mechanisms and how they can influence global atmospheric temperature. Here the El Niño and Southern Oscillation phenomenon is used to demonstrate the physics associated with changes in the oceanic distribution of heat and how it is redistributed through the atmosphere. This includes a calculation to show that the heat released from only a part of the warm anomaly associated with the 2015–2016 El Niño could be solely responsible for a spike in atmospheric temperature that appears in the monthly record of the satellite-derived forty-year temperature record for the global lower atmosphere.

The chapter then discusses prominent and familiar oceanic cycles, including their background and the potential to have an influence on global temperatures over the timescale of decades. This chapter also highlights how the PDO and AMO could interact with each other and be related to global temperature. Then it reviews a relatively new theory about the long-term connections between sequential changes in all these cycles, called the "stadium wave" hypothesis, and how these changes relate to global temperature trends. Finally, it discusses the NAO, which is a prominent atmospheric teleconnection, in relation to the fundamental dynamics of short-term atmospheric variability and long-term variations in this index as forced by ocean cycles. The information this index conveys is commonly misunderstood.

One implication of this review is that the oceanic cycles discussed here can influence changes in global atmospheric temperature on timescales commonly attributed to changes in atmospheric greenhouse gas concentrations. Thus, it may be premature to attribute all or most of the current changes in climate to human activity.

References

Ahrens, C. D, and R. Henson (2022). *Meteorology Today: An Introduction to Weather and Climate.* 13th ed. Boston, Massachusetts: Cengage.

Bjerknes, J. (1966). "A Possible Response of the Atmospheric Hadley Circulation to Equatorial Anomalies of Ocean Temperature." *Tellus* 18, no. 4 (November): 820–29. Online at https://onlinelibrary.wiley.com/doi/abs/10.1111/j.2153-3490.1966.tb00303.x.

———. (1969). "Atmospheric Teleconnections from the Equatorial Pacific." *Monthly Weather Review* 97, no. 3 (March): 163–72. Online at https://journals.ametsoc.org/view/journals/mwre/97/3/1520-0493_1969_097_0163_atftep_2_3_co_2.xml.

Camargo S. J., et al. (2010). "The Influence of Natural Climate Variability on Tropical Cyclones, and Seasonal Forecasts of Tropical Cyclone Activity." *Global Perspectives on Tropical Cyclones, World Scientific Series on Asian Pacific Weather and Climate* 4:325–60. Online at https://www.worldscientific.com/doi/10.1142/9789814293488_0011.

Carlson, A. (2010). "What Caused the Younger Dryas Cold Event?" *Geology* 38, no. 4 (April): 383–84. Online at https://pubs.geoscienceworld.org/gsa/geology/article/38/4/383/130267/What-Caused-the-Younger-Dryas-Cold-Event.

Cook, B. I., et al. (2014). "Pan-Continental Droughts in North America over the Last Millennium." *Journal of Climate* 27, no. 1 (January): 383–97. Online at https://journals.ametsoc.org/view/journals/clim/27/1/jcli-d-13-00100.1.xml.

Da Costa, E. D., and A. C. De Verdiere (2002). "The 7.7-year North Atlantic Oscillation." *Quarterly Journal of the Royal Meteorological Society* 128, no. 581 (April): 797–818. Online at https://rmets.onlinelibrary.wiley.com/doi/abs/10.1256/0035900021643692.

Delworth, T. L., and M. E. Mann (2000). "Observed and Simulated Multidecadal Variability in the Northern Hemisphere." *Climate Dynamics* 16, no. 9 (September): 661–76. Online at https://link.springer.com/article/10.1007/s003820000075.

Diaz, H. F., and V. Markgraf (2000). *El Niño and the Southern Oscillation: Multiscale Variability and Global and Regional Impacts.* Cambridge, United Kingdom: Cambridge University Press.

Foltz, G. R., M. J. McPhaden, and R. Lumpkin (2012). "A Strong Atlantic Meridional Mode Event in 2009: The Role of Mixed

Layer Dynamics." *Journal of Climate* 25, no. 1 (January): 363–80. Online at https://journals.ametsoc.org/view/journals/clim/25/1/jcli-d-11-00150.1.xml.

Gershunov, A., and T. P. Barnett (1998). "Interdecadal Modulation of ENSO Teleconnections." *Bulletin of the American Meteorological Society* 79, no. 12 (December): 2715–25. Online at https://journals.ametsoc.org/view/journals/bams/79/12/1520-0477_1998_079_2715_imoet_2_0_co_2.xml.

Jensen, A., A. R. Lupo, I. I. Mokhov, M. G. Akperov and F. Sun (2018). "The Dynamic Character of Northern Hemisphere Flow Regimes in a Near-Term Climate Change Projection." *Atmosphere* 9, no. 1 (January): 27

JISAO (n.d.) "The Pacific Decadal Oscillation (PDO)." University of Washington, Joint Institute for the Study of the Atmosphere and Ocean/National Oceanic and Atmospheric Administration. Online at http://research.jisao.washington.edu/pdo.

Klotzbach P. J., and W. M. Gray (2008). "Multidecadal Variability in North Atlantic Tropical Cyclone Activity." *Journal of Climate* 21, no. 15 (August): 3229–35. Online at https://journals.ametsoc.org/view/journals/clim/21/15/2008jcli2162.1.xml.

Knauss, J. A. (1978). *Introduction to Physical Oceanography*. New Jersey: Prentice-Hall.

Kononova, N. K., and A. R. Lupo (2020). "Changes in the Dynamics of the Northern Hemisphere Atmospheric Circulation and the Relationship to Surface Temperature in the 20th and 21st Centuries." *Atmosphere* 11, no. 3 (March): 255. Online at https://www.mdpi.com/2073-4433/11/3/255.

Kravtsov, S., A. W. Robertson, and M. Ghil (2005). "Bimodal Behavior in the Zonal Mean Flow of a Baroclinic β-Channel Model." *Journal of the Atmospheric Sciences* 62 (June): 1746–69. Online at https://journals.ametsoc.org/view/journals/atsc/62/6/jas3443.1.xml.

Lüdecke, H.-J., et al. (2020). "Decadal and Multidecadal Natural Variability in European Temperature." *Journal of Atmospheric and Solar-Terrestrial Physics* 205, no. 5 (May): 105294. Online at https://doi.org/10.1016/j.jastp.2020.105294.

Luo, D., A. R. Lupo, and H. Wan (2007). "Dynamics of Eddy-Driven Low-Frequency Dipole Modes. Part I: A Simple Model of North Atlantic Oscillations." *Journal of the Atmospheric Sciences* 64, no. 1 (January): 29–51. Online at https://journals.ametsoc.org/view/journals/atsc/64/1/jas3818.1.xml.

Lupo, A. R., et al. (2019). "Changes in Global Blocking Character during Recent Decades." *Atmosphere* 10, no. 2 (February): 92. Online at https://www.mdpi.com/2073-4433/10/2/92.

MacDonald, G. M., and R.A. Case (2005). "Variations in the Pacific Decadal Oscillation over the Past Millennium." *Geophysical Research Letters* 32, no. 8 (April): L08703. Online at https://agupubs.onlinelibrary.wiley.com/doi/full/10.1029/2005GL022478.

Mantua, N. J., et al. (1997). "A Pacific Interdecadal Climate Oscillation with Impacts on Salmon Production." *Bulletin of the American Meteorological Society* 78, no. 6 (June): 1069–79. Online at https://journals.ametsoc.org/view/journals/bams/78/6/1520-0477_1997_078_1069_apicow_2_0_co_2.xml.

Maruyama, F. (2019). "Influence of the Atlantic Multidecadal Oscillation and the Pacific Decadal Oscillation on Global Temperature by Wavelet-Based Multifractal Analysis." *Journal of Geoscience and Environment Protection* 7, no. 8 (August): 105–17. Online at https://www.scirp.org/journal/paperinformation.aspx?paperid=94379.

Mestas-Nuñez, A. M., and D. B. Enfield (2001). "Eastern Equatorial Pacific SST Variability: ENSO and Non-ENSO Components and Their Climatic Associations." *Journal of Climate* 14, no. 3 (February): 391–402. Online at https://journals.ametsoc.org/view/journals/clim/14/3/1520-0442_2001_014_0391_eepsve_2.0.co_2.xml.

Miller, A. J., et al. (1994). "The 1976–77 Climate Shift of the Pacific Ocean." *Oceanography* 7, no. 1 (October): 21–26. Online at https://tos.org/oceanography/article/the-1976-77-climate-shift-of-the-pacific-ocean.

Minobe, S. (1997). "A 50–70 Year Climatic Oscillation over the North Pacific and North America." *Geophysical Research Letters* 24, no. 6 (March): 683–86. Online at https://agupubs.onlinelibrary.wiley.com/doi/10.1029/97GL00504.

Mokhov, I. I., and D. A. Smirnov (2006). "El Niño–Southern Oscillation Drives North Atlantic Oscillation as Revealed with Non-Linear Techniques from Climatic Indices." *Geophysical Research Letters* 33, no. 3 (February): 3708–11. Online at https://agupubs.onlinelibrary.wiley.com/doi/full/10.1029/2005GL024557.

Newman, M., et al. (2016). "The Pacific Decadal Oscillation, Revisited." *Journal of Climate* 29, no. 12 (June): 4399–4427. Online at https://journals.ametsoc.org/view/journals/clim/29/12/jcli-d-15-0508.1.xml.

NOAA Climate Prediction Center (2022). "North Atlantic Oscillation (NAO)." Online at https://www.cpc.ncep.noaa.gov/products/precip/CWlink/pna/nao.shtml.

O'Reilly, C. H., et al. (2016). "The Signature of Low-Frequency Oceanic Forcing in the Atlantic Multidecadal Oscillation." *Geophysical Research Letters* 43, no. 6 (February) 2810–18. Online at https://agupubs.onlinelibrary.wiley.com/doi/full/10.1002/2016GL067925.

Pedlosky, J. (1987). *Geophysical Fluid Dynamics*. 2nd ed. New York: Springer-Verlag Press.

Peixoto, J. P., and A. H. Oort (1992). *Physics of Climate*. New York: American Institute of Physics.

Philander, S. G. (1990). *El Niño, La Niña, and the Southern Oscillation*. London: Academic Press.

Rohli, R. V., and A. J. Vega (2017). *Climatology*. 4th ed. Burlington, Massachusetts: Jones and Bartlett.

Shi, W., M. L'Heureux, and E. LaJoie, eds. (2022) *Climate Diagnostics Bulletin.* Washington, D.C.: U.S. Department of Commerce. Online at https://www.cpc.ncep.noaa.gov/products/CDB/editors.shtml.

Tilly, D. E., et al. (2008). "Calculated Height Tendencies in Two Southern Hemisphere Blocking and Cyclone Events: The Contribution of Diabatic Heating to Block Intensification." *Monthly Weather Review* 136, no. 9 (September): 3568–78. Online at https://journals.ametsoc.org/view/journals/mwre/136/9/2008mwr2374.1.xml.

Trenberth, K., R. Zhang, et al. (2021). "Atlantic Multi-Decadal Oscillation (AMO)." NCAR | Climate Data Guide. Online at https://climatedataguide.ucar.edu/climate-data/atlantic-multi-decadal-oscillation-amo.

Van Geel, B., and P. A. Ziegler (2013). "IPCC Underestimates the Sun's Role in Climate Change." *Energy and Environment* 24 (3–4): 431–54. Online at https://www.jstor.org/stable/43735181.

Vimont, D. J., and J. P. Kossin (2007). "The Atlantic Meridional Mode and Hurricane Activity." *Geophysical Research Letters* 34, no. 7 (April): L07709. Online at https://agupubs.onlinelibrary.wiley.com/doi/10.1029/2007GL029683.

Wang, Y.-H., et al. (2012). "Decadal Variability of the NAO: Introducing an Augmented NAO Index." *Geophysical Research Letters* 39, no. 21 (November): L21702. Online at https://agupubs.onlinelibrary.wiley.com/doi/full/10.1029/2012GL053413.

Wilby, R. L., G. O'Hare, and N. Barnsley (1997). "The North Atlantic Oscillation and British Isles Climate Variability, 1865–1996." *Weather* 52, no. 9 (April): 266–76. Online at https://www.semanticscholar.org/paper/The-North-Atlantic-Oscillation-and-British-Isles-Wilby-O'Hare/ef95aa3b91c850c91ed08bce70e708dc31ebc423.

Woollings, T., et al. (2014). "Contrasting Interannual and Multidecadal NAO Variability." *Climate Dynamics* 45, no. 1–2 (July): 539–56. Online at https://link.springer.com/article/10.1007/s00382-014-2237-y.

Wyatt, M. G., and J. A. Curry (2014). "Role for Eurasian Arctic Shelf Sea Ice in a Secularly Varying Hemispheric Climate Signal during the 20th Century." *Climate Dynamics* 42, no. 9–10 (May): 2763–82. Online at https://link.springer.com/article/10.1007/s00382-013-1950-2.

Wyatt, M. G., S. Kravtsov, and A. A. Tsonis (2012). "Atlantic Multidecadal Oscillation and Northern Hemisphere's Climate Variability." *Climate Dynamics* 38, no. 5 (March): 929–49. Online at https://link.springer.com/article/10.1007/s00382-011-1071-8.

Xie, S.-P. (1999). "A Dynamic Ocean-Atmosphere Model of the Tropical Atlantic Decadal Variability." *Journal of Climate* 12, no. 1 (January): 64–70. Online at https://journals.ametsoc.org/view/journals/clim/12/1/1520-0442_1999_012_0064_adoamo_2.0.co_2.xml.

Yuan, T., et al. (2016). "Positive Low Cloud and Dust Feedbacks Amplify Tropical North Atlantic Multidecadal Oscillation." *Geophysical Research Letters* 43, no. 3 (January): 1349–56. Online at https://ntrs.nasa.gov/api/citations/20170003432/downloads/20170003432.pdf.

Zhang, Y., J. M. Wallace, and D. S. Battisti (1997). "ENSO-Like Interdecadal Variability: 1900–93." *Journal of Climate* 10, no. 5 (May): 1004–20. Online at https://journals.ametsoc.org/view/journals/clim/10/5/1520-0442_1997_010_1004_eliv_2.0.co_2.xml.

CHAPTER 7

The Role of Evaporation, Precipitation, and Clouds

BY ROY W. SPENCER

CHAPTER SUMMARY

It is easy to overlook water vapor as the strongest of Earth's greenhouse gases. Together with the clouds we see, water vapor accounts for about 75 percent of the greenhouse effect. Without greenhouse gases, the Earth would be a ball of ice. Therefore, an understanding of the processes controlling water vapor in the atmosphere is critical to analyzing warming effects. Rising temperatures contribute to evaporation but also affect precipitation processes, thus significantly enhancing or suppressing vapor exchanges. Cloud types, altitude, and location are important parts of that cycle. None of these are understood well enough to predict how weak

CO_2 warming will create net positive or negative water vapor feedbacks to total warming.

Details of precipitation physics are poorly understood, and they take place on spatial scales too small for climate models to represent from first principles. Therefore, the models can only crudely represent clouds and precipitation by using mathematical representations approximating anticipated effects but subject to uncertain and subjective statistical relationships. With continuing speculation over uncertainties in water vapor, clouds, and precipitation processes, the range of net warming projections from climate models continues to grow. Science can hardly be considered settled amid these controversies.

One of the unique features of Earth's climate system is the presence of water, in all of its phases: liquid (rivers, lakes, oceans, and rainfall), solid (snow and ice), and gas (water vapor). The atmosphere's hydrologic cycle includes water vapor from the evaporation of surface water (providing Earth's main greenhouse gas), then clouds condensed from that water vapor, and finally precipitation falling from some of those clouds. These processes are intricately interrelated, and how they will change with global warming remains uncertain.

Water vapor is Earth's strongest greenhouse gas, and together with clouds it accounts for about 75 percent of the total greenhouse effect, with CO_2, methane, and other non-condensing gases providing the remaining 25 percent (Lacis et al. 2010). Without the greenhouse "blanket" surrounding Earth, our planet would likely be encased in ice. Obviously, the processes controlling how much water vapor resides in the atmosphere are critical for understanding climate and climate change. As we shall see, the processes that limit how much water vapor accumulates in the atmosphere—precipitation—are not known in enough detail to predict how the weak direct-warming effect of increasing CO_2 will be either amplified or reduced by precipitation limits on water vapor. Climate models only crudely represent the conversion from water vapor to precipitation, with statistical approximations made to produce approximately the average amounts of water vapor and precipitation. The actual physics that will determine how precipitation will change with warming are not even understood, let alone represented in climate models.

How Is Water Vapor Controlled in the Climate System?

The mainstream view of most climate scientists is that water vapor is controlled by temperature, and that temperature is, in turn, controlled by how much carbon dioxide and other non-condensing greenhouse gases are in the atmosphere. In this simplistic view, CO_2 is then the principal "control knob" of the climate system (Lacis et al. 2010), and water vapor provides a strong positive feedback, amplifying the warming caused by CO_2.

But as Rennó, Emanuel, and Stone (1994) showed, precipitation processes also have a huge impact on how much water vapor resides in the atmosphere. Atmospheric water vapor (and thus a large part of Earth's greenhouse effect) is not only controlled by surface temperature driving evaporation, but also by precipitation processes removing water vapor from the atmosphere.

Most of the atmospheric water vapor produced by surface evaporation remains at low altitudes, in the atmosphere's boundary layer (Figure 7.1). This layer has variable thickness up to a 1–2 km depth, where turbulent mixing of the air is driven by solar heating of the surface. If you have flown in an aircraft on a sunny day, you might have noticed the turbulent ride at lower altitudes within the boundary layer and a smoother ride at higher altitudes.

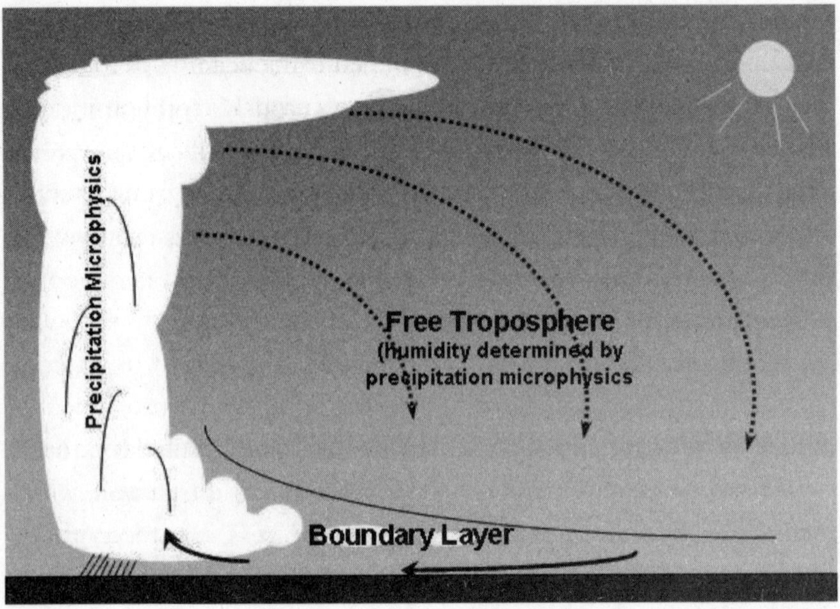

Figure 7.1. Schematic representation of the atmospheric hydrologic cycle, with near-surface winds picking up water vapor from surface evaporation, which then leads to cloud formation, and precipitation falling from some of those clouds. The return air circulation in the free troposphere is largely cloud-free and has low humidity. Earth's water vapor–induced greenhouse effect, even in clear sky regions, thus depends upon complex precipitation formation processes. *Image by the author. Used by permission.*

As the atmosphere fills with water vapor from surface evaporation, clouds form. Those clouds reflect sunlight back to outer space, a cooling effect on the climate system, but they also slow the loss of infrared radiation to outer space, thus helping to warm the planet through their contribution to the greenhouse effect. In the global average, the cooling effect of clouds dominates (Ramanathan et al. 1989). Only thin, high-altitude cirrus clouds have a net warming effect on our climate. These different cloud types can have large regional differences around the world. For example, low-altitude marine stratus clouds, which dominate the eastern ends of the subtropical ocean basins, have a strong cooling effect on the climate system.

Finally, the formation of precipitation within some clouds limits the buildup of atmospheric water vapor by returning water back to Earth's surface, thus limiting the strength of Earth's natural greenhouse effect. The microphysical processes involved in precipitation formation are understood in only a general sense, involving tiny cloud water droplets and ice particles of various sizes, all interacting in complex ways in turbulent cloud updrafts and downdrafts.

Evaporation of water from the surface requires heat, thus cooling the surface, as we are all aware of from the cooling effect of water on our skin. The faster the surface wind blows, the faster the rate of evaporation. When water vapor condenses to form clouds, that "latent heat" is released to the atmosphere, causing warming of air parcels, which then rise. The higher the parcels rise, the greater the amount of precipitation formed, which then depletes water vapor in the atmosphere.

Importantly, all the condensation-driven warm updrafts in clouds force an equal amount of sinking air in the so-called "free troposphere," which is the deep layer of air above the boundary layer. That sinking air is usually clear, with low humidity. Since it is driven by cloud updrafts, we can see that clear, cloud-free air is not controlled separately from cloudy air but is a result and a necessary part of the total cloud circulation. For example, the mostly clear and dry skies over the Sahara Desert are due to sinking air that is being forced to sink by updrafts in precipitation systems thousands of kilometers away. These processes together complete the atmospheric portion of the global hydrologic cycle—evaporation, cloud formation, precipitation, and then starting over with evaporation.

Each of these features of the atmospheric hydrologic cycle provides potential impacts on estimates of global warming through so-called feedbacks, that is, warming-driven changes in other processes that either amplify or reduce the original warming. So, while the direct warming effect of a doubling of atmospheric CO_2 ("$2xCO_2$") is around

1°C, negative feedbacks could reduce that value, or positive feedbacks could amplify it. Some climate researchers tend to believe that many of these feedbacks are positive, amplifying the weak CO_2-only warming by up to several times, to as much as 5°C of total warming for a doubling of atmospheric CO_2. Sherwood et al. (2020) examined a wide range of previously published estimates of future warming from $2xCO_2$ and claimed a range from 2.0 to 5.7°C. A minority of scientists think the feedbacks that amplify the initial warming will be weaker, producing less than 2°C of warming (Lewis and Curry 2018). A few scientists even think the feedbacks are possibly negative, reducing the initial warming to below 1°C (for example, Lindzen and Choi 2009). Chapter 9 of this book addresses this issue in depth.

These feedbacks are by no means certain or well quantified. Indeed, the latest computerized climate models (CMIP6; Meehl et al. 2020) produce a greater range of potential warming than in any previous assessment produced by the United Nations over the last thirty years. The uncertainties associated with water vapor, cloud, and precipitation processes regarding their impact on global warming estimates cannot be overemphasized.

The Effect of Warming on Water Vapor, Clouds, and Precipitation

Water Vapor

Because water vapor, clouds, and precipitation are intricately linked together, it is difficult to address them separately. A change in one will affect the others.

It is widely believed that warming temperatures will lead to global-average increases in atmospheric water vapor and thus an increase in the greenhouse effect. This is called positive water vapor feedback, and in computer climate models it leads to at least a doubling of the rate of warming due to increasing CO_2 alone (IPCC 2007).

Assume that warming is associated with increased rates of surface evaporation and then boundary layer water vapor, which is highly likely. While increasing surface evaporation with warming means extra cooling of Earth's surface (since evaporation requires heat energy to occur), the extra water vapor could enhance the greenhouse effect, which is widely believed to be a strong net warming effect in global warming theory.

But because evaporation, clouds, and precipitation are interrelated, it becomes less certain just how much (if any) increasing water vapor will amplify the small, 1°C warming from a doubling of CO_2. Let us follow through the hydrologic cycle to examine how a warming-induced increase in water vapor might change cloud and precipitation processes.

The extra heat energy required for more surface evaporation with warming is released to the atmosphere when clouds form, driving either more clouds to form, or stronger updrafts within those clouds, or both. It is even possible for there to be even fewer clouds if the clouds become narrower and more scattered but with even stronger updrafts.

Thus, the amount and altitude of clouds could either increase or decrease with warming. No one really knows. The uncertainties associated with warming-induced cloud changes are widely known in the climate research community (Meehl et al. 2020; Zelinka et al. 2020). Some climate models produce positive cloud feedback, while others produce negative cloud feedback. We do know that the net effect of clouds on the climate system is a cooling effect, so it is reasonable to surmise that warming from increasing CO_2 could cause a small increase in cloudiness, thus reflecting more solar energy to outer space. This would function as a negative feedback, thus reducing warming. This remains uncertain, however.

Precipitation

Let us examine the next step in the hydrologic cycle: precipitation. Increased surface evaporation must be matched by increased rates of precipitation; otherwise, the atmosphere would continually fill with ever-increasing amounts of water vapor. But even if the global rates of evaporation and precipitation increase and are exactly equal in a warmer world, this does not tell us how much water vapor will reside in the atmosphere.

What is often overlooked is the potential effect of warming on the efficiency of precipitation systems, which in turn could greatly affect global warming estimates. Rennó, Emanuel, and Stone (1994) showed that a climate system with low precipitation efficiency is warmer and moister, while a climate system with higher precipitation efficiency is cooler and dryer. While it might sound counterintuitive to have high precipitation efficiency leading to less precipitation, the important process is how water vapor in the atmosphere is regulated, and anything that reduces atmospheric water vapor will cool the climate system. Thus, higher precipitation efficiency removes more water vapor from the atmosphere before it can build up, which leads to a weaker greenhouse effect, thus cooler global temperatures, thus less evaporation, and so less precipitation.

It is common knowledge, to those who travel the world and watch the weather, that warm, tropical rain systems are more efficient than cool, high-latitude systems (Lutsko and Cronin 2018). Relatively shallow cloud systems in the tropics can produce huge amounts of rain. On one summer's night in Townsville, Australia, I personally witnessed heavy rain falling from a clear, cloudless sky. Obviously, clouds must have formed to produce the rain, but they must have been completely depleted of water by highly efficient rainfall processes. We might expect that global warming would be accompanied by increasing precipitation efficiency, with lower rates of warming through a negative feedback on water vapor, potentially reducing rather than increasing initial warming from added atmospheric CO_2.

Nevertheless, it has been observed that globally warm years have more water vapor in the boundary layer, especially if one averages over the global oceans. These increases are likely driven by increased rates of surface evaporation, which has led many researchers to conclude that water vapor feedback is positive. But what happens in the free troposphere is much more uncertain, and it has long been known that a very small reduction of free tropospheric vapor can have a larger cooling effect than the warming effect of substantial vapor increases in the boundary layer (Spencer and Braswell 1997). Since free tropospheric water vapor is controlled more by precipitation processes, we see once again that global warming predictions depend critically on how precipitation processes will change with warming.

Climate models that predict future rates of global warming represent cloud and precipitation processes only crudely. They have parameterizations—indirect statistical, rather than direct physical, relationships—that estimate the net cloud and precipitation amounts on a relatively coarse spatial scale, say, 100 km or so. The models cannot resolve individual clouds, so those cloud and precipitation effects are only approximated with highly uncertain statistical relationships. Even in the most sophisticated cloud-resolving models, the onset of precipitation is initiated when the cloud water reaches a certain threshold, called the auto-conversion threshold (the point at which cloud water is converted to precipitation). That threshold is often a single number, with no connection to the cloud microphysics that control it. It has been optimized to produce a realistic average amount of precipitation (and free-tropospheric water vapor), but no one knows how that threshold might change in a quantitative sense with warming.

If the foregoing discussion seems difficult to follow, rest assured that I have only scratched the surface. The interplay between evaporation, cloud circulations, and precipitation is endlessly complex. There are known unknowns (for example, what controls precipitation efficiency in a warming world), and there are, no doubt, unknown unknowns. After more than thirty years of climate model development, the warming predictions made by two dozen models are in greater disagreement than ever before (Meehl et al. 2020). This demonstrates that there are great uncertainties remaining in the processes controlling how much warming the climate system will experience as atmospheric CO_2 concentrations increase (see chapter 9).

References

IPCC (2007). "Chapter 8.6.3.1: Water Vapor and Lapse Rate." In *IPCC Fourth Assessment Report: Climate Change 2007: Working Group I: The Physical Science Basis*. Cambridge, United Kingdom, and New York. Cambridge University Press. Online at https://archive.ipcc.ch/publications_and_data/ar4/wg1/en/ch8s8-6-3-1.html.

Lacis, A. A., et al. (2010). "Atmospheric CO_2: Principal Control Knob Governing Earth's Temperature." *Science* 330, no. 6002 (October): 356–59. Online at https://doi.org/10.1126/science.1190653.

Lewis, N., and J. Curry (2018). "The Impact of Recent Forcing and Ocean Heat Uptake Data on Estimates of Climate Sensitivity." *Journal of Climate* 31, no. 15 (August): 6051–71. Online at https://doi.org/10.1175/JCLI-D-17-0667.1.

Lindzen, R., and Y.-S. Choi (2009). "On the Determination of Climate Feedbacks from ERBE Data." *Geophysical Research Letters* 36, no. 16 (August): L16075. Online at https://doi.org/10.1029/2009GL039628.

Lutsko, N. J., and T. W. Cronin (2018). "Increase in Precipitation Efficiency with Surface Warming in Radiative-Convective

Equilibrium." *Journal of Advances in Modeling Earth Systems* 10, no. 11 (November): 2992–3010. Online at https://doi.org/10.1029/2018MS001482.

Meehl, G. A., et al. (2020). "Context for Interpreting Equilibrium Climate Sensitivity and Transient Climate Response from the CMIP6 Earth System Models." *Science Advances* 6, no. 26 (June). Online at https://doi.org/10.1126/sciadv.aba1981.

Ramanathan, V., et al. (1989). "Cloud-Radiative Forcing and Climate: Results from the Earth Radiation Budget Experiment." *Science* 243, no. 4887 (January): 57–63. Online at https://www.science.org/doi/10.1126/science.243.4887.57.

Rennó, N. O., K. A. Emanuel, and P. H. Stone (1994). "Radiative-Convective Model with an Explicit Hydrological Cycle 1. Formulation and Sensitivity to Model Parameters." *Journal of Geophysical Research: Atmospheres* 99, no. D7 (July): 14429–41. Online at https://agupubs.onlinelibrary.wiley.com/doi/abs/10.1029/94JD00020.

S. C. Sherwood et al. (2020). "An Assessment of Earth's Climate Sensitivity Using Multiple Lines of Evidence." *Reviews of Geophysics* 58, no. 4 (July). Online at https://agupubs.onlinelibrary.wiley.com/doi/full/10.1029/2019RG000678.

Spencer, R. W., and W. D. Braswell (1997) "How Dry Is the Tropical Free Troposphere? Implications for Global Warming Theory." *Bulletin of the American Meteorological Society* 78, no. 6 (June): 1097–1106. Online at https://doi.org/10.1175/1520-0477(1997)078<1097:HDITTF>2.0.CO;2.

Zelinka, M. D., et al. (2020) "Causes of Higher Climate Sensitivity in CMIP6 Models." *Geophysical Research Letters* 47, no. 1 (January): e209GL085782. Online at https://doi.org/10.1029/2019GL085782

CHAPTER 8

The Role of Greenhouse Gases

BY DAVID R. LEGATES

CHAPTER SUMMARY

Of the several gases making up Earth's atmosphere, nitrogen and oxygen comprise 99 percent of dry air and argon most of the remaining 1 percent. These gases don't contribute to the "greenhouse effect." Only trace amounts of the greenhouse gases (CO_2, O_3, CH_4, N_2O) are present. Water (H_2O) is added to these, varying in concentration by volume from nearly 0 percent (polar dry air) to 4 percent (humid tropics). CO_2 concentration is very small (0.04 percent), which is why it is reported in parts per million (ppm).

While "greenhouse" terminology is commonly used, it is a misnomer because atmospheric mechanisms are more numerous and complex than what occurs in a greenhouse.

> Nevertheless, the general idea of warming the Earth's surface to a habitable condition applies, coming primarily from H_2O (75 percent) and CO_2 (20 percent). A differential energy capture occurs because greenhouse gases absorb and emit radiation in the infrared wavelength bands at which energy is radiated back into space after incoming solar energy, at shorter wavelengths, enters the system. As CO_2 concentration doubles from pre-industrial 280 ppm, the next 280 ppm absorbs only 1 percent of the energy of the original 280 ppm. The earlier concentration has done most of the job, and the addition operates with a logarithmic decay for little incremental energy absorption. So, temperature change due to CO_2's rising from 560 ppm to 1120 ppm will be similar to that from the previous doubling. But 1120 ppm will be centuries away, if ever.

Greenhouse gases are important to Earth's climate, as they make the surface warmer than it would be otherwise. But what are greenhouse gases, why do they absorb thermal infrared radiation (that is, heat), and how important are these gases in changing climatic conditions if their concentrations increase? These questions will be addressed in this chapter.

Greenhouse Gases Warm the Surface of Earth

Consider a simple, zero-dimensional energy balance climate model (for example, Budyko 1969) of a hypothetical planet. To be in thermodynamic equilibrium—that is, the temperature of the modeled planet does not change over time—the energy that comes to the planet from the Sun must equal the energy that is emitted by the planet to space. Thus, when the incoming energy is balanced by the outgoing energy, the temperature of the planet remains constant. For simplicity, our planet will be zero-dimensional, or just a single point in space.

First, consider the energy that comes from the Sun to our planet. At the mean distance from Earth to the Sun, the energy received by a plane held perpendicular to the Sun's rays is 1365.2 W/m^2. Climatologists call this the *solar constant*, but it is not really a constant, because the Sun is a variable star and Earth traverses an elliptical orbit around it. Nevertheless, for a simple, zero-dimensional climate model, a constant value will be assumed. Even though the planet is merely a point in space, this energy must be distributed across the surface of a spherical planet. Thus, the solar constant is multiplied by the ratio of the area of a circle (what is seen by the Sun) to the surface area of a sphere having the same radius (the surface area over which the solar energy is distributed). This results in a value of 341.3 W/m^2, which is the energy received by our planet from the Sun (Trenberth, Fasullo, and Kiehl 2009—see Figure 3.1 of chapter 3 of this book).

Where does that number—341.3 W/m^2—come from? (This and the following four paragraphs will incorporate a bit of higher math, but fear not. Even if you're not a mathematician, you'll be able to grasp their substance.) If the radius of the planet is r_e, then the area of its disk is πr_e^2 and its surface area is $4\pi r_e^2$. Taking the ratio of these two yields a value of 0.25, which is then multiplied by the solar constant to get the value of 341.3 W/m^2.

To calculate the energy given off by the planet, the Stefan-Boltzmann radiation law indicates that the total energy emitted by an object at temperature T is simply a function of the fourth power of the absolute temperature (T in Kelvins). The constant of proportionality is the Stefan-Boltzmann constant—5.67 x 10^{-8} W/m^{2}K^4. The Stefan-Boltzmann radiation law assumes the object is a *blackbody*—that is, a perfect emitter. This is a reasonable assumption for our simple, zero-dimensional energy balance model.

Now, first assume that the atmosphere of our simple planet consists of just three gases—nitrogen (N_2—78 percent), oxygen (O_2—21 percent), and argon (Ar—1 percent). This is actually the chemical makeup of pure dry air (that is, water vapor neglected) with the value of argon increased to 1 percent from 0.93 percent (to account for the deletion of all other gases and to keep atmospheric pressure nearly the same). As will be shown in the next section, none of these three gases absorbs significant amounts of thermal infrared radiation (that is, heat), which are the wavelengths of energy that are given off by an object at temperatures found on Earth's surface.

Since the simple, zero-dimensional energy balance model must be in thermal equilibrium, the energy coming from the Sun (that is, 341.3 W/m^2) must equal the energy given off by the planet (that is, $[5.67 \times 10^{-8}]\ T^4$). However, not all of the energy received at Earth's surface is absorbed by the planet—some is reflected to space. This is called the *albedo* of the planet and is approximately 12.5 percent (Trenberth, Fasullo, and Kiehl 2009). The amount absorbed is therefore 87.5 percent, which yields a surface temperature of 254.9K (−3.75°C) (solving for T in $(0.875\ x\ 341.3) = \left[\left(5.67\ x\ 10^{-8}\right) T^4\right]$). This is colder than the average surface temperature of Earth (~287.6K or 14.5°C [58.1°F]).

Water vapor (H_2O) is a complicated molecule. It is a greenhouse gas, but it also condenses in our atmosphere to form clouds (see chapter 7 above). With respect to solar energy (that is, visible light), clouds reflect the incoming solar radiation by raising the planetary albedo to about 29.9 percent (Trenberth, Fasullo, and Kiehl 2009). If we introduce clouds into our simple, zero-dimensional energy balance model but, for now, ignore the fact that water vapor is a greenhouse gas, we calculate a surface temperature of 269.4K (−18.3°C [−0.4°F]), which is even colder (solving for T in $(0.701\ x\ 341.3) = \left[\left(5.67\ x\ 10^{-8}\right) T^4\right]$. Note, then, that with respect to solar energy, clouds dramatically cool the planet.

Warming the planet from approximately 269.4K to about 287.6K (14.5°C)—a warming of about 18.2K—is accomplished by greenhouse gases. On Earth, the biggest contributors to this warming are H_2O and carbon dioxide (CO_2). These gases, along with ozone (O_3), methane (CH_4), nitrous oxide (N_2O), and others absorb the thermal infrared radiation emitted by the surface, thereby warming the atmosphere (see Figure 3.1 in chapter 3 of this book). Since the atmosphere then is at a temperature above absolute zero (that is, 0K or −273.15°C), it too emits energy, some of which escapes to space but a majority of which is absorbed by Earth's surface. Thus, Earth's surface is warmed by the Sun and by the energy emitted by the atmosphere. All of this energy came from the Sun originally, but the atmosphere prevents some of the emitted thermal radiation (from the surface) from escaping to space and, instead, serves to warm Earth's surface.

Why Do Greenhouse Gases Absorb Infrared Radiation?

Why is it that when it comes to the "greenhouse effect," the focus is placed on H_2O, CO_2, O_3, CH_4, and N_2O and not on the three gases that comprise 99.93 percent of dry air—N_2, O_2, and Ar? The simple answer is that the first five gases—the "greenhouse gases"—absorb energy in the thermal infrared portion of the spectrum, whereas the latter three do not. Thus, greenhouse gases are often called "trace gases," because they (with the exception of H_2O vapor in some areas of the planet) constitute a very small portion of the atmosphere (by volume). Greenhouse gases, nevertheless, play a significant role in defining the climate of Earth.

But a longer answer is needed to explain why greenhouse gases absorb and emit thermal infrared energy and why N_2, O_2, and Ar do not. First, it must be recognized that gases behave differently than liquids and solids. Emission spectra (that is, the energy emitted by an object across the wavelengths of the electromagnetic spectrum) for liquids and solids follow Planck's radiation law, usually near the blackbody emission curve. Thus, energy is emitted across the entire electromagnetic spectrum with a preferred wavelength that is inversely proportional to the temperature of the object. Gases, however, behave differently, in that they absorb and emit energy in specific wavelength bands. These bands depend on a number of characteristics of a molecule that is moving freely in space, since gases are not bound by structural rigidity (as in a solid) or by intermolecular bonds (as in a liquid).

Absorption of energy in the thermal infrared portion of the electromagnetic spectrum by a gas depends largely on the vibration or rotation of an electric dipole moment (van Wijngaarden and Happer 2020, 2021). (A molecule that exhibits an electric dipole is one within which there is a separation of positive and negative electrical charges; that is, the molecule is polarized, having a distinct polarity due to the non-coincidence of the positive and negative charges within it.) Simply put, a molecule that is a good candidate for a greenhouse gas must have a separation of charges (the negative from the positive, or an electric dipole) that can move (relative to the center of mass of the molecule) with various vibrations and/or rotations that the molecule can exhibit. Argon is simply a single-atom molecule, so a significant separation of charges cannot occur within it. By contrast, N_2 and O_2 are diatomic molecules (that is, two atoms constitute each molecule), and while they undergo stretching and twisting, those motions do not significantly result in a separation of charges. Thus, these three molecules are not greenhouse gases, because they do not absorb a significant amount of energy in the thermal infrared.

Three-atom molecules are better candidates to be effective greenhouse gases, because they exhibit three pairs of possible vibrational modes (Szalay 2014)—symmetrical and asymmetrical stretching, bending and rocking, and wagging and twisting (Figure 8.1). Stretching

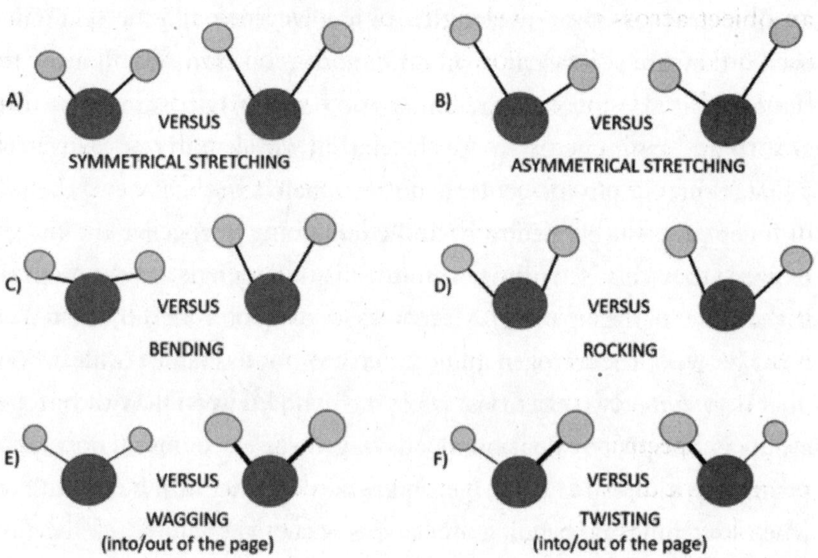

Figure 8.1. The six ways in which a three-atom molecule can vibrate. The example shown here is for a gas with a symmetric, bent molecular shape (for example, water vapor). *Source: Redrawn from https://en.wikipedia.org/wiki/Molecular_vibration. Public domain.*

involves changes in the length of the bonds between atoms (Figure 8.1 A and B); bending and rocking arise from a change in the angle between the bonds (Figure 8.1 C and D); and wagging and twisting arise when the angle formed by the three atoms changes (Figure 8.1 E and F). These motions result in a temporal separation of charges which leads to absorption bands in thermal infrared wavelengths. Ozone is even more complex since there is one single covalent bond and there is one double covalent bond between the oxygen atoms. This creates two charge separations—one resulting from the bent molecular shape and one from the asymmetry of the single covalent bond (with a positive charge on the center molecule). Thus, gases with a bent molecular shape (for example, H_2O and O_3) are greenhouse gases.

Linear three-atom molecules also involve these vibrational modes, even if they are symmetric. Carbon dioxide is a symmetric, linear molecule, but it also involves stretching and bending oscillations that also absorb and emit energy in the thermal infrared. Nitrous oxide, also a linear three-atom molecule, is not symmetric in that one of the two nitrogen atoms is bonded to both the remaining nitrogen atom and the oxygen atom (that is, a nitrogen atom and not the single oxygen atom lies in the center of the molecule). Moreover, the two bonds are not equal—the bond between the nitrogen and oxygen atom is a double covalent bond (that is, it shares two electrons) while the bond between the two nitrogen atoms is a triple covalent bond (sharing three electrons). This lack of symmetry allows for a charge separation to exist and be modulated when stretching and bending oscillations occur. Methane is an even more complex molecule as it involves four hydrogen atoms bonded to a central carbon atom. This provides for more complex stretching and bending oscillations and is why the global warming potential of each CH_4 molecule is twenty-five (that is, twenty-five times that of CO_2; Boucher et al. 2009).

But why are they called "greenhouse gases"? The usual narrative is that visible light enters a greenhouse and warms the objects therein, which subsequently emit energy in the thermal infrared portion of the electromagnetic spectrum. Like the atmosphere, the glass in the greenhouse is largely transparent to visible light (about 54 percent of the energy reaching the top of Earth's atmosphere reaches the surface) while it is largely opaque to thermal infrared (only about 10 percent of the energy emitted by Earth's surface escapes to space) (Trenberth, Fasullo, and Kiehl 2009).

Unfortunately, the name "greenhouse effect" is a misnomer (as is the phrase "the atmosphere works like a blanket"), because the atmosphere does not behave in the same way a greenhouse does. In a greenhouse, radiation is not the primary mechanism by which warming occurs. The primary mechanism is the suppression of convection—preventing air heated by the incoming radiation from leaving the greenhouse. In addition to the radiation balance, energy can be exchanged from the surface to the atmosphere through sensible heat (that is, heat you can sense through moving air) and the evaporation of water, or latent heat (see Trenberth Fasullo, and Kiehl 2009). The atmosphere facilitates energy exchange from the surface by moving air; a greenhouse (as well as a blanket) warms the surface by preventing the sensible heat from being removed. This distinction has been known for almost a century, but the misconception continues.

Greenhouse Gases and Climate Change

The concentration of H_2O varies considerably across Earth's surface; it can be as large as 4 percent of the atmosphere by volume in a humid, tropical environment or as little as near 0 percent in cold or dry climates. In contrast, CO_2 concentrations are generally well mixed throughout the atmosphere and are currently about 412.5 ppm. Note that this concentration of CO_2 is a very small number—it is the equivalent of about forty-one seats in a stadium that seats one hundred thousand! But the combined effect of H_2O and CO_2 is substantial, causing Earth's surface to be warmer by about 18.2K.

Does that mean a doubling of CO_2 would raise Earth's surface temperature by another 18.2K? Before jumping to that conclusion, it is important to determine first the relative impact of H_2O and CO_2 as greenhouse gases and to understand their respective contribution to this 18.2K of warming. It is difficult to quantify exactly what proportion of the greenhouse effect comes from any particular molecule or compound because many of their absorption bands overlap in the thermal infrared. Carbon dioxide is responsible for about 20 percent of the greenhouse warming, while small liquid and solid particles (that is, aerosols) and other minor gases (for example, CH_4, N_2O, and O_3) account for about

5 percent (NASA 2011). The most important greenhouse compound, however, is clearly H_2O, with water vapor (H_2O in gaseous form) accounting for about 50 percent and clouds (H_2O in liquid or solid form) about 25 percent.

So, does this therefore mean that if CO_2 is responsible for about 20 percent of the greenhouse warming, then a doubling of CO_2 will result in about 3.6K (that is, 20 percent of 18.2K) of additional warming? Indeed, climate models provide an estimate of the equilibrium climate sensitivity (ECS) to doubled CO_2 concentrations—the change in global surface air temperatures following a doubling of atmospheric CO_2—of between 2K and 5.5K (Meehl et al. 2020; Sherwood et al. 2020; Zelinka et al. 2020). Thus, a value of 3.6K would fall near the midpoint of that range. The IPCC *Sixth Assessment Report* (AR6) suggests a value between 2.5K and 4K with a best estimate of 3K (Williamson et al. 2023).

However, far from being diagnostic, climate models are *tuned* to provide a targeted equilibrium climate sensitivity (Voosen 2016; Hourdin et al. 2017; see chapter 4 above). As Hourdin et al. (2017, 599) explained, "One can imagine changing a parameter which is known to affect the sensitivity, keeping both this parameter and the ECS in the *anticipated acceptable range*" [emphasis added]. The problem with using models to determine ECS, then, is that by definition, models are parameterized to yield "acceptable" results—but what is "acceptable" cannot be determined by the models, for that would be circular reasoning. Thus, models cannot be used to assess ECS, and observational data must be relied upon exclusively.

Observational estimates of ECS also are difficult to assess, because Earth is never in thermodynamic equilibrium, and it can be problematic to distinguish the effect of CO_2 from natural variability or other forcings. Nevertheless, several researchers have attempted to estimate ECS from the observational record, and recent estimates seem to fall into three categories: "low" estimates of around 1.5K with a range near 1K to 2.5K (for example, Christy and McNider 2017; Lewis and Curry 2018), "medium" estimates near 2.5K with a range between about 1.8K and 3.7K (for example, Hébert et al. 2021), and "high" estimates near 3.5K with a range of approximately 2.3K to 4.5K (for example, Dessler and Forster 2018; Sherwood et al. 2020). Tokarska et al. (2020) offer an outlier in that their estimate lies between the low and medium groups with a range between 1.3K and 3.1K. This demonstrates that considerable uncertainty exists with respect to estimating the impact of a doubling of atmospheric CO_2. Chapter 9 of this book offers a much more detailed discussion of efforts to determine ECS.

Note that the "high" estimates are in line with the model estimates of climate sensitivity and are commensurate with the value of 3.6K calculated earlier (that is, 20 percent of 18.2K). There is, however, a strong argument that ECS is likely to be well below 3.6K. In particular, the sensitivity of the climate to changes in CO_2 concentrations is not linear; that is, a quadrupling of CO_2 is not likely to produce twice the warming that a doubling would produce. That is because the impact of a doubling of CO_2 depends considerably on the starting point (that is, how much CO_2 exists in the atmosphere prior to the doubling), which in turn affects how much infrared in CO_2's absorption bands (wavelengths) remains to be absorbed by any additional CO_2.

Consider, as done earlier, a planet with an atmosphere devoid of greenhouse gases. When a small amount of, say, CO_2 is added to that atmosphere, it will begin to absorb those wavelengths of thermal infrared radiation that correspond to the vibration or rotation of the electric dipole moment of CO_2 previously discussed. But as more CO_2 is added to the atmosphere, the ability to absorb those wavelengths decreases because some of the radiation in that wavelength has already been absorbed by the molecules of CO_2 added earlier. Thus, going from 0 ppm to 20 ppm of CO_2 has a much greater effect on air temperature

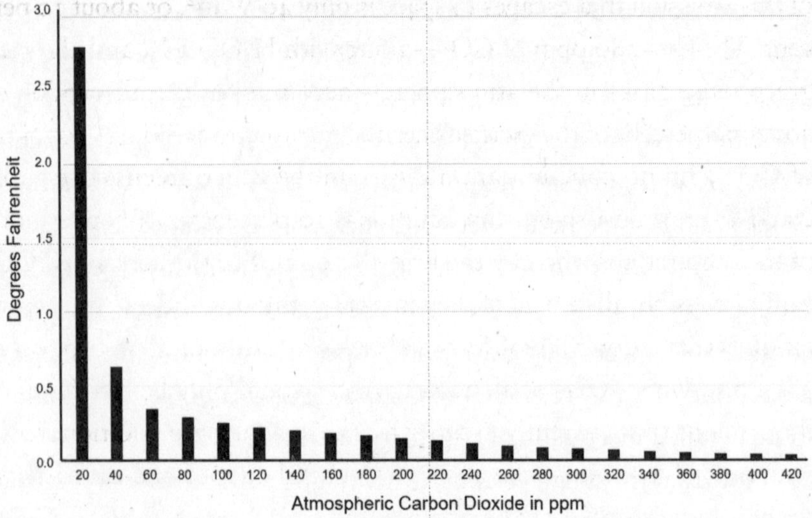

Figure 8.2. Increase in atmospheric temperature per 20 ppm increment in carbon dioxide. *Source: Data from Figure 3 of Archibald (2007). Courtesy of David R. Legates.*

than going from 400 ppm to 420 ppm—because the amount of infrared of the appropriate wavelength that remains available for absorption is much less.

The effect of greenhouse gases on atmospheric temperature is a strongly logarithmic decay; therefore, climate sensitivity decreases with increasing concentration (Archibald 2007). At pre-industrial levels of carbon dioxide (that is, approximately 280 ppm), most of the thermal infrared radiation that CO_2 *can* absorb has already *been* absorbed. Why? Because CO_2 can only absorb specific wavelengths of thermal infrared radiation, and when CO_2 concentrations approach 100 percent absorption, very little infrared radiation remains to be absorbed by newly added CO_2.

Using the global energy balance of Trenberth, Fasullo, and Kiehl (2009—Figure 3.1 in chapter 3 of this book), the energy emitted by Earth's surface (in the thermal infrared) is 390 W/m^2, but the amount of this emission that escapes to space is only 40 W/m^2, or about 10 percent. The first 280 ppm of CO_2—along with H_2O, CH_4, and all other greenhouse gases in the atmosphere—accounts for the absorption of about 90 percent of the emitted thermal infrared radiation. A doubling of CO_2 with no concomitant increase in the other greenhouse gases could *at most* absorb only an additional 10 percent or only one-ninth of the amount absorbed by the first 280 ppm. But the additional CO_2 cannot possibly absorb *all* of the remaining amount; indeed, the expectation is that a doubling of CO_2 will cause an additional absorption of 3.9 ± 0.5 W/m^2 (Arias et al. 2021), which would only be one-tenth of the amount that currently escapes to space. Thus, the additional 280 ppm of CO_2 will cause the absorption of only about one-ninetieth of the amount absorbed by the first 280 ppm.

Archibald (2007) used MODTRAN (http://modtran.spectral.com) to calculate the effect of each 20 ppm increase in CO_2 from 0 ppm to 420 ppm (Figure 8.2). Note that the curve exhibits a very strong exponential decay with more than half of the *combined* current warming of all 420 ppm achieved by the first 20 ppm. This implies that climate sensitivity decreases logarithmically with increasing CO_2 (and other greenhouse gas) concentrations.

Conclusion

This chapter has investigated what makes a gas absorb thermal infrared radiation (that is, heat), why molecules that absorb thermal infrared radiation are called greenhouse gases, and the importance of these gases in changing climatic conditions if their concentrations increase. The greenhouse effect is an important component of Earth's climate. While CO_2 is an important player in the greenhouse effect, the impact of a doubling of CO_2 provides only a minor effect on climate change.

References

Archibald, D. C. (2007). "Climate Outlook to 2030." *Energy & Environment* 18, no. 5 (September): 615–19. Online at https://www.jstor.org/stable/44397307.

Arias, P. A., et al. (2021). "Technical Summary." *Climate Change 2021: The Physical Science Basis; Working Group I Contribution to the Sixth Assessment Report of the Intergovernmental Panel on Climate Change.* (*Sixth Assessment Report*) 33–144. Cambridge, United Kingdom, and New York: Cambridge University Press. Online at https://report.ipcc.ch/ar6/wg1/IPCC_AR6_WGI_FullReport.pdf.

Boucher, O., et al. (2009). "The Indirect Global Warming Potential and Global Temperature Change Potential Due to Methane Oxidation." *Environmental Research Letters* 4, no. 4 (October): 044007. Online at https://iopscience.iop.org/article/10.1088/1748-9326/4/4/044007/meta.

Budyko, M. I. (1969). "The Effect of Solar Radiation Variations on the Climate of the Earth." *Tellus* 21, no. 5 (October): 611–19. Online at https://onlinelibrary.wiley.com/doi/10.1111/j.2153-3490.1969.tb00466.x.

Christy, J. R., and R. T. McNider (2017). "Satellite Bulk Tropospheric Temperatures as a Metric for Climate Sensitivity." *Asia-Pacific Journal of Atmospheric Science* 53, no. 4 (November): 511–18. Online at https://link.springer.com/article/10.1007/s13143-017-0070-z.

Dessler, A. E., and P. M. Forster (2018). "An Estimate of Equilibrium Climate Sensitivity from Interannual Variability." *Journal of Geophysical Research: Atmospheres* 123, no. 16 (August): 8634–45. Online at https://agupubs.onlinelibrary.wiley.com/doi/full/10.1029/2018JD028481.

Hébert, R., S. Lovejoy, and B. Tremblay (2021). "An Observation-Based Scaling Model for Climate Sensitivity Estimates and Global Projections to 2100." *Climate Dynamics* 56, no. 3 (February): 1105–29. Online at https://link.springer.com/article/10.1007/s00382-020-05521-x.

Hourdin, F., et al. (2017). "The Art and Science of Climate Model Tuning." *Bulletin of the American Meteorological Society* 98, no. 3 (March): 589–602. Online at https://journals.ametsoc.org/view/journals/bams/98/3/bams-d-15-00135.1.xml.

Lewis, N., and J. A. Curry (2018). "The Impact of Recent Forcing and Ocean Heat Uptake Data on Estimates of Climate Sensitivity." *Journal of Climate* 31, no. 15 (August): 6051–71. Online at https://journals.ametsoc.org/view/journals/clim/31/15/jcli-d-17-0667.1.xml.

Meehl, G. A., et al. (2020). "Context for Interpreting Equilibrium Climate Sensitivity and Transient Climate Response from the CMIP6 Earth System Models." *Science Advances* 6, no. 26 (June): eaba1981. Online at https://www.science.org/doi/10.1126/sciadv.aba1981.

NASA (2011). "Effects of Changing the Carbon Cycle." NASA Earth Observatory, June 16. Online at https://earthobservatory.nasa.gov/features/CarbonCycle/page5.php.

Sherwood, S. C., et al. (2020). "An Assessment of Earth's Climate Sensitivity Using Multiple Lines of Evidence." *Reviews of Geophysics* 58, no. 4 (July): e2019RG000678. Online at https://agupubs.onlinelibrary.wiley.com/doi/full/10.1029/2019RG000678.

Szalay, V. (2014). "Eckart-Sayvetz Conditions Revisited." *Journal of Chemical Physics* 140, no. 23 (June): 234107. Onlne at https://pubmed.ncbi.nlm.nih.gov/24952523.

Tokarska, K. G., et al. (2020). "Observational Constraints on the Effective Climate Sensitivity from the Historical Period." *Environmental Research Letters* 15, no. 3 (March): 034043. Online at https://iopscience.iop.org/article/10.1088/1748-9326/ab738f.

Trenberth, K. E., J. T. Fasullo, and J. Kiehl (2009). "Earth's Global Energy Budget." *Bulletin of the American Meteorological Society* 90, no. 3 (March): 311–24. Online at https://journals.ametsoc.org/view/journals/bams/90/3/2008bams2634_1.xml.

Van Wijngaarden, W. A., and W. Happer (2020). "Dependence of Earth's Thermal Radiation on Five Most Abundant Greenhouse

Gases." arXiv:2006.03098 [physics.ao-ph], June 8. Online at https://arxiv.org/abs/2006.03098.

———. (2021). "Relative Potency of Greenhouse Molecules." arXiv:2103.16465v1 [physics.ao-ph], March 31. Online at https://arxiv.org/abs/2103.16465.

Voosen, P. (2016). "Climate Scientists Open Up Their Black Boxes to Scrutiny." *Science* 354, no. 6311 (October): 401–2. Online at https://www.science.org/doi/10.1126/science.354.6311.401.

Williamson, M. S., et al. (2023). "Testing the Assumptions in Emergent Constraints: Why Does the 'Emergent Constraint on Equilibrium Climate Sensitivity from Global Temperature Variability' Work for CMIP5 and Not CMIP6?" *EGUSphere*, May 30. Online at https://egusphere.copernicus.org/preprints/2023/egusphere-2023-1093/egusphere-2023-1093.pdf.

Zelinka, M. D., et al. (2020). "Causes of Higher Climate Sensitivity in CMIP6 Models." *Geophysical Research Letters* 47, no. 1 (January): e2019GL085782. Online at https://agupubs.onlinelibrary.wiley.com/doi/full/10.1029/2019GL085782.

Chapter 9

The Holy Grail of Climate Change: Quantifying Climate Sensitivity

by Nicola Scafetta

Chapter Summary

The key parameter at the heart of the global warming controversy is the sensitivity of climate to a change in CO_2 (and other greenhouse gas) concentration. While it's a complex scientific question, it simply comes down to how much warming will occur after a doubling of CO_2. It has thus far risen about halfway from a 280 ppm pre-industrial level towards a doubling (560 ppm) later in this century. Fundamental physics demonstrates that, at minimum, about 1°C of warming will have occurred upon doubling. About that much has occurred to date, so sensitivity is apparently more than 1°C per 2xCO_2. The question is how much more. If around 1.5°C/2xCO_2, then the IPPC's <2°C warming target for late this century is attainable with little concern for adverse effects.

Two investigative approaches are available to scientists: climate models, which the IPCC embraces, and empirical analyses (which IPCC assessments ignore). After thirty years of effort, climate modeling has been unable to narrow its wide range of uncertainty, currently 1.8°–5.7°C/2xCO_2. A central estimate has varied around 3.5°C/2xCO_2. Methodologies employing empirical methods cluster to around 1.5°C/2xCO_2, and they reveal natural temperature oscillations that climate modeling is unable to reproduce. Only a low-end sensitivity assumption yields warming statistically compatible with observations. Clearly this is unsettled science, challenging climate alarmism and the necessity of urgent and expensive mitigation policies.

Editors' note: It is essential to include this chapter in this book, but it is not easily understood by nonscientists. Thus, we provide a brief overview of the chapter as a prelude to the scientific discussion laid out by Dr. Scafetta.

As Scafetta indicates, when the Earth gains more energy than it gives off, it warms—and vice versa. Climate sensitivity, then, is the rate at which the Earth warms or cools as a result of this temperature imbalance. He argues that climate sensitivity is the most important climatic parameter and projections of anthropogenic climate change depend on model estimates of this parameter.

Climate sensitivity is defined as the average warming of the Earth's surface due to a doubling of carbon dioxide in the atmosphere. Scafetta distinguishes between the transient climate response (the change in surface air temperature when the doubling is completed) and the equilibrium climate sensitivity (the change in surface air temperature when, later, the Earth has come to thermal equilibrium after the doubling). His analysis in this chapter focuses only on the equilibrium climate sensitivity. Scafetta then explains that the calculation of the equilibrium climate sensitivity is complicated because of the myriad of feedbacks and interacting processes that affect the Earth's climate. He goes through the history of estimates of the equilibrium climate sensitivity, including model and observational estimates.

In section two, Scafetta provides an estimate of the equilibrium climate sensitivity based on an update of research by Lacis et al. (2010) and suggests it is consistent with more complex analyses made by a variety of different methodologies. In section three, he compares this observational value with numerous estimates from climate model simulations. He concludes that the real value of the equilibrium climate sensitivity lies between 1°C and 2°C, with values smaller than 1.5°C being more probable. Moreover, none of the models reproduces the observed fluctuations in air temperature correctly, usually failing to reproduce cooling periods, underestimating the warming in the early twentieth century, and overestimating warming in the twenty-first century. They appear to faithfully reproduce the warming in the late twentieth century, but it is likely they are "tuned" to do so—that is, elements are added to the model specifically to force it to achieve that result, without knowing whether those elements accurately represent what's happening in the real climate system, rather like knowing the answers to a test before taking it. In section four, Scafetta discusses some of the policy implications of using higher values of equilibrium climate sensitivity derived from climate models.

Overall, the key to understanding this chapter is to understand the concept behind equilibrium climate sensitivity. Simply put, it is the response of the Earth's climate system to a doubling of carbon dioxide concentrations from pre-industrial levels. Higher values imply that a significant warming would result from a doubling of carbon dioxide, while lower values imply a reduced impact of greenhouse gases. That the models have much higher values than obtained through observations is why climate alarmists are so adamant that a doubling of carbon dioxide concentrations will have a devastating effect on the Earth's climate. For the same reason, climate realists, like Scafetta and the other contributors to this volume, disagree.

Some parts of this chapter involve fairly advanced mathematics, which is included to demonstrate the mathematical basis for the overall argument.

—David R. Legates and E. Calvin Beisner

Introduction

A crucial question in the controversy over anthropogenic climate change and what, if anything, should be done about it is this: How much can our emissions of carbon dioxide and other greenhouse gases be expected to raise Earth's temperature? The answer to this question depends on climate sensitivity—a term conventionally referring not to all aspects of climate, including temperature, humidity, wind, and precipitation, and not to all parts of the climate system, including the atmosphere, oceans, cryosphere, soil, and biosphere (as meteorologists and climatologists usually mean by climate), but solely to global-average surface temperature of the atmosphere.

Paleotemperature reconstructions of planet Earth show that the global surface air temperature of the past 540 million years—that is, since the Cambrian period, when the first major proliferation of complex life formed—has varied from 6°C below to 14°C above the 1960–1990 average (Gerg 2015). From the pre-industrial period (1850–1900) to 2010–2020, a global warming of about 0.9–1.0°C (or less) has been observed.

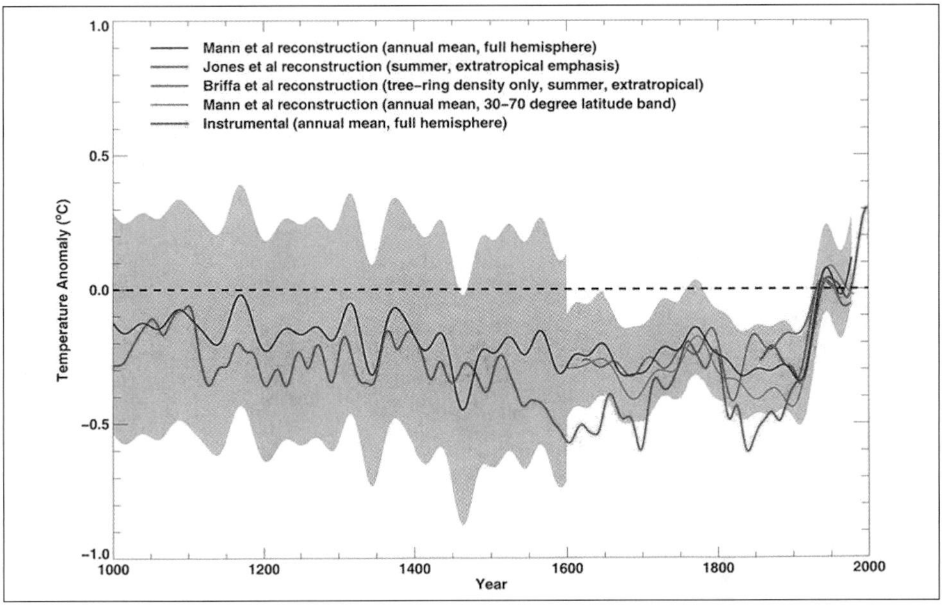

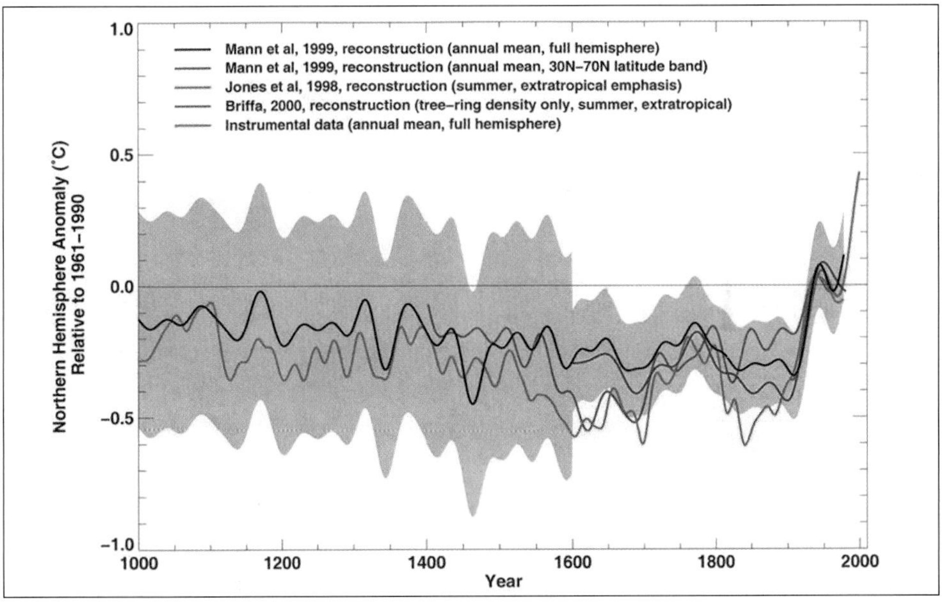

Figure 2.3. Global air temperature reconstructions, Northern Hemisphere anomaly (°C) relative to 1961–1990 mean, for the draft (1999) version (top, unpublished) and final (2001) version (bottom, published) of Figure 2.21 of the IPCC *Third Assessment Report* (Houghton et al. 2001) for Working Group 1. Note the height of the red line (instrumental data) at far right in the unpublished and published versions.

Top: *Courtesy of W. Soon.* Bottom: *Courtesy of the IPCC.*

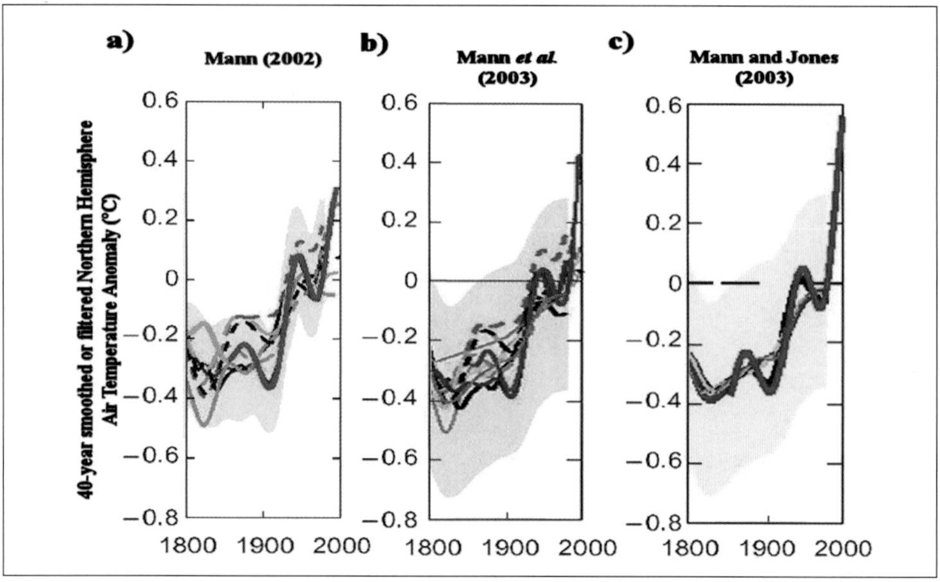

Figure 2.4. Representations of air temperature reconstructions as published by Mann (2002—a), Mann et al. (2003—b), and Mann and Jones (2003—c). Note the height of the red line (instrumental data) in 1999 (at the right of each pane).

Source: Adapted from Soon et al. (2004). Courtesy of Willie Soon.

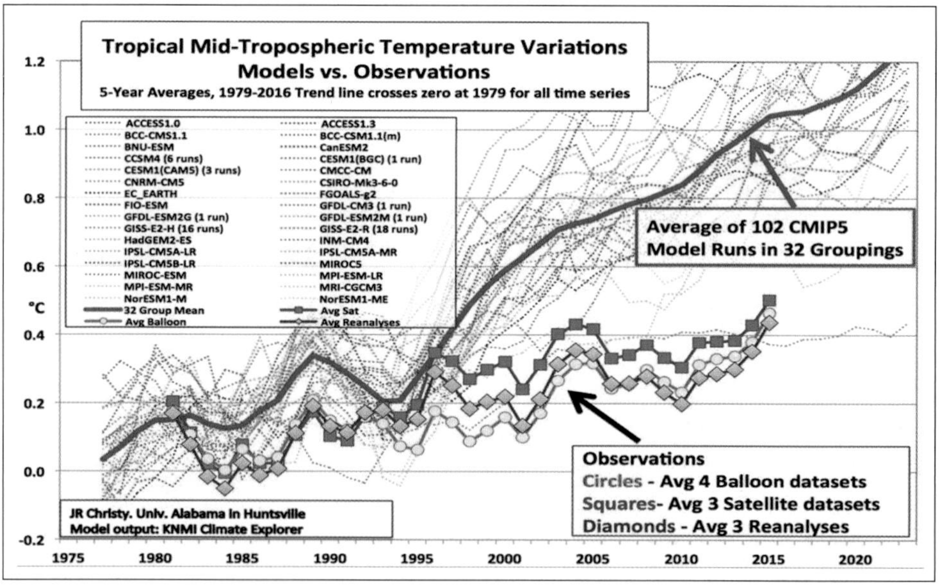

Figure 4.1a. Solid red line: average of all CMIP5 climate models; thin colored lines: average of individual CMIP5 model groups; solid figures: weather balloon, satellite, and reanalysis data for the tropical troposphere. Data are in tabular form in Christy, Po-Chedley, and Mears, "Tropospheric Temperature," in Hartfield, Blunden, and Arndt (2018), S16–S18.

Source: J. R. Christy, University of Alabama in Huntsville. Used by permission.

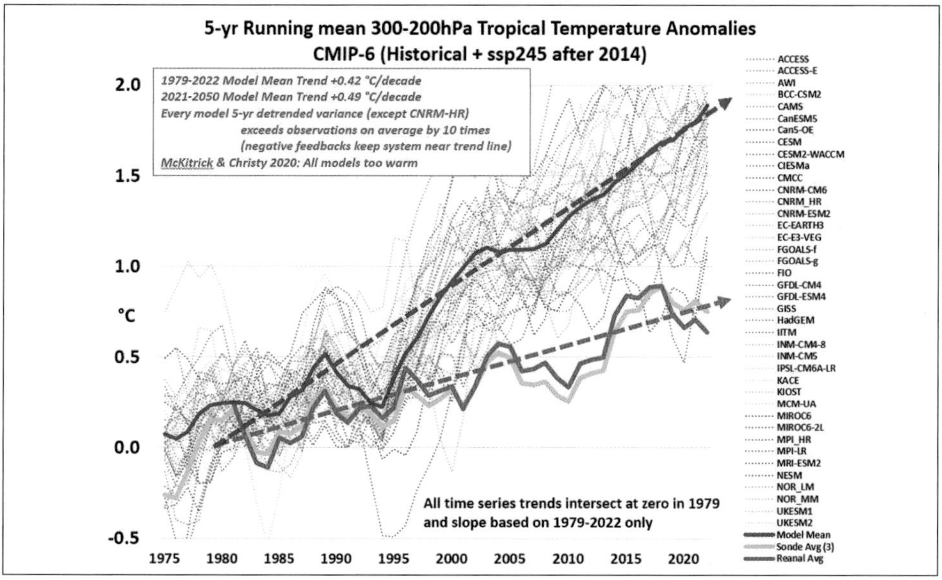

Figure 4.1b. Solid red line: average of all CMIP6 climate models; thin colored lines: individual CMIP6 models; dashed red line: trend of all CMIP6 climate models; solid figures: weather balloon, satellite, and reanalysis data.

Source: J. R. Christy, University of Alabama in Huntsville. Used by permission.

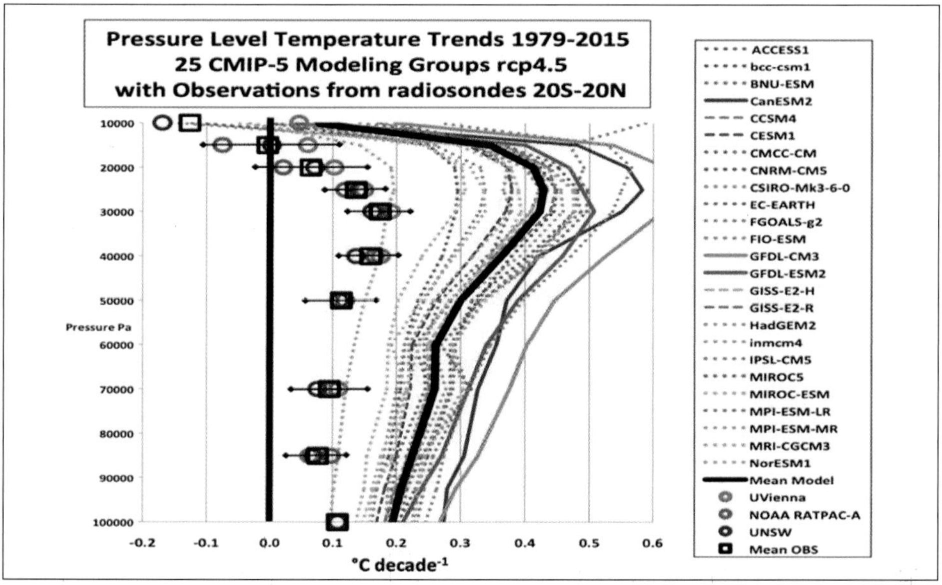

Figure 4.2a. Predicted tropical temperature change in degrees per decade on the x-axis and pressure altitude on the y-axis. The surface corresponds to 100,000 Pa (Pascals), and the top of the y-axis is around 60,000 feet in altitude. Colored thin lines: individual models; solid black: model average; circles and squares are observations.

Source: Christy and McNider (2017). Courtesy of John R. Christy.

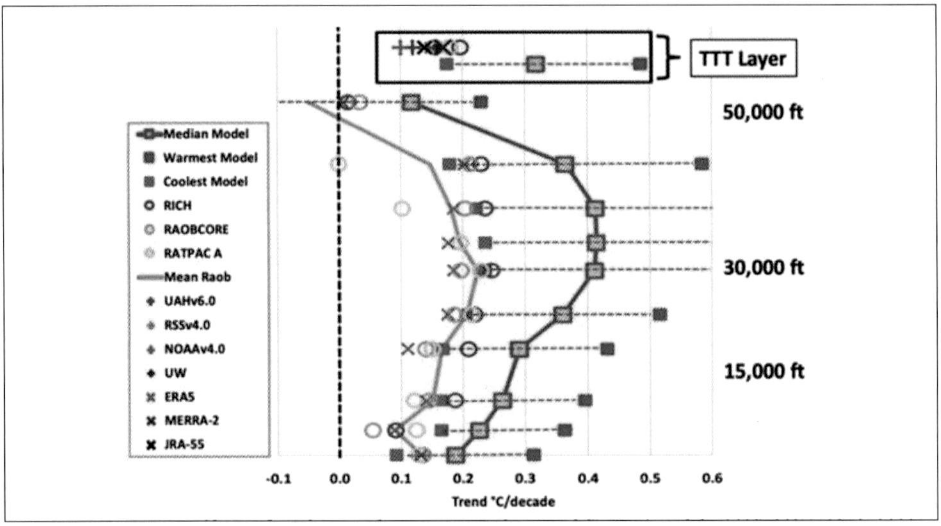

Figure 4.2b. Predicted tropical temperature change of CMIP6 models, 20°S–20°N, 1979–2022, in degrees per decade on the x-axis and altitude on the y-axis. The surface corresponds to 100,000 Pa (Pascals), and the top of the y-axis is around 50,000 feet in altitude. Green line: average of observational datasets, which are individually represented by circles (balloon datasets) and x's (reanalyses). Red line: average of models with horizontal dotted lines indicating the range of the model simulations at each altitude from blue box (coldest model) to red box (hottest model). The top box represents essentially the average of the entire layer with diamonds added, which depict observations from satellites, which only measure the deep layer.

Source: Updated from Christy and McNider (2017) and Christy et al. (2020). Courtesy of John R. Christy.

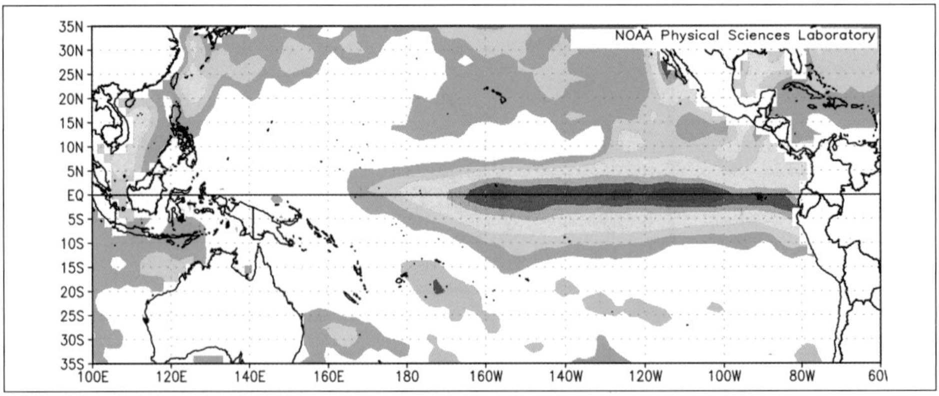

Figure 6.1. The tropical Pacific Ocean sea surface temperature anomaly (SST—°C) for December 2015. The anomalies are the difference between the December 2015 observations and the 1981–2010 mean temperature. The colors in the Eastern Tropical Pacific are positive SST anomalies of 0.5–1.0°C, up to greater than 3.0°C in the darkest shade.

Source: National Oceanic and Atmospheric Administration Physical Science Laboratory NCEP/NCAR reanalyses data (https://psl.noaa.gov/data/gridded/data.ncep.reanalysis.html). Courtesy of NOAA (National Oceanic and Atmospheric Administration).

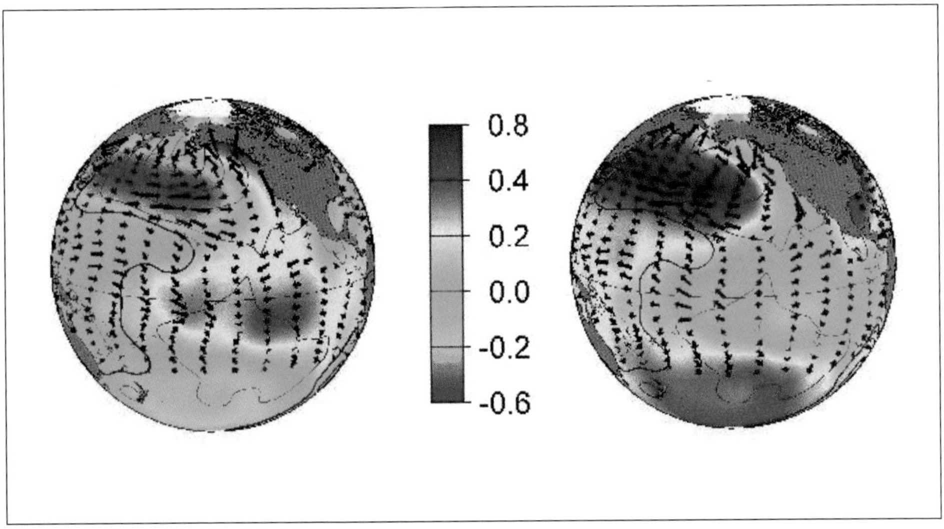

Figure 6.3. The Pacific Ocean SST patterns during the warm or positive (left) and cold or negative (right) phase of the PDO.

Courtesy of JISAO, University of Washington (http://research.jisao.washington.edu/pdo). Image credit: Steve Hare.

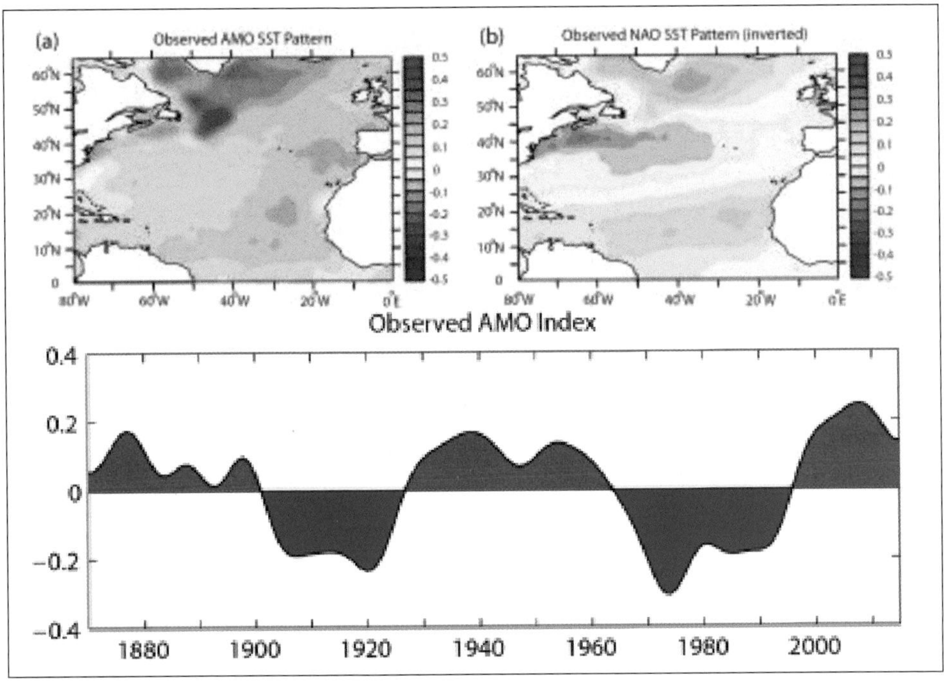

Figure 6.4. The Atlantic-wide SSTs (upper left) and SST anomalies (upper right) and AMO index (bottom), adapted from Trenberth and Zhang et al. (2021).

Courtesy of UCAR (University Corporation for Atmospheric Research).

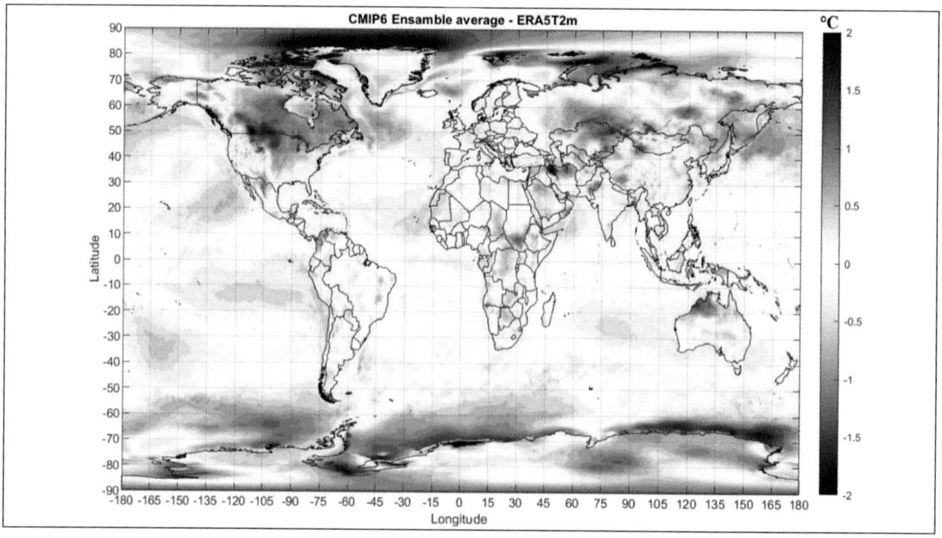

Figure 9.3. Difference between the warming predicted on average by the CMIP6 GCMs and that by ERA5-T2m.

Source: Scafetta (2022). Courtesy of Nicola Scafetta.

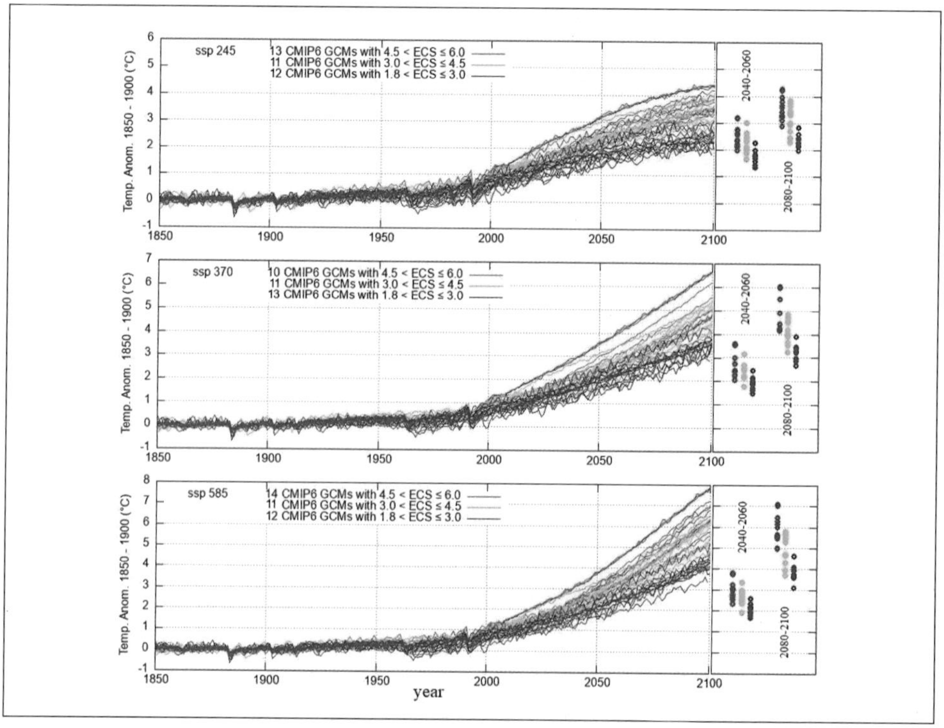

Figure 9.5. All available CMIP6 GCM average simulations for different SSPs: low-ECS GCMs (blue), medium-ECS GCMs (green), and high-ECS GCMs (red). The right panels show the model mean warming levels in 2040–2060 and 2080–2100.

Source: Scafetta (2022). Courtesy of Nicola Scafetta.

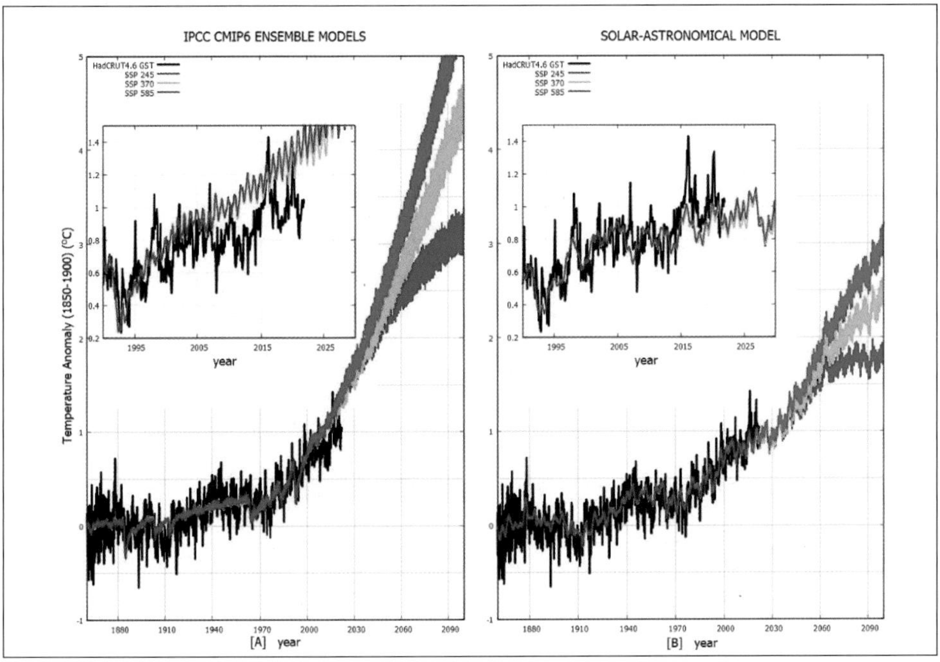

Figure 9.6. Ensemble CMIP6 GCM simulations for different SSPs versus the HadCRUT global surface temperature record. [A] Original records. [B] Comparison with the solar-astronomical harmonic climate model first proposed in Scafetta (2013) and updated with more harmonics and the CMIP6 GCMs.

Source: Scafetta and Bianchini (2023). Courtesy of Nicola Scafetta.

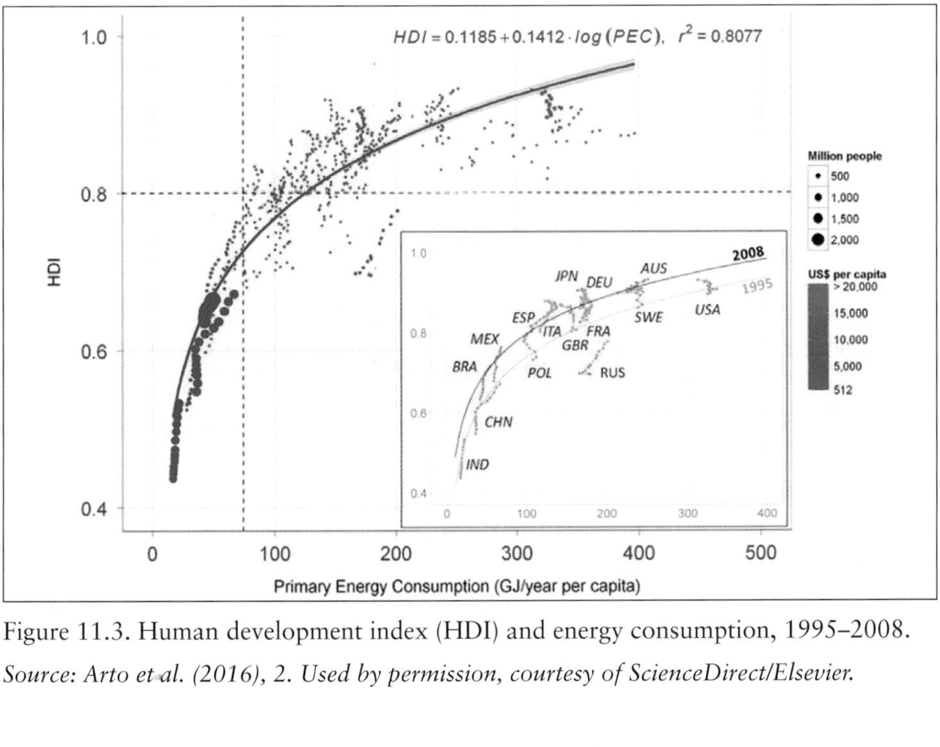

Figure 11.3. Human development index (HDI) and energy consumption, 1995–2008.

Source: Arto et al. (2016), 2. Used by permission, courtesy of ScienceDirect/Elsevier.

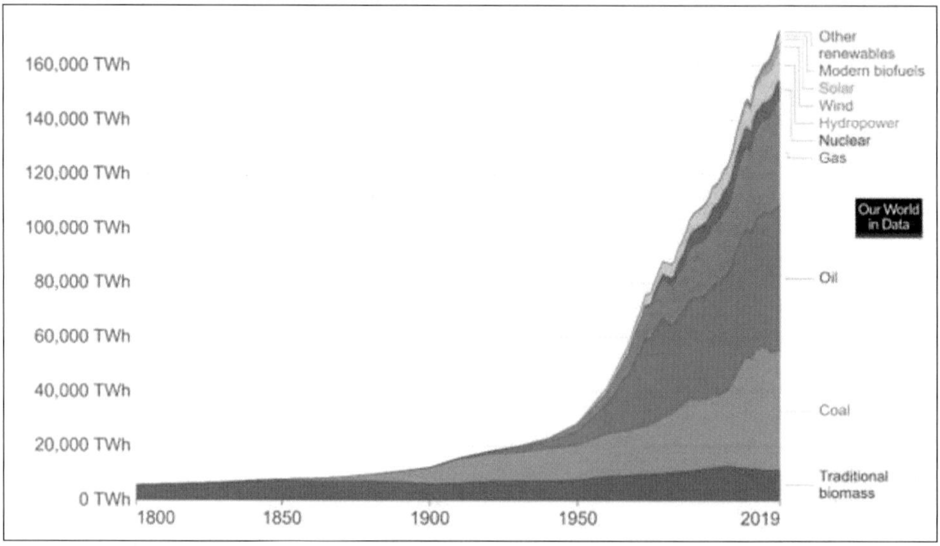

Figure 12.1. Global primary energy consumption by source. Primary energy is calculated based on the "substitution method," which takes into account the inefficiencies in fossil fuel production by converting non-fossil energy, not the energy inputs required if they had the same conversion losses as fossil fuels.

Sources: Data from Vaclav Smil and BP Statistical Review of World Energy; graph by Our World in Data. Licensed under Creative Commons (https://creativecommons.org/licenses/by/4.0/legalcode.en).

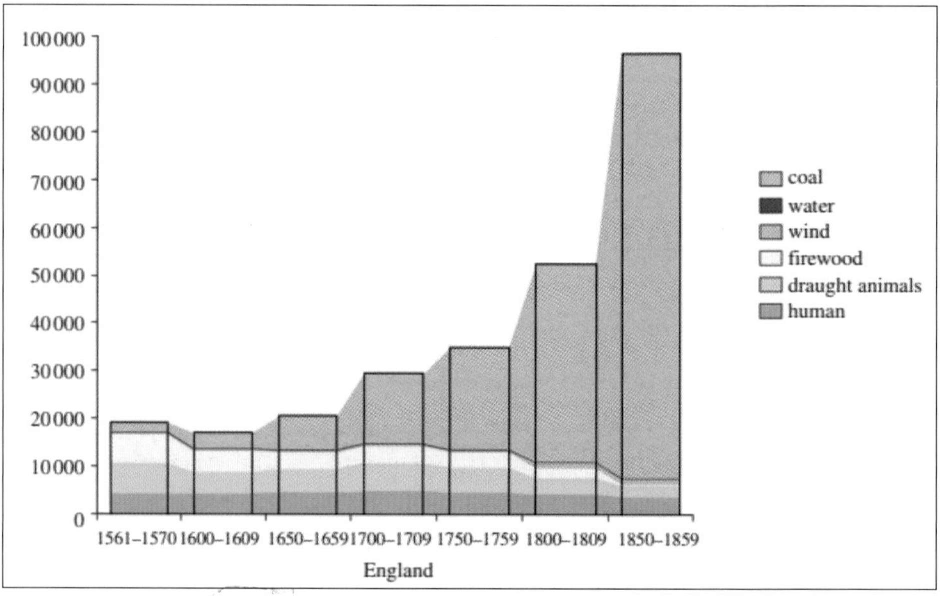

Figure 13.2. Energy consumption in England and Wales (1561–1859).

Source: E. Wrigley, Energy and the English Industrial Revolution, 7. Courtesy of Cambridge University Press.

Key to Symbols and Abbreviations

$2xCO_2$ = Doubled Atmospheric CO_2 Concentration
CMIP = Coupled Model Intercomparison Project(s), numbered by generation
F = Radiative Forcing
I = Irradiance
SSP = Shared Socioeconomic Pathway(s)
T = Temperature
W/m^2K^4 = Watts/square meter in °Kelvin^4
α = Albedo (proportion of the incident light or radiation that is reflected by a surface)
Δ = Change
σ = Stefan-Boltzmann Constant, $\sigma = 5.67 \times 10^{-8}$ W/m^2K^4

Several external, internal, and, recently, anthropogenic (human-induced) factors are responsible for global climate changes. The climate warms when the radiative energy absorbed by the system is larger than the thermal infrared radiation emitted by Earth to space—that is, when there is a positive energy imbalance and Earth gains energy—and cools when the energy imbalance is negative. Climate sensitivity is defined as a measure of how much Earth's climate cools or warms in response to changes in radiative forcing. Climate sensitivity is the most important climatic parameter, and it determines, for example, the climatic impact of anthropogenic greenhouse gas emissions.

Water vapor (H_2O) and carbon dioxide (CO_2) are greenhouse gases because they absorb and emit infrared radiation. It is common to define climate sensitivity using a metric based on the radiative forcing $\Delta F_{2xCO_2} = 3.77$ W/m^2, where ΔF_{2xCO_2} means change (Δ) in forcing (F) from doubling of atmospheric CO_2 concentration ($2xCO_2$), which corresponds to the radiation increase induced by doubling the CO_2 atmospheric concentration from its pre-industrial concentration value of 280 ppm to 560 ppm. In 2021, the CO_2 concentration was about 415 ppm (directly measured in the atmosphere), compared to 277 ppm in 1750 (according to ice-core estimates), an increase of nearly half. The radiative forcing by CO_2 is a *logarithmic function* (the inverse of the more familiar exponential function) of the atmospheric CO_2 concentration. Thus, if the radiative forcing of doubling CO_2 is ΔF_{2xCO_2} (that is, change in forcing from doubling atmospheric CO_2), the radiative forcing of quadrupling CO_2 is not $(2 \times 2) = 4\Delta F_{2xCO_2}$ but $2\Delta F_{2xCO_2}$, the radiative forcing of $8xCO_2$ is not $(2 \times 2 \times 2) = 8F_{2xCO_2}$ but $3\Delta F_{2xCO_2}$, and so on. It is important to keep this in mind. To raise the temperature by radiative forcing from a second doubling of CO_2 as much as from the first doubling (277 to 554 ppm) would require adding not the same amount of CO_2 again (277 ppm) but twice that much (554 ppm); and to raise temperature the same amount again would require adding 1,108 ppm.

Distinguishing Transient from Equilibrium Climate Sensitivity

Two primary types of climate sensitivity are defined: the shorter-term *transient climate response* (TCR) and the longer-term *equilibrium climate sensitivity.* Transient climate response is defined as the global mean temperature change (ΔT) that occurs at the time of CO_2 doubling for the specific case of a 1 percent per year increase of CO_2. Equilibrium climate sensitivity is defined as the change in global mean temperature resulting when a climate system attains a new thermodynamic equilibrium (balance between energy input and output)after doubling of atmospheric CO_2 concentration (ΔT_{2xCO_2}) with the change of forcing from doubling of atmospheric CO_2 (ΔF_{2xCO_2}). Since evaluating equilibrium climate sensitivity requires very long simulations to reach equilibrium, climate scientists also define an *effective climate sensitivity* using model or real-world observations from a system that is not yet in equilibrium.

In any case, in the following we focus on equilibrium climate sensitivity since all alternative climate sensitivity definitions depend on it.

If Earth were a blackbody, its equilibrium climate sensitivity could be easily calculated using the Stefan-Boltzmann law, which holds that "total radiant heat power emitted from a surface is proportional to the fourth power of its absolute temperature" (*Britannica* n.d.). At equilibrium, incoming energy must balance outgoing. The outgoing radiation (F) is proportional to the fourth power of the temperature of the body (that is, $F = sT^4$), where the constant of proportionality is the Stefan-Boltzmann constant, $\sigma = 5.67 \times 10^{-8}$ W/m^2K^4. Because the incoming total solar irradiance (I) = 1361 W/m^2 and Earth's albedo (α) = 0.3 and Earth is spherical, F (outgoing radiation) = $(1 - \alpha)I/4 = 238.2$ W/m^2 (that is, outgoing radiation $1 - 0.3 = 0.7$; $0.7 \times 1361 = 952.7$; $952.7 / 4 = 238.175$ W/m^2, often rounded to 240 W/m^2) and the average temperature of Earth's surface would be 255K ($T = \sqrt[4]{(1-\alpha)I/4}$. Using this value of 255K, an increase of radiative forcing equal to a doubling of CO_2 induces an increase in the forcing of 3.77 W/m^2 ($4\sigma T^3 \Delta T$), which yields an equilibrium climate sensitivity of about 1K.

However, the global surface temperature of Earth is about T = 288K (14.85°C or 58.73°F), which requires an input of 390 W/m^2 (from $F = \sigma[288K]^4$) while the Sun contributes only 240 W/m^2. The additional 150 W/m^2 are claimed to be added by the warming effect of the atmosphere, which includes the radiative effect of the greenhouse gases plus the cloud system, which together absorb and radiate back the infrared radiation emitted by Earth.

The climatic system is also made of several components responding to radiative perturbations. These mechanisms activate positive or negative feedbacks. For example, a temperature rise can reduce the ice albedo (thus increasing absorption of incoming radiation) and increase atmospheric water vapor, which is a powerful greenhouse gas (thus reducing outgoing radiation) and influences the cloud system, which then also changes the albedo and other climate parameters. Evaluating or modeling accurately all feedback mechanisms of the climate system is still not possible. Therefore, the equilibrium climate sensitivity problem is still unresolved, as is acknowledged by the Intergovernmental Panel on Climate Change (IPCC 2021); recent literature proposes equilibrium climate sensitivity values ranging from 0.5 to 6°C (cf. Knutti, Rugenstein, and Hegerl 2017).

Debating the Value of Climate Sensitivity

Indeed, the equilibrium climate sensitivity problem has been debated for more than 140 years, because its value strongly depends on the physical assumptions of the adopted climate models. In 1896, Arrhenius estimated that a CO_2 doubling could potentially induce a global surface temperature increase of 5–6°C; however, ten years later, he (1906) concluded that his previous estimate was erroneous and proposed lower equilibrium climate sensitivity values ranging between 1.6 and 3.9°C. Möller (1963) showed that equilibrium climate sensitivity could vary greatly, up to one order of magnitude, according to how water vapor and/or cloudiness responded to the CO_2 perturbation, and concluded that "the theory that climatic variations are affected by variations in the CO_2 content becomes very questionable." Manabe and Wetherald (1967) developed a one-dimensional climate model and estimated equilibrium climate sensitivity = 2°C. Later, however, with a different model, the same authors (1975) estimated equilibrium climate sensitivity = 2.93°C. Syukuro Manabe was awarded the 2021 Nobel Prize in Physics "for the physical modelling of Earth's climate, quantifying variability and reliably predicting global warming" (Nobel Prize 2021), but he did not really quantitatively solve the equilibrium climate sensitivity physical problem; he just pointed out that a problem could rise from continuous emission of greenhouse gases because it would have had a climatic effect that, however, could not be accurately quantified.

Since then, more powerful global circulation models have been developed such as those collected by the World Climate Research Programme Coupled Model Intercomparison Projects (CMIP). The IPCC used its third version (CMIP3) in the 2007 *Assessment Report*, its fifth version (CMIP5) in the 2013 report, and its sixth and latest version (CMIP6) in the sixth report (AR6) (IPCC 2021). However, the equilibrium climate sensitivity of these advanced climate models still varies greatly from model to model. The CMIP5 global circulation model equilibrium climate sensitivities span from 2.1 to 4.7°C, while CMIP6 global circulation model equilibrium climate sensitivities span even more, from 1.8 to 5.7°C. This is a huge and still unresolved uncertainty and indicates that, according to the CMIP6 global circulation models, the same increase of CO_2 could induce by itself a warming ranging from a given amount to three times more (cf. Huntingford Williamson, and Nijsse 2020).

The situation remains problematic also using alternatives to the global circulation model approaches. Some studies suggest that high-equilibrium climate sensitivity values (for example, larger than 4.5°C) are not supported (Nijsse, Cox, and Williamson 2020; Jiménez-de-la-Cuesta and Mauritsen 2019; Zelinka et al. 2020; Zhu, Poulsen, and Otto-Bliesner 2020); others suggest that only low-equilibrium climate sensitivity (for example, 0.5–2.5°C) is consistent with the observations (Bates 2016; Christy and McNider 2017; van Wijngaarden and Happer 2020; Kluft et al. 2019; Lewis and Curry 2018; Lindzen and Choi 2011; McKitrick and Christy 2020; Monckton et al. 2015; Scafetta 2012, 2013; Smirnov and Zhilyaev 2021; Stefani 2021).

Estimates of the types and magnitudes of changes to weather and climate that could be driven by changes in CO_2 concentration depend heavily on quantifying equilibrium climate sensitivity. Hence, the uncertainty about equilibrium climate sensitivity must be reduced if those estimates are to improve. However, the physical problem cannot be solved yet. Hence, one needs to find indirect approaches to constrain the uncertainty.

Most Global Circulation Models Overstate Climate Sensitivity

Indeed, most global circulation models appear to overestimate the surface warming observed since 1980 (Scafetta, 2013, 2021a, 2021c, 2022; Nijsse, Cox, and Williamson 2020; Wang et al. 2021) in the global (McKitrick and Christy 2020) and tropical troposphere (Mitchell et al. 2020) and, in particular, at the top of the troposphere (200–300 hPa), where the global circulation models predict a hot spot that has not been observed (McKitrick and Christy 2018). Other evidence suggesting low-equilibrium climate sensitivity values derives from the failure of the global circulation models to reproduce natural climatic oscillations from the decadal to the millennial scale—oscillations revealed by several climatic reconstructions throughout the Holocene (Alley 2004; Christiansen and Ljungqvist 2012; Esper et al. 2012; Kutschera et al. 2017; Ljungqvist 2010; Matskovsky and Helama 2014).

For example, Scafetta (2021a) showed that with the current radiative forcing functions adopted by the global circulation models, these models are not able to reproduce the known warm periods of the past—for example, the Medieval Warm Period—even versus early paleoclimatic reconstructions (Moberg 2005). These results question the reliability of the current global circulation models even if they appear to approximately reconstruct the modern warm period (IPCC 2021). In fact, as discussed in chapters 4 and 8 of this book, the internal parameters of the models are carefully tuned with the aim to reproduce the observed climatic trends (cf. Golaz et al. 2019).

Another important source of uncertainty is that solar/astronomical forcings are still debated since there are Coupled Model Intercomparison Project records that show a very small secular variability (for example, Matthes et al. 2017, which was the solar record adopted for the CMIP6 global circulation model simulations), while others show a secular variability up to ten times larger (Egorova et al. 2018). Also, the global surface temperature reconstructions are uncertain. In fact, land-use and urban changes impact the observed land records, and the homogenization techniques adopted to filter off such non-climatic biases are not perfect. Consequently, the real global and local climatic warming trends may be lower (for example, by 20 percent on average) than those currently claimed (cf. Scafetta and Ouyang 2019; Scafetta 2021b). All these uncertainties affect the estimation of equilibrium climate sensitivity because the larger the solar forcing, and/or the smaller the global warming, the smaller equilibrium climate sensitivity must be. Connolly et al. (2021) discuss in detail several of the latter issues.

Why Climate Sensitivity Is Important to Policy

Constraining equilibrium climate sensitivity has important political implications because the global surface temperature could warm between 1 and 3.3°C (depending on which CMIP6 global circulation model is adopted) above the pre-industrial period (1850–1900) even if anthropogenic emissions stopped today (Huntingford, Williamson, and Nijsse 2020). Higher equilibrium climate sensitivity values imply faster warming as anthropogenic greenhouse gas accumulates in the atmosphere in the next decades.

Solving this issue is urgent, because if global warming exceeds 2°C above the pre-industrial period by 2050, it may be harmful (IPCC 2018). To prevent climate change–related hazards, expensive mitigation policies are being proposed and implemented by several nations. Western countries even aim to be climate-neutral—an economy with net-zero greenhouse gas emissions—by 2050 by completely substituting "Green" energy sources (primarily wind and solar) for fossil fuels, a controversial policy that could needlessly harm and impoverish these countries, while slowing economic development of poorer countries, if implemented.

However, if equilibrium climate sensitivity is low, equivalent greenhouse gas emissions would produce less warming, and moderate climatic changes could be better addressed using comparatively inexpensive adaptation policies. Thus, it is crucial to narrow the equilibrium climate sensitivity range to determine the best policies to address future climatic changes.

In the next sections, I argue that equilibrium climate sensitivity must be relatively small, probably between 1 and 2°C. This eventuality should exclude the necessity of urgent and expensive mitigation policies.

A Tentative Estimate of Equilibrium Climate Sensitivity

The condensing greenhouse gas forcing (water vapor and clouds) and the non-condensing greenhouse gas forcing (CO_2, O_3, N_2O, CH_4, and others) account for about 75 percent and 25 percent, respectively, of the total greenhouse effect of Earth's atmosphere, which raises the global mean surface temperature from the blackbody temperature of 255K (−18.15°C; −0.67°F) to the observed 288K (14.85°C; 58.73°F) (Lacis et al. 2010). However, the condensing greenhouse gas forcing does not emerge only because of the existence of the non-condensing greenhouse gas forcing, as erroneously claimed in Lacis et al. (2010)—a fact that would imply that the non-condensing greenhouse gas forcing should be amplified by four because of the feedback response of water vapor and clouds, which would yield equilibrium climate sensitivity = 4°C, which is what the CMIP6 global circulation models predict on average (IPCC 2021).

In fact, by improving and correcting Lacis et al.'s argument, it must be considered that water vapor and cloudiness respond also to the total solar irradiance input, which contributes 240 W/m^2 of the required 390 W/m^2. If the non-condensing greenhouse gas total forcing contributes 25 percent of the additional 150 W/m^2—that is, 37.5 W/m^2—to obtain the observed global surface temperature, the condensing greenhouse gas total forcing should induce an amplification of the total radiative input (240 + 37.5 = 277.5 W/m^2) equal to 390 / 277.5 = 1.4.

This simple consideration may suggest that water vapor and cloud feedback could amplify the warming of the surface induced by the Sun plus the non-condensing greenhouse gases by a factor of about 1.5, which corresponds to an equilibrium climate sensitivity of about 1.5°C or slightly less.

Although such an estimate is very rough, it approximately agrees with complex empirical evaluations derived using different methodologies (Bates 2016; Christy and McNider 2017; van Wijngaarden and Happer 2020; Kluft et al. 2019; Lewis and Curry 2018; Lindzen and Choi 2011; McKitrick and Christy 2020; Monckton et al. 2015; Scafetta 2012, 2013; Smirnov and Zhilyaev 2021; Stefani 2021). However, the advanced CMIP global circulation models have always produced significantly larger equilibrium climate sensitivity values. This divergence has been noted also by Knutti, Rugenstein, and Hegerl (2017), who concluded that "evidence from climate modelling favors values of equilibrium climate sensitivity in the upper part of the 'likely' range, whereas many recent studies based on instrumentally recorded warming—and some from paleoclimate—favor values in the lower part of the range."

However, it is possible to check whether low-equilibrium climate sensitivity values could be inferred also by directly testing the CMIP6 global circulation models' performance in reproducing the observed warming from 1980 to 2021. Let us see how.

Testing Global Circulation Model Predictions versus Temperature Data

Scafetta (2021c, 2022) analyzed in detail the performance of thirty-eight CMIP6 global circulation models in reconstructing the temperature changes observed from 1980 to 2021 both globally and locally. Herein we briefly present and further discuss those results. All synthetic and observational data are freely available from KNMI Climate Explorer (https://climexp.knmi.nl/start.cgi).

The monthly reanalysis from the ERA5 Near-Surface Air Temperature (T2m) record (Hersbach et al. 2020) for 1980 to June 2021 is herein preferred to other options (for example, HadCRUT, the Hadley Centre/Climatic Research Unit; GISTEMP, the NASA Goddard Institute for Space Studies; and NOAA, the National Oceanic and Atmospheric Administration, surface temperature records) because it covers the entire world surface and may be used to properly test the simulations (cf. Scafetta 2021c). The ERA5 records are reanalysis temperature data modeled from other observed data, that is, they are derived from a combination of in-situ and model simulations and may be considered a good compromise among all available temperature reconstructions.

The thirty-eight global circulation models are listed in Figure 9.1 as a function of their equilibrium climate sensitivity values, which span from 1.8 to 5.7°C. It is noteworthy to emphasize that none of the CMIP5 global circulation models discussed in the IPCC AR5 in 2013 had an equilibrium climate sensitivity greater than 4.7°C, while fourteen CMIP6 global circulation models have an equilibrium climate sensitivity greater than 4.5°C. Among the latter, twelve were developed in Western countries (France, United States, United Kingdom, and Canada) and only two (CIESM and NESM3) are from China. In contrast, the INM-CM global circulation models have the lowest equilibrium climate sensitivity and were developed in Russia. (Might

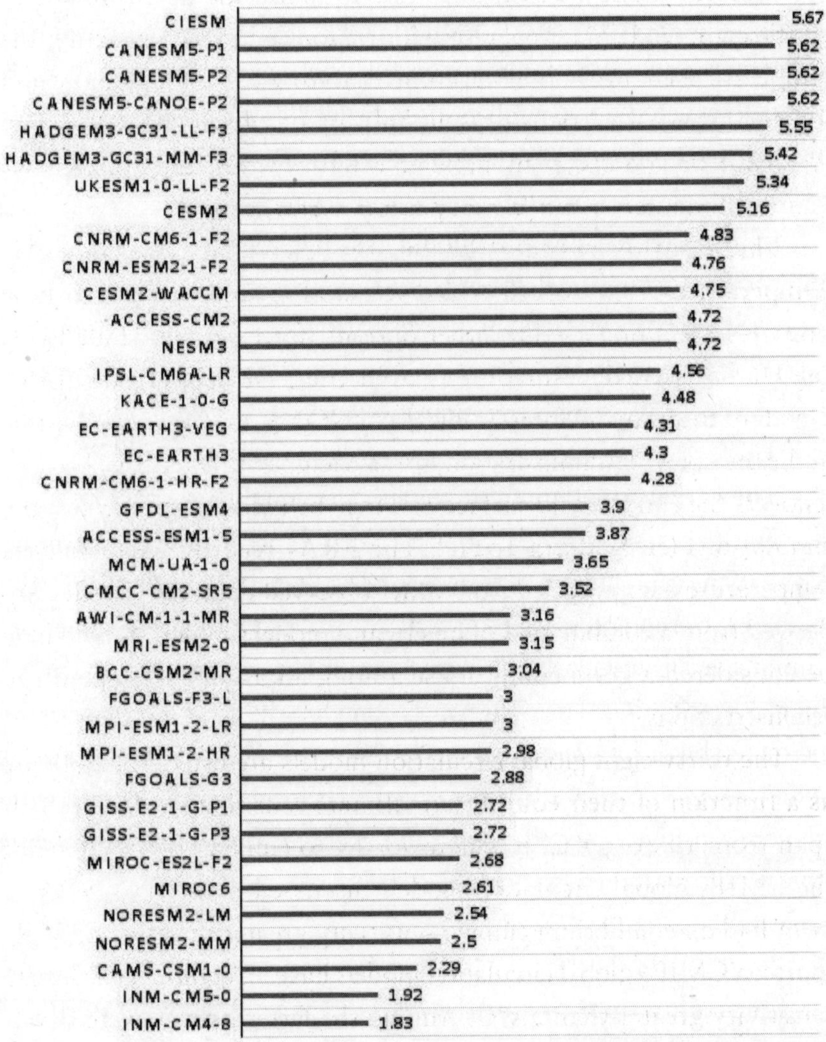

Figure 9.1. Equilibrium climate sensitivity (ECS) in °C for thirty-eight CMIP6 GCMs. *Source: Scafetta (2021c), data from IPCC (2021). Courtesy of Nicola Scafetta.*

the political distribution of these models suggest why climate change alarmism is more strongly advocated in Western countries?)

The model simulations cover the period from 1850 to 2100 and were produced using common historical forcings (1850–2014) continued with different shared socioeconomic pathway (SSP) scenarios (2015–2100). In the following SSPs, the numbers after the hyphen are the levels of forcing from 1750 to 2100 in W/m^2 (Hausfather and Peters 2020):

SSP1-2.6 (very low greenhouse gas emissions)
SSP2-4.5 (intermediate emissions)
SSP4-6.0 (moderately high emissions)
SSP3-7.0 (high emissions)
SSP5-8.5 (very high emissions)

The various simulations are practically equal up to 2021.

Figure 9.2 shows the global surface temperature model average simulations (thin lines) versus the ERA5-T2m record (thick line) relative to the 1980–1990 period. The models are grouped into three equilibrium climate sensitivity classes (low, 1.80–3.00°C; medium, 3.01–4.50°C; high, 4.51–6.00°C). The right panels compare the 2011–2021 warming predicted by the models (dots) versus the warming of ERA5-T2m (bar), which is $\Delta T \approx 0.56$°C. It is observed that only the low-equilibrium climate sensitivity models predict, on average, a warming statistically compatible with the observations.

The Relevance of Land versus Ocean Measurements

However, Scafetta (2021c) showed that the simulations and the data differ significantly over large regions if local trends are considered. Figure 9.3 (in the color figures section between pages 240 and 241) shows the areal distribution of the difference between the warming of

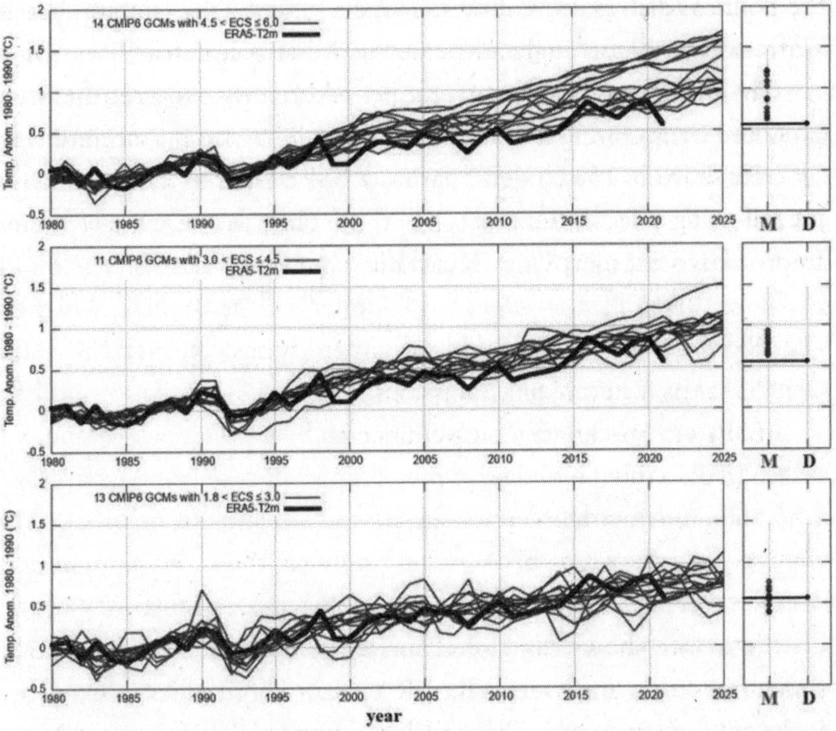

Figure 9.2. Left: Typical CMIP6 GCM surface temperature average simulations (thin) against ERA5-T2m (thick). Right: model forecast (M, thin) and observed data (D, thick, $\Delta T \approx 0.56$ °C) mean global surface warming 2011–2021 (1980–1990 anomalies). *Source: Scafetta (2022). Courtesy of Nicola Scafetta.*

1980–1990 and 2011–2021 predicted on average by the CMIP6 global circulation models and by ERA5-T2m. The models usually predict a larger warming (the orange areas predominate), but there are also regions where the models predict less warming than was observed (blue areas). The discrepancies are important because most of the extended blue areas (where models predict less warming than observed) are found over land, while over the ocean the orange areas (where models predict more warming than observed) predominate. Moreover, a clear asymmetry between the Arctic (more bluish) and Antarctic (more reddish) regions is observed. The land-ocean asymmetry was noted also in Scafetta (2021b) and suggests the presence of non-climatic warming biases over land. The Arctic-Antarctic asymmetry suggests the existence of physical internal and external (astronomical) mechanisms not considered by the models but that are unrelated to the greenhouse gas warming effect. Moreover, given the observed north-south and land-ocean asymmetries, it is unlikely that the discrepancies found could be solved by the internal variability of the models, which is smoothed out by considering their average. On the contrary, the result suggests the existence of physical biases in the global circulation models.

In any case, Scafetta (2021c) also analyzed the performance of each CMIP6 global circulation model, in each case using its average simulation in regionally reconstructing the warming from 1980–1990 to 2011–2021 shown by ERA5-T2m. Figure 9.4 shows scatterplots and linear regressions between the equilibrium climate sensitivity of the CMIP6 global circulation models and the percentage of the world area where they disagree with the ERA5-T2m record by at least 0.2°C, 0.5°C, and 1.0°C, respectively. The analysis suggests that the model-data agreement improves as the equilibrium climate sensitivity of the models becomes lower and lower. Moreover, since even the global circulation models with the lowest equilibrium climate sensitivity still disagree significantly (at least by 0.2°C) from the observation over about 50 percent of the world's surface, it may be inferred that the real equilibrium climate sensitivity could be even smaller than the smallest value of the CIMP6 model, which is about 1.8°C.

The Importance of Natural Oscillations

Another simple empirical approach that yields low-equilibrium climate sensitivity values exists. Several researchers have noted that the climate system presents numerous decadal and multidecadal natural

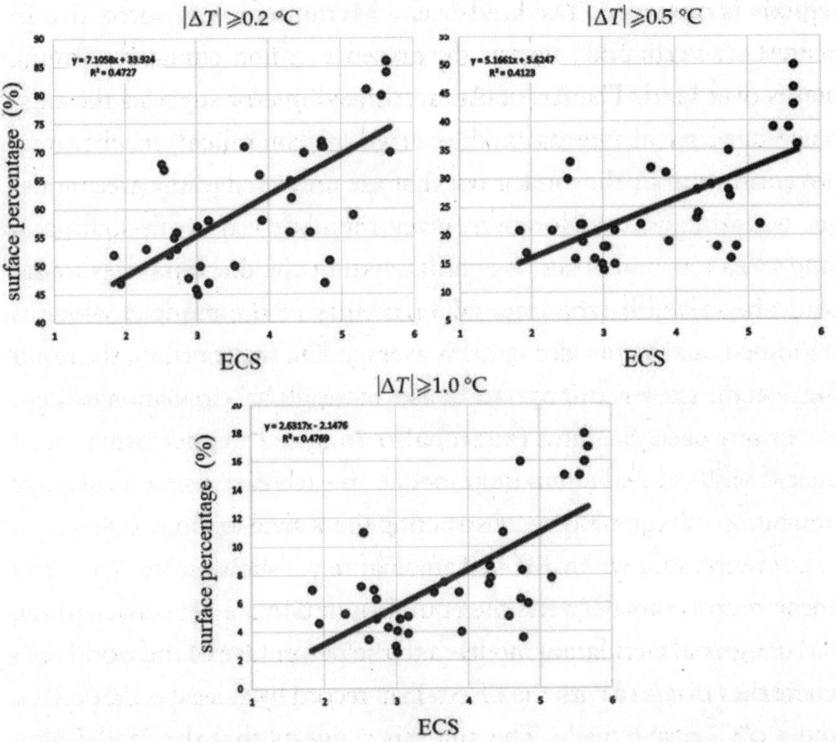

Figure 9.4. Scatterplots and linear regressions between the ECS of the CMIP6 GCMs and the percentage of the world area where they disagree with the ERA5-T2m record by at least 0.2°C, 0.5°C, and 1.0°C, respectively. *Source: Scafetta (2021c). Courtesy of Nicola Scafetta.*

oscillations. The typical climatic oscillations have periods of about 9, 10–11, 20, 60, and 115 years, and all of them have an astronomical origin (Scafetta 2010, 2014a). Longer oscillations up to the millennial scale are also present (Alley 2004; Christiansen and Ljungqvist 2012; Esper et al. 2012; Kutschera et al. 2017; Ljungqvist 2010; Matskovsky and Helama, 2014).

The 60-year oscillation is particularly important for our purpose because it is sufficiently short to be identified with precision in numerous climatic records (global and local temperature, sea level,

North Atlantic Oscillation, Atlantic Meridional Oscillation, Pacific Decadal Oscillation, and so forth) and because it presents 30-year periods of warming and cooling, which modulate climatic changes (Scafetta 2014b; Wyatt and Curry 2014). Such oscillation is quite evident in the global surface temperature records because 1850–1880, 1910–1940, and 1970–2000 were warming periods, while 1880–1910 and 1940–1970 were cooling periods and the period from 2000–2020 had only a slight warming. Thus, the global warming curve since 1850 does not rise monotonically, as would be suggested by anthropogenic forcings, but appears to be made of a quasi-60-year oscillation superimposed on a longer upward trend, which can be due to much longer natural oscillations (for example, the millennial ones) plus some warming induced by the anthropogenic radiative forcings.

Scafetta (2013) showed that none of the CMIP5 global circulation models can reproduce the observed oscillations. The CMIP6 global circulation models appear to have the same problem. Consequently, a common feature of these models is that they significantly underestimate the warming observed from 1910–1940, fail to reproduce the cooling from 1880–1910 and 1940–1970, and overestimate the warming observed since 2000. However, the global circulation models usually reproduce the warming from 1970–2000 well, but this result appears accidental and due to tuning of their internal parameters, which can be optimized to reproduce that warming trend using the adopted radiative forcings.

Scafetta (2013) and, later, Scafetta (2021a) showed that the global surface temperature records since 1850 could be better modeled with a number of oscillations. In particular, the 60-year oscillation appears to be responsible for at least 50 percent of the 1970–2000 warming. Thus, only the residual 50 percent of that warming could have been produced by the global circulation model–adopted radiative forcings. Since the average equilibrium climate sensitivity of the CMIP5 global circulation models was about 3°C, if 50 percent of the 1970–2000 warming was induced by a natural oscillation not reproduced by the models, then the models must on average overestimate equilibrium climate sensitivity by at least a factor of two. Thus, Scafetta (2013) concluded that the real equilibrium climate sensitivity had to be around 1.5°C. This estimate could still be too large, since 20 percent of the apparent *global* warming since 1950 could be spurious because induced by non-climatic warming biases such as those related to urbanization (Scafetta 2021b; Connolly et al. 2021). This would imply equilibrium climate sensitivity not of 3°C or even of 1.5°C but of 1.2°C.

In conclusion, by considering all evidence, the present author suggests that the real equilibrium climate sensitivity of Earth could roughly be between 1 and 2°C, but values smaller than 1.5°C could be more probable.

Implication for Policy

Results like those shown in Figures 9.2 and 9.4 suggest that high– and medium–equilibrium climate sensitivity global circulation models (equilibrium climate sensitivity greater than 3°C) do not appear to be consistent with observations and should not be used for implementing economic policies based on their scenario forecasts for the twenty-first century.

To evaluate the importance of the result, Figure 9.5 (in the color figures section between pages 240 and 241) shows all available CMIP6 global circulation model average simulations for three different SSPs: low-equilibrium climate sensitivity (blue), medium-equilibrium climate sensitivity (green), and high-equilibrium climate sensitivity (red). The right panels show the model mean warming levels in 2040–2060 and 2080–2100.

Note that the 2°C global warming threshold by 2040–2060—above which the IPCC says serious climatic hazards could occur (IPCC

2018)—is usually crossed only by the simulations produced by the global circulation models with equilibrium climate sensitivity > 3°C. In contrast, most of the global circulation models with equilibrium climate sensitivity < 3°C do not cross or, at most, are very close to such a threshold (and then only in the worst scenario).

However, as discussed above, the real equilibrium climate sensitivity could be even lower than what the CMIP6 global circulation models predict. Figure 9.6 (in the color figures section between pages 240 and 241) shows the ensemble of CMIP6 global circulation model average simulations for three different SSP scenarios versus the Hadley Center/Climatic Research Unit global surface temperature record since 1850 (Morice et al. 2012). Panel A shows the original records and the fast warming that these models predict for the twenty-first century. The 2°C warming threshold would be crossed as soon as 2035–2045, which confirms that the present climatic alarmism (advocated by political activists like Al Gore, Greta Thunberg, and many others) is based on the CMIP global circulation model climate computer simulations promoted by the IPCC (2018, 2021).

In contrast, panel B shows the comparison with the solar-astronomical harmonic climate model proposed in Scafetta (2013) that used natural harmonics (with periods of 9.1, 10.5, 20, 60, 115, and 983 years) plus the volcanic and anthropogenic signature deduced from the CMIP6 global circulation models but reduced by half (reflecting the discussion above of equilibrium climate sensitivity). The simulations shown are derived using the improved model made by adding some high frequency harmonics to better capture the ENSO fluctuations, as proposed in Scafetta (2021a). It is evident that the curves in B agree better with the observed data since 1850 and, in particular, as shown in the figure inserts, from 2000 to 2021 when the warming bias of the global circulation models has become more and more evident. This result also demonstrates that the solar-astronomical harmonic climate model is a very reliable alternative to the global circulation models and that climate change could be determined by still unknown or poorly understood physical mechanisms responsible for the identified oscillations. Figure 9.6 also shows that, in just a few years, the failure of the global circulation models should become indisputable if the temperature remains nearly constant as predicted by the semi-empirical model.

The important result is that, by using the same SSP scenarios for the twenty-first century, the proposed solar-astronomical harmonic climate model predicts moderate warning: the 2°C threshold would eventually be crossed by the SSP5-8.5 scenario around 2065 and by SSP3-7.0 around 2080 but not at all by the SSP2-4.5 simulations. Moreover, the warming predicted by the depicted simulations should be reduced by about 20 percent if, as appears to be the case, the adopted global surface temperature record is affected by non-climatic warming biases such as those associated with urbanization (Scafetta 2021b; McKitrick and Michaels 2007).

Conclusion

As discussed in the introduction, the equilibrium climate sensitivity value of Earth is still unknown, and, very likely, it is not constant either. However, several lines of empirical evidence suggest that it should be between 1 and 2°C, as estimated, for example, in Scafetta (2013), Lewis and Curry (2018), van Wijngaarden and Happer (2020), and many others using different approaches. In contrast, the most advanced CMIP6 global circulation models used to guide policies predict equilibrium climate sensitivity ranging between 1.8 and 5.7°C. Yet this large uncertainty indicates that such models are very different from each other and that their predictions for the twenty-first century must be handled with caution, because their large uncertainty proves that climate science is not settled yet.

Empirical evidence shows that high– and medium–equilibrium climate sensitivity global circulation models simulate more warming than is observed in global surface temperature records like ERA5-T2m (Scafetta 2021c, 2022). The low–equilibrium climate sensitivity global circulation models, although still not sufficiently reliable, do appear to better agree with the observations only when the global surface temperature averages are considered, while still performing poorly when regional patterns are analyzed. In any case, the low–equilibrium climate sensitivity global circulation models are already found unalarming because their predicted global surface warming remains close to or below 2°C by the middle of the twenty-first century even in the worst emission scenario.

However, by considering that there likely exist climatic oscillations not reproduced by the global circulation models, the real equilibrium climate sensitivity could be even lower than that predicted by the lowest equilibrium climate sensitivity global circulation models. The result is depicted in Figure 9.6, panel B, which uses a solar-astronomical harmonic climate, which actually fits the data since the Medieval Warming Period (Scafetta 2021a). Since the SSP3-7.0 and SSP2-4.5 are considered the most realistic emission scenarios for the twenty-first century, it is highly unlikely that the alarming 2°C threshold will be crossed by 2050.

The equilibrium climate sensitivity of the CMIP6 global circulation models could be seriously overestimated because the solar forcing currently adopted in the global circulation models could be severely erroneous (see the detailed discussion in Connolly et al. 2021), or there may be additional forcings such as an interplanetary-dust forcing that could directly and harmonically modulate the cloud cover (Scafetta, Milani, and Bianchini 2020). Missing or erroneous forcings would require different models and/or different tuning of their internal parameters. Indeed, spectral coherence analysis between astronomical and climatic oscillations from the interannual to the multi-millennial scale appears very robust (Scafetta 2014a, 2020), and none of these oscillations is reproduced by the global circulation models.

Moreover, since the climatic records are likely affected by non-climatic warming biases, in particular over land (Scafetta 2021b; Connolly et al. 2021; McKitrick and Michaels 2007), future climate changes will be even more moderate because the anthropogenic component of the semi-empirical model shown in Figure 9.6, panel B, would also need to be scaled down.

The argument presented above demonstrates that there are still important open and unresolved physical issues in climate science and justifies questioning climate change alarmism and the necessity of implementing urgent and expensive mitigation policies.

References

Alley, R. B. (2004). *GISP2 Ice Core Temperature and Accumulation Data. IGBP PAGES/World Data Center for Paleoclimatology Data Contribution Series #2004-013*. Boulder, Colorado: NOAA/NGDC Paleoclimatology Program. Online at ftp://ftp.ncdc.noaa.gov/pub/data/paleo/icecore/greenland/summit/gisp2/isotopes/gisp2_temp_accum_alley2000.txt.

Arrhenius, S. (1896). "On the Influence of Carbonic Acid in the Air upon the Temperature of the Ground." *London, Edinburgh, and Dublin Philosophical Magazine and Journal of Science*, 5th ser., 41 (April): 237–75. Online at https://www.rsc.org/images/Arrhenius1896_tcm18-173546.pdf.

———. (1906). "Die vermutliche Ursache der Klimaschwankungen" [The Probable Cause of Climate Fluctuations]. *Meddelanden från K. Vetenskapsakademiens Nobelinstitut* 1 (2): 1–12. Translation online at https://friendsofscience.org/assets/documents/Arrhenius%20 1906,%20final.pdf.

Bates, J. R. (2016). "Estimating Climate Sensitivity Using Two-Zone Energy Balance Models." *Earth and Space Science* 3, no. 5 (May): 207–25. Online at https://agupubs.onlinelibrary.wiley.com/doi/full/10.1002/2015EA000154.

Christiansen, B., and F. C. Ljungqvist (2012). "The Extra-Tropical Northern Hemisphere Temperature in the Last Two Millennia: Reconstructions of Low-Frequency Variability." *Climate of the Past* 8, no. 2 (April): 765–86. Online at https://cp.copernicus.org/articles/8/765/2012/cp-8-765-2012.html.

Christy, J. R., and R. T. McNider (2017). "Satellite Bulk Tropospheric Temperatures as a Metric for Climate Sensitivity." *Asia-Pacific Journal of Atmospheric Sciences* 53, no. 4 (November): 511–18. Online at https://sealevel.info/christymcnider2017.pdf.

Connolly, R., et al. (2021). "How Much Has the Sun Influenced Northern Hemisphere Temperature Trends? An Ongoing Debate." *Research in Astronomy and Astrophysics* 21, (6): 131 (68 pages). Online at https://iopscience.iop.org/article/10.1088/1674-4527/21/6/131.

Egorova, T., et al. (2018). "Revised Historical Solar Irradiance Forcing." *Astronomy & Astrophysics* 615 (July): A85. Online at https://www.aanda.org/articles/aa/full_html/2018/07/aa31199-17/aa31199-17.html.

Encyclopaedia Britannica Online (n.d.). "Stefan-Boltzmann Law." Online at https://www.britannica.com/science/Stefan-Boltzmann-law.

Esper, J., et al. (2012). "Orbital Forcing of Tree-Ring Data." *Nature Climate Change* 2 (July): 862–66. Online at https://www.nature.com/articles/nclimate1589.

Gerg's Net (2015). "Temperature of Planet Earth." June 2. Online at http://gergs.net/all_palaeotemps. (Retrieved June 10, 2022).

Golaz, J.-C., et al. (2019). "The DOE E3SM Coupled Model Version 1: Overview and Evaluation at Standard Resolution." *Journal of*

Advances in Modeling Earth Systems 11, no. 7 (March): 2089–2129. Online at https://agupubs.onlinelibrary.wiley.com/doi/full/10.1029/2018MS001603.

Hausfather, Z., and G. Peters (2020). "RCP8.5 Is a Problematic Scenario for Near-Term Emissions." *Proceedings of the National Academy of Sciences of the United States of America* 117, no. 45 (October): 27791–92. Online at https://www.pnas.org/doi/10.1073/pnas.2017124117.

Hersbach, H., et al. (2020). "The ERA5 Global Reanalysis." *Quarterly Journal of the Royal Meteorological Society* 146, no. 730 (May): 1999–2049. Online at https://rmets.onlinelibrary.wiley.com/doi/full/10.1002/qj.3803.

Huntingford, C., M. S. Williamson, and F. J. M. M. Nijsse (2020). "CMIP6 Climate Models Imply High Committed Warming." *Climatic Change* 162 (October): 1515–20. Online at https://link.springer.com/article/10.1007/s10584-020-02849-5.

IPCC (2018). *Global Warming of 1.5°C: An IPCC Special Report on the Impacts of Global Warming of 1.5°C above Pre-Industrial Levels and Related Global Greenhouse Gas Emission Pathways, in the Context of Strengthening the Global Response to the Threat of Climate Change, Sustainable Development, and Efforts to Eradicate Poverty.* Cambridge, United Kingdom, and New York: Cambridge University Press. Online at https://www.ipcc.ch/sr15.

———. (2021). *Climate Change 2021: The Physical Science Basis; Working Group I Contribution to the Sixth Assessment Report of the Intergovernmental Panel on Climate Change* (*Sixth Assessment Report*). Cambridge, United Kingdom, and New York: Cambridge University Press. Online at https://report.ipcc.ch/ar6/wg1/IPCC_AR6_WGI_FullReport.pdf.

Jiménez-de-la-Cuesta, D., and T. Mauritsen (2019). "Emergent Constraints on Earth's Transient and Equilibrium Response to Doubled CO_2 from Post-1970s Global Warming." *Nature Geoscience* 12, no. 11 (October): 902–5. Online at https://www.nature.com/articles/s41561-019-0463-y.

Kluft, L., et al. (2019). "Re-Examining the First Climate Models: Climate Sensitivity of a Modern Radiative–Convective Equilibrium Model." *Journal of Climate* 32, no. 23 (December): 8111–25. Online at https://journals.ametsoc.org/view/journals/clim/32/23/jcli-d-18-0774.1.xml.

Knutti, R., M. A. A. Rugenstein, and G. C. Hegerl (2017). "Beyond Equilibrium Climate Sensitivity." *Nature Geoscience* 10, no. 10 (September): 727–36. Online at https://www.nature.com/articles/ngeo3017.

Kutschera, W., et al. (2017). "The Tyrolean Iceman and His Glacial Environment during the Holocene." *Radiocarbon* 59, no. 2 (April): 395–405. Online at https://www.cambridge.org/core/journals/radiocarbon/article/abs/tyrolean-iceman-and-his-glacial-environment-during-the-holocene/B4CBBBF4A23BDBE4EC5B305EA526E46A.

Lacis, A. A., et al. (2010). "Atmospheric CO_2: Principal Control Knob Governing Earth's Temperature." *Science* 330, no. 6002 (October): 356–59. Online at https://www.science.org/doi/10.1126/science.1190653.

Lewis, N., and J. Curry (2018). "The Impact of Recent Forcing and Ocean Heat Uptake Data on Estimates of Climate Sensitivity." *Journal of Climate* 31, no. 15 (August): 6051–71. Online at https://journals.ametsoc.org/view/journals/clim/31/15/jcli-d-17-0667.1.xml.

Lindzen, R. S., and Y.-S. Choi (2011). "On the Observational Determination of Climate Sensitivity and Its Implications." *Asia-Pacific Journal of Atmospheric Sciences* 47, no. 4 (August): 377–90. Online at https://link.springer.com/article/10.1007/s13143-011-0023-x.

Ljungqvist, F. C. (2010). "A New Reconstruction of Temperature Variability in the Extra-Tropical Northern Hemisphere during the Last Two Millennia." *Geografiska Annaler*, Ser. A, 92, no. (3): 339–51. Online at https://agbjarn.blog.is/users/fa/agbjarn/files/ljungquist-temp-reconstruction-2000-years.pdf.

Manabe, S., and R. T. Wetherald (1967). "Thermal Equilibrium of the Atmosphere with a Given Distribution of Relative Humidity." *Journal of the Atmospheric Sciences* 24, no. 3 (May): 241–59. Online at https://journals.ametsoc.org/view/journals/atsc/24/3/1520-0469_1967_024_0241_teotaw_2_0_co_2.xml.

———. (1975). "The Effects of Doubling the CO_2 Concentration on the Climate of a General Circulation Model." *Journal of the Atmospheric Sciences* 32, no. 1 (January): 3–15. Online at https://journals.ametsoc.org/view/journals/atsc/32/1/1520-0469_1975_032_0003_teodtc_2_0_co_2.xml.

Matskovsky, V. V., and S. Helama (2014). "Testing Long-Term Summer Temperature Reconstruction Based on Maximum Density Chronologies Obtained by Reanalysis of Tree-Ring Data Sets from Northernmost Sweden and Finland." *Climate of the Past* 10, no. 4 (August): 1473–87. Online at https://cp.copernicus.org/articles/10/1473/2014.

Matthes, K., et al. (2017). "Solar Forcing for CMIP6 (v3.2)." *Geoscientific Model Development* 10, no. 6 (June): 2247–2302. Online at https://gmd.copernicus.org/articles/10/2247/2017.

McKitrick, R., and J. R. Christy. (2018). "Test of the Tropical 200- to 300-hPa Warming Rate in Climate Models." *Earth and Space Science* 5, no. 9 (July): 529–36. Online at https://agupubs.onlinelibrary.wiley.com/doi/full/10.1029/2018EA000401.

———. (2020). "Pervasive Warming Bias in CMIP6 Tropospheric Layers." *Earth and Space Science* 7, no. 9 (July): e2020EA001281. Online at https://agupubs.onlinelibrary.wiley.com/doi/full/10.1029/2020EA001281.

McKitrick, R., and P. J. Michaels (2007). "Quantifying the Influence of Anthropogenic Surface Processes and Inhomogeneities on Gridded Global Climate Data." *Journal of Geophysical Research* 112, no. D24 (December): D24S09. Online at https://agupubs.onlinelibrary.wiley.com/doi/full/10.1029/2007JD008465.

Mitchell, D. M., et al. (2020). "The Vertical Profile of Recent Tropical Temperature Trends: Persistent Model Biases in the Context of Internal Variability." *Environmental Research Letters* 15, no. 10 (October): 1040b4. Online at https://iopscience.iop.org/article/10.1088/1748-9326/ab9af7.

Moberg, A., et al. (2005). "Highly Variable Northern Hemisphere Temperatures Reconstructed from Low- and High-Resolution Proxy Data." *Nature* 433, no. 7026 (February): 613–17. Online at https://www.nature.com/articles/nature03265.

Möller, F. (1963). "On the Influence of Changes in the CO_2 Concentration in Air on the Radiation Balance of the Earth's Surface and on the Climate." *Journal of Geophysical Research* 68, no. 13 (July): 3877–86. Online at https://agupubs.onlinelibrary.wiley.com/doi/abs/10.1029/JZ068i013p03877.

Monckton, C., et al. (2015). "Why Models Run Hot: Results from an Irreducibly Simple Model." *Science Bulletin* 60, no. 15 (August): 1378–90. Online at https://www.sciencedirect.com/science/article/pii/S2095927316303589.

Morice, C. P., et al. (2012). "Quantifying Uncertainties in Global and Regional Temperature Change Using an Ensemble of Observational Estimates: The HadCRUT4 Data Set." *Journal of Geophysical Research: Atmospheres* 117, no. D8 (April): D08101. Online at https://agupubs.onlinelibrary.wiley.com/doi/full/10.1029/2011JD017187.

Nijsse, F. J. M. M., P. M. Cox, and M. S. Williamson (2020). "Emergent Constraints on Transient Climate Response (TCR) and Equilibrium Climate Sensitivity (ECS) from Historical Warming in CMIP5 and CMIP6 Models." *Earth System Dynamics* 11, no. 3 (August): 737–50. Online at https://esd.copernicus.org/articles/11/737/2020.

Nobel Prize (2021)."The Nobel Prize in Physics 2021." Press release. October 5. Online at https://www.nobelprize.org/prizes/physics/2021/press-release.

Scafetta, N. (2010). "Empirical Evidence for a Celestial Origin of the Climate Oscillations and Its Implications." *Journal of Atmospheric and Solar-Terrestrial Physics* 72, no. 13 (August): 951–70. Online at https://www.sciencedirect.com/science/article/abs/pii/S1364682610001495.

———. (2012). "Testing an Astronomically Based Decadal-Scale Empirical Harmonic Climate Model Versus the IPCC (2007) General Circulation Climate Models." *Journal of Atmospheric and Solar-Terrestrial Physics* 80 (May): 124–37. Online at https://www.sciencedirect.com/science/article/abs/pii/S1364682611003385.

———. (2013). "Discussion on Climate Oscillations: CMIP5 General Circulation Models versus a Semi-Empirical Harmonic Model Based on Astronomical Cycles." *Earth-Science Reviews* 126 (November): 321–57. Online at https://www.sciencedirect.com/science/article/abs/pii/S0012825213001402.

———. (2014a). "Discussion on the Spectral Coherence between Planetary, Solar and Climate Oscillations: A Reply to Some Critiques." *Astrophysics and Space Science* 354, no. 2 (November): 275–99. Online at https://arxiv.org/abs/1412.0250.

———. (2014b). "Multi-Scale Dynamical Analysis (MSDA) of Sea Level Records versus PDO, AMO, and NAO Indexes." *Climate Dynamics* 43, no. 1–2 (April): 175–92. Online at https://arxiv.org/abs/1304.6148.

———. (2020). "Solar Oscillations and the Orbital Invariant Inequalities of the Solar System." *Solar Physics* 295, no. 2

(February): article 33. Online at https://link.springer.com/article/10.1007/s11207-020-01599-y.

———. (2021a). "Reconstruction of the Interannual to Millennial Scale Patterns of the Global Surface Temperature." *Atmosphere* 12, no. 2 (January): 147. Online at https://www.mdpi.com/2073-4433/12/2/147.

———. (2021b). "Detection of Non-Climatic Biases in Land Surface Temperature Records by Comparing Climatic Data and Their Model Simulations." *Climate Dynamics* 56, no. 9–10 (May): 2959–82. Online at https://ui.adsabs.harvard.edu/abs/2021ClDy...56.2959S/abstract.

———. (2021c). "Testing the CMIP6 GCM Simulations versus Surface Temperature Records from 1980–1990 to 2011–2021: High ECS Is Not Supported." *Climate* 9, no. 11 (October): 161. Online at https://www.mdpi.com/2225-1154/9/11/161.

———. (2022). "Advanced Testing of Low, Medium, and High ECS CMIP6 GCM Simulations versus ERA5-T2m." *Geophysical Research Letters* 49, no. 6 (March): e2022GL097716. Online at https://agupubs.onlinelibrary.wiley.com/doi/full/10.1029/2022GL097716.

Scafetta, N., and A. Bianchini (2023). "Overview of the Spectral Coherence between Planetary Resonances and Solar and Climate Oscillations." *Climate* 11, no. 4 (March): 77. Online at https://doi.org/10.3390/cli11040077.

Scafetta, N., F. Milani, and A. Bianchini (2020). "A 60-Year Cycle in the Meteorite Fall Frequency Suggests a Possible Interplanetary Dust Forcing of the Earth's Climate Driven by Planetary Oscillations." *Geophysical Research Letters* 47, no. 18 (September): e2020GL089954. Online at https://agupubs.onlinelibrary.wiley.com/doi/full/10.1029/2020GL089954.

Scafetta, N., and S. Ouyang (2019). "Detection of UHI Bias in China Climate Network Using Tmin and Tmax Surface Temperature Divergence." *Global and Planetary Change* 181 (October): 102989.

Online at https://www.sciencedirect.com/science/article/abs/pii/S092181811930102X.

Smirnov, B. M., and D. A. Zhilyaev (2021). "Greenhouse Effect in the Standard Atmosphere." *Foundations* 1, no. 2 (October): 184–99. Online at https://www.mdpi.com/2673-9321/1/2/14.

Stefani, F. (2021). "Solar and Anthropogenic Influences on Climate: Regression Analysis and Tentative Predictions." *Climate* 9, no. 11 (November): 163. Online at https://www.mdpi.com/2225-1154/9/11/163.

Van Wijngaarden, W. A., and W. Happer (2020). "Dependence of Earth's Thermal Radiation on Five Most Abundant Greenhouse Gases." arXiv:2006.03098 [physics.ao-ph], June 8. Online at https://arxiv.org/abs/2006.03098.

Wang, C., et al. (2021). "Compensation between Cloud Feedback and Aerosol-Cloud Interaction in CMIP6 Models." *Geophysical Research Letters* 48, no. 4 (January): e2020GL091024. Online at https://agupubs.onlinelibrary.wiley.com/doi/full/10.1029/2020GL091024.

Wyatt, M. G., and J. A. Curry (2014). "Role for Eurasian Arctic Shelf Sea Ice in a Secularly Varying Hemispheric Climate Signal during the 20th Century." *Climate Dynamics* 42 (May): 2763–82. Online at https://link.springer.com/article/10.1007/s00382-013-1950-2.

Zelinka, M. D., et al. (2020). "Causes of Higher Climate Sensitivity in CMIP6 Models." *Geophysical Research Letters* 47, no. 1 (January): e2019GL085782. Online at https://agupubs.onlinelibrary.wiley.com/doi/full/10.1029/2019GL085782.

Zhu, J., C. J. Poulsen, and B. L. Otto-Bliesner (2020). "High Climate Sensitivity in CMIP6 Model Not Supported by Paleoclimate." *Nature Climate Change* 10, no. 5 (April): 378–79. Online at https://www.nature.com/articles/s41558-020-0764-6.

Chapter 10

Effects of Human-Induced Global Warming

by Anthony R. Lupo

Chapter Summary

The climate modeling community produces a wide range of climate projections based on socioeconomic scenarios leading to increased greenhouse gas concentrations that induce radiative forcings (energy differentials) and temperature change. They still detail a wide range—from no more than what has already occurred to as much as 5.7°C. However, the recent IPCC report does acknowledge the implausibility of the highest radiative forcing, which was used in previous impact analyses and should be reassessed. The most probable warming now indicated by the IPCC is less than 2.7°C by 2100.

Previous chapters discussed how climate models have routinely over-forecast observed trends. It is therefore reasonable to assume that extreme events (often included under "impacts" of climate change) will occur in a similar or only slightly enhanced manner relative to historical experience rather than increase greatly. Media and policymakers highlight only negative impacts of global warming on biodiversity and human health, ignoring positive effects. For example, increasing vegetative production comes with longer growing seasons, CO_2 fertilization, and more efficient vegetative water use in warmer climates. Many analyses show that greater human mortality and agricultural losses arise from colder climates than warm ones.

Successful civilizations have learned to adapt to impacts of climate change. Wealthy and technologically advanced societies adapt better than poorer, less advanced ones, making them less vulnerable and better prepared for future changes. All parts of our civilization should be similarly enabled to deal with climate change.

Introduction

In human history, civilizations have risen and fallen because the climate became more or less favorable to their existence, occasionally over comparatively short periods of time. These changes in past climate were caused by natural variability, and some civilizations contributed to their own demise by failing to adapt. However, successful civilizations have learned to adapt or mitigate the impacts of climate change.

Climate change is a serious issue. Our understanding of climate and how it changes has advanced enough to project the future reasonably well using models, especially if we use them with full awareness of what they do well and what they do not do well.

Chapter 4 of this book explained how climate models work and how simulations compare to reality. Stated briefly, a climate model is a hypothesis, frequently in the form of mathematical statements, that describes some process or processes we think are physically important for the climate, climatic change, or both, with physical consistency of the model formulation and agreement with observations serving to "test" the hypothesis (that is, the model) (Oglesby 2010). This is what students learn when they take classes about climate modeling. Since models have already been discussed in chapters 4 and 9, this chapter will not review them.

Models are tools that are used by scientists to advise policymakers, who then use these results to formulate recommendations for legislation. Often policies and recommendations are based on mid-range or even higher-end scenarios (for example, USGCRP 2017). In the Intergovernmental Panel on Climate Change (IPCC) *Sixth Assessment Report* (AR6) (IPCC 2021), modeled possible futures are called Shared Socioeconomic Pathways (SSPs) (for example, Riahi et al. 2017; Rogelj et al. 2018). They were generated for the Coupled Model Intercomparison Project—Phase 6 (CMIP6) (Eyring et al. 2016). These SSPs are scenarios of projected socioeconomic global changes up to the year 2100. They assume that societies collectively make policies with respect to climate and the environment that are then used to drive model projections that include atmospheric concentrations of carbon dioxide and other greenhouse gases, as well as the rates of change for these concentrations.

The IPCC uses five SSP scenarios to present possible outcomes based on population growth and other demographic drivers such as education, urbanization, land-use policies, gross domestic product data, and economic development policies (Riahi et al. 2017) that lead to increases in atmospheric greenhouse gases corresponding to increases in atmospheric radiative forcing (W/m^2) and hence to future global-average temperatures. These increases in radiative forcing represent energy retained by the atmosphere that can be associated with increases in global temperature as projected by the climate models. While the models can be run with a myriad of possible future scenarios, a few were routinely presented in peer reviewed literature and the IPCC AR6 (IPCC 2021; IPCC-SPM 2021). These are described below.

Scenarios 1–5 are based on socioeconomic and governmental policy assumptions about population growth, with Scenarios 1 and 5 ("Sustainability and Fossil Fueled Development") resulting in slower population growth and lower world populations (approximately 8.2–8.5 billion) by the year 2100. Scenario 3 ("Regional Rivalry—A Rocky Road") assumes the most rapid population growth with 11.1 billion people by the year 2100. Scenarios 2 and 4 are called "Middle of Road" and "Inequality—A Road Divided," respectively. These represent moderate population growth that levels during the twenty-first century. The five radiative forcing scenarios generally presented are 1.9, 2.6, 4.5, 7.0, and 8.5 W/m^2, which correspond to low (1.9 and 2.6), intermediate (4.5), and high (7.0 and 8.5) greenhouse gas emissions scenarios. Each represents the "excess" value for longwave radiation that results in energy retained by the climate system as associated with a certain amount of greenhouse gas concentrations in Earth's radiation budget. Naturally, if more energy is retained by the climate system, the Earth would warm. Each scenario is then identified using the notation of SSPa-b, where *a* is the population-growth scenario and *b* is the amount of radiative forcing (in W/m^2).

The first two scenarios (SSP1-1.9, and SSP1-2.6) are associated with policies resulting in net-zero greenhouse emissions by the years 2050 and 2075, respectively, and global temperature increases by the year 2100 as projected by climate models of 1.0–1.8°C (1.8–3.4°F) and 1.3–2.4°C (2.3–4.3°F), respectively. The intermediate scenario (SSP2-4.5) assumes increases in greenhouse gas emissions to the year 2050 and then decreases until the year 2100, resulting in a projected global increase in temperature of 2.1–3.5°C (3.8–6.3°F) by the year 2100. Lastly, the high-emission scenarios (SSP3-7.0 and SSP5-8.5) result in a doubling of atmospheric global greenhouse gas concentrations (relative to pre-industrial times) by the year 2100 for the former, and a tripling of greenhouse gas concentrations by the year 2075 for the latter, respectively. These are associated with global temperature increases by the year 2100 of 2.8–4.6°C (5.0–8.3°F) and 3.3–5.7°C (5.9–10.3°F), respectively. RCPs 8.5 (yielding 3.2–5.4°C warmer than 1850–1900 by 2100) and 6 (yielding 2.0–3.7°C warmer) are implausible, anticipating far greater dependence on coal than widespread national policies are likely to yield (RCP = Representative Concentration Pathway). RCP 4.5 (yielding 1.7–3.2°C warmer) is at the upper end of the plausible, thus both less likely and warmer than SSP4-3.4 ("baseline") and RCP 2.6 ("goal"). Consequently, the most probable scenario, according to the IPCC, is for warming relative to 1850–1900 in the range of 0.9–~2.7°C by 2100. That lower likely range of warming would yield lower increases of the probability of the warming-driven extreme events discussed below.

Chapters 4 and 9 demonstrated that global temperatures are increasing closer to the lowest end of the range of projected temperature scenarios described here. Recent articles by Pielke, Burgess, and Ritchie (2022) and Scafetta (2022) analyze the full range of scenarios similar to those presented above. The former analyzed model scenarios produced for the IPCC *Fifth Assessment Report* and AR6. They found that historical conditions and observations in the most recent fifteen years (2005–2020) are consistent with scenarios that project 2–3°C of warming. The latter study examined the simulations produced by thirty-eight climate models used in the CMIP6 project to hindcast observed global temperature from the decade of the 1980s to the most recent decade from several organizations. This paper reports that models projecting less future warming (lower to intermediate scenarios above) performed better in these hindcasts. In short, future warming is more likely to be toward the lower than toward the higher end of model forecasts.

In this chapter, discussion will focus on the likely effects of human-induced global warming on extreme weather events, plant growth, agriculture, sea level, sea ice and glacial ice, biodiversity, and human health and economy as presented in IPCC (2021) or IPCC-SPM (2021) and the peer reviewed literature. The terminology that is used to describe changes as projected by the models is virtually certain (99–100 percent), very likely (90–99 percent), likely (66–90 percent), and as likely as not (33–66 percent). Similar terminology is adopted for changes that are unlikely: virtually impossible (0–1 percent), very unlikely (1–10 percent), unlikely (10–34 percent), and as likely as not (33–66 percent). Lastly, the discussion in this chapter will cover the full range of scenarios in spite of the results of Pielke, Burgess, and Ritchie (2022) and Scafetta (2022), that is, despite the likelihood that higher-end scenarios are wrong. Since the media and policymakers often report high-end, that is, pessimistic scenarios, ignoring or downplaying the lower-end scenarios despite their higher likelihood, this chapter will allow the reader to put these reports in the proper context.

Climate Change Projections and Observations

It is important to remember, in considering all of the projections below of the effects of climate change, that the higher-end projections are less likely than the lower-end projections.

Sea Level Change

Sea level change can be measured relative to the sea floor or local terrain using instruments based on Earth, or relative to the center of the Earth using space-borne instruments (IPCC 2021). Future sea level change would be the result of both glacier melt and the expansion of ocean water due to heating.

Ocean water is a fluid and expands when it warms. The amount of ocean expansion depends on temperature (for example, PRI 2022), expanding approximately 4 percent from 20°C (room temperature) to 100°C (boiling) but only about 0.5 percent from 20°C to 40°C (about 0.5 cm). Thus, a one-meter column of water at room temperature will expand to 1.04 m at the boiling point of water, but to only 1.005 m at 40°C. The rate of volume expansion is not linear and will also increase with temperature. As a side note and for comparison, to heat the topmost 1 m of ocean by 1°C would require 1.5×10^{21} Joules of energy, or three times the 0.580×10^{21} Joules of energy consumed by humanity in a year (TWC 2023). Alternatively, if the midrange SSP scenario (4.5 W/m^2) were chosen as an example, a temperature increase of 3°C in the atmosphere would provide 1.5×10^{22} Joules of energy. If that energy were completely transferred to the ocean, it would be enough to warm the top 10 m of water by 1°C, which would expand the ocean by approximately 0.25 cm.

Sea level will also change locally with respect to terrain subsiding or rising at the coastline (PRI 2022). Causes of land subsidence and rising include tectonic movements (leading to either rising or subsiding); removal of understructure, such as groundwater (leading to subsidence); and removal of overstructure, such as glacial ice (leading to land's rising).

Barring an unforeseen major decline in global-average surface temperature, it is certain that sea level will rise over the twenty-first century as it did over the twentieth century. In the IPCC's *Sixth Assessment Report* (2021), sea level is projected likely to rise about 0.3–0.55 m (0.98–1.80 ft.) under the most optimistic scenario (SSP1-1.9) to about 0.6–1.0 m (1.97–3.28 ft.) under the most pessimistic (SSP5-8.5). This is compared to the values from 1995 to 2014. The combined range in English units would be about 12–40 inches. While the numbers in the upper part of the scenario may raise some eyebrows, they are not the extreme values some occasionally state.

In IPCC (2021), global sea level rise was reported to be 1.4 millimeters annually for most of the twentieth century. This translates to about six inches of rise globally during the twentieth century, and the National Aeronautics and Space Administration (NASA) reports a sea level increase of about eight inches since 1900 (to about 2020—see NASA 2020). These observed changes have been on the lower side of what has been observed historically, and even the middle of the range of IPCC (2021) sea level changes reported above would be consistent with historical values.

Historically, sea level has been higher, and sea level change has been more rapid, than today. For example, during the last interglacial period (about 120,000 years ago), sea level could have been 20–30 feet higher than today (for example, Dutton and Lambeck 2012). During the last ice age, the sea level is thought to have been about 390 feet lower than today (for example, Stanford et al. 2010). If sea level rose at a constant rate from the end of the ice age to today, that increase would translate to about one to two feet per century, depending on when the end of the ice age was identified. Further, researchers (for example, Stanford et al. 2010) believe that this sea level rise was not constant and may have been very little for some centuries, but as much as 7–15 feet for other centuries.

Sea Ice

The amount of area covered by sea ice in the Arctic is expected to retreat (IPCC 2021). With sea ice, the relevant measures are (a) the amount of sea ice cover during the warmest part of the season (August and September—approximately 4,000 km^2) and (b) the typical time of surface melt in the spring and freeze-up in the fall. The IPCC (2021) projects about 50 percent loss of warm-season sea ice under the optimistic scenarios by the year 2100 and near complete loss of warm-season sea ice by that year under the most pessimistic scenarios (for example, Boe et al. 2009). The summer season would be considered ice-free at approximately 1,000 km^2 of ice cover.

It is difficult to make a historical reference to Arctic sea ice because direct estimates of this value have been available only since the mid-twentieth century, and satellite measurements since the late 1970s. Arctic sea ice cover is estimated to have decreased by about 33 percent between the late 1970s and the mid-2010s, which was a period of observed warming globally, for the minimum part of the ice season (IPCC 2021). However, this value varies annually, and one study (Comiso, Meier, and Gersten 2017a) showed a decrease of about 2.5 percent per decade during the maximum extent period and about 4.5 percent per decade annually.

In the Antarctic, there is low confidence in model projections of sea ice cover for various reasons, but the model spread is reported to be large (IPCC 2021). While the CMIP6 models have improved their ability to reproduce the seasonal cycle of Antarctic sea ice, they have not been able to reproduce observed trends very well. The models routinely overestimate low ice concentrations and underestimate high ice concentrations since the late 1970s when compared to satellite records (IPCC 2021).

While there are more observations and for a longer period in the Arctic, there is little information available for Antarctic sea ice before the satellite era. There is no significant trend in Antarctic sea ice since the satellite era, according to studies cited by the IPCC (2021), as studies have shown mixed trends, but there has been significant interannual variability. The results of Comiso et al. (2017b) show an increase in sea ice extent of 1.7 percent per decade since the late 1970s, and they point out this is consistent with a warming climate.

Land Ice

The IPCC (2021) also projects how much will be lost from ice sheets (Greenland and Antarctica) and glaciers worldwide, and the resulting contributions to global sea level, by 2100 and compares that to modern losses. In Greenland, the losses of ice mass are virtually certain and are projected to add approximately 1–10 cm (0.39–3.94 inches) to sea level under optimistic and 9–18 cm (3.54–7.09 inches) for pessimistic scenarios. In Antarctica, the comparable numbers are 3–27 cm (1.18–10.63 inches) for the optimistic and 3–34 cm (1.18–13.39 inches) under the pessimistic scenarios. The observed quantities over the last three decades have been 1.1–1.5 cm (0.43–0.59 inches) for Greenland and 0.5–1.0 cm (0.19–0.39 inches) for the Antarctic according to IPCC (2021).

However, there is not unanimous agreement that these ice sheets are shrinking quickly. A recent study by Zwally et al. (2015) demonstrated that the Antarctic ice sheet may not have lost ice mass during the late twentieth and early twenty-first century but may have gained mass. Recent work examining the melting of continental ice at the end of the last ice age demonstrates that natural processes can also drive relatively rapid ice sheet loss (for example, Menounos et al. 2017).

For the land and mountain glaciers, melting is projected to continue throughout the twenty-first century, and under optimistic scenarios they are projected to lose 5–31 percent of their current mass, and 16–56 percent under pessimistic scenarios (IPCC 2021). During the last few decades, these glaciers have lost enough ice to contribute 1.3–2.2 cm (0.51–1.26 inches) to sea level rise.

Extreme Events

The IPCC (2021) generally projects an increase in drought, extreme heat events, flooding events, and heavy precipitation events. These are quantified in terms of how much more likely these are to occur given a certain increase in global temperature (IPCC 2021, introduction). Droughts are classified as meteorological (precipitation minus evaporation), agricultural, and hydrologic (for example, Ahrens and Henson 2022). Also, all the extreme events named here can be defined differently by region or season. Their occurrence can be expressed as a once-in-ten-year or once-in-fifty-year event during a time when human influence was thought to be low, that is, the second half of the nineteenth century.

For *hot extremes*, the IPCC (2021) projects that by 2100 what occurred once in ten years in the late nineteenth century will occur 4–9 times in ten years for the range of optimistic (1.5°C) to pessimistic (4.0°C) scenarios for the increase in global mean temperature, compared to 3 times currently. In this case, projections are not for certain timelines, but for reaching the designated temperature-increase thresholds. The once-in-fifty-year event is projected to occur 9–39 times, compared to 5 times currently. For heavy precipitation, a once-in-ten-year event relative to baseline currently occurs 1.3 times now but is expected to occur 1.5–2.7 times in the warmer world. Agricultural drought is thought to occur 1.7 times now in ten years compared to the nineteenth-century baseline and may occur 2–4 times per decade in the warmer world.

The increase in occurrence globally of warm events over the twentieth century has occurred on all continents and many regions with high confidence in the literature (for example, Perkins-Kirkpatrick and Lewis 2020) for the Eastern Hemisphere, but comparatively lower confidence for some regions (for example, Canada, and southern South America). However, for drought, fewer parts of the world exist where increases during the twentieth century are reported (for example, the western United States and the Mediterranean). Only medium confidence in these results exists because the research has produced inconclusive results regarding trends in drought. For example, Spinoni et al. (2020)

found no trend in drought occurrence and severity globally since the mid-twentieth century. An interesting study by Ionita et al. (2021) demonstrated that past "megadroughts" over Central Europe were decadal in nature and linked to natural cycles when examining the current decadal drought influencing Central and Eastern Europe (for example, Zolotokrylin 2013). Even in the United States, natural variability is strongly related to the occurrence of drought (for example, Rajagopalan 2000). Lupo et al. (2021) indicated that during the past fifty years, drought occurred less often during the middle part of that period than for the first decade and as of late when examining agriculturally productive regions in the United States and Eastern Europe. Drought has even occurred in cycles and over long periods of time since the end of the late ice age (for example, Chendev et al. 2015).

Increases in *heavy precipitation events* can be discussed in terms of increases in frequency or amount per event. For increases in the amount per event, medium confidence is found in the central United States and high confidence for Northern Europe only (for example, Fischer and Knutti 2016), although other regions have reported increases in the literature. However, changes in precipitation patterns are quite complex, as some areas have become wetter while others have become drier (for example, USGCRP 2017, chapter 7). Flooding events are projected to increase by about 25 percent by 2100 due to storm surge and wave events, or to precipitation events, compared to the present worldwide. Given the observed increases in sea level and heavy rain events, there is medium confidence that flooding has increased globally (IPCC-SPM 2021).

The literature cited in the IPCC (2021) projects an increase in the number of intense *tropical cyclones* while the total overall number may not change dramatically, but there is low confidence in the future frequency of such events. In the last few decades, there has been an increase in the number of tropical cyclones events globally, but the overall trend is not statistically significant, and trends have been very different in each ocean basin (for example, Lupo et al. 2020). For example, the Atlantic and Indian Ocean basins have observed an increase in the number of tropical cyclones in the last four decades, while other ocean basins (West and East Pacific and the Southern Hemisphere) have observed few changes or decreases.

The occurrence of events such as *severe weather* (tornadoes, hail, high winds) is difficult to glean from models, but as they are associated typically with extratropical cyclones or landfalling cyclones, they can be estimated from the projection of these events. The global models underestimate the strength and occurrence of extratropical storm tracks while projecting their poleward movement (for example, Eichler et al. 2013), although there has been marginal improvement recently (for example, Priestley et. al. 2020). Thus, it would be difficult to project changes in the occurrence of severe weather other than that its occurrence would move poleward. There have been observed increases in severe weather events across the globe, but confidence in these trends is low due to increases in population and better remote sensing techniques (for example, Nouri et al. 2021); that is, some or all of the apparent increases may be due to improved observation and reporting rather than to actual increases.

The frequency of *atmospheric blocking* events (long-lived, quasi-stationary ridging in the jet stream) is projected to remain about the same as today according to two recent review articles (Woollings et al. 2018; Lupo 2021), although the projected confidence in future occurrence of blocking is low. Atmospheric blocking events are relevant to extreme events because they are associated with cold waves, drought, forest fire weather, and heat waves. Weather and climate models tend to underestimate the duration and intensity of blocking, and this is due to the ability of general circulation models to capture the character of the storm tracks and/or individual cyclone events (especially cyclones that deepen more rapidly) since they contribute greatly to the life cycles and intensity of atmospheric blocking events (Lupo 2021). Improvements in modeling and in predicting blocking have progressed with the latest CMIP6 results as shown in Lupo (2021). In recent years, the number of these events has increased globally, but Lupo (2021) and references therein have demonstrated strong interdecadal variability.

An examination of extreme events is important because of the outsized attention paid to these singular events when they occur. Also, many of these events (for example, cold waves) might be the result of changes in the general circulation (for example, blocking), which are influenced by longer-term cycles discussed in chapter 6.

Fire and Fire Weather

Trends in fire events are difficult to observe and project since many fires are caused by humans and due to capricious activity (for example, recreation and carelessness—Balch et al. 2017). Consequently, fire weather, rather than fire, is examined. The chances of a background increase in fire weather would be due to the combination of warm extremes and drought as described above. Based on the IPCC (2021) projections, there is a medium to high confidence in the increased occurrence of fire weather in regions where fires are more frequent and in the expansion of regions that are fire-prone. However, the observations have shown only medium confidence in the currently observed increase in fire weather.

Weather, Climate, Wealth, and Mortality

For most of human history, dangerous weather and extreme climate have taken their toll on civilizations, destroying infrastructure and agriculture and causing human casualties. However, the twentieth century bore witness to some positive trends as technology has advanced and the wealth of nations globally has increased. Many studies have shown very strong upward trends in agricultural production and yield due to technology (for example, Henson et al. 2017). This has made agriculture less vulnerable to weather and climate, while at the same time feeding more people. Technology and the increase in global wealth have meant that the fraction of economic loss due to disasters compared to overall wealth has decreased (Watts et al. 2019) The best news from the twentieth century is the strong decline in human casualties due to weather and climate (for example, Goklany 2011) as forecasting and warning technologies have allowed for much longer lead times before the occurrence of dangerous weather, and improved structures have sheltered rising percentages of the human population.

Conclusions

In chapters 4 and 9 of this book, the models used to project increases in global temperature were examined in detail. In this chapter, we describe how these models are used to project quantitatively and qualitatively the effects of human influence on the climate by using increased greenhouse gases as a surrogate for human activity, including the growth in population, the introduction of technologies, and the implementation of policies. While the modeling community (for example, CMIP6) produces a range in future climate scenarios, generally the upper half of the scenarios are shown by the media and policymakers, and the lower half are ignored. Too frequently, the most extreme scenarios are presented. In order to access the full range of scenarios, one must go to the published technical literature or the IPCC (2021) report itself.

In this chapter, the full range of modeled scenarios and their impact on human activity were shown. In chapters 4 and 9, it was demonstrated that models routinely over-forecast the observed trends. Thus, it is reasonable to assume that extreme events (for example, extreme heat, drought, or heavy rains) may occur similarly to today, or increase slightly, but it is unlikely that they will increase greatly.

Typically, only the negative impacts of climate warming on biodiversity (for example, Weiskopf et al. 2020) or human health (for example, Minor et al. 2022) are reported, and it is implied that there are few to no positive influences. This can be misleading, as many have shown that human populations suffer greater mortality (for example, Gasparrini et al. 2015) and agricultural loss in colder climates than in warmer. Also, growing seasons can be longer for many plant species and water use more efficient in warmer climates (for example, Jones 2014). Additionally, atmospheric phenomena such as El Niño were once thought to bring negative economic impacts to local communities in the United States, for example, through increases in flooding in some regions along with the associated damage. However, Changnon et al. (1999) showed that the occurrence of El Niño was a net positive for the United States economy through the reduction in the cost of energy required for winter heating. Finally, warnings of dire consequences for many species are proving to be exaggerated or overblown (for example, Clark et al. 2020).

This review does not hold that the climate is not changing or that nothing can be done about it. Human adaptation to climate change has worked for millennia. Our society is the wealthiest and most technologically advanced in history, and as a result humanity is less vulnerable to weather and climate, and we are better prepared to protect ourselves from future changes in climate and extreme events. Models can thus be used to help us make informed decisions about economic activity in areas such as energy demand and use, or food production.

References

Ahrens, C. D., and R. Henson (2022). *Meteorology Today: An Introduction to Weather, Climate, and the Environment.* 13th ed. Boston, Massachusetts: Cengage Learning.

Balch, J. K., et al. (2017). "Human-Started Wildfires Expand the Fire Niche across the United States." *Proceedings of the National Academy of Sciences of the United States of America* 114, no. 11 (February): 2946–51. Online at https://www.pnas.org/doi/10.1073/pnas.1617394114.

Boé, J., A. Hall, and X. Qu (2009). "September Sea-Ice Cover in the Arctic Ocean Projected to Vanish by 2100." *National Geoscience* 2, no. 5 (March): 341–43. Online at https://www.nature.com/articles/ngeo467.

Changnon, D., et al. (1999). "Interactions with a Weather-Sensitive Decision Maker: A Case Study Incorporating ENSO Information into a Strategy for Purchasing Natural Gas." *Bulletin of the American Meteorological Society* 80, no. 6 (June): 1117–26. Online at https://journals.ametsoc.org/view/journals/bams/80/6/1520-0477_1999_080_1117_iwawsd_2_0_co_2.xml.

Chendev, Y. G., et al. (2015). "Regional Specificity of the Climatic Evolution of Soils in the Southern Part of Eastern Europe in the Second Half of the Holocene." *Eurasian Soil Science* 48 (December): 1279–91. Online at https://link.springer.com/article/10.1134/S1064229315120042.

Clark, T. D., et al. (2020). "Ocean Acidification Does Not Impair the Behaviour of Coral Reef Fishes." *Nature* 577, no. 7790 (January): 370–75. Online at https://doi.org/10.1038/s41586-019-1903-y.

Comiso, J. C., W. N. Meier, and R. Gersten (2017). "Variability and Trends in the Arctic Sea Ice Cover: Results from Different Techniques." *Journal of Geophysical Research: Oceans* 122, no. 8 (July): 6883–6900. Online at https://agupubs.onlinelibrary.wiley.com/doi/10.1002/2017JC012768.

Comiso, J. C., et al. (2017). "Positive Trend in the Antarctic Sea Ice Cover and Associated Changes in Surface Temperature." *Journal of Climate* 30, no. 6 (March): 2251–67. Online at https://journals.ametsoc.org/view/journals/clim/30/6/jcli-d-16-0408.1.xml.

Dutton, A., and K. Lambeck (2012). "Ice Volume and Sea Level during the Last Interglacial." *Science* 337, no. 6091 (July): 216–19. Online at https://eps.harvard.edu/files/eps/files/duttonlambeck2012science.pdf.

Eichler, T. P., N. Gaggini, and Z. Pan (2013). "Impacts of Global Warming on Northern Hemisphere Winter Storm Tracks in the CMIP5 Model Suite." *Journal of Geophysical Research: Atmosphere* 118, no. 10 (February): 3919–32. Online at https://agupubs.onlinelibrary.wiley.com/doi/full/10.1002/jgrd.50286.

Eyring, V., et al. (2016). "Overview of the Coupled Model Intercomparison Project Phase 6 (CMIP6) Experimental Design and Organization." *Geoscientific Model Development* 9, no. 5 (May): 1937–58. Online at https://gmd.copernicus.org/articles/9/1937/2016.

Fischer, E., and R. Knutti (2016). "Observed Heavy Precipitation Increase Confirms Theory and Early Models." *Nature Climate Change* 6, no. 11 (October): 986–91. Online at https://doi.org/10.1038/nclimate3110.

Gasparrini, A., et al. (2015). "Mortality Risk Attributable to High and Low Ambient Temperature: A Multicountry Observational Study." *The Lancet* 386, no. 9991 (May): 369–75. Online at https://doi.org/10.1016/S0140-6736(14)62114-0.

Goklany, I. M. (2011). *Wealth and Safety: The Amazing Decline in Deaths from Extreme Weather in an Era of Global Warming, 1900–2010. Policy Study 393*. Los Angeles: Reason Foundation. Online at https://reason.org/wp-content/uploads/files/deaths_from_extreme_weather_1900_2010.pdf.

Henson, C., et al. (2017). "ENSO and PDO-Related Climate Variability on Midwestern United States Crop Yields." *International Journal of Biometeorology* 61, no. 5 (May): 857–67. https://pubmed.ncbi.nlm.nih.gov/27787628.

Ionita, M., et al. (2021). "Past Megadroughts in Central Europe Were Longer, More Severe, and Less Warm Than Modern

Droughts." *Communications Earth & Environment* 2, no. 1 (March): article 61. Online at https://www.nature.com/articles/s43247-021-00130-w.

IPCC (2021). *Climate Change 2021: The Physical Science Basis; Working Group I Contribution to the Sixth Assessment Report of the Intergovernmental Panel on Climate Change.* (*Sixth Assessment Report*) Cambridge, United Kingdom, and New York: Cambridge University Press. Online at https://report.ipcc.ch/ar6/wg1/IPCC_AR6_WGI_FullReport.pdf.

IPCC-SPM (2021). *Climate Change 2021: The Physical Science Basis; Summary for Policymakers.* Cambridge, United Kingdom, and New York: Cambridge University Press. Online at https://www.ipcc.ch/report/ar6/wg1/downloads/report/IPCC_AR6_WGI_SPM.pdf.

Jones, N. (2014). "CO_2 Makes Growing Seasons Longer." *Nature*, April 23. Online at https://doi.org/10.1038/nature.2014.15081.

Lupo, A. R. (2021). "Atmospheric Blocking Events: A Review." *Annals of the New York Academy of Sciences* 1504, no. 1 (November): 5–24. Online at https://pubmed.ncbi.nlm.nih.gov/33382135.

Lupo, A. R., et al. (2020). "The Interannual and Interdecadal Variability in Tropical Cyclone Activity: A Decade of Changes in the Climatological Character." In *Current Topics in Tropical Cyclone Research*, edited by A. R. Lupo, chapter 1. London: IntechOpen. Online at https://www.intechopen.com/chapters/72703.

Lupo, A. R., et al. (2021). "A Comparison of the Characteristics of Drought during the Late 20th and Early 21st Centuries over Eastern Europe, Western Russia and Central North America." *Atmosphere* 12, no. 8 (August): 1033. Online at https://www.mdpi.com/2073-4433/12/8/1033.

Menounos, B., et al. (2017). "Cordilleran Ice Sheet Mass Loss Preceded Climate Reversals near the Pleistocene Termination." *Science* 358, no. 6364 (November): 781–84. Online at https://www.science.org/doi/10.1126/science.aan3001.

Minor, K., et al. (2022). "Rising Temperatures Erode Human Sleep Globally." *One Earth* 5, no. 5 (May): 534–39. Online at https://www.sciencedirect.com/science/article/pii/S2590332222002093.

NASA (2020). "NASA-Led Study Reveals the Causes of Sea Level Rise since 1900." NASA Sea Level Change Observations from Space, August 21. Online at https://sealevel.nasa.gov/news/191/nasa-led-study-reveals-the-causes-of-sea-level-rise-since-1900.

Nouri, N., et al. (2021). "Explaining the Trends and Variability in the United States Tornado Records Using Climate Teleconnections and Shifts in Observational Practices." *Scientific Reports* 11, no. 1 (January): 1741. Online at https://doi.org/10.1038/s41598-021-81143-5.

Oglesby, R. J. (2010). "Assessing the Role of Climate in Environmental Systems Analysis and Modeling." In *Environmental Systems*. Vol. 2, edited by A. Sydow. Oxford, United Kingdom: EOLSS Publishers. Online at http://www.eolss.net/sample-chapters/c09/E4-20-03-06.pdf.

PRI (2022). "Thermal Expansion of Water." Paleontological Research Institution. Online at https://www.priweb.org/teach-cl-sci/thermal-expansion-of-water.

Perkins-Kirkpatrick, S. E., and S. C. Lewis (2020). "Increasing Trends in Regional Heatwaves." *Nature Communications* 11, no. 1 (July): article 3357. Online at https://doi.org/10.1038/s41467-020-16970-7.

Pielke, R., Jr., M. G. Burgess, and J. Ritchie (2022). "Plausible 2005–2050 Emissions Scenarios Project between 2 °C and 3 °C of Warming by 2100." *Environmental Research Letters* 17, no. 2 (February): 024027. Online at https://iopscience.iop.org/article/10.1088/1748-9326/ac4ebf/pdf.

Priestley, M. D. K., et al. (2020). "An Overview of the Extratropical Storm Tracks in CMIP6 Historical Simulations." *Journal of Climate* 33, no. 15 (August): 6315–43. Online at https://journals.ametsoc.org/view/journals/clim/33/15/JCLI-D-19-0928.1.xml.

Rajagopalan, B., et al. (2000). "Spatiotemporal Variability of ENSO and SST Teleconnections to Summer Drought over the United States during the Twentieth Century." *Journal of Climate* 13, no. 24 (December): 4244–55. Online at https://journals.ametsoc.org/view/journals/clim/13/24/1520-0442_2000_013_4244_svoeas_2.0.co_2.xml.

Riahi, K., et al. (2017). "The Shared Socioeconomic Pathways and Their Energy, Land Use, and Greenhouse Gas Emissions Implications: An Overview." *Global Environmental Change* 42 (January): 153–68. Online at https://www.sciencedirect.com/science/article/pii/S0959378016300681.

Rogelj, J., et al. (2018). "Scenarios towards Limiting Global Mean Temperature Increase below 1.5°C." *Nature Climate Change* 8, no. 4 (March): 325–32. Online at https://doi.org/10.1038/s41558-018-0091-3.

Scafetta, N. (2022). "CMIP6 GCM Ensemble Members versus Global Surface Temperatures." *Climate Dynamics* 60 (September): 3091–3120. Online at https://doi.org/10.1007/s00382-022-06493-w.

Spinoni, J., et al. (2020). "Future Global Meteorological Drought Hot Spots: A Study Based on CORDEX Data." *Journal of Climate* 33, no. 9 (May): 3635–61. Online at https://journals.ametsoc.org/view/journals/clim/33/9/jcli-d-19-0084.1.xml.

Stanford, J. D., et al. (2010). "Sea-Level Probability for the Last Deglaciation: A Statistical Analysis of Far-Field Records." *Global and Planetary Change* 79, no. 3–4 (December): 193–203. Online at https://www.sciencedirect.com/science/article/abs/pii/S0921818110002419.

TWC (2023). "Global Energy Consumption." The World Counts. Accessed May 8, 2023. Online at https://www.theworldcounts.com/challenges/climate-change/energy/global-energy-consumption.

USGCRP (2017). *Climate Science Special Report: Fourth National Climate Assessment.* Vol. 1. Washington, D.C.: U.S. Global Change Research Program. Online at https://science2017.globalchange.gov.

Watts, N., et al. (2019). "The 2019 Report of The *Lancet* Countdown on Health and Climate Change: Ensuring That the Health of a Child Born Today Is Not Defined by a Changing Climate." *The Lancet* 394, no. 10211 (November): 1836–78. Online at https://doi.org/10.1016/S0140-6736(19)32596-6.

Weiskopf, S. R., et al. (2020). "Climate Change Effects on Biodiversity, Ecosystems, Ecosystem Services, and Natural Resource Management in the United States." *Science of the Total Environment* 733 (September): 137782. Online at https://www.sciencedirect.com/science/article/pii/S0048969720312948.

Woollings, T., et al. (2018). "Blocking and Its Response to Climate Change." *Current Climate Change Reports* 4, no. 3 (September): 287–300. Online at https://link.springer.com/article/10.1007/s40641-018-0108-z.

Zolotokrylin, A. N. (2013). "Droughts and Desertification in Sub-Boreal Landscapes of Russia." Izvestiya Russian Academy of Sciences: Geographic Series 5:64–73. Online (in Russian) at https://izvestia.igras.ru/jour/article/view/93/89v.

Zwally, H., et al. (2015). "Mass Gains of the Antarctic Ice Sheet Exceed Losses." *Journal of Glaciology* 61, no. 230 (July):1019–36. Online at https://www.cambridge.org/core/journals/journal-of-glaciology/article/mass-gains-of-the-antarctic-ice-sheet-exceed-losses/983F196E23C3A6E7908E5FB32EB42268.

Chapter 11

The Role of Energy in Human Thriving

by Timothy D. Terrell

Chapter Summary

The average American family 150 years ago spent more than 90 percent of its income on essentials for survival. Today it requires only about 37 percent, thereby freeing up significant income for improved quality of life. This was only possible with abundant, reliable, and affordable energy. Developing countries seek similar economic progress and improved living standards.

Almost 40 percent of the world burns biomass for heat and cooking, and about 3.8 million people die annually of illnesses resulting from indoor air pollution. Other costs from low energy availability include lost time for education and missed income generation necessary for economic growth, not to mention lost wildlife habitats and other environmental impacts these societies cannot afford to address.

Rather than contributing to effective power projects, wealthy countries and development banks impose ill-conceived energy policies that aggressively limit fossil fuel investments and instead emphasize unreliable, expensive, and inadequate wind and solar. Developing countries see their hypocrisy and view the low-development trap as new colonialism and carbon imperialism. They also note the convenient ideological cover for crony-capitalist wealth accumulation that defeats benefits of well-functioning markets and the rule of law. If the correct priority is facilitation of faster economic progress and human prosperity for all, such policies should be set aside. They cannot be shown to change the CO_2 trend anyhow.

The industrialized world tends to forget its own development history. Despite voicing concern for the world's poor, it often fails to understand the energy challenges now faced by the developing world. Industrialized nations, having long ago provided cheap and productivity-enhancing electricity for themselves, now tend to focus discussions about energy on issues of environmental sustainability rather than access. Whether from ignorance, environmentalist fervor, or crony-capitalistic avarice, these wealthier countries have been using influence over international aid and lending organizations to induce the developing world to sacrifice access to energy, and all its benefits to human prosperity, health, and life, for notions of sustainability.

In poorer nations, applicants for aid from foreign governments and NGOs recognize that they must use the vocabulary of environmental sustainability in their appeals. But some sustainability goals may be a poor fit for developing economies. Too often, the policies advocated by the richer nations of the world have a paternalistic and condescending quality. Energy that is clean according to the metrics of the industrialized world is sometimes beyond the economic reach of the poor. If we care about the conquest of poverty in developing economies, it behooves us to remember our own past.

In the mid-1870s, a U.S. census survey of wage-earning families in Massachusetts revealed that out of an average income of $763 per month, the average family spent $694, or over 90 percent, on essentials—what the census categorized as "subsistence, clothing, rent, and fuel" (U.S. Census 1975, 322). Comparisons of consumer spending across long spans of time are difficult, but according to the Bureau of Labor Statistics, the average American family in 2019 spent $8,169 on food, $20,679 on housing, and $1,883 on clothing, out of an average pre-tax income of $82,852—about 37 percent (BLS 2021). Adding health care, which was not a separate category in the 1874–75 survey and was part of "sundry expenses," brings the 2019 percentage to 43 percent. ("Housing" in current BLS surveys includes items that would have been included in "sundry expenses" in the 1874–75 survey, such as furniture and home maintenance.)

Not only have the quality and quantity of food, housing, and clothing improved greatly since the late 1800s, but much income has been freed up for spending on goods and services that are not essential for bare survival but improve the quality of life, such as arts and entertainment, education, vacation travel, and communication with distant family and friends.

This vast improvement in living standards since the 1870s has been accompanied by a twenty-one-fold increase in total primary energy consumed by the nation and an approximately 250 percent increase in per capita primary energy consumption (EIA 2012, 341; EIA 2021, 3)—and could not have taken place otherwise. Abundant, reliable, affordable, and relatively clean energy is both a contributor to household incomes in the United States and other developed countries and a consequence of that prosperity. As energy usage increases, extreme poverty declines, and in the countries that use the most energy, extreme poverty has almost completely disappeared (Figure 11.1). Energy is thus a key ingredient in human thriving, and making energy more affordable worldwide is critical to reducing global poverty and improving human development (Pîrlogea 2012; Jeremiah, Adiat, and Ekong 2019). In this chapter, we consider the path of energy-supported development, the consequences of developed-nation opposition to low-cost fuels, and the problems of centrally planned energy policies.

The Energy Ladder

While we see encouraging technological progress that may allow a less stark trade-off between *cheap* and *clean* energy than prevailed from the late 1700s to the mid-1900s, energy usage is typically marked by steps up an "energy ladder" (Figure 11.2, on page 247). With faster economic progress facilitated by cheap energy, the world's poor can move more quickly up the ladder toward cleaner energy sources—and enjoy higher living standards in several dimensions. And yet the industrialized world sometimes advocates for ill-conceived energy policies in the developing world that would slow economic growth rates, compromising both energy availability and environmental quality.

Global health is linked to energy availability and source type, with energy poverty being responsible for millions of deaths each year. Without access to reliable electric power or liquid fuels, around three billion people worldwide use biomass (for example, wood, charcoal, dung, crop waste) to heat their homes and cook their food. The concentrated toxins and particulates in these indoor spaces can damage lungs and eyes and create other health problems. The World Health Organization

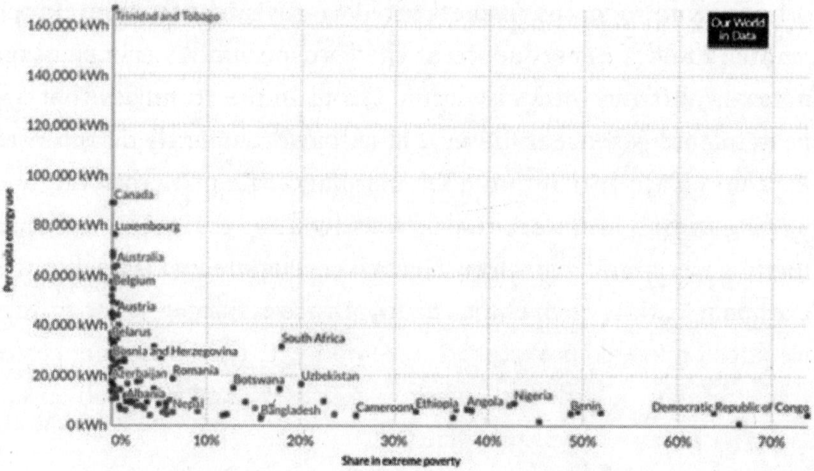

Figure 11.1. Energy Use and Extreme Poverty: Energy use per capita versus share of population in extreme poverty, 2015. Per capita energy use is measured in kilowatt-hours (kWh) per year. Extreme poverty is defined as living within a consumption (or income) level below 1.90 international dollars per day. International dollars are adjusted for price differences between countries and price changes over time (inflation). *Sources: Data from International Energy Agency via World Bank; graph by Our World in Data, licensed under Creative Commons (https://creativecommons.org/licenses/by/4.0/legalcode.en).*

(WHO) estimated in 2018 that 3.8 million people—mostly women, children, and the elderly who spend disproportionate time indoors—die each year from respiratory illnesses and other diseases caused by indoor air pollution (Gordon et al. 2014; Aemro, Moura, and Almeida 2021).

Additionally, biomass energy sources often require the expenditure of significant amounts of time from members of the household—woodcutting, gathering crop waste, and so forth. This is time that could be spent in income-earning activities or in education. Affordable, readily available energy means that households are able to avoid toxic indoor environments, spend more time in education and productive employment, and benefit from cheaper household lighting and cooking.

Considering the opportunity costs of biomass, it can be far more expensive than modern energy sources. There are also indirect impacts on human health and life satisfaction. For example, as reliable energy infrastructure is brought online, higher-paying, safer manufacturing jobs can replace agricultural jobs. But building electric power grids and natural gas pipelines for reliable baseload power requires immense amounts of capital. This in turn requires economic growth. But the developing world is often pushed to adopt policies that slow that growth and force prolonged poverty.

Do as I Say, Not as I Do: The Hypocrisy of Energy Colonialism

All the world was once energy poor, relying on energy sources that created indoor (and outdoor) air pollution as well as requiring extensive land conversion. Pre-modern Europe obtained about half of its power from animal muscle—mainly horses and oxen used in plowing and pulling wagons—and another fourth from wood (Keay 2007, 5). The rest came from water, human muscle, peat, and wind. Estimates suggest that Europe employed about 15 GW of power, largely in the production of food and heat for homes. This was a lot of power relative to the amount of economic output generated at the time. Though it is difficult to measure GDP with accuracy in centuries past, one study indicates that "it is very probable that the energy intensity of Shakespearean England, measured in terms of joules per unit of GDP, was higher than that of the UK today" (Tooze and Warde 2005; cf. Warde 2007). And though most of pre-modern Europe's energy sources were what we would call "renewable," the environment was substantially changed by these energy demands. One study shows that each European required about five acres to meet energy needs (Warde and Lindmark 2006), and another notes the impact on the land: "During the late twelfth and

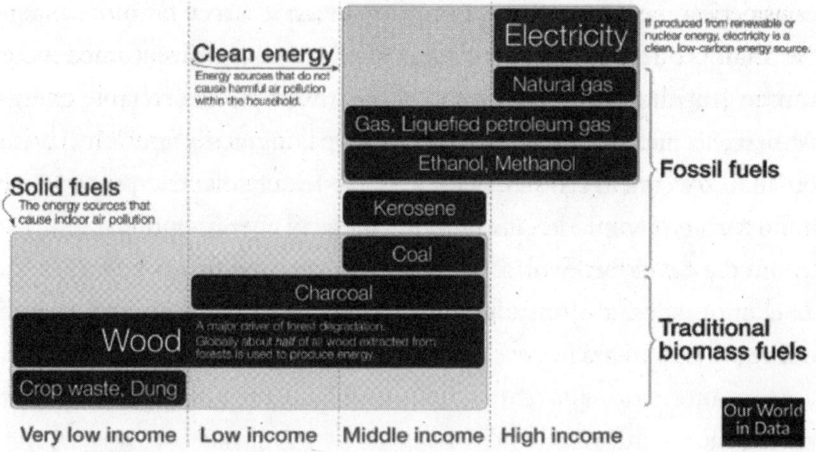

Figure 11.2. The Energy Ladder. Dominant energy source for cooking and heating, by level of income. *Data sources: World Health Organization, Our World in Data. Chart by Our World in Data, licensed under Creative Commons (https://creativecommons.org/licenses/by/4.0/legalcode.en), courtesy of Max Roser, adapted.*

thirteenth centuries, Europe rapidly cut down its forests, consumed its timber, and burned its brushwood for fuel" (Fischer 1996).

The Industrial Revolution would bring new sources of energy and, with them, rapid advancements in the standard of living, as well as higher life expectancy. Coal became the dominant fuel of the Industrial Revolution, and although burning coal was inevitably dirty (though, because of its much higher energy density, it was cleaner than biomass per unit of energy generated), its adoption—perhaps surprisingly—brought environmental benefits. In Europe, since coal substituted for firewood and animal muscle, the need to clear land for grazing and animal fodder was reduced, and deforestation slowed. Tilling and other land-use change can lead to the release of carbon dioxide and methane (Post and Kwon 2008, Terrell 2020), so for those concerned about such emissions, the shift to coal did not produce the net effects (increased greenhouse gas emissions) that might be imagined. (As Keay has noted, "[T]he renewables-based energy economy was...not a low carbon system" [2007, 10].) Furthermore, the economic growth this transportable energy source generated eventually led to alternatives that tended to be cleaner. At first this meant petroleum, its derivative liquid fuels, and natural gas, but in the twentieth century, nuclear, photovoltaic solar cells, and modern wind turbines would be added to the range of energy options.

In the developed world, energy sources moved up the energy ladder as economic conditions changed and technology improved. But for many policymakers in developed countries today, and their supporters among international organizations and industry groups, this efficient progression—informed and driven largely by market forces—is not for poorer countries to follow.

In 2020, UN Secretary General António Guterres called for India to stop investing in coal-fired power immediately, which, according to scholars from two Indian think tanks, "amounts to asking for the virtual de-industrialization of India, and stagnation in a low-development trap for the vast majority of its population" (Jayaraman and Kanitkar 2020).

Former Indian chief economic adviser Arvind Subramanian has called this anti–fossil fuel push "carbon imperialism" (Prasad 2017), and Indian prime minister Narendra Modi has complained of a new colonialism, in which the developed countries of the world, having used fossil fuels to achieve prosperity, now promote energy policies that would deny growth to countries like his own. Speaking at an Indian Constitution Day event not long after the 2021 international climate conference in Glasgow, Modi said,

> Attempts are made to shut the path and resources for developing nations through which developed nations reached where they are today....In past decades, a web of different terminologies was spun for this. But the aim has always been one to stop the progress of developing nations. The issue of the

> environment is also being...hijacked for this purpose. We saw an example of this in the recent COP26 Summit....Today no nation exists as a colony to any other nation. [That] doesn't mean that [the] colonial mindset ended. (Jayaraj 2021)

"If we talk of absolute cumulative emissions," Modi continued, "developed nations caused 15 times more emissions than India since 1850. Still, India is lectured on environmental conservation." Modi also pointed out that, "Sadly, we also have such people in our country who stall the development of the nation in the name of freedom of expression without understanding the aspirations of the nation. Such people don't bear the brunt, but those mothers who get no electricity for their children bear it" (Jayaraj 2021; *Times of India* 2021).

Nigeria's former finance minister Kemi Adeosun has voiced the same concern:

> I am going to point fingers at multinational institutions and the West (for [their] double standard). A good example is the coal-fired power plants. In Nigeria, we have coal but we have power problem[s], yet we've been blocked because it is not green. It is hypocrisy because we have the entire western industrialisation built on coal energy; that is the competitive advantage that they have been using. Now, Africa wants to use coal and suddenly they are saying, "Oh, you have to use solar and wind (renewable energy)," which are the most expensive, after polluting the environment for hundreds of years. Now that Africa wants to use coal, they deny us. (Fadare 2019)

As Lakshman Guruswamy (2011, 140) has pointed out, "[A] disturbingly large swath of humanity is caught in a time warp." Lack of access to the energy alternatives that became common in the industrialized world in the twentieth century, or even earlier, has left the world's poor on the lower rungs of the energy ladder, and thereby with lower levels of human development (see Figure 11.3 in the color figures section between pages 240 and 241). While some developing countries, such as India, have readily available fossil fuels that could generate electricity to alleviate indoor air pollution and produce economic growth toward the top rungs, some advocacy groups suggest that it is preferable to shift directly to solar, wind, or other renewable sources of electric power.

The Tradeoffs of Energy

Since burning fossil fuels results in emissions, some of which are directly harmful to human health and others, perhaps, indirectly because they contribute to climate change, attempts to reduce their use might at first appear to be a morally and environmentally appropriate course of action, particularly from the point of view of industrialized nations. But for the energy-poor in developing countries, these moralistic pronouncements mean only prolonged poverty and disease, which impose greater risks to them than either type of emissions. To put it simply, critics of fossil fuels tend to focus only on their unintended harmful byproducts while ignoring their intended, and much greater, benefits.

Indiscriminate opposition to all fossil fuels in all applications is the kind of "carbon imperialism" that shows a reckless disregard for the needs of some of the world's poorest people. Liquefied petroleum gas (LPG), for example, is an important rung on the energy ladder for many poor countries, offering reductions in deforestation, faster economic growth, and significant reductions in the health problems associated with cooking with solid fuels (Tamba 2020). Expanding LPG access is an achievable goal in the near term, promising relatively rapid returns on investment. And yet, policymakers and environmental groups who want to end all fossil fuel extraction demand an end to LPG's use. Nigeria's vice president, Yemi Osinbajo, cautioned that pressure from wealthy nations to reduce investment in fossil fuels does not adequately account for the needs of the developing world:

> Such policies often do not distinguish between different kinds of fossil fuels, nor do they consider the vital role some of these fuels play in powering the growth of developing economies, especially in sub-Saharan Africa. . . .
>
> As development finance institutions try to balance climate concerns against the need to spur equitable development and increase energy security, the United Kingdom, the United States, and the European Union have all taken aggressive steps to limit fossil fuel investments in developing an[d] emerging economies.
>
> The World Bank and other multilateral development banks are being urged by some shareholders to do the same. The African Development Bank, for instance, is increasingly unable to support large natural gas projects in the face of European shareholder pressure. (Ugbodaga 2021)

More-productive, higher-paying jobs are desperately needed in the developing world, and for that, an uninterrupted flow of electricity is vital. Investment in solar and wind has become increasingly viable, especially for small-scale needs, but they do not provide the necessary reliable baseload power. Producing that requires power plants that use coal or gas, on which the United States itself still depends for most of its electricity, not to mention nuclear plants. Assurances of compromise by international development finance agencies to people like Osinbajo are best looked at with skepticism. Development banks have already effectively stopped funding coal-fired power plants, and gas appears to be next, regardless of its profound benefits for poorer countries. While saying they are willing to fund limited natural gas power plants in developing countries, the burden of fighting the anti–fossil fuel trend to get projects approved means a ban in practice, if not on paper (Moss 2021). Trophy renewable energy projects that satisfy shareholders thousands of miles away are of limited use in economies where extreme poverty is still widespread. A senior official at Tamil Nadu Generation and Distribution Corporation, an electric utility in India, emphasized the inability of renewables to power a growing economy: "We cannot depend on just solar and wind. You can have the cake of coal and an icing of solar" (Reuters 2021).

The push for renewables has other adverse consequences for the developing world. While many may argue that modern renewable energy technologies are better for the environment, the case is not as open-and-shut as many believe, as other authors in this book argue (see chapters 12–16). Slower, more expensive development of renewable energy, when energy from fossil fuels could be distributed more quickly, means deforestation in poor areas. "People cut down our trees because they don't have electricity," observed Ugandan Gordon Mwesigye. "Our country loses its wildlife habitats, as well as the health and economic benefits that abundant electricity brings" (Spencer, Driessen, and Beisner 2005). These are some of the hidden costs of holding back energy development around the world.

Alongside locals searching for more available, and more dangerous, fuels, the renewable technology itself can lead to serious environmental problems at different stages of its life cycle. This begins with the mining and processing of raw materials that go into wind turbines and solar panels—a highly polluting process that takes place largely in developing countries and often uses child or forced labor (Hongqiao 2016; Kara 2023)—and ends with the disposal of worn out or degraded equipment. Ironically, the construction of wind turbines requires the use of large amounts of concrete, steel, and carbon fiber, the production of which currently requires energy-dense fossil fuels. Then there is the end-of-life disposal problem. Solar panel waste alone is expected to be about 78 million metric tons by 2050 (Weckend, Wade, and Heath 2016), and waste from other components of renewable technologies, such as wind turbines and battery storage units, will add many more tons of waste. Poorer countries typically send the waste to a landfill rather than recycle it, since they do not have the facilities to carry out recycling effectively. Some of the waste is toxic, such as cadmium, lead, and silicon tetrachloride (Bronstein 2020).

Bootleggers and Baptists in Climate Policy

Developing nations are fighting not only misconceptions among well-intentioned international organizations, but also powerful incentives driven by the interests of industry groups in wealthy countries. For example, the U.S. International Development Finance Corporation approved $500 million of loans to an American solar module manufacturer for the construction of a factory in Tamil Nadu, India (USAID 2021). Are purely environmental concerns driving the transfer of U.S. taxpayer dollars to a U.S. company, or have industry representatives simply found a convenient ideological cover for what is nothing more than a crony-capitalistic wealth transfer? Could fossil fuel companies themselves be using climate policy as a way to gain market share? A recent report produced jointly by Indian think tank TERI and Royal Dutch Shell outlined a plan for India to achieve net-zero carbon emissions by 2050. Optimistically projecting developments of new industries like green hydrogen, and—even more optimistically—counting on the Indian government to efficiently steer the economy with subsidies, taxes, regulations, and infrastructure development, the report's strategy seems to be based more on imagination than economic reality. That is, if the strategy is really about net-zero carbon and not about enlisting the Indian government to fight a competitor. Unsurprisingly, given that Royal Dutch Shell is an oil and natural gas producer, its plan to transition to net-zero carbon emissions in India involves an increase in natural gas usage for decades to come as policy pushes industry away from coal (Dhawan and Prasad 2021).

It would not be the first time that environmental policy was used to stifle competition. Economist Bruce Yandle (1983, 1999) has likened alliances between environmental advocacy groups and industry to the benefits both religious groups (motivated by the desire to reduce alcohol consumption) and illegal producers of alcohol (motivated by the desire for higher prices for their product) receive from regulations that suppress alcohol sales. This "bootleggers and Baptists" framework helps us understand that when industries support regulations that restrict their own activities, it could be "rent-seeking" behavior—using politically created barriers to exclude competition and raise their own profits (Stigler 1971; Buchanan and Tullock 1975; Peltzman 1976; Buchanan 1980; McChesney 1997). This could be the driving force behind, for example, hazardous waste incinerators funding environmental groups that sued competitors using the Clean Air Act (Terrell and Barnett 2001, 26–29), large light bulb manufacturers lobbying governments to ban incandescent light bulbs (Young 2011), or city governments outlawing new gas stations in the name of climate change (Mitchell 2021).

The Path Forward: Energy Efficiency and Market Economies

While per capita energy usage has increased since the beginning of the Industrial Revolution, energy consumption per unit of output (energy intensity) has fallen (O'Connor and Cleveland 2014, 7978). As the dominant share of output shifts from manufacturing to less energy-intense services, and as technological progress allows for more energy-efficient manufacturing processes, it takes less energy to create a dollar of GDP. But lowering energy intensity may be difficult, particularly in countries where economic institutions do not create strong incentives to save and invest in modern energy infrastructure.

Ultimately, then, resolving energy poverty—on our way to alleviating poverty in general—is linked to institutional change. History has shown that some of the most effective institutions for promoting economic growth are well-functioning markets and the rule of law. While some increases in energy efficiency may be seen even in the least market-friendly countries, shifting toward markets generally facilitates a faster progression toward lower energy intensity.

The relatively rapid shift toward markets among some Eastern European countries in the 1990s provided an opportunity to see the impact of marketization more clearly. Under communism, technological progress was slow (and partly dependent on employing innovations from non-communist countries). Highly polluting and inefficient factories were kept open, and energy prices were set artificially low by the government for political reasons. Prices were political fiction rather than reflections of real consumer priorities or the availability of various resources. Manufacturers thus used obsolete and wasteful production processes to make goods that were chosen by political officials rather than by consumers. Free markets incentivized entrepreneurs to innovate and meet needs efficiently, without ham-fisted interference from poorly informed and corrupt bureaucracies. Before market reforms, the energy consumed by the transition economies per dollar of GDP was four to eight times that of the OECD (Organization for Economic Cooperation and Development) countries (Gray 1995). A study covering the period 1990–2010 found significant energy efficiency improvements in these economies as central planning gave way to markets (Nepal, Jamasb, and Tisdell 2014). For the developing world, moving toward market institutions could lead to the kind of capital accumulation that allows for the construction of initially expensive networks like power grids and natural gas pipelines.

Market reform—moving toward freer markets—is easier said than done. Well-functioning markets are typically rooted in cultural habits and perceptions of work, trade, and wealth, and these may change only slowly. The temptation is ever present to bypass markets and force change, imposing a vision of human thriving through top-down political institutions. This is a mistake. Politicians and their friends in developmental and environmental organizations should resist the urge to tinker with developing economies, which can ill afford the waste inherent in politicized central planning. Foreign aid is no substitute for growth—especially when the aid may itself incentivize the destruction of efficient market functioning (Moyo 2009). Centrally planned industrial policy, whether linked to climate goals or not, often leads to fruitless dead ends while more promising ventures get crowded out, as Japan experienced following World War II:

> In the 1950s, MITI [Ministry of International Trade and Industry] attempted to prevent a small firm from acquiring manufacturing rights from Western Electric to produce semiconductors. The firm persisted and was eventually allowed to acquire the technology. That firm, Sony, went on to become a highly successful consumer electronics company. MITI also attempted to prevent firms in the auto industry from entering the export market and tried to force ten firms in this industry to merge into two: Nissan and Toyota. These attempts failed, and automobile manufacturing went on to become one of Japan's most successful industries. (Powell 2021)

Thus, what may seem like an acceleration of technological progress via subsidies and other policy inducements may actually slow improvement. Even energy subsidies that are intended to favor the poor may have adverse consequences, as one study of Yemeni energy poverty has indicated (El-Katiri and Fattouh 2011, 16–20). While the authors stopped short of recommending that subsidies be abolished and recommended other kinds of government intervention, several problems common to central planning came to light. The study indicated that (1) energy subsidies reduce incentives for suppliers to expand their infrastructure or improve reliability, (2) price distortion creates new incentives for people to shift resources in directions the planners did not foresee, (3) energy subsidies can encourage overconsumption, and (4) many of the benefits end up in the hands of the nonpoor.

Empowering government to steer the economy may simply encourage interest groups to use policies to quash competitors rather than promote growth and environmental quality. And even if elected officials and bureaucracy staffs are somehow able to resist the siren call of lobbyist dollars and the temptation to abuse their power to promote their personal objectives, the requisite information to make appropriate decisions will be elusive. As the Austrian economist Ludwig von Mises pointed out over a century ago, rejecting markets means rejecting the information about individual priorities that markets provide and replacing the plans that individuals make for their own lives with the plans strangers make for them. His student Friedrich Hayek, who won the Nobel Prize in economics in 1974, argued that central planners, however brilliant, cannot know what they would need to know to make efficient decisions for society because of the difficulties in communicating some of the most important information (Hayek 1945). This is no less true when central planning is centered on environmental quality.

Conclusion

Moving up the energy ladder toward abundant, reliable, and lower-cost energy means, first, that we avoid top-down regulatory approaches that cut the lower rungs off the ladder for the world's poor. Expensive clean energy may be out of reach in the near term for people using traditional biomass fuels. The wealthier countries of the world would do well to put aside their "carbon imperialism" and recognize that fossil fuels could improve health for those afflicted by indoor air pollution and generate economic growth. Growth, in turn, allows for the expansion of electric grids and cleaner, life-promoting technologies that the developed world now enjoys. Whether the intentions of the climate policymakers are pure or corrupted by industry lobbyists, their propensity for rejecting market signals slows growth and prolongs poverty. As Yemi Osinbajo (2021) wrote, "[O]ur citizens cannot be forced to wait for battery prices to fall or new technologies to be created in order to have reliable energy and live modern, dignified lives."

If we seek human thriving for the whole world, we would do well to resist climate central planning and the rent-seeking of well-connected industry groups. Instead, let us respect the individuals in developing countries who can find a better path than we might imagine. Politicians, scientists, and activists should remember that relief from energy poverty in India, Nigeria, Yemen, and other developing countries is likely to originate in the same changes that relieved energy poverty in the developed world: movement toward beneficial institutions that respect individual and national aspiration, and freedom.

References

Aemro, Y. B., P. Moura, and A. T. Almeida (2021). "Inefficient Cooking Systems a Challenge for Sustainable Development: A Case of Rural Areas of Sub-Saharan Africa." *Environment, Development, and Sustainability* 23, no. 10 (October): 14697–721. Online at https://ideas.repec.org/a/spr/endesu/v23y2021i10d10.1007_s10668-021-01266-7.html.

Arto, I., et al. (2016). "The Energy Requirements of a Developed World." *Energy for Sustainable Development* 33 (August): 1–13.

Online at https://www.sciencedirect.com/science/article/pii/S0973082616301892.

Bronstein, K. (2020). "The Good, Bad, and Ugly about Renewable Energy in Developing Countries." RTI International, June 11. Online at https://www.rti.org/insights/renewable-energy-developing-countries.

Buchanan, J. M. (1980). "Rent Seeking and Profit Seeking." In *Toward a Theory of the Rent-Seeking Society*, edited by J. Buchanan, R. Tollison, and G. Tullock. College Station, Texas: Texas A&M University Press.

Buchanan, J. M., and G. Tullock (1975). "Polluters' Profit and Political Response: Direct Controls versus Taxes." *American Economic Review* 65, no. 1 (March): 139–47.

BLS (2021). *Consumer Expenditure Surveys*. Bureau of Labor Statistics. Online at https://www.bls.gov/cex.

Dhawan, V., and N. Prasad (2021). *India: Transforming to a Net-Zero Emissions Energy System*. London: Shell International B.V.; New Delhi: The Energy and Resources Institute (TERI). Available at https://www.teriin.org/sites/default/files/2021-03/India_Transforming_to_a_net-zero_emissions_energy_system.pdf.

El-Katiri, L., and B. Fattouh (2011). *Energy Poverty in the Arab World: The Case of Yemen*. Oxford, United Kingdom: Oxford Institute for Energy Studies. Online at https://www.oxfordenergy.org/publications/energy-poverty-in-the-arab-world-the-case-of-yemen.

EIA (Energy Information Administration) (2012). *Annual Energy Review 2011*. Washington, D.C.: U.S. Department of Energy. Online at https://www.eia.gov/totalenergy/data/annual/pdf/aer.pdf.

———. (2021). *April 2021 Monthly Energy Review*. Washington, D.C.: U.S. Department of Energy. Online at https://www.eia.gov/totalenergy/data/monthly/archive/00352104.pdf.

Fadare, S. (2018). "The Magic of Smokeless Coal." *The Nation*, December 27. Online at https://thenationonlineng.net/magic-smokeless-coal.

Fischer, D. (1996). *The Great Wave: Price Revolutions and the Rhythm of History*. Oxford, United Kingdom: Oxford University Press.

Gordon, S.B., et al. (2014). "Respiratory Risks from Household Air Pollution in Low and Middlc Income Countries." *The Lancet: Respiratory Medicine* 2, no. 10 (October): 823–60. Online at https://pubmed.ncbi.nlm.nih.gov/25193349.

Gray, D. (1995). *Reforming the Energy Sector in Transition Economies: Selected Experience and Lessons*. World Bank Discussion Papers, no. 296. Washington, D.C.: World Bank. Online at https://elibrary.worldbank.org/doi/abs/10.1596/0-8213-3424-7.

Guruswamy, L. (2011). "Energy Poverty." *Annual Review of Environment and Resources* 36 (November): 139–61. Online at https://www.annualreviews.org/doi/pdf/10.1146/annurev-environ-040610-090118.

Hayek, F. A. (1945). "The Use of Knowledge in Society." *American Economic Review* 35, no. 4 (September): 519–30.

Hongqiao, L. (2016). "The Dark Side of Renewable Energy." Earth Journalism Network, August 25. Online at https://earthjournalism.net/stories/the-dark-side-of-renewable-energy.

Jayaraj, V. (2021). "The East Slams the West's Climate 'Colonialism.'" Cornwall Alliance for the Stewardship of Creation, December 19. Online at https://cornwallalliance.org/2021/12/the-east-slams-the-wests-climate-colonialism.

Jayaraman, T., and T. Kanitkar (2020). "Reject This Inequitable Climate Proposal." *The Hindu*, September 18. Online at https://www.thehindu.com/opinion/lead/reject-this-inequitable-climate-proposal/article32634171.ece.

Jeremiah, E., Q. Adiat, and E. Ekong (2019). "Energy Usage, Internet Usage and Human Development in Selected West African Countries." *International Journal of Energy Economics and Policy* 9 (5): 316–21. Online at https://www.econjournals.com/index.php/ijeep/article/view/7611.

Johnson, R. A. (2005). *Six Men Who Built the Modern Auto Industry*. Saint Paul, Minnesota: Motorbooks.

Kara, S. (2023). *Cobalt Red: How the Blood of the Congo Empowers Our Lives*. New York: Macmillan.

Keay, M. (2007). *Energy: The Long View*. Oxford, United Kingdom: Oxford Institute for Energy Studies. Online at https://www.oxfordenergy.org/wpcms/wp-content/uploads/2010/11/SP20-EnergyThelLongView-MalcolmKeay-2007.pdf.

McChesney, F. S. (1997). *Money for Nothing: Politicians, Rent Extraction, and Political Extortion*. Cambridge, Massachusetts: Harvard University Press.

Mitchell, D. J. (2021). "The Economics of Unholy Alliances: Bootleggers and Baptists." International Liberty, March 2. Online at https://danieljmitchell.wordpress.com/2021/03/02/the-economics-of-unholy-alliances-bootleggers-and-baptists.

Moss, T. (2021). "The DFC, World Bank, and How a Nuanced Compromise on Gas Financing for Poor Countries Could Quietly Become a Blanket Ban (Hint: Ask the Kosovars)." Center for Global Development, September 27. Online at https://www.cgdev.org/blog/dfc-world-bank-and-how-nuanced-compromise-gas-financing-poor-countries-could-blanket-ban.

Moyo, D. (2009). *Dead Aid: Why Aid Is Not Working and How There Is a Better Way for Africa*. London: Allen Lane.

Nepal, R., T. Jamasb, and C. Tisdell (2014). "Market-Related Reforms and Increased Energy Efficiency in Transition Countries: Empirical Evidence." *Applied Economics* 46, no. 33 (August): 4125–36. Online at https://www.tandfonline.com/doi/abs/10.1080/00036846.2014.952894.

O'Connor, P. A., and C. J. Cleveland (2014). "U.S. Energy Transitions 1780–2010." *Energies* 7, no. 12 (November): 7955–93.

Osinbajo, Y. (2021). "The Divestment Delusion: Why Banning Fossil Fuel Investments Would Crush Africa." *Foreign Affairs*, August 31. Online at https://www.foreignaffairs.com/articles/africa/2021-08-31/divestment-delusion.

Peltzman, S., (1976). "Toward a More General Theory of Regulation." *Journal of Law and Economics* 19, no. 2 (August): 211–40. Online at https://www.jstor.org/stable/725163.

Pîrlogea, C. (2012). "The Human Development Relies on Energy: Panel Data Evidence." *Procedia Economics and Finance* 3:496–501. Online at https://www.sciencedirect.com/science/article/pii/S2212567112001864.

Post, W. M., and K. C. Kwon (2008). "Soil Carbon Sequestration and Land-Use Change: Processes and Potential." *Global Change Biology* 6, no. 3 (October): 317–27. Online at https://onlinelibrary.wiley.com/doi/abs/10.1046/j.1365-2486.2000.00308.x.

Powell, B. (2021). "Japan." Econlib.org. Accessed Dec. 27, 2021. Online at https://www.econlib.org/library/Enc/Japan.html.

Prasad, G. C. (2017). "Arvind Subramanian Slams Carbon Imperialism, Calls for Global Coal Alliance." Mint, August 17. Online at https://www.livemint.com/Politics/obWqbtfIao8hmrs8tpezTN/Arvind-Subramanian-slams-carbon-imperialism-calls-for-globa.html.

Reuters (2021). "INSIGHT: COP26 Aims to Banish Coal but Asia Is Building Hundreds of Power Plants to Burn It." Energyworld.com, November 1. Online at https://energy.economictimes.indiatimes.com/news/coal/insight-cop26-aims-to-banish-coal-but-asia-is-building-hundreds-of-power-plants-to-burn-it/87450532\.

Spencer, R. W., P. K. Driessen, and E. C. Beisner (2005). *An Examination of the Scientific, Ethical, and Theological Implications of Climate Change Policy.* Collierville, Tennessee: Cornwall Alliance for the Stewardship of Creation. Online at http://www.cornwallalliance.org/docs/an-examination-of-the-scientific-ethical-and-theological-implications-of-climate-change-policy.pdf.

Stigler, G. J. (1971). "The Theory of Economic Regulation." *Bell Journal of Economics and Management Science* 2, no. 1 (Spring): 3–21. Online at https://www.jstor.org/stable/3003160.

Tamba, J. G. (2020). "LPG Consumption and Economic Growth, 1975–2016: Evidence from Cameroon." *International Journal of Energy Sector Management* 15, no. 1 (October): 195–208. Online at https://www.researchgate.net/publication/346155769_LPG_consumption_and_economic_growth_1975-2016_evidence_from_Cameroon.

Terrell, T. D. (2020). "Carbon Flux and N- and M-Shaped Environmental Kuznets Curves: Evidence from International Land Use Change." *Journal of Environmental Economics and Policy* 10, no. 2 (August): 155–74. Online at https://www.tandfonline.com/doi/abs/10.1080/21606544.2020.1809527.

Terrell, T. D., and A. H. Barnett (2001). "Economic Observations on Citizen-Suit Provisions of Environmental Legislation." *Duke Environmental Law Policy Forum* 12, no. 1 (Fall): 1–38. Online at https://scholarship.law.duke.edu/delpf/vol12/iss1/1.

Times of India (2021). "Breaking News Live Updates: 'India Is Lectured on Environmental Conservation,' PM Slams Colonial Mindset." November 26. Online at https://timesofindia.indiatimes.com/india/breaking-news-live-updates-india-and-world-november-25/liveblog/87918494.cms.

Tooze, A., and P. Warde (2005). "A Long Run Historical Perspective on the Prospects for Uncoupling Economic Growth and CO_2 Emissions." Submission to *Stern Review*, December. The National Archives (United Kingdom). Online at https://webarchive.nationalarchives.gov.uk/ukgwa/+/http://www.hm-treasury.gov.uk/media/2/1/climatechange_drjatooze_1.pdf.

Ugbodaga, K. (2021). "Why LPG Should Be Transition Fuel in Developing Countries—Osinbajo." *PM News*, December 7. Online at https://pmnewsnigeria.com/2021/12/07/why-lpg-should-be-transition-fuel-in-developing-countries-osinbajo.

USAID (2021). "On DFC Financing for First Solar." Press Release. U.S. Agency International Development, December 7. Online at https://www.usaid.gov/news-information/press-releases/dec-07-2021-dfc-financing-first-solar.

US Census (1975). "Consumer Income and Expenditures: Family and Individual Income (Series G 1-415)." Census.gov. Online at https://www2.census.gov/library/publications/1975/compendia/hist_stats_colonial-1970/hist_stats_colonial-1970p1-chG.pdf?#.

Warde, P. (2007). "Facing the Challenge of Climate Change: Energy Efficiency and Energy Consumption." History and Policy, October 19. Online at https://www.historyandpolicy.org/policy-papers/papers/facing-the-challenge-of-climate-change-energy-efficiency-and-energy-consump.

Warde, P., and M. Lindmark (2006). "Energy and Growth in the Long Run." Proceedings of XIV International Economic Congress, Helsinki, Finland.

Weckend, S., A. Wade, and G. Heath (2016). *End-of-Life Management: Solar Photovoltaic Panels* Abu Dhabi: International Renewable Energy Agency (IRENA). Online at https://www.irena.org/-/media/Files/IRENA/Agency/Publication/2016/IRENA_IEAPVPS_End-of-Life_Solar_PV_Panels_2016.pdf.

Yandle, B. (1983). "Bootleggers and Baptists—The Education of a Regulatory Economist." *Regulation* 7, no. 3 (May). Online at https://www.cato.org/sites/cato.org/files/serials/files/regulation/1983/5/v7n3-3.pdf.

———. (1999). "Bootleggers and Baptists in Retrospect." *Regulation* 22, no. 3 (January): 5–7. Online at https://www.researchgate.net/publication/285439337_Bootleggers_and_Baptists_in_Retrospect.

Young, R. (2011). "CEI Podcast for July 14, 2011: The Incandescent Light Bulb Ban." Competitive Enterprise Institute, July 14. Online at http://www.openmarket.org/2011/07/14/cei-podcast-for-july-14-2011-the-incandescent-light-bulb-ban.

CHAPTER 12

Sources of Primary Energy

BY ROBERT A. HEFNER V

CHAPTER SUMMARY

Ninety-five percent of world energy today is sourced from coal, oil, gas, hydro, and nuclear. The balance comes from wind, solar, biofuels, and other renewables, which forty years ago provided less than 1 percent. Can an increasing share of renewables be expected in the future?

Sequential technological developments since the Industrial Revolution have consistently been towards more energy-dense fuels (energy per unit weight or volume). Natural gas, recently responsible for significant U.S. CO_2 reductions, has trillions of times the energy density of solar and a million times more than wind. The land used to produce power differs widely by fuel. In this regard, nuclear, natural gas,

> and fossil fuels are hundreds to thousands of times more efficient than wind or solar systems. Until now, no society has reverted to a less energy-efficient primary fuel.
>
> Forced energy replacements have only made progress with government subsidies and tax incentives, thereby distorting economic viability. Economically efficient energy sources are more likely to be successful in the long run. Looking ahead, other than nuclear, hydrogen has the highest energy density of candidate fuels, and a nuclear-hydrogen pairing might be the next naturally viable step forward to an energy future free of CO_2 concerns.

Bill McKibben, founder of 350.org, tweets regularly about fossil fuels ruining the world—from his petroleum-based iPhone (Apple Inc. 2022) and computer (SciMed n.d.). Twitter stores his tweets on its petroleum-based servers powered largely by fossil fuels. (If the information technology sector, of which Twitter is a part, were a country, it would be the third-largest consumer of electricity in the world—behind only China and the United States [Tinker 2019].) Women complain that fossil fuels cause devastating global warming by adding carbon dioxide to the atmosphere—while they wear petroleum-based yoga pants and sip carbonated beverages. The North Face refuses to put the logos of fossil fuel companies on its apparel, even though its product is 90 percent petroleum (Habeeb 2021; Smith 2021; North Face 2021).

Sometimes we are blissfully ignorant of our surroundings, no matter how vital they are. Hence the joke:

> Two young fish are passing by an older, wiser fish. "How's the water today, boys?" the old fish asks. The two young fish turn to each other, puzzled, as the older fish continues

swimming along. One of the younger fish finally gets the courage to ask, "What's water?"

Energy is to us what water is to fish. We depend on it for practically everything, but we're largely blind to it. That blindness is dangerous. It can lull us into accepting deadly ideas. Ridding us of that blindness is this chapter's purpose. It will (1) define energy and review and compare the sources of primary energies; (2) explain the importance of energy density and power density; (3) discuss energy's environmental impact; (4) review and compare government subsidies and tax incentives for different energy sources; and (5) draw lessons for the future.

What Is Energy, and What Are Its Primary Sources?

Energy is *the ability to do work*. Simple as that is, it should alert us to the importance of comparing how much work different energy sources can do.

Historically speaking, the world was largely a carbohydrate economy before the Industrial Revolution of the 1800s. Crops got energy from the Sun, converting a relatively small amount of it into carbohydrates. People and livestock ate those crops, and that gave them their energy. They used that energy to do work. People got some energy, too, from wind (via windmills and ships' sails) and running water (via watermills), but those played relatively minor roles.

Everything changed with the Industrial Revolution. Steam engines, powered initially by wood and later by coal, did work previously done by human and animal muscle. Those led to engines powered by petroleum, natural gas, hydroelectricity, and later uranium and other radioactive materials. Later fuels were more energy dense than earlier ones, meaning they contained more energy, capable of doing more work, per unit of weight. For example, typical dry wood contains about 15

Table 12.1
World Energy Consumption by Source, Percent, 1980 and 2019

Source	1980	2019
Oil	45.85	33.06
Coal	26.88	27.04
Gas	18.35	24.23
Nuclear	2.55	4.27
Hydropower	6.2	6.45
Wind	<0.01	2.18
Solar	0	1.11
Biofuels	0	0.68
Other renewables	0.18	1
Combined wind, solar, biofuels, & other renewables	<0.19	4.97
Combined thermal (oil, coal, gas, nuclear) and hydro	99.83	95.05

Source: Our World in Data.

Megajoules per kilogram (MJ/kg), and typical bituminous coal contains about 29 MJ/kg (Engineering ToolBox n.d.), which explains why train operators favored coal over wood.

Hydrocarbon fuels include coal, petroleum, natural gas (the three so-called "fossil fuels"), and ethanol. Pure hydrogen, too, can be burned as a fuel. These and nuclear power perform work by heating water into steam to drive turbines to generate electricity, or by internal combustion driving pistons and similar motor mechanisms. Turbines driven by running water also generate electricity. And turbines are very important to a power operator's ability to manage the grid because of what is called *grid inertia*.

Grid inertia is a form of storing energy that is used to address imbalances between supply and demand on electricity grids over very short time periods. In plain terms, hydrocarbon fuels and nuclear generate electricity with turbines, and it takes energy to get those large, heavy turbines spinning. When one form of energy goes down unexpectedly, inertia keeps those heavy turbines spinning, providing the grid operator time to balance the load before a brownout or blackout occurs. Managers of control rooms need time to react when something goes wrong. You can think of grid inertia as a large battery that stores energy for the grid operators if power goes offline.

In recent decades, growing numbers of people hope to substitute wind, solar, and other "renewable" fuels for fossil fuels, either because we risk running out of fossil fuels or because emissions from burning them are bad for the environment—especially carbon dioxide, blamed for causing global warming. The most important renewable fuels include biofuels (mainly for transport), wind, solar, and hydroelectric. Wind and solar, however, do not have grid inertia, so grid operators do not have time to react if the power goes offline. Thus, wind and solar inherently increase grid instability.

Despite the popularity of renewables, the composition of fuels powering global society has changed little since 1980 (Table 12.1).

Roughly one-third of primary energy goes toward generating electricity. Virtually all of wind, solar, nuclear, and coal energy is used for electricity generation. Approximately 38 percent of natural gas end-use is for electrical generation. By contrast, less than 1 percent of oil is allocated to generating electricity.

However, Table 1 is missing something—scale. The world consumed 87,599 terawatt-hours (TWh) in 1980 and 173,340 TWh in 2019 (Our World in Data). So, while thermal fuels plus hydropower declined slightly as a percent of total energy consumed over the past forty years (from 99.83 percent to 95.05 percent), they nearly doubled in total consumption—by 82,380 TWhs (Figure 12.1 in the color figures section between pages 240 and 241).

What are the end uses for oil and more than 60 percent of natural gas, then? The majority of each barrel of oil is used to create fuels for transportation as well as refined products that we would not otherwise have. Without petroleum we would not have internal combustion vehicles, contact lenses, glasses, solar panels, wind turbines, batteries, computers, nylon, and, ironically, electric vehicles—the list runs to thousands of items we all take for granted every day. Natural gas, too, is converted into drugs, fabrics, fertilizers, and many other products, and it is also used to manufacture many different chemicals. The impact of natural gas's refined products is paramount to modern society, too. For example, natural gas is used to produce two nitrogen-based fertilizers—ammonia and urea. As the Russian war on Ukraine has shown, when natural gas supplies are disrupted, so are fertilizers and, thus, food, so the war increased the risk of famine around the world.

The Importance of Energy Density

As we saw above, different fuels have different energy densities. The differences determine how much work a given quantity of them can do. Consider a barrel of oil for illustration. If energy is the ability to do work, how much work does a barrel of oil do?

A barrel of oil contains 5.8 million British Thermal Units (BTU) of energy (IPAA n.d.). A human in peak physical condition can generate about 750 BTU per hour of physical work. That means a barrel of oil can produce 7,733 hours of optimal human labor. At the January 2022 average wage of $26.92 per hour in the United States, that means a single barrel of oil generates $208,172.36 worth of work. Yet it sells for less than an equivalent amount of soda. How so? A barrel of oil contains 42 gallons; the average price of oil in 2021 was $67.99 per barrel, or $1.62 per gallon. At the time, Costco sold 8 liters of soda for $6, or $2.85 per gallon.

As people consider substituting wind or solar energy for fossil fuels, an important consideration is whether the energy derived from them must be used instantly when generated or stored for later use. Because wind and solar are intermittent (the wind doesn't always blow; the Sun doesn't always shine), electricity generated from them must be used instantly—or stored. If at a given moment the electric grid is receiving all the electricity needed, electricity from wind and solar must be stored for use at a later time. Electricity used in vehicles must be stored in batteries, too.

Compared with the energy density of oil, that of batteries is low. Consequently, battery storage is more expensive. Oil stores its own energy, known as *potential energy*, in a 42-gallon barrel that costs roughly $68 and weighs about three hundred pounds when full. A Tesla Powerwall 2 with equivalent energy storage capacity would cost $1.3 million (19,118 times as much) and weigh nearly 34,000 pounds (113.3 times as much). These cost and weight comparisons must be adjusted, of course, for the fact that you can only burn the oil once but can recharge the battery many times. What difference does that make? In Australia, Tesla warrants the Powerwall 2 for ten years or 37,800 kWh of throughput energy, or 2,800 charging cycles (Skyline Solar n.d.). This reduces the price ratio of the Powerwall 2 versus oil from 19,118:1 to 6.83:1 and changes the weight ratio from 113.3:1 to 0.04:1.

As the number of humans inhabiting this planet increases, more resources are required to keep them alive and flourishing. This is why energy density matters. The less dense an energy source is, the more of it is required to do a given amount of work; the more dense it is, the less of it is required. The comparative energy densities of primary fuels are captured well by Vaclav Smil (Figure 12.2, on p. 273). Note that solar, geothermal, and wind are not shown. Why? Because they are so

Table 12.2. Energy Density: Solar to Oil

Source	Joules per cubic meter
Geothermal	0.05
Wind at 10 mph (5 m/s)	7
Tidal water	0.5–50
Human	1,000
Fat (food)	30,000,000
Natural gas	40,000,000
Automobile unoccupied (5,000 lbs.)	40,000,000
Gasoline	10,000,000,000
Oil	45,000,000,000

Data source: Layton 2008.

energy diffuse that they don't even register on the perpendicular axis. Their inherent *lack* of energy is captured well in Table 12.2.

A typical human body has energy density equivalent to 1,000 joules per cubic meter. That is about 20–2,000 times greater than tidal water, 140 times greater than 10-mile-an-hour wind, and 667 million times greater than solar. Gasoline is ten *quadrillion* times more energy dense than solar radiation, one *billion* times more energy dense than wind and tidal water, and ten *million* times more energy dense than human power. And nuclear, depending on how highly enriched, is a hundred to a thousand times more energy dense than natural gas.

By substituting wind and solar for fossil fuels and nuclear, modern society would be moving backward toward an unreliable, carbohydrate economy dictated by the weather. Not surprisingly, then, no society

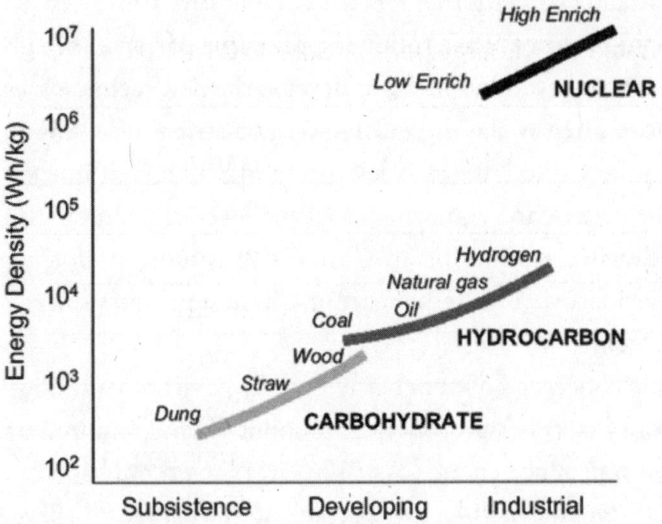

Figure 12.2. Energy density of primary fuels. *Figure source: Huber and Mills (2006), from data in Smil (1999) and Spletzer (1999). Courtesy of Basic Books/Hachette Book Group.*

in history has attempted to revert to a more energy-diffuse primary fuel—until recently.

Energy's Environmental Impact: Land Use

Pollution from extracting, refining, delivering, and using energy is what most people think of as energy's environmental impact, and it is important. However, in a phenomenon sometimes called the environmental transition, technological advances result in a pattern in which early development brings increased pollution, while later development reduces that even to below what it was at the start. As a result, pollution per unit of energy produced and used now is much, much lower than in decades or generations past. In wealthy, developed countries, it is already so slight that it poses comparatively little risk to health. Developing countries are following the same pattern, though at a faster rate, since they do not need to develop the new technologies but can use those already developed (Goklany 2007; Simon 1995). Coal burned in the United States is less polluting than coal burned in China due to American regulations and the level of technologies deployed. Offshoring production to China is thus more polluting, particularly considering that 85 percent of Chinese primary energy consumption is coal.

Many people concerned about energy and the environment, however, often overlook another problem: the amount of land required by various sources to produce energy. As Bill Gates's team published in *How to Avoid a Climate Disaster*, and in contrast to what most believe, wind and solar are very land-intensive (and therefore environmentally destructive) technologies.

Table 12.3 provides an opportunity to distinguish between energy density and power density. As Robert Bryce explains,

> *Power density* refers to the amount of *power* that can be harnessed in a given unit of volume, area, or mass. Examples . . . include horsepower per cubic inch, watts per square meter, and watts per kilogram. . . . *Energy density* refers to the amount of *energy* that can be contained in a given unit of volume, area, or mass. Common energy density metrics include Btu per gallon and joules per kilogram. (Bryce 2010, 40)

Energy density is the *amount* of energy per unit weight (gravimetric energy density) or volume (volumetric energy density) and is shown in Table 12.2. Energy density can explain many things in everyday life. For example, if you want to pack the minimum volume of food for a

Table 12.3. Land Use by Energy Source

Energy Source	Watts per square meter
Fossil fuels	500–10,000
Nuclear	500–1,000
Solar*	5–20
Hydropower (dams)	5–50
Wind	1–2
Wood and other biomass	Less than 1

*The power density of solar could theoretically reach 100 watts per square meter, but no one has accomplished this yet.

Source: Gates 2021.

mountain hike you take a granola bar (17 J/g), not carrots (1.7 J/g) (Smil 2010). *Power density* refers to the *rate* of energy release per unit of volume or weight. Smil argues that this definition should be measured in W/m^2 of the horizontal area of the required land or water surface rather than per unit of the working surface of a converter. This explains why a wind farm composed of 3 MW Vestas turbines with a rotor diameter of 112 meters and spaced six diameters apart will have a peak power density of 6.6 W/m^2. However, at a relatively high capacity factor of 30 percent (because wind speed is not always optimal), that is just 2.2 W/m^2, which is in line with Gates's research. Solar photovoltaic (PV) plants can generate electricity with a much higher power density than wind. Solar PV's power density is generally 10–20 W/m^2. But when all ancillary space requirements are included, the typical density range declines to 4–9 W/m^2 (Smil 2010). Therefore wind produces only 1–2 watts per square meter due to its energy-diffuse nature, and solar is

Table 12.4. Hydrocarbon Fuel Energy Content and CO_2 Emissions

	H:C Ratio	Energy Content (kJ/g)	CO_2 Released (mol/103kJ)
Ethanol	3:1	27.3	1.6
Coal	1:1	39.3	2.0
Petroleum	2:1	43.6	1.6
Natural gas	4:1	51.6	1.2
Hydrogen	-	120	-

Source: Anonymous n.d.

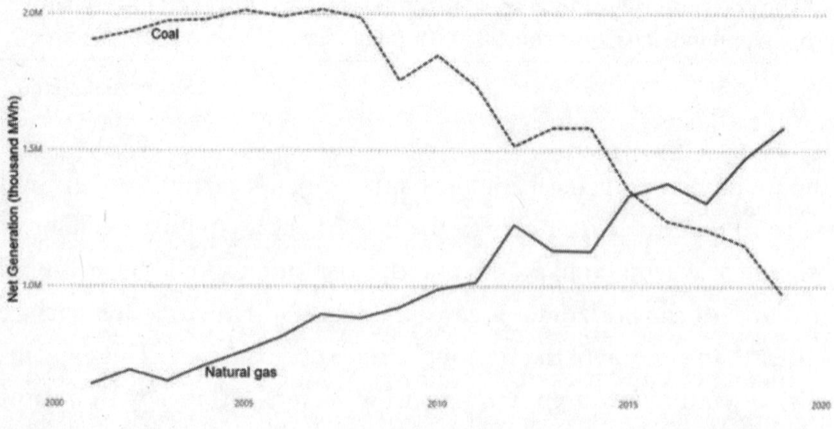

Figure 12.3. The inverse relationship between coal and natural gas consumption. *Source: Hefner.Energy, BP Statistical Review (2020). Used by permission.*

similarly abysmal. Natural gas is precisely the opposite, producing up to 10,000 W/m^2.

To meet President Biden's 2030 Net Zero electricity goals—before boosting demand by electrifying all our vehicles—the United States would have to cover the entire states of New York, California, and Vermont with turbines and panels to satisfy demand (Shellenberger 2021). And that is just for today's use; the EIA (U.S. Energy Information

Administration) projects electricity demand to explode from about 4 billion kilowatt-hours to about 5.5 billion kilowatt-hours by 2050 (EIA 2021a). If we say we care about the environment, land use should be pivotal to our understanding. Again, this metric is rooted in energy density.

Energy's Environmental Impact: Carbon Dioxide Emissions

The environment is also impacted by carbon dioxide. Each fuel has a different relationship to carbon dioxide emissions, as Table 12.4 illustrates.

For example, natural gas is 31 percent more energy dense, by weight, than coal. However, it emits nearly 50 percent less carbon dioxide than coal. That hydrogen does not contain carbon in its molecular formula while being the most prevalent molecule in the universe and more than twice the energy density of natural gas makes for a potentially game-changing formula.

Natural gas has been the driving force behind America's great decarbonization. As Figure 12.3 illustrates, there is a reduction in coal generation for every upward movement in gas generation.

Since about 2005, the combination of hydraulic fracturing and horizontal drilling—often simply called "fracking"—has enabled us to extract oil and natural gas from shale at declining costs. Since the Shale Revolution, the United States has lowered its overall CO_2 emissions by roughly the same percentage as Germany, but the United States bests Germany in reduction of CO_2 per capita by 14,500 percent (BP 2020). Thus, natural gas from shale is responsible for the world's most significant carbon dioxide emissions reduction. More importantly, instead of the German taxpayer paying $580 billion (Nelson and Czerwinski 2018), America's reduction was paid for without a single dollar of taxpayer funds.

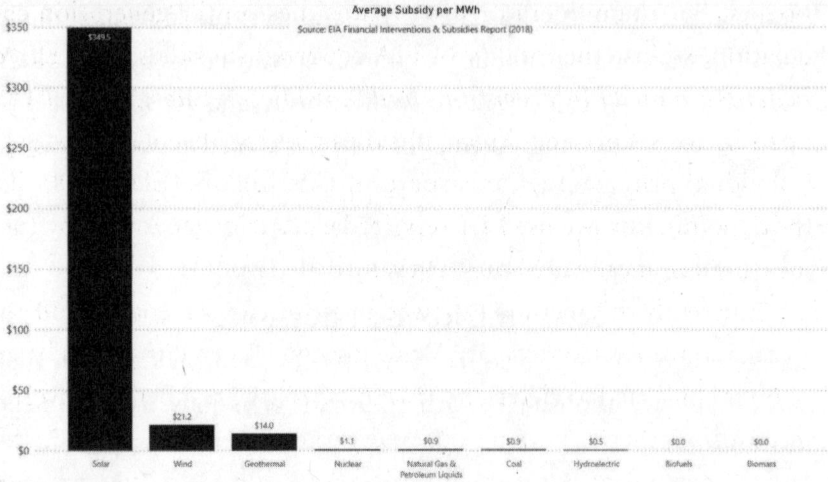

Figure 12.4. Subsidy per MWh by fuel. *Sources: EIA; Hefner.Energy (2021). Used by permission.*

Government Subsidies and Tax Incentives for Fossil Fuels versus Renewables

The cost of generating energy in usable form depends to a large extent on the energy density of the source. When certain products are too expensive, the government can subsidize them to make them more competitive in the marketplace. The energy field provides clear examples of this phenomenon, with billions of dollars in play. This makes it important to measure the effects of subsidies and tax incentives against amounts of energy delivered in return.

Recall that energy is the ability to do work. The EIA provides data to (a) measure how much the government subsidizes each fuel and (b) how much each fuel contributes to society in the form of power generation. The resulting metric is *subsidy per power generation unit*, or dollars per megawatt-hour (MWh).

Different groups define subsidies differently, causing much confusion. *Merriam-Webster* defines a subsidy as *a grant or gift of money*. However, the EIA expands the dictionary's definition to include tax breaks. For the numerator in our subsidies/power generation calculation, we use the totality of EIA-reported subsidies from *Direct Federal Financial Interventions and Subsidies in Energy Fiscal Year 2016* in 2018, covering direct subsidies plus tax incentives, for each individual primary fuel, measured in U.S. dollars (EIA 2018). For the denominator, we use EIA-reported electricity generation by fuel, measured in megawatt-hours (MWh).

Inherently this method is flawed because 100 percent of wind and solar is converted to electricity, while less than 1 percent of each barrel of oil is converted to electricity (EIA 2021b) (the rest being converted to gasoline, diesel, heating oil, and thousands of other products), and 38 percent of natural gas end-use is for electricity generation (EIA 2021c) (the rest being converted to drugs, fabrics, fertilizers, and many other products, and used in manufacturing many different chemicals). Thus, this method is heavily skewed in favor of wind and solar. But, since the EIA does not report total subsidies for natural gas and petroleum liquids independent of one another, we are forced to use this method. The resulting conclusions are nonetheless remarkable (Figure 12.4).

To provide context to these numbers, the average price of U.S. electricity in fiscal year 2020 was $66.60 per MWh., meaning taxpayers were *subsidizing* solar companies over five times the average price of electricity—and then paying again for it through their utility bills.

Some significant findings from Hefner.Energy's and EIA's research include:

- Despite receiving 73.61 percent of all federal subsidies in the United States, wind and solar only produced 5.4 percent of power generation in the most recent year reported.
- Solar receives 38,833 percent more subsidies per MWh than natural gas and petroleum liquids; wind receives

2,356 percent more subsidies per MWh than natural gas and petroleum liquids.

- Globally, fossil fuels account for 87 percent of energy supply yet only receive subsidies equal to 0.7 percent of global GDP (that is, work).
- In the three most recent years reported, direct subsidies (actual cash handouts) to natural gas and petroleum liquids totaled zero dollars from the U.S. government, while wind and solar received $14 billion (Hefner.Energy 2022). Billions have been lost in solar-industry bankruptcies over the years, including but not limited to Solyndra (Baker 2011), SoloPower (Groom 2020), Tonopah Solar Energy (Puko and Randles 2020), SolarWorld AG (Enkhardt 2018), Abound Solar (Reuters 2012), and Beacon Power (Hals and Rampton 2011), as well as in bankruptcies of other ventures pursued in the effort to reduce reliance on fossil fuels, like Fisker Automotive (Greene 2013) and A123 Systems (Seetharaman and Rascoe 2012).
- In an email to Hefner.Energy, the EIA confirmed that it is "not aware that there are any direct federal subsidies for generating electricity with petroleum liquids (or for natural gas)" (EIA, email to author, March 16, 2022).
- In the three most recent years reported, tax breaks provided to biofuels, wind, and solar amounted to $20 billion, dwarfing the $5 billion reported for the oil and gas industry.
- In the most recent fiscal year, natural gas and petroleum liquids were a tax break revenue source for the federal government—providing $940 million of federal income. As the EIA reported, "Natural gas and petroleum-related U.S. tax expenditures decreased from $2.3 billion in FY

2013 to an estimated revenue inflow (versus a positive tax expenditure) of $940 million in FY 2016, thus in aggregate becoming a set of revenue-generating tax provisions to the government in that fiscal year."

- Big Oil—comprising ExxonMobil, Chevron, Shell, and BP—is often targeted by political leaders for receiving "generous" subsidies. But Big Oil has already been excluded or severely limited from the two largest tax breaks. Percentage depletion was removed in 1975 (Cox and Wright 1976). Since 1986, oil and gas corporations have been able to deduct immediately only 70 percent of intangible drilling costs (IDCs—the equivalent of cost of goods sold [COGS] to other industries, 100 percent of which can be deducted immediately), spreading the balance over five years.

After all of this, remember, the method is already skewed, as explained above, in favor of wind and solar, so the actual contrasts are even more stark.

The findings from our research should not be surprising, if energy density is properly understood and respected. The energy density of nuclear, coal, oil, and natural gas provides the most benefit to society without requiring government intervention (while storing their own energy in the form of potential energy). Energy diffuse fuels like geothermal, wind, and, in particular, solar provide the least benefit to society in the form of reliable work and thus require government intervention (without the ability to inherently store their own energy).

Leveraging the Lessons of Energy Density for the Future

The EIA projects that global energy demand will increase 50 percent by 2050 (EIA 2019), mostly due to an ever-increasing global

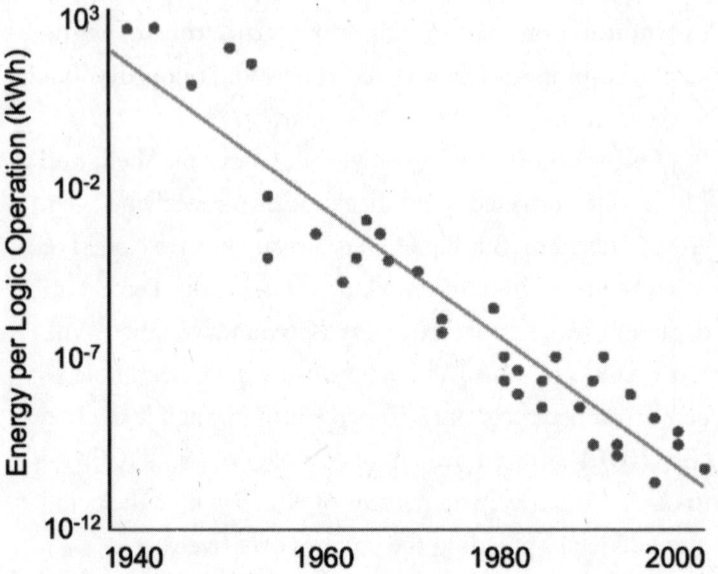

Figure 12.5. Energy use (kilowatt-hours) per logic operation. *Source: Isaac (2001), via Huber and Mills (2006). Courtesy of Basic Books/Hachette Book Group.*

population. It is also partly due to the Jevons paradox, which states that the more energy efficient we become, the more energy we will use. (Why? Because, as the law of demand in economics explains, people buy more of something at a lower price than a higher price, and increasing efficiency in producing something enables its price to fall.) The relationship between efficiency and consumption in computer processing illustrates the paradox.

As Figure 12.5 shows, the amount of energy it takes to perform a computation decreased by orders of magnitude from 1940 through 2000. But as Figure 12.6 shows, that resulted in explosive energy demand for computation.

As computer chips became one quadrillion times more efficient, their costs fell dramatically. Computers became more affordable and accessible to common people, whose demand for them, and hence for

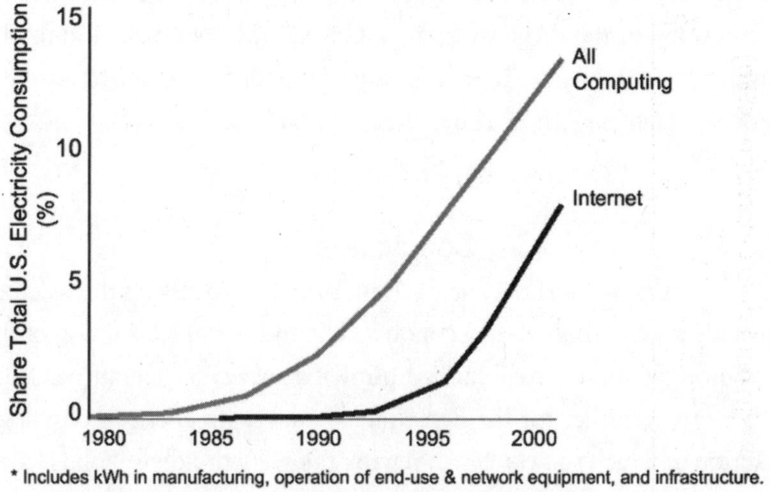

Figure 12.6. Share of total United States energy consumption by internet and all computing (1980–2000). *Source: Huber and Mills (2002) via Huber and Mills (2006). Courtesy of Basic Books/Hachette Book Group.*

the energy they use, consequently rose even faster than the chips' energy efficiency rose, thus increasing total energy demand.

Likewise, our homes have become much more energy efficient. Our lightbulbs have become incredibly efficient (LED technology), but they have also become less expensive and smaller, increasing the number of bulbs per home and the amount of time they are left on. Similar to households, transportation has become more efficient, yet we continue to demand more fuel to move more things around the world. So global energy demand is set to spike by 2050.

In the 170 years since 1850, mankind's energy use has progressed from very low-density sources like wood, hay, and dung (dominant for thousands of years) to increasingly dense sources like whale oil, coal, petroleum, natural gas, hydrogen, and nuclear. The demand that we replace the latter sources with wind and solar is a demand to regress to lower-density sources. If history is any indication, and the importance of energy density is to be leveraged, the energy transition of the future likely resides in the "Age of Energy Gases" (Hefner 2000), namely, hydrogen, which has the highest energy content by weight of any fuel other than nuclear—three times that of diesel.

Conclusion

Prior to the nineteenth century, humanity had to rely on the weather to provide for a carbohydrate economy. The Industrial Revolution of the 1800s brought about a step-change, allowing society to operate independently of the weather for the first time. This was an energy technology revolution in which society began relying upon energy-dense solids (coal) and liquids (petroleum) to power themselves into the future. During the twentieth century, technological breakthroughs in solids (nuclear) and liquids (hydroelectric) continued. However, it was the breakthrough with energy gases (natural gas and liquified natural gas) that began the ultimate energy transition. The "Grand Energy Transition" in fossil fuels moves from solids to liquids, and then to gases (Hefner 2009).

The importance of energy density for each of these primary fuels cannot be ignored. Energy density saved taxpayers billions of dollars, helped the Allies to win World War II, and provides unprecedented amounts of work (that is, wealth, which leads to freedom). Moreover, contrary to popular beliefs of the twenty-first century, the energy density of thermal energies (nuclear, petroleum, natural gas, and coal) protects the environment by eliminating the need for sprawling land use to meet the energy demands of modern society. While diffuse energies like wind and solar (including batteries) have a role in the energy ecosystem, any movement to adopt them as a baseload at the expense of other technologies contradicts centuries of precedent. The more society decides to lean on wind and solar, the more at-risk our energy systems are to the whims of the weather.

For thousands of years, literally from the beginning of human life through to the 1800s, society was underpinned by the limitations of physical labor. Technological breakthroughs in energy- and power-dense fuels have ushered in an era of global abundance never before imagined. Today, in large part because we take advantage of the energy and power densities of coal, oil, natural gas, and nuclear, child cancer survival, girls' school attendance, water quality, air quality, vaccines, the democratization of information, scientific breakthroughs, the amount of protected nature, women's rights, crop yields, literacy, and democracy are all at their highest levels in history. Conversely, bad things are at their lowest: percentage of humanity living in poverty, legal slavery, deaths due to war, child deaths, smallpox, child labor, deaths from natural disasters, and hunger.

An appreciation for the fundamentals of primary energy is paramount to society's continuing to thrive. These lessons must inform our national energy policies.

References

Anonymous (n.d.). "Energy From Fossil Fuels." Western Oregon University. Online at https://people.wou.edu/~courtna/GS361/Energy_From_Fossil_Fuels.htm.

Anonymous (2021). "Fossil Fuels Received $5.9 Trillion in Subsidies in 2020, Report Finds." Yale Environment 360, October 6. Online at https://e360.yale.edu/digest/fossil-fuels-received-5-9-trillion-in-subsidies-in-2020-report-finds.

Apple Inc. (2022). "Product Environmental Report: iPhone 14 Pro." Online at https://www.apple.com/environment/pdf/products/iphone/iPhone_14_Pro_PER_Sept2022.pdf.

Baker, D. R. (2011). "Solyndra Files Bankruptcy, Employees Sue." *San Francisco Chronicle*, September 7. Online at https://

www.sfgate.com/bayarea/article/solyndra-files-bankruptcy-employees-sue-2311147.php.

Beisner, E. C. (2014). *What Is the Most Important Environmental Task Facing American Christians Today?* Collierville, Tennessee: Cornwall Alliance for the Stewardship of Creation.

BP (2020). *Statistical Review of World Energy.* London: British Petroleum. Online at https://www.bp.com/en/global/corporate/energy-economics/statistical-review-of-world-energy.html.

Bryce, R. (2010). *Power Hungry: The Myths of "Green" Energy and the Real Fuels of the Future.* New York: PublicAffairs.

Cox, J. C., and A. W. Wright (1976). "The Impact of the Tax Reduction Act of 1975 on the Petroleum Industry." *Boston College Industrial and Commercial Law Review* 17, (5): 805–30. Online at https://lira.bc.edu/work/ns/ecd0e7ce-a6d1-4f7d-aa13-5e4dffb2503d.

Dayaratna, K. (2021). "Why 'Social Cost of Carbon' Is the Most Useless Number You've Never Heard Of." The Heritage Foundation. March 2. Online at https://www.heritage.org/energy-economics/commentary/why-social-cost-carbon-the-most-useless-number-youve-never-heard.

Dayaratna, K., R. McKitrick, and D. Kreutzer (2017). "Empirically Constrained Climate Sensitivity and the Social Cost of Carbon." *Climate Change Economics* 8, no. 2 (April): 1750006. Online at https://doi.org/10.1142/S2010007817500063.

EIA (2018). *Direct Federal Financial Interventions and Subsidies in Energy in Fiscal Year 2016.* Washington, D.C.: Energy Information Administration. Online at https://www.eia.gov/analysis/requests/subsidy/archive/2016/pdf/subsidy.pdf.

———. (2019). "EIA Projects Nearly 50% Increase in World Energy Usage by 2050, Led by Growth in Asia." Energy Information Administration, September 24. Online at https://www.eia.gov/todayinenergy/detail.php?id=41433.

———. (2021a). *Annual Energy Outlook 2021*. Washington, D.C.: U.S. Department of Energy. Online at https://www.eia.gov/outlooks/aeo/tables_side.php.

———. (2021b). "Oil and Petroleum Products Explained: Use of Oil." Energy Information Administration. Online at https://www.eia.gov/energyexplained/oil-and-petroleum-products/use-of-oil.php.

———. (2021c). "Natural Gas Explained: Use of Natural Gas." Energy Information Administration. Online at https://www.eia.gov/energyexplained/natural-gas/use-of-natural-gas.php.

———. (2023). "Federal Financial Interventions and Subsidies in Energy in Fiscal Years 2016–2022." Energy Information Administration, August 1. Online at https://www.eia.gov/analysis/requests/subsidy.

The Engineering ToolBox (n.d.). "Fuels—Higher and Lower Calorific Values." Online at https://www.engineeringtoolbox.com/fuels-higher-calorific-values-d_169.html.

Enkhardt, S. (2018). "SolarWorld files for Insolvency—Again." *PV Magazine*, March 28. Online at https://www.pv-magazine.com/2018/03/28/solarworld-files-for-insolvency-again.

FAO (2020). "Land Use in Agriculture by the Numbers." Food and Agriculture Organization of the United Nations, May 7. Online at https://www.fao.org/sustainability/news/detail/en/c/1274219.

Gates, B. (2021). *How to Avoid a Climate Disaster: The Solutions We Have and the Breakthroughs We Need*. New York: Alfred A. Knopf.

Goklany, I. M. (2007). *The Improving State of the World: Why We're Living Longer, Healthier, More Comfortable Lives on a Cleaner Planet*. Washington, D.C.: Cato Institute.

Greene, R., M. Mosk, and B. Ross (2013). "Energy Department 'Bet' on Fisker Automotive Ends in Bankruptcy." Center for Public Integrity,

November 27. Online at https://publicintegrity.org/environment/energy-department-bet-on-fisker-automotive-ends-in-bankruptcy.

Groom, N. (2020). "U.S. Solar Power Plant Backed by over $700 Million in Government Loans Goes Bust: Filing." Reuters, July 30. Online at https://www.reuters.com/article/us-usa-solar-bankruptcy/u-s-solar-power-plant-backed-by-over-700-million-in-government-loans-goes-bust-filing-idUSKCN24V3C4.

Habeeb, L. (2021). "The True Face of the North Face." *Newsweek*, March 16. Online at https://www.newsweek.com/true-face-north-face-1576659.

Hals, T., and R. Rampton (2011). "Beacon Power Bankrupt; Had U.S. Backing like Solyndra." Reuters, October 30. Online at https://www.reuters.com/article/us-beaconpower-bankruptcy/beacon-power-bankrupt-had-u-s-backing-like-solyndra-idUSTRE79T39320111031.

Hefner.Energy (2022). "Subsidies Series: Part I." May 6. Online at https://www.hefner.energy/articles/subsidies-series-part-i.

Hefner, R. A., III (2009). *The Grand Energy Transition: The Rise of Energy Gases, Sustainable Life and Growth, and the Next Great Economic Expansion*. Hoboken, New Jersey: John Wiley & Sons.

Hirsch, J. (2015). "Elon Musk's Growing Empire Is Fueled by $4.9 Billion in Government Subsidies." *Los Angeles Times*, May 30. Online at https://www.latimes.com/business/la-fi-hy-musk-subsidies-20150531-story.html.

Huber, P. W., and M. P. Mills (2002). "Silicon & Electrons." Digital PowerGroup.com, cited in Huber and Mills (2006).

———. (2006). *The Bottomless Well: The Twilight of Fuel, the Virtue of Waste, and Why We Will Never Run Out of Energy*. New York: Basic Books.

IPAA (n.d.). "Energy Conversions." Independent Petroleum Association of America. Online at https://www.ipaa.org/reference-tools.

IEA (2006). "Carrots and Sticks: Taxing and Subsidising Energy." International Energy Agency, January 17. Online at https://www.iea.org/reports/carrots-and-sticks-taxing-and-subsidising-energy.

———. (2022). "Energy Subsidies: Tracking the Impact of Fossil-Fuel Subsidies." International Energy Agency. Online at https://www.iea.org/topics/energy-subsidies.

Isaac, R. (2001). *Influence of Technology Directions on System Architecture.* IBM Research Division. Online at https://www.yumpu.com/en/document/read/32046904/influence-of-technology-directions-on-system-architecture.

Lalljee, J. (2021). "Elon Musk Is Speaking Out against Government Subsidies. Here's a List of the Billions of Dollars His Businesses Have Received." Insider, December 15. Online at https://www.businessinsider.com/elon-musk-list-government-subsidies-tesla-billions-spacex-solarcity-2021-12.

Layton, B. E. (2008). "A Comparison of Energy Densities of Prevalent Energy Sources in Units of Joules per Cubic Meter." *International Journal of Green Energy* 5:438–455. Online at https://drexel.edu/~/media/Files/greatworks/pdf_sum10/WK8_Layton_EnergyDensities.ashx.

McLean, B. (2019). "'He's Full of Shit': How Elon Musk Fooled Investors, Bilked Taxpayers, and Gambled Tesla to Save SolarCity." *Vanity Fair*, August 25. Online at https://www.vanityfair.com/news/2019/08/how-elon-musk-gambled-tesla-to-save-solarcity.

Nelson, M., and M. Czerwinski (2018). "With Nuclear Instead of Renewables, California & Germany Would Already Have 100% Clean Electricity." Environmental Progress, September 11. Online at https://environmentalprogress.org/big-news/2018/9/11/california-and-germany-decarbonization-with-alternative-energy-investments.

North Face (2021). "Our Position on Co-Branding." June 8. Online at https://www.thenorthface.com/en-us/approach/response-co-branding.

Perry, M. J. (2016). "New US Homes Today Are 1,000 Square Feet Larger Than in 1973 and Living Space per Person Has Nearly Doubled." American Enterprise Institute, June 5. Online at https://www.aei.org/carpe-diem/new-us-homes-today-are-1000-square-feet-larger-than-in-1973-and-living-space-per-person-has-nearly-doubled.

Puko, T., and J. Randles (2020). "Energy Department Poised to Lose Up to $225 Million on Solar Project Bankruptcy." *Wall Street Journal*, July 30. Online at https://www.wsj.com/articles/energy-department-poised-to-lose-up-to-225-million-on-solar-project-bankruptcy-11596145244.

Reuters (2012). "Abound Solar Files to Liquidate in Bankruptcy." July 2. Online at https://www.reuters.com/article/us-aboundsolar-bankruptcy/abound-solar-files-to-liquidate-in-bankruptcy-idUSBRE86118020120702.

Ritchie, H. (2017). "How Much of the World's Land Would We Need in Order to Feed the Global Population with the Average Diet of a Given Country?" Our World in Data, October 3. Online at https://ourworldindata.org/agricultural-land-by-global-diets.

SciMed (Scientific and Medical Products, Ltd.) (n.d.) "What Products Are Made from Petroleum?" Online at https://www.scimed.co.uk/education/what-products-are-made-from-petroleum.

Seetharaman, D., and A. Rascoe, "Battery Maker A123 Systems Files for Bankruptcy." Reuters, October 16. Online at https://www.reuters.com/article/us-a123systems-bankruptcy/battery-maker-a123-systems-files-for-bankruptcy-idUSBRE89F0UA20121016.

Shellenberger, M. (2021). "Finally They Admit Renewables Are Terrible for the Environment." Public (Substack), May 2. Online at https://michaelshellenberger.substack.com/p/finally-they-admit-renewables-are.

Simon, J. L., (ed.) (1995). *The State of Humanity*. Oxford, United Kingdom, and Cambridge, Massachusetts: Blackwell.

Skidmore, Z. (2021). "IMF: Fossil Fuel Industry the Recipient of Subsidies of $5.9tn per Year." Power Technology, October 6. Online at https://www.power-technology.com/news/imf-fossil-subsidies.

Skyline Solar (n.d.). "Tesla Powerwall Lifespan: How Long Do They Last?" Online at https://www.skylinesolar.com.au/tesla-powerwall-lifespan-how-long-do-they-last.

Smil, V. (1999). *Energies: An Illustrated Guide to the Biosphere and Civilization*. Cambridge, Massachusetts: MIT Press.

Smith, E. (2021). "A Closer Look at the PR Feud between Liberty Oilfield and the North Face." Outside, July 12. Online at https://www.outsideonline.com/business-journal/brands/what-happens-when-an-oil-company-publicly-accuses-the-north-face-of-hypocrisy.

Spletzer, B. (1999). "Power Systems Comparisons, Intelligent Systems and Robotics Center." Sandia National Laboratories, cited in Huber and Mills (2006).

Tinker, S. (2019). "Global Electricity." Switch Energy Alliance. Online at https://switchon.org/presentations.

CHAPTER 13

The Energy-Climate Connection

BY BILL PEACOCK

CHAPTER SUMMARY

Assaults on the energy consumer's freedom of choice result in higher costs, a lower standard of living, unintended consequences, and the failure of regulators to achieve intended goals. These are generally ignored in framing climate policy. Significant gasoline price increases followed environmental policy changes and executive orders in the first year of the Biden administration. The intermittent nature of "renewable" systems necessitates construction of backup generating capacity from fossil fuels. But double-investing for the same energy market elevates consumer costs and defeats emission goals, as seen in some European countries already experiencing energy poverty. Government's choices of energy winners and losers have repeatedly failed over the last fifty years. Financial losses and bankruptcies continue amidst electric vehicle (EV) mandates, while their projected CO_2 reductions are minuscule in the context of the problem. And yet capital investments will be misallocated and an entire industry distorted without actually contributing to human welfare.

Governments are formed to "secure these rights," yet their market interventions degrade human rights. Substituting regulators' judgment for that of free citizens leads to failure, for which another remedial intervention must be imposed, serially compounding market distortions. The moral and effective way to improve mankind and the planet is through citizens' free choices, from which optimal solutions evolve naturally.

Introduction

On May 26, 1285, Edward I of England commissioned Roger de Northwode, John de Cobbeham, and Henry le Galeys to investigate the use of "sea-coal" in lime kilns in London and its suburbs. The commission was driven by complaints "that whereas formerly the lime used to be burnt with wood, it is now burnt with sea-coal, whereby the air is infected and corrupted to the peril of those frequenting and dwelling in those parts" (Edward I 1893, 207).

This was not the first time Edward and his family had dealt with what we know today simply as coal. In 1257, his mother Eleanor was forced to leave Nottingham Castle because "she found it impossible to stay there by reason of the smoke from the sea coal" (Green 1901, 378). About fifteen years later, Edward had (unsuccessfully) banned the burning of sea-coal in London "on the urging of important noblemen and clerics" (Urbinato 1994). The rich were upset at the smog resulting from the heavy use of sea-coal for heating by commoners, who were driven to it as wood became scarce and more expensive due to population growth and restricted access to forests.

Describing this situation from an economic perspective, we can say that thirteenth-century energy consumers turned to a substitute product (sea-coal) for heating because wood prices had increased due to high demand in the face of decreasing supply. The subsequent interventions of Edward I and later monarchs into the nascent British energy market may have reduced smog in London, but they came at the cost of making most of their subjects poorer, colder, and less adequately housed.

Responses of officials across the world to COVID-19 have reminded us that the actions of rulers—be they medieval kings or modern bureaucrats—do not always benefit their citizens. In large part, this is because they approach public health (and other) concerns with pride and arrogance, often revealed by their failure to seek wide counsel from people outside their own spheres of expertise, rather than with wisdom and justice. Prideful rulers ignore or oppose their citizens' "unalienable Rights," including "Life, Liberty and the pursuit of Happiness," to use the words of America's Declaration of Independence. As we will explore in this chapter, this assault on rights—and correspondingly on energy markets—most often results not only in a lower standard of living but also in the failure of regulators to achieve their intended goals.

The High Cost of Intervention in Energy Markets

Just as in medieval England, the unintended consequences of intervention in markets by today's regulators attempting to address public health challenges are rarely considered. Along with our fundamental rights, consumer costs such as higher prices for energy, housing, transportation, and other consumer goods are generally ignored when adopting modern environmental policies.

Consider, for example, environmental policy changes related to climate change and energy implemented in the first year of the Biden administration. Less than a month into office, President Joe Biden issued an "Executive Order on Tackling the Climate Crisis at Home and Abroad" "to avoid the most catastrophic impacts of that crisis." Included in that order was a ban on new oil and natural gas leasing on public lands and in offshore waters (later overturned by a federal court). The order also sought to develop policies that would bring the United States into compliance with the Paris Accords, from which President Trump had withdrawn the United States in 2020, and into which President Biden returned us.

The order also required the immediate development of a climate finance plan "promoting the flow of capital toward climate-aligned investments and away from high-carbon investments" (Biden 2021). At least $100 billion of funding (Taranto et. al. 2021) in the $1.2 trillion infrastructure bill Biden signed into law in November 2022 was in accord with the principles behind the finance plan.

These and other potential interventions into energy markets had an immediate effect on energy costs. The price of regular gasoline, for instance, rose by about 43 percent in Biden's first year in office (AAA 2021). Overall, energy prices were up 33 percent in the first eleven months of the administration, by far the biggest cost driver in the Consumer Price Index (Figure 13.1; BLS 2021).

Biden's energy policies limiting the development of fossil fuels harken back to those of other Democrat administrations, most of which have been set aside during Republican years. However, Biden's policies promoting renewable and other alternative sources of energy have been mirrored across most administrations—Republican and Democrat alike—for the last five decades.

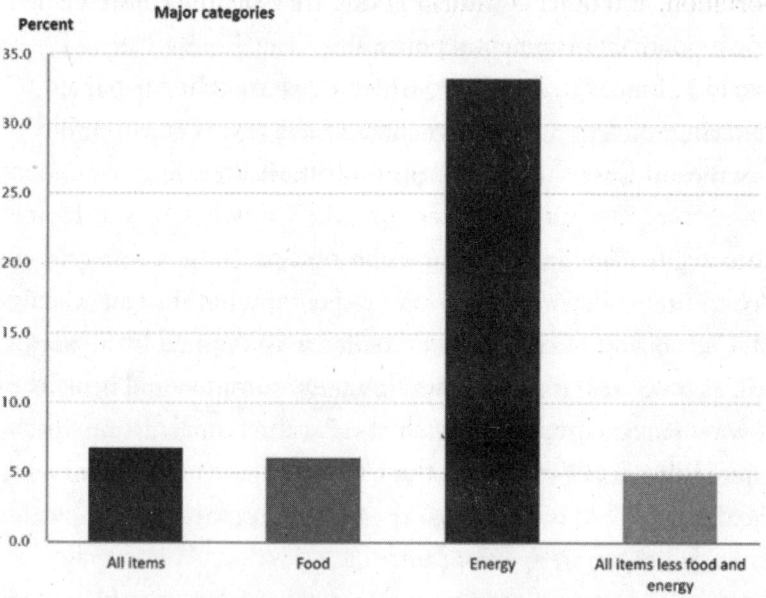

Figure 13.1. Twelve-month percentage change, Consumer Price Index, selected categories, November 2021, not seasonally adjusted. *Source: U.S. Bureau of Labor Statistics.*

Subsidies for energy research and development are part of a long-running effort by the federal government to find alternatives to fossil fuels. In the 1970s, as Robert Bradley writes, "Politicians, experts, and leading oil and gas executives were convinced that mineral energies were inexorably depleting, leaving the U.S. with a national security problem of increasing oil imports." He continues,

> The energy crisis, which began with natural gas shortages in the winter of 1971–72 and oil shortages two years later, revitalized interest in wind power in the United States. The American Wind Energy Association (AWEA) was formed in 1974; six years later the nation's first wind farm was constructed in Vermont, consisting of 20 turbines generating

> 600 kilowatts (0.6 megawatts) at its peak. Still, the industry's embryonic status was evident in President Jimmy Carter's 1977 National Energy Plan, which emphasized solar-panel energy, nuclear fusion, synthetic fuels (from coal), and municipal waste—not wind power. (Bradley 2018)

Renewable generation began to be commercially feasible in the 1990s because of federal income tax credits for wind (Production Tax Credit) and solar (Investment Tax Credit). It was not until the 2000s, though, as states mandated renewable energy subsidies and benefits of their own—particularly the building of subsidized transmission lines—that these sources began to make significant inroads into the nation's electrical grids. That is also when the cost to taxpayers of renewable energy subsidies began to skyrocket.

From 2006 through 2021, federal subsidies for renewable energy cost taxpayers more than $95 billion (Table 13.1; Peacock 2021b, 8). Most of that cost came from tax credits for wind ($35.9 billion) and solar ($25.4 billion). Other costs came through stimulus payments, research and development expenditures, and direct payments. These figures do not include the billions of dollars spent on state and local subsidies for renewables. Texas subsidies and benefits, for example, totaled about $11.9 billion over the same period (Peacock 2021b, 5).

With more potential intervention in the energy market on the way through laws like the multi-trillion-dollar Build Back Better bill proposed in 2021 (which failed but was in part resurrected in 2022's Inflation Reduction Act), the citizens of the United States are on the brink of joining their counterparts in Europe in living in energy poverty with perpetually high energy costs. Witness that the price of a gallon of regular gasoline was $7.87 in Great Britain, $8.29 in Switzerland, $7.41 in Spain, and $8.21 in France (Auto Traveler 2021).

Table 13.1. U.S. Renewable Energy Subsidies ($), 2006–2021

Year	Texas	Federal
2006	92,128,828	819,787,483
2007	101,391,806	774,377,878
2008	150,947,289	941,206,121
2009	149,204,682	2,871,823,209
2010	183,340,478	6,043,832,734
2011	1,107,364,716	6,205,217,990
2012	1,095,869,837	8,102,387,628
2013	1,068,677,094	9,410,222,995
2014	981,879,340	6,308,038,807
2015	970,429,660	6,265,650,731
2016	996,290,622	5,501,384,467
2017	997,446,561	7,907,228,371
2018	979,873,756	8,947,643,596
2019	999,972,993	8,438,500,000
2020	1,015,050,072	8,300,000,000
2021	1,000,634,014	8,200,000,000
Total	**11,890,501,746**	**95,037,302,010**

Source: Peacock (2021b), 7–8.

The Failure of Intervention in Energy Markets

The high cost of government-supported alternatives to consumer-selected fuels is not the only problem with intervention in energy markets. The truth is that the alternatives never work very well, either.

The efforts under President Carter's National Energy Plan serve as one example:

> [T]here is a long history of government attempting to choose "winners" and "losers," and invariably making the wrong choices. Following on the second OPEC oil embargo in 1979, for example, the Carter Administration launched U.S. Synfuels Corporation in early 1980. The goal was to produce cheap synthetic crude oil and reduce the country's dependence on OPEC. The company was shut down in 1984, having spent $25 billion in taxpayer money and producing far less synthetic crude oil than was promised (Continental Economics 2011).

The life span of renewables has been longer, but only because their subsidies did not suffer the same fate as those for synthetic fuels. From a market standpoint, however, their performance has been even worse. Not only does the inefficiency of turning wind and sunlight into electricity mean they come with the same uncompetitive high costs, but also their intermittency results in their being an unreliable source for providing power at a utility-grid scale:

> The value of a generator is, in part, determined by its nameplate capacity (maximum output) but also on its productivity and availability. Productivity is the ratio of physical output (MWh) to physical input (e.g., MMBTU of gas burned), sometimes referred to as technical efficiency. A wind turbine's output depends on both its scale and its availability factor, the latter defined as the average percentage of all hours in a year that it is capable of generating. The value of that output is determined by demand and cost. A wind

> unit that injects power into the grid at peak hours is more valuable than one that operates during hours of low demand because its output displaces higher-cost conventional power. Wind's intermittency, however, means that additional costs of backup generation must be incurred to transform a turbine's output into reliable megawatt-hours, since most consumers place far higher values on dependable (firm) than on interruptible power. . . .
>
> [Wind's] actual output per hour depends on wind speed, which ranges from zero (still air) to limits imposed by design. Wind's low productivity when power is most valuable is not unique to Texas. Looking at ERCOT [Electric Reliability Council of Texas], the Pennsylvania New Jersey Maryland Interconnection (PJM), and the Mid-Continent Independent System Operator (MISO) in 2012, between 82 percent and 86 percent of wind generation capacity did not operate during their top 10 peak demand days. During peak periods, only 10 percent or less of conventional generation capacity is typically unavailable. (Michaels 2019, 4)

Intermittency not only reduces the value of electricity generated but also forces the construction of additional generation from reliable sources (primarily natural gas) to compensate for wind's lack of availability during peak demand. Grid operators must ensure that there is an adequate amount of reliable backup generation on standby in case renewables fail to generate their expected contribution. Michaels explains what this looks like in practice:

> All electric grids require reserves, but wind is unique because it necessitates additional backup that would be unnecessary, absent intermittency. Necessary backup varies with

> generation conditions, load, and other region-specific data, and no quick summaries are available.... The details of estimating gas-fired capacity value (for actual generation) relative to the cost of maintaining availability are situation-dependent. Most major states impose surcharges on wind power and include them as "uplift" amounts for accommodating intermittency. 2016 uplift costs averaged over ERCOT (including the system administrative fee) accounted for \$1.03 per MWh, up from \$0.74 per MWh in 2015. (Michaels 2019, 8; internal citations omitted)

At \$1.03 per MWh, the cost of backing up wind generation would add about \$1.50 to the average monthly electricity bill in Houston.

The problems caused by the intermittency of solar generation are somewhat less when compared with wind because it generates electricity only during the day, when demand for power is usually higher. However, during the blackouts that hit Texas in February 2021, solar and wind both proved that their intermittency can lead to disastrous consequences.

At about 1:00 a.m. on Monday, February 15, 2021, ERCOT announced "there is not enough generation available to meet current demand" and that it would "instruct utilities to begin rotating outages." Wind was operating at 16.8 percent of its capacity—still much lower than natural gas and coal. And solar—as designed—was operating at zero percent of its capacity. Thus, 85 percent of renewable capacity was missing in action; wind and solar were providing only 8.2 percent of the 65,256-megawatt load (demand), a situation that would soon shut down most of the Texas grid (Peacock 2021a). If all the money that had been invested in solar and wind had been invested in natural gas, Texans likely would have suffered at most only rolling blackouts rather than days without power and water.

In light of the fact of renewables' inability to provide affordable and reliable power to the grid—and the subsequent reduction of the purchasing power of consumers faced with higher energy bills—why do governments worldwide continue to distort markets through subsidies and mandates in an effort to force continued investment in renewables? Long and Steinberger (2016) provided the rationale of supporters of the Clean Power Plan announced by President Barack Obama in 2015:

> Renewable energy is one of the most effective tools we have in the fight against climate change, and there is every reason to believe it will succeed....
>
> In the longer term, the U.S. Environmental Protection Agency's Clean Power Plan to establish the first national limits on carbon pollution from power plants will continue to drive renewable energy growth. Wind and solar energy will play a central role in achieving the emissions cuts required, and carbon policies like the Clean Power Plan will be critical to ensuring that low-carbon resources are prioritized over higher-emitting power plants.
>
> The non-market benefits of renewable energy also are considerable. The LBNL [Lawrence Berkeley National Laboratory] researchers estimated that renewables supported nearly 200,000 jobs, provided $5.2 billion worth of health benefits through improved air quality, and resulted in global climate benefits of $2.2 billion.

Other chapters in this book will deal with the claimed environmental benefits of renewables related to climate change. Here, we focus on why claims of improved human welfare through government intervention in energy markets to address climate change and other concerns do not stand up to close inspection.

The Blessings of Capitalism and Energy Markets

To understand the benefit of markets to human health and economic prosperity, it is necessary to venture into late fifteenth-century medieval Europe, two to three hundred years before the widespread use of modern energy sources began. John Flynn describes the vast social and economic changes taking place at that time:

> The long struggle to break up the old feudal system and the primitive guild ethics of the towns and set in motion the capitalist society lengthened out into a series of steps. First there was the slow infiltration of money. Next came the shattering of public acceptance of the ethics of trading and banking. Then came the rise of free competition and the long retreat of the old guild trade monopolies. Next was the development of modern banking. Then came the rise of the large-scale industrial operator. It is because [Jacob] Fugger played a leading role in all these stages that he stands as the most important figure at the dawn of the capitalist era. (Flynn 1941, 21)

We take this brief detour from the beginnings of modern energy markets and the Industrial Revolution in England because it is important to understand that their birth did not happen spontaneously. While barely noticed today, underlying modern energy markets are enormous investments of capital made over the last five hundred years. Just one example: before commercial-scale energy production from coal, oil, and natural gas was possible, massive investments in machines were needed to produce the products necessary to extract, refine, transport, and use the energy stored in these products. The benefits to human health and prosperity brought about by these investments are astounding in the context of human history. But they really should not be surprising once we examine the factors more closely. For millennia, humans had relied largely on power from organic sources to provide enough food and shelter to survive; human strength was supplemented with power from draft animals and firewood. Solar power was harnessed only to provide food through photosynthesis and the consumption of plants by people and livestock and of livestock by people. Water and wind also provided mechanical power at various times and places, but in comparatively small quantities.

As the seventeenth century headed to its conclusion, wood, human muscle, and draught animals accounted for most of the energy consumed. But the introduction of fossil fuels, made possible by the accumulation of capital through the development of capital markets starting in Italy, spreading early through Germany and England, and gradually reaching around the globe, brought radical changes in life for humans. The use of fossil fuel mechanical power, starting with coal, multiplied many times over.

For example, as illustrated in Figure 13.2 (in the color figures section between pages 240 and 241), while total energy consumption in England and Wales multiplied by almost five times from the mid-sixteenth century to the mid-nineteenth, energy from firewood fell by about nine-tenths, from draught animals by about half, and from human muscle by perhaps 10 percent (despite about a sevenfold increase in human population [Wikipedia n.d.]). There was little change in the amount derived from water and a slight increase from wind. But the amount from coal increased by over forty times.

The benefits stemming from the increased use of fossil fuel are laid out by Kathleen Hartnett White:

> Use of the energy in fossil fuels unleashed economic productivity on a scale previously unimaginable. When innovative minds developed a steam engine which could convert the stored heat energy in coal into mechanical energy, the economic limits under which all human societies had formerly existed were blown apart. A life of back-breaking drudgery

> was no longer the inescapable condition of the overwhelming majority of mankind.
>
> Life expectancy had changed little throughout all human history until the Industrial Revolution; it thereafter tripled. Income per capita has since increased 11-fold. Not coincidentally, man-made emissions of carbon dioxide have risen three-fold since the beginning of the Industrial Revolution. Fossil-fuel powered mechanization revolutionized economic productivity, increased incomes, population, and life expectancy across all classes. (White 2014)

At present, the United States is the embodiment of the Industrial Revolution and its reliance on fossil fuels, as well as of the system of capitalism that gave it birth. The benefits to Americans of this heritage are captured in the correlation we see in Figure 13.3 between increasing emissions of CO_2 and population growth, affluence, and life expectancy.

Rights Exercised through Markets Provide Superior Outcomes

There certainly have been challenges with capitalism and the use of fossil fuels over the last several centuries—pollution and relationships between owners and workers among them. Even so, the benefits of capitalism and fossil fuels are indisputable in terms of human prosperity and health. Also indisputable is the history of failure by government officials who attempt to override consumer preferences—and rights—by intervening in markets, particularly when it comes to energy sources. Yet the interventions—and failures—continue unabated.

The alleged justification for these assaults on the rights of consumers to express their preferences through markets has perversely evolved into support for positive "human rights," which "impos[e]

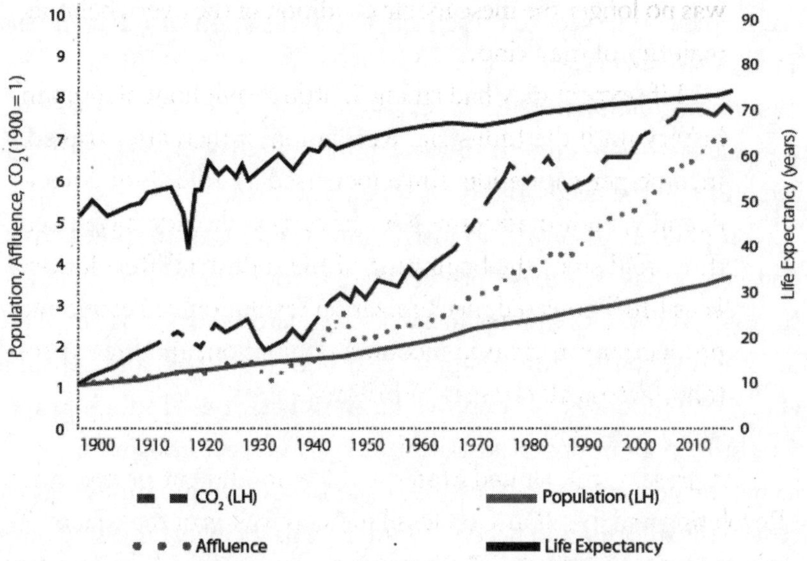

Figure 13.3. U.S. carbon dioxide emissions, population, GDP, and life expectancy (1900–2009). *Source: Goklany (2012), 8. Courtesy of Indur Goklany.*

corresponding obligations on governmental duty-bearers" (Meier 2018). The obligations of government officials include providing citizens "the enjoyment of the highest attainable standard of health," defined as "a state of complete physical, mental, and social well-being and not merely the absence of disease or infirmity" (WHO 2006).

Yet a long line of philosophers, theologians, and political thinkers—such as Augustine, Thomas Aquinas, Martin Luther, John Calvin, John Locke, and Thomas Jefferson—have understood that humanity's "unalienable Rights" are not supplied by government but instead are "endowed by their Creator," as noted in the Declaration of Independence. These rights are to be exercised individually and collectively by people. Outside the family, the primary way they do this collectively is through executing their decisions about their lives, liberty, and property through markets.

Most interventions in markets, then, do not improve human rights but degrade them, in opposition to the purpose for which governments are formed—"to secure these rights" (Declaration of Independence). This is not surprising, given how government intervention through regulations, mandates, and taxes stands in stark contrast to the voluntary nature of interactions between market participants that focuses attention on the needs and desires of consumers.

Proponents also seek to justify interventions in market activities on the grounds that they "protect the environment, workers, and consumers" (Pew 2015). In some instances, regulators purport to act in order to "improve market information" that both regulators and consumers can use to monitor and improve business activity: "Today's proposal would help us understand better how to protect consumers' access to mortgage credit...." (CFBP 2014). However, regulations generally reduce the information needed for market participants to carry out the efficient and fair operation of markets.

The reason for this is simple: market prices of goods and services transmit important information through the marketplace to market participants, that is, buyers and sellers.

> Prices are crucial for setting priorities. Without prices, we fly blind. We do not know what things cost. We do not know what people have recently bid in order to buy or rent scarce resources. In a world governed by scarcity, prices are tools of understanding and therefore tools of action. Prices are the most important sources of information that lead to the coordination of competing economic plans of action.
>
> Prices are objective. They are the product of competitive bidding in the market. They are the results of the people with specific information who are willing to put money on the line by buying or selling assets. The information conveyed by prices is highly specific. (North 2020, 63)

Market intervention by government distorts market prices, thus distorting and reducing the information available to buyers and sellers—and reducing the quality of the decisions they make.

An extension of this is that intervention, by design, changes or even prohibits the market outcomes that would have resulted through the voluntary actions of buyers and sellers in the market. The result is that intervention replaces consumer preferences (to a greater or lesser extent) with the preferences of regulators and other parties, usually those seeking to profit through regulation.

Friedrich Hayek explains why the substitute decisions of regulators will always be inferior to those made by buyers and sellers acting on information (knowledge) transmitted by market prices:

> [T]he sort of knowledge with which I have been concerned is knowledge of the kind which by its nature cannot enter into statistics and therefore cannot be conveyed to any central authority in statistical form. . . . It follows from this that central planning based on statistical information by its nature cannot take direct account of these circumstances of time and place. . . .
>
> If we can agree that the economic problem of society is mainly one of rapid adaptation to changes in the particular circumstances of time and place, it would seem to follow that the ultimate decisions must be left to the people who are familiar with these circumstances, who know directly of the relevant changes and of the resources immediately available to meet them. We cannot expect that this problem will be solved by first communicating all this knowledge to a central board which, after integrating *all* knowledge, issues its orders. (Hayek 1945) [Emphasis added]

The harm to human health and prosperity caused by the substitution of the preferences of monarchs, politicians, and bureaucrats for those of millions of subjects, citizens, and consumers is incalculable. Yet even a cursory review of economies where substantial restrictions on rights and markets are endemic establishes that the harm is real and continues to this day.

Conclusion

The high price of increased prosperity and advances in human health throughout history has been the messy business of people exercising their God-given rights through markets. This enables them to absorb information and convert it to useful means of satisfying their needs and wants. Though costly, only in this way has mankind been able to build up enough capital to access the tremendous benefits of the energy stored in fossil fuels.

Since well before Edward I, rulers and experts have attempted to clean up the mess of humanity—for many reasons, including concerns about diminishing supplies of fuel, pollution, or climate change—by substituting their judgments for those of common citizens. But as this article demonstrates, these efforts are destined to fail and leave humanity in a worse state. The moral and most effective way to improve the condition of mankind and his planet is through man's exercise of his "unalienable Rights" through markets, including energy markets.

References

AAA (2021). "Gas Prices." American Automobile Association. Accessed December 13, 2021. Online at https://gasprices.aaa.com.

Auto Traveler (2021). "Fuel Prices in Europe." Accessed December 13, 2021. Online at https://autotraveler.ru/en/spravka/

fuel-price-in-europe.html#.YbfYD5HMK3A. For archived page from December 13, 2021, see https://web.archive.org/web/20211213085743/https://autotraveler.ru/en/spravka/fuel-price-in-europe.html#.YbcLEy3P32c.

Biden, Joe (2021). "Executive Order on Tackling the Climate Crisis at Home and Abroad." White House.gov, January 27. Online at https://www.whitehouse.gov/briefing-room/presidential-actions/2021/01/27/executive-order-on-tackling-the-climate-crisis-at-home-and-abroad.

BLS (2021). "12-month Percentage Change, Consumer Price Index, Selected Categories." U.S. Bureau of Labor Statistics, December. Online at https://web.archive.org/web/20211231223942/https://www.bls.gov/charts/consumer-price-index/consumer-price-index-by-category.htm.

Bradley, R. L., Jr. (2018). *The Economic Fall & Political Rise of Renewable Energy*. Austin, Texas: Texas Public Policy Foundation. Online at https://www.texaspolicy.com/wp-content/uploads/2018/11/The-Economic-Fall-and-Political-Rise-of-Renewable-Energy-ACEE-Bradley.pdf.

CFBP (2014). "CFPB Proposes Rule to Improve Information about Access to Credit in the Mortgage Market." Consumer Financial Protection Bureau, July 24. Online at https://www.consumerfinance.gov/about-us/newsroom/cfpb-proposes-rule-to-improve-information-about-access-to-credit-in-the-mortgage-market.

Continental Economics (2011). *Electricity Competition at Work: The Link between Competitive Electricity Markets, Job Creation, and Economic Growth*. Report prepared for COMPETE Coalition. Edgewood, New Mexico: Continental Economics. Online at https://images.edocket.azcc.gov/docketpdf/0000146818.pdf.

Edward I (1893). *Calendar of the Patent Rolls*. London: Eyre and Spottiswoode. Online at https://babel.hathitrust.org/cgi/pt?id=mdp.39015031081162&view=1up&seq=223.

Flynn, J. T. (1941). *Men of Wealth: The Story of Twelve Significant Fortunes from the Renaissance to the Present Day*. New York: Simon and Schuster. Online at https://mises.org/library/men-wealth-story-twelve-significant-fortunes-renaissance-present-day.

Goklany, I. M. (2012). *Humanity Unbound: How Fossil Fuels Saved Humanity from Nature and Nature from Humanity*. Washington, D.C.: Cato Institute. Online at https://www.cato.org/sites/cato.org/files/pubs/pdf/pa715.pdf.

Green, E. (1901). "Nottingham Castle." *Archaeological Journal* 58 (1): 365–97. Online at https://ur.booksc.eu/book/36642673/767cea.

Hayek, F. A. (1945). "The Use of Knowledge in Society." *American Economic Review* 35, no. 4 (September): 519–30. Online at https://fee.org/articles/the-use-of-knowledge-in-society.

Long, N., and K. Steinberger (2016). "Renewable Energy Is Key to Fighting Climate Change." Natural Resources Defense Council, July 26. Online at https://www.nrdc.org/experts/noah-long/renewable-energy-key-fighting-climate-change.

Meier, B. M., et. al. (2018). "Human Rights in Public Health." *Health and Human Rights Journal* 20, no. 2: (December): 85–91. Online at https://www.ncbi.nlm.nih.gov/pmc/articles/PMC6293343.

Michaels, R. (2019). *Intermittent Generation Comes to Texas: The High Cost of Renewable Energy*. Austin, Texas: Texas Public Policy Foundation. Online at https://www.texaspolicy.com/wp-content/uploads/2019/03/2019-02-RR-Michaels-ACEE-Intermittent-Generation.pdf.

North, G. (2020). *Christian Economics*. Vol. 4. Scholar's ed. Dallas, Georgia: Point Five Press. Online at https://www.garynorth.com/CE4-1.pdf.

Peacock, B. (2021a). "The Numbers Point to the Causes of the Texas Blackouts." ExcellentThought, February 28. Online at https://

www.excellentthought.net/the-numbers-point-to-the-causes-of-the-texas-blackouts.

———. (2021b). *Subsidies to Nowhere: A Year-by-Year Estimate of Renewable Energy Subsidy Costs for Texas and the U.S.* Houston, Texas: Energy Alliance. Online at https://static1.squarespace.com/static/5f08b9b336577f152f2c5c3e/t/6143c0845d7fd84c28ac5a6d/1631830153863/Subsidies-to-Nowhere.pdf.

Pew Charitable Trusts (2015). "Government Regulation: Costs Lower, Benefits Greater Than Industry Estimates." May 26. Online at https://www.pewtrusts.org/en/research-and-analysis/fact-sheets/2015/05/government-regulation-costs-lower-benefits-greater-than-industry-estimates.

Taranto, R., et. al. (2021). "Comprehensive $1.2 Trillion Infrastructure Bill to Provide Critical Support for Clean Energy." *National Law Review*, November 16. Online at https://www.natlawreview.com/article/comprehensive-12-trillion-infrastructure-bill-to-provide-critical-support-clean-0.

Urbinato, D. (1994). "London's Historic 'Pea-Soupers.'" U.S. Environmental Protection Agency. Online at https://archive.epa.gov/epa/aboutepa/londons-historic-pea-soupers.html.

White, K. H. (2014). *Fossil Fuels: The Moral Case*. Austin, Texas: Texas Public Policy Foundation. Online at https://www.texaspolicy.com/wp-content/uploads/2018/08/Fossil-Fuels-The-Moral-Case.pdf.

Wikipedia (n.d.). "Demography of England." Online at https://en.wikipedia.org/wiki/Demography_of_England.

WHO (2006). *Constitution of the World Health Organization*. Geneva, Switzerland: World Health Organization. Online at https://apps.who.int/gb/bd/PDF/bd47/EN/constitution-en.pdf.

Wrigley, E. A. (2010). *Energy and the English Industrial Revolution*. Cambridge, United Kingdom: Cambridge University Press.

———. (2016). *The Path to Sustained Growth: England's Transition from an Organic Economy to an Industrial Revolution.* Cambridge, United Kingdom: Cambridge University Press.

Chapter 14

Climate Change and the Economics of an Energy Transition

by G. Cornelis van Kooten

Chapter Summary

Recent blackouts illustrate the intermittency problem of solar and wind power. The problem begins with peak power demand when wind and solar fall dramatically short of expected contributions. Sufficient battery backup is unavailable due to excessive costs, and baseload power response (coal, natural gas, nuclear) may be inadequate due to shuttered facilities or fuel shortages. If importing power from other jurisdictions is restricted or unavailable, a blackout ensues. Failing to meet expectations of power availability in a wealthy society is an unforgivable failure.

Investments in wind and solar might appear attractive under first cost estimates and when subsidies distort true economics. However, nuclear and gas variable costs remain marginally better than renewables. Often overlooked is the lifespan of wind and solar systems, typically only a third of nuclear and fossil fuel facilities. Furthermore, plant decommissioning costs and waste disposal are not assessed on equal terms, and the intermittency issue imposes variable and fixed cost impacts on operation of baseload assets.

Groups of citizens increasingly oppose location of renewable facilities due to real or perceived costs to human health, bird, bat, and insect strikes, aesthetic considerations, and excessive land requirements. This could be a significant obstacle to scalability. Energy security is causing reconsideration of global fuel supply channels amid international tensions. History has shown that energy transitions take many decades to evolve. Although many countries have agreed to a "Net Zero" target, eliminating fossil fuel emissions by 2050, significant issues place that goal in question.

Introduction

Under the December 2015 Paris Agreement to the United Nations' 1992 Framework Convention on Climate Change (UNFCCC 1992), countries pledged to reduce their carbon dioxide (CO_2) and other greenhouse gas emissions in their intended nationally determined contributions (UNFCCC 2022). Since then, many countries have agreed to eliminate entirely emissions from fossil fuel burning by 2050—a target referred to as "Net Zero." Any CO_2 emissions remaining at that time are to be offset either by sequestering the carbon in forest sinks or by carbon capture and storage (CCS). Both of these offsetting techniques are expensive and remain untried at a large scale (IEA 2021; Brouwer and Bergkamp 2021).

Countries' climate change policies have focused primarily on the electricity sector (see chapter 15). In 2019, 25,900 terawatt hours (TWh) of electricity were generated, while primary energy consumption totaled 173,340 TWh, which means that electricity accounted for only about 15 percent of the primary energy consumed globally (Ritchie and Roser n.d.). Yet the electricity sector has been targeted because power can be generated from a large variety of energy sources, including fossil fuels, hydraulics, wind, solar, biomass, geothermal, tides, and nuclear. Electricity can then be used to power electric vehicles, heat homes and commercial properties, power manufacturing facilities, and produce hydrogen fuel from water through a process of electrolysis.

Because coal is cheap, ubiquitous, often domestically available, and more reliable than wind and solar sources of energy, China, India, Russia, and most developing countries are ramping up coal capacity and production. Yet because coal releases more CO_2 to the atmosphere per unit of heat generated than any other energy source, except for biomass (van Kooten, Withey, and Johnston 2021), current policies of most countries require the phaseout of coal-fired power by as early as 2030. However, replacing coal-fired power plants with intermittent renewable energy sources, such as wind and solar, would impose significant economic costs and still require backup power, as wind and solar cannot be switched on and off at will due to their intermittency.

Consider recent electricity blackouts experienced in the United Kingdom, California, and Texas—jurisdictions that have all significantly increased their reliance on renewable energy in recent years (Wolff, Kahn, and Colman 2021). While several factors affected the reliability of these electricity grids, renewable energy is largely to blame. Why? Because the wind doesn't always blow and the Sun doesn't always shine—and the energy from these sources cannot be stored at adequate levels (van Kooten, Withey, and Duan 2020).

Unreliable wind and solar generating sources require conventional backup power, which is generally provided by natural gas. The introduction of intermittent renewable energy sources into electricity grids stymies investment in reliable, conventional fossil fuel or hydroelectric capacity, thus exposing power networks to occasional imbalances between demand and supply that can only be covered by having sufficient fast-responding generation (normally gas plants) available when renewable sources are inadequate due to low wind speeds, too much cloudiness, or, of course, nighttime. This is largely what happened during recent blackouts—electricity from renewable sources fell while there was insufficient fast-responding backup generation to cover the loss. The United Kingdom, California, and Texas cases are briefly discussed in the section below on "The Problem of Intermittency: Illustrations."

The European Union and the United Kingdom have gone further than most regions in passing legislation to intensify reliance on renewable sources for generating electricity, with natural gas increasingly relied upon for meeting gaps between load (demand) and supply. Much to the disappointment of environmental groups, the EU recently declared gas and nuclear power to constitute "green energy," with the former needed to transition to Net Zero (European Commission 2022). Natural gas is also used for heating and industrial purposes, particularly in the production of fertilizer.

In light of Russia's invasion of Ukraine in February 2022 and the reliance of countries in Western Europe on Russian oil and gas, the interplay between energy security and greater reliance on intermittent renewable energy is increasingly important to policymakers. Energy security is considered a major issue, if not the major issue, when countries attempt to apply sanctions on belligerent countries to bring them in line with what are considered international norms (Blackwill and Harris 2017). This issue is discussed further in the section below on "Energy Security."

Finally, proponents of wind and solar energy argue that the costs of these energy sources have been reduced enough that society should transition to them as fast as possible. In a sense, they are partly correct: the life-cycle costs of wind and solar sources of energy appear to have fallen by some 70 percent and 90 percent, respectively, over the past decade (Lazard 2020). Even on a variable cost basis, solar and wind energy are competitive with fossil fuels. However, this thinking ignores certain costs related to the intermittent nature of wind and solar that makes them much less attractive sources of energy than promoted. These issues are discussed in the section below on "Economic Costs of Transitioning to Net Zero."

The Problem of Intermittency: Illustrations

Various models of electricity grids have demonstrated how difficult and costly it is to replace fossil fuel–generated power with power from intermittent sources (for example, Brouwer and Bergkamp 2021; van Kooten, Withey, and Duan 2020; Hughes 2020a, 2020b; van Kooten and Mokhtarzadeh 2019; van Kooten 2017). While some wind and solar energy can be easily integrated into existing electricity grids, models indicate that, at high degrees of penetration, renewable sources create the types of problems experienced by the United Kingdom, California, and Texas.

United Kingdom

The United Kingdom has gone further than other jurisdictions in its reliance on renewable energy to produce electricity. However, fluctuations in power from intermittent renewable sources have contributed to an energy crisis. During 2021, United Kingdom wind output peaked at 17,600 MW on May 4 but fell by 98 percent to only 409 MW on September 6, with the difference of over 17,000 MW representing the electricity that would normally be produced by some twenty coal- or gas-fired power plants. But such fossil fuel plants have essentially been shuttered, with the required backup power sourced along transmission interties with Ireland and the Continent. When the Irish interconnect could not deliver, blackouts occurred, and prices skyrocketed due to the low supply and high demand.

With much less wind than expected, the United Kingdom was forced to reopen some fossil fuel plants. Because natural gas prices had nearly quadrupled since the beginning of the year, coal was a much cheaper option, even with coal providers paying more than $100 per ton of CO_2 (€75/tCO_2) for carbon offset permits. The cost of power rose to $3,067/MWh on September 9, 2021, with the wholesale price rising to nearly $420/MWh (Mellor 2021)—or $0.42/kWh as measured on consumers' utility bills. Critically low wind power in the first few days of November led to extremely high wholesale prices, with coal and other fossil fuel assets receiving some $5,300/MWh for the power they produced for three hours early on November 3, nearly one hundred times the normal wholesale price. The daily cost of balancing the grid hit $84.0 million on November 4, nearly thirty times the normal cost (Constable 2020; Net Zero Watch 2021). The annual cost of the United Kingdom's Balancing Mechanism reached $2.4 billion in 2020–21 and was expected to rise in 2021–22. Of course, these costs are eventually borne by ratepayers.

California

The share of renewables in California's electricity grid has been increasing more rapidly than elsewhere in the United States. In August 2020, California suffered a heat wave that resulted in blackouts as generation was insufficient to meet the load (Singh 2021). For much of a week, a shortfall of some 4,400 megawatts of power existed. At one point, the system lost 470 MW of capacity due to an unexpected plant shutdown and a downfall of 1,000 MW of energy from wind turbines due to less wind. However, the loss of solar power when the Sun went down likely had the greatest impact as demand for cooling increased precipitously during the hottest part of the day and into the evening, because people were arriving home from work and turning their thermostats down. Because surrounding states were experiencing the same heat wave, no electricity was available across transmission interties. California's grid operator planned for power outages again in 2021 as wildfires threatened transmission lines between Oregon and northern California and another heat wave was underway (Baker, Wade, and Chediak 2021).

In response to these developments, the grid operator delayed the retirement of several gas plants, encouraged people to conserve by implementing a higher temperature setting for air conditioning units, incentivized the import of more power during peak-demand periods, and encouraged power companies to install utility-scale batteries to store solar power for use in the evening and night—steps supposed to boost available electricity by some 2,000 MW (Baker, Wade, and Chediak 2021). At the same time, the state was planning to shut down the 2,200 MW capacity Diablo Canyon nuclear power plant beginning in 2024, later postponed to 2025, with the potential for a twenty-year extension (Lopez 2023). Its closure would end California's reliance on nuclear energy. California legislation prevents the system operator from replacing power from Diablo Canyon with electricity from any source that would increase CO_2 emissions. Replacing reliable (nuclear) power with unreliable intermittent sources of power will only aggravate the likelihood of blackouts in the future.

Texas

A severe winter storm hit Texas in February 2021, resulting in major blackouts that lasted upwards of several weeks in some areas (Wolff, Kahn, and Colman 2021; Wikipedia n.d.). Several factors contributed to the problem. One was the loss of wind power caused by ice on turbine blades, along with solar power lost due to snow and ice on solar panels. These failures were exacerbated by a reduction in natural gas availability and an inability to access electricity from other jurisdictions. At times, the wholesale price of electricity spiked to the system's price ceiling of $9,000/MWh ($9/kWh), compared to a typical price of $50/MWh (5¢/kWh)—a factor of 180.

The woes experienced by jurisdictions that replaced conventional power sources with wind and solar were predictable. For example, using information about the Alberta electricity grid, van Kooten (2021) and van Kooten, Withey, and Duan (2020) demonstrated that it would be impossible for Alberta to produce all of its power requirements using renewable sources only. It was not surprising therefore that, in late 2021, the problem of intermittency came into particular focus in Europe and the United States as some of the slowest wind speeds in decades intensified reliance on fossil fuels for electricity. This was then exacerbated by the Russian invasion of Ukraine.

Energy Security

The European Union and the United Kingdom have long depended on Russia for natural gas, oil, and even coal. This reliance on Russia varies across countries, but Germany is a bellwether in this regard. Prior to the Russian invasion of Ukraine, Germany obtained 55 percent of its natural gas, 35 percent of its oil, and 50 percent of its bituminous (thermal) coal from Russia, but it was able to reduce its respective dependencies on gas, oil, and coal to 40 percent, 25 percent, and 25 percent after the invasion (Reuters 2022). Prices of all three fossil fuel sources of energy have increased rapidly as Western (and Asian) economies recover from the COVID-19 pandemic and the invasion of Ukraine.

Although President Biden promised to supply Europe with more liquefied natural gas (LNG), Europe must compete with resurging Asian economies for LNG shipments from the United States and elsewhere. This has resulted in high gas prices, which, in turn, led to much higher electricity rates and overall heating costs. It has also threatened the viability of manufacturers reliant on natural gas, particularly chemical companies that produce ammonia fertilizer, which in turn plays an important role in food production, with repercussions for food prices globally.

Oil refineries in Europe began paying more for oil, whether it came from Russia, Norway, the Middle East, or elsewhere. One impact has been an increase in the costs of transportation, with some countries reducing taxes on gasoline and diesel fuel in an attempt to keep prices and inflation in check. And, as noted above, electricity system operators (ESOs) have moved to accept coal-fired power; even though coal prices have also risen, coal is less expensive and more readily available than oil and gas as a source for generating electricity. Indeed, coal is globally so pervasive that the EU will eliminate all coal imports from Russia as one means to reduce Russia's ability to finance its war in Ukraine. But the EU is unwilling to eliminate oil and gas imports from Russia because these are more difficult to source internationally.

Overall, increases in energy costs brought about increased inflation, which approached 12 percent on an annualized basis in many European countries. They have also resulted in rethinking the 2050 Net Zero target, with some arguing for faster adoption of wind and solar energy sources and others arguing for more time to meet Net Zero. The issue is likely to be impacted by the costs of adopting a carbon-free electricity system.

Economic Costs of Transitioning to Net Zero

The shibboleth promoted by the environmental establishment is that an electricity system based on renewable sources of energy will reduce overall generation costs. This fallacy was exposed by the real-world examples provided above. The case for lower costs is based on two considerations: (a) the declining costs of wind turbines and solar photovoltaic (PV) panels and (b) estimates of the levelized cost of energy (LCOE).

Cost of Electricity

Some notion of the *life-cycle costs* of electricity is provided in Table 14.1, which suggests that onshore wind and solar PV panels are now, *at first blush*, the least costly sources for generating electricity. When *variable costs* of energy are considered, however, the costs of fossil fuel and nuclear power generation are much closer to, and sometimes less than, those of wind and solar. From an asset management point of view, investing in wind and solar projects might make sense (especially in light of the subsidies for building wind and solar projects), but that may not be true for society.

The LCOE is based on assumptions that include fuel costs, asset lifespans, rates of return on assets, and, importantly, assumed *capacity factors* (CF). The CF is defined as the electricity produced over some period divided by the potential electricity that could be produced under perfect conditions over the same period (say, 8,760 hours for a year). Suppose a wind farm has a capacity of 10 MW, meaning it could potentially produce 87,600 MWh (= 10 MW × 8,760 hours) of energy nonstop under perfect conditions of ideal wind speed throughout the year without hindrance by temperature or ice; if it actually generates 16,381 MWh over the year, its CF is 18.7 percent (= 16,381 / 87,600). Onshore wind assets rarely achieve CFs exceeding 30 percent, with most yielding 20–25 percent or much less; offshore wind assets achieve higher CFs but are more costly to build and maintain and have shorter lifespans. For comparison, coal-fired plants operate with CFs exceeding

Table 14.1. Unsubsidized Levelized Cost of Energy (LCOE), Change in Costs, and Marginal Cost of Electricity, 2020

Asset Type	LCOE ($/MWh[a])	Change in LCOE 2009–2020 (%)	Marginal cost of energy ($/MWh)
Nuclear	$143–$200	+33%	$25–$32
Peak-gas (OCGT)[d]	$113–$198	–36%	n.a.[c]
CCGT (gas)[e]	$53–$63	–29%	$23–$32
Coal	$82–$134	+1%	$34–$48
Wind (onshore)	$34–$45	–70%	$26–$54
Solar thermal	$103–$172	–16%	n.a.
Solar PV	$28–$44	–90%	$29–$38
Storage[b]	$165–$305	n.a.[c]	n.a.[c]

[a] Includes costs of decommissioning fossil fuel plants and disposal of nuclear waste
[b] Lithium-ion battery with capacity of 100 MW and energy storage of 400 MWh.
[c] n.a. = not available
[d] Open-cycle gas turbine; peak gas plants ramp up and down to reflect the rise and fall of demand
[e] Combined-cycle gas turbine
Source: Lazard (2020) except storage, which is available from Lazard (2019).

80 percent, while the CFs of nuclear plants exceed 90 percent. Higher CFs imply lower average costs.

While CFs are important, they tell us nothing about the *timing* of wind or solar output. Recall that California suffered blackouts when air-conditioning requirements peaked as the Sun went down. Likewise, wind output is often lower during peak hours (early morning/late afternoon), but higher at night when demand is low. While storage devices (discussed below) could help in these situations, the LCOE for storage systems is higher than the LCOE associated with peak gas plants, for example.

LCOE data also ignore other issues. First, the lifespans of utility-level wind turbines and solar PV units are a third to half of those for coal, nuclear, and gas facilities. For thermal plants (fossil fuel and nuclear), costs of plant decommissioning and nuclear waste disposal are taken into account in calculating LCOE. For proper comparison, analogous costs should be considered in calculating LCOE for wind and solar as well, but they are not. Neither are issues related to the disposal of toxic wastes associated with wind turbine components and solar panels; for example, solar panel wastes are considered to be three hundred times more hazardous per unit of energy produced than nuclear waste (Atasu, Duran, and Wassenhove 2021; IER 2017). Both these costs should be taken into account in calculating wind and solar's LCOE.

Second, intermittency imposes costs on other assets in the system. Because wind and solar power must be used by the system as it is produced (in the parlance of power engineering, wind and solar output are *non-dispatchable*), other assets in the system must change their output to track changes in intermittent output in addition to changes in load. That is, as the output from wind or solar assets rises or falls, the output from other sources must do the opposite—equally and instantly. This is not a problem if peak gas or hydroelectric assets are affected, but, in many cases, intermittency affects *baseload* power plants, which do not easily ramp up and down; rapid ramping of these assets greatly increases operating and maintenance costs. Further, baseload facilities are often forced to operate below their optimal capacity as power from intermittent renewables enters the grid, which also increases costs.

Third, investment in gas assets occurs only if fixed costs—costs that do not vary regardless of how much energy the assets are producing and selling at a given time—can be recovered. As more wind energy enters a grid, the wholesale price of electricity falls while gas plants are called upon less often. Unless a gas plant earns enough surplus through much higher prices during the reduced hours it operates, the gas plant will eventually close and not be replaced, as investors recognize they are unlikely to make a profit. This problem can be resolved by operating a capacity market in addition to the market where load (demand) and supply determine the wholesale price of electricity—this balancing market is known as the energy market. Where the system operator employs a capacity market, the operator will pay the lowest bidder to construct required backstop capacity, although this leads to higher retail prices as these investment costs must be paid by ratepayers. However, some system operators only employ an energy market, which can lead to insufficient capacity to backstop intermittent wind and solar. In that case, the system may need to rely on imports from other jurisdictions to cope with intermittency; lack of adequate transmission capacity along interties with other jurisdictions, or insufficient generation available for export in adjacent systems, could result in system blackouts, as occurred in the regions discussed above.

There are other costs that will vary greatly across a landscape. Some have been taken into account in the LCOE, but many have not. Land costs are often ignored, although they are likely small. In Alberta, for example, the value of farmland averaged C$3,008/acre (US$2,377/acre) in 2020 (Statistics Canada 2022). It is estimated that one acre can support a solar facility with maximum capacity of 7.9 MW (Ong et al. 2013). Then, given an annual land rental value of perhaps $250/acre and an average CF of 33 percent, the added cost is an insignificant $0.02/MWh.

Political opposition to wind and solar is hard to measure in economic terms. Citizens increasingly oppose the location of wind and solar facilities and transmission lines due to the perceived or real cost to human health, bird and bat strikes (Peiser 2019; van Kooten 2016), and aesthetic considerations. Indeed, citizen opposition to wind and solar developments and transmission lines might be the greatest obstacle to overcome (Bryce 2021; Merrill 2021).

Policymakers look to batteries (or some other storage option) to address the intermittency problem. However, research suggests that the required battery would need to be excessively large and expensive (Duan, van Kooten, and Liu 2020). As an example, consider the 17,000 MW shortfall experienced by the United Kingdom discussed above. Suppose that the low wind regime lasts for 30 days, or 720 hours. In that case, a battery would need to be capable of storing 12,240,000 MWh (12.24 GWh) of energy. A Tesla "Powerwall" battery has a capacity of 13.5 kWh and costs about $11,000, excluding installation and other costs (Foushee 2023). Battery storage of the energy shortfall in the United Kingdom would then cost about $10 trillion! While costs might be somewhat lower if there exist economies of scale, it is unlikely that the battery size or its capacity to store energy will improve by leaps and bounds over the next decade or so to warrant greater investments in intermittent energy sources in anticipation of such improvements. Even a perfect storage device would need to be too large and expensive to warrant construction.

Even if a "reasonable" storage device were forced on the system, baseload coal, gas, or nuclear assets (if allowed) would outcompete wind for access to it (van Kooten and Mokhtarzadeh 2019). Indeed, significant gas plant capacity must be added to eliminate coal-fired power even if adequate wind, solar, and storage capacity were developed.

Finally, van Kooten and Mokhtarzadeh (2019, 71) concluded that "when wind and/or solar energy enters the Alberta electricity grid, the maximum emissions reduction that can be achieved is about 56%, but, when nuclear power is permitted, emissions could be reduced by as much as 97%." Given that nuclear power plants take time to build, it would seem that an energy transition away from fossil fuels will require reliance on natural gas as a bridge to a nuclear future (Prins 2021; European Commission 2022). Even then, attaining Net Zero CO_2 emissions is unlikely at any time in the near future.

Table 14.2. Land-Use Intensities by Energy Source, W/m²

Energy Type	Energy Density (W/m^2)
Corn ethanol	0.1
United States gas well	53.0
Biomass-fueled power plant	0.4
Wind	1.2
Solar PV	6.7
Nuclear power plant	56.0
Oil stripper well (10 bbls per day)[a]	27.0
Oil stripper well (2 bbls per day)[a]	5.5
Gas stripper well[a]	28.0

[a] An oil stripper well is defined as producing less than 10 barrels (bbl) per day; a gas stripper well produces less than 60,000 cubic feet of natural gas per day.

Source: Bryce (2010), 86, 93.

Energy Densities

There remains an additional powerful argument favoring fossil fuels. Renewable sources fail to deliver sufficient energy per unit of mass, with too large a physical footprint when it comes to land use. Currently, pumped storage is considered the best available utility-grade storage option, accounting for more than 99 percent of the world's storage capacity, even though it entails an energy loss of about 25 percent (the amount of the generated electricity that must be expended on pumping water to elevated storage before it can flow down through turbines to generate new electricity; Smil 2020, 167–68). Batteries are also a poor alternative, not only because of their cost but also because

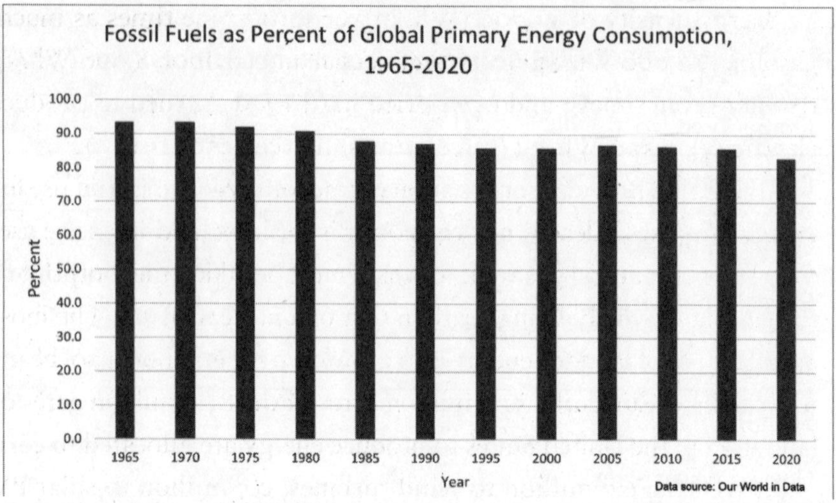

Figure 14.1. Fossil fuels as percent of global primary energy consumption, 1965–2020. *Data source: Our World in Data.*

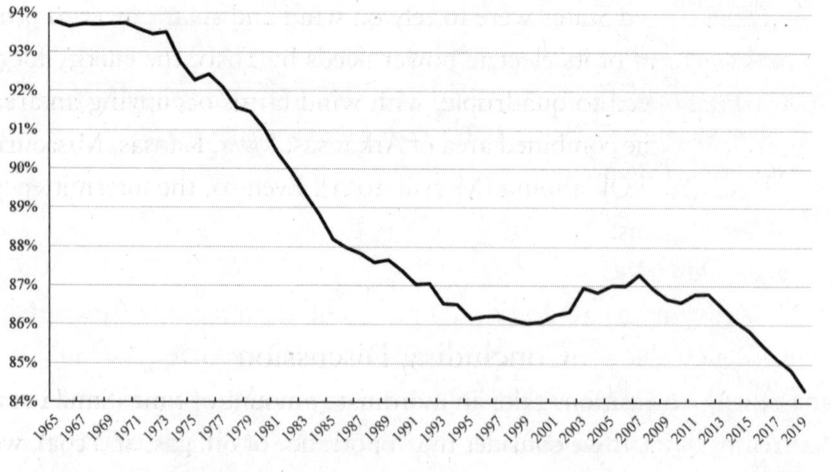

Figure 14.2. Global reliance on fossil fuels, 1965–2019. *Data source: Our World in Data.*

they have a low energy density compared with fossil fuels. Lithium-ion batteries have an energy density of only 300 watt-hours per kilogram (Wh/kg), which is why electric vehicles require a battery weighing 500 kg (Smil 2020, 169). In contrast, low-quality residual oil or diesel has an energy density of 11,700 (Wh/kg), or thirty-nine times as much; gasoline, 12,000 Wh/kg (forty times); coal and ethanol, 8,000 Wh/kg (twenty-seven times); and oven-dried hardwood (burned to produce electricity), 4,500 Wh/kg (fifteen times) (Bryce 2010, 191).

Table 14.2 provides some notion of tradeoffs regarding land use for energy purposes. Clearly, nuclear power is the least land-intensive use, followed by a natural gas well, to which must be added the footprint of the gas plant (which is smaller than that of a nuclear plant). The most extensive use of land for energy is to grow corn for ethanol or soybeans for biodiesel. Currently, 51.5 million acres of the 81.0 million acres of land used in the United States to produce energy are allocated to corn and soybeans; 6.7 million to wind turbines; 0.5 million to solar PV panels; 4.8 million to transmission lines; and 0.6 million to the production of coal-fired power (Merrill 2021).

If the United States were to rely on wind and solar power to provide 98 percent of its electric power needs by 2050, the energy footprint would need to quadruple, with wind farms occupying an area equivalent to the combined area of Arkansas, Iowa, Kansas, Missouri, Nebraska, and Oklahoma (Merrill 2021). Even so, the intermittency problem remains.

Concluding Discussion

Energy transitions take an inordinate amount of time (Smil 2017, 2020, 174–77). If we consider the importance of oil, gas, and coal, we find that, as a portion of total energy consumption, fossil fuel consumption declined 10.5 percent over the past six decades (from 93.5 percent to 83.0 percent) (Figure 14.1).

But the greatest reduction in relative reliance on fossil fuels occurred between 1970 and 1995, prior to the implementation of policies to reduce CO_2 emissions. A further but smaller decline occurred after

2007 (Figure 14.2). Indeed, although their relative contribution to the energy mix has declined slightly, consumption of fossil fuels increased by more than 337 percent since 1965 and by 145 percent since 2000. It is unlikely that fossil fuels will decline below 50 percent of primary energy consumption in the near future.

As Smil (2019) pointed out, "[C]omplete decarbonization of the global energy supply will be an extremely challenging undertaking of an unprecedented scale and complexity that will not be accomplished—even in the case of sustained, dedicated and extraordinarily costly commitment—in a matter of a few decades." Yet, politicians continue to pursue policies that are costly and might even threaten our way of life—policies that are not rational.

References

Atasu, A., S. Duran, and L. N. Van Wassenhove (2021). "The Dark Side of Solar Power." *Harvard Business Review*, June 18. Online at https://hbr.org/2021/06/the-dark-side-of-solar-power.

Baker, D. R., W. Wade, and M. Chediak (2021). "California Orders Grid Emergency, Power Shortfalls Loom." Bloomberg, July 9. Online at https://www.bloomberg.com/news/articles/2021-07-10/california-orders-stage-2-grid-emergency-power-shortfalls-loom.

Blackwill, R. D., and J. M. Harris (2017). *War by Other Means: Geoeconomics and Statecraft*. Cambridge, Massachusetts: Harvard University Press.

Brouwer, K. M., and L. Bergkamp, eds. (2021). *Road to EU Climate Neutrality by 2050: Spatial Requirements of Wind/Solar and Nuclear Energy and Their Respective Costs*. Brussels: ECR Group and Renew Europe, European Parliament. Online at https://roadtoclimateneutrality.eu/Energy_Study_Full.pdf.

Bryce, R. (2010). *Power Hungry: The Myths of "Green" Energy and the Real Fuels of the Future.* New York: PublicAffairs.

———. (2021). *Not in Our Backyard: Rural America Is Fighting Back against Large-Scale Renewable Energy Projects.* Golden Valley, Minnesota: Center of the American Experiment. Online at https://www.americanexperiment.org/reports/not-in-our-backyard.

Constable, J. (2020). *The Brink of Darkness: Britain's Fragile Power Grid.* Briefing 47. London: The Global Warming Policy Foundation.

Duan, J., G. C. van Kooten, and X. Liu (2020). "Renewable Electricity Grids, Battery Storage and Missing Money." *Resources, Conservation and Recycling* 161 (October): 105001. Online at https://www.sciencedirect.com/science/article/abs/pii/S0921344920303189.

European Commission (2022). "EU Taxonomy: Commission Begins Expert Consultations on Complementary Delegated Act Covering Certain Nuclear and Gas Activities." Press release, January 1. Online at https://ec.europa.eu/commission/presscorner/detail/en/ip_22_2.

Foushee, F. (2023). "Tesla Powerwall Review." saveonenergy, June 8. Online at https://www.saveonenergy.com/solar-energy/tesla-powerwall-review.

Hughes, G. (2020a). *Wind Power Economics: Rhetoric & Reality.* Vol. I, *Wind Power Costs in the United Kingdom.* Salisbury, United Kingdom: Renewable Energy Foundation. Online at https://www.ref.org.uk/Files/performance-wind-power-uk.pdf.

———. (2020b). *Wind Power Economics Rhetoric & Reality.* Vol. II, *The Performance of Wind Power in Denmark.* Salisbury, United Kingdom: Renewable Energy Foundation. Online at https://www.ref.org.uk/Files/performance-wind-power-dk.pdf.

IER (2017). "Will Solar Power Be at Fault for the Next Environmental Crisis?" Institute for Energy Research, August 15. Online at https://www.instituteforenergyresearch.org/uncategorized/will-solar-power-fault-next-environmental-crisis.

IEA (2021). *Net Zero by 2050: A Roadmap for the Global Energy Sector.* Paris: International Energy Agency. Online at https://www.iea.org/reports/net-zero-by-2050.

Lazard (2019). *Lazard's Levelized Cost of Storage Analysis—Version 5.0.* London: Lazard. Accessed November 3, 2021. Online at https://web.archive.org/web/20211215170414/https://www.lazard.com/media/451087/lazards-levelized-cost-of-storage-version-50-vf.pdf. Updated in Lazard (2021). *Lazard's Levelized Cost of Storage Analysis—Version 7.0.* London: Lazard. Online at https://www.lazard.com/media/42dnsswd/lazards-levelized-cost-of-storage-version-70-vf.pdf.

———. (2020). *Lazard's Levelized Cost of Energy Analysis—Version 14.0.* London: Lazard. Online at https://www.lazard.com/media/kwrjairh/lazards-levelized-cost-of-energy-version-140.pdf.

Lopez, N. (2023). "Feds Allow Diablo Canyon to Stay Open While Seeking 20-year Extension." CalMatters, March 2. Online at https://calmatters.org/environment/2023/03/diablo-canyon-nuclear-power-plant.

Mellor, S. (2021). "Europe's Ambitious Net-Zero Pledges Hit Home—with Eye-Watering Energy Bills." *Fortune*, September 10. Online at https://fortune.com/2021/09/10/europe-net-zero-energy-bills-nord-stream-2-russia.

Merrill, D. (2021). "The U.S. Will Need a Lot of Land for a Zero-Carbon Economy." Bloomberg, June 3. Online at https://www.bloomberg.com/graphics/2021-energy-land-use-economy.

Net Zero Watch (2021). "Britons Face Record Bill as Wind Farms Perform Poorly Again." Press Release, November 25. Online at https://www.netzerowatch.com/britons-face-record-bill-as-wind-farms-perform-poorly-again.

Ong, S., et al. (2013). *Land-Use Requirements for Solar Power Plants in the United States.* Golden, Colorado: National Renewable Energy Laboratory. Online at https://www.nrel.gov/docs/fy13osti/56290.pdf.

Our World in Data (n.d.). "Energy Consumption by Source, World." Accessed May 10, 2023. Online at https://ourworldindata.org/grapher/energy-consumption-by-source-and-country?time=2020. latest.

Peiser, B. (ed.) (2019). *The Impact of Wind Energy on Wildlife and the Environment: Papers from the Berlin Seminar.* GWPF Report 35. London: The Global Warming Policy Foundation. Online at https://www.thegwpf.org/content/uploads/2019/07/wind-impact-1.pdf.

Prins, G. (2021). "The Worm in the Rose." NetZero Watch, October 23. Online at https://www.netzerowatch.com/the-worm-in-the-rose.

Reuters (2022). "Germany Makes Progress in Cutting Back on Russian Energy, Minister Says." March 25. Online at https://www.reuters.com/business/energy/germany-made-progress-reducing-russian-energy-imports-2022-03-25.

Ritchie, H., and M. Roser (n.d.) "Energy Production and Consumption." Our World in Data. Accessed May 10, 2023. Online at https://ourworldindata.org/energy-production-consumption.

Singh, M. (2021). "'California and Texas Are Warnings': Blackouts Show US Deeply Unprepared for the Climate Crisis." *The Guardian*, February 19. Online at https://www.theguardian.com/environment/2021/feb/19/power-outages-texas-california-climate-crisis.

Smil, V. (2017). *Energy and Civilization: A History.* Cambridge, Massachusetts: The MIT Press.

———. (2019). "What We Need to Know about the Pace of Decarbonisation." Supplement, *Substantia* 3, no. 2 (September): 69–73. Online at https://www.torrossa.com/en/resources/an/4618471#page=70.

———. (2020). *Numbers Don't Lie: 71 Stories to Help Us Understand the Modern World*. New York: Penguin Books.

Statista (2023). "Share of Fossil Fuels in Primary Energy Consumption Worldwide from 1965 to 2020." Online at https://www.statista.com/statistics/1302762/fossil-fuel-share-in-energy-consumption-worldwide.

Statistics Canada (2022). "Value per Acre of Farm Land and Buildings at July 1." Online at https://www150.statcan.gc.ca/t1/tbl1/en/tv.action?pid=3210004701.

UNFCCC (1992). *United Nations Framework Convention on Climate Change*. New York: United Nations. Online at https://unfccc.int/resource/docs/convkp/conveng.pdf.

———. (2022). "Nationally Determined Contributions (NDCs): The Paris Agreement and NDCs." Online at https://unfccc.int/process-and-meetings/the-paris-agreement/nationally-determined-contributions-ndcs/nationally-determined-contributions-ndcs.

Van Kooten, G. C. (2016). "The Economics of Wind Power." *Annual Review of Resource Economics* 8 (October): 181–205. Online at https://www.annualreviews.org/doi/abs/10.1146/annurev-resource-091115-022544.

———. (2017). "California Dreaming: The Economics of Renewable Energy." *Canadian Journal of Agricultural Economics* 65, no. 1 (January): 19–41. Online at https://onlinelibrary.wiley.com/doi/abs/10.1111/cjag.12132.

———. (2021). "Canadian Climate Policy and Its Implications for Electricity Grids." Fraser Institute, October 21. Online at https://www.fraserinstitute.org/studies/canadian-climate-policy-and-its-implications-for-electricity-grids.

Van Kooten, G. C., and F. Mokhtarzadeh (2019). "Optimal Investment in Electric Generating Capacity under Climate Policy." *Journal of Environmental Management* 232 (February): 66–72. Online at https://www.sciencedirect.com/science/article/abs/pii/S0301479718313033.

Van Kooten, G. C., P. Withey, and J. Duan (2020). "How Big a Battery?" *Renewable Energy* 146:196–204. Online at https://ideas.repec.org/a/eee/renene/v146y2020icp196-204.html.

Van Kooten, G. C., P. Withey, and C. M. T. Johnston (2021). "Climate Urgency and the Timing of Carbon Fluxes." *Biomass and Bioenergy* 151 (August): 106162. Online at https://www.sciencedirect.com/science/article/abs/pii/S0961953421001987?via%3Dihub.

Wikipedia (n.d.) "2021 Texas Power Crisis." Accessed May 10, 2023. Online at https://en.wikipedia.org/wiki/2021_Texas_power_crisis.

Wolff, E., D. Kahn, and Z. Colman (2021). "Texas and California Built Different Power Grids, but Neither Stood Up to Climate Change." *Politico*, February 21. Online at https://www.politico.com/news/2021/02/21/texas-california-climate-change-power-grids-470434.

Chapter 15

How Economic Thinking Can Help Tackle Climate Change

by G. Cornelis van Kooten

Chapter Summary

Developing countries often question climate policies imposed by wealthy countries because they restrict the use of fossil fuels to reduce poverty. The poor discount theoretical, future risks posed by climate change because they deal with real, present risks. Greenhouse gas emissions by wealthy countries have leveled off or declined over recent decades, while those from populous developing countries have risen significantly, raising the total. Unless the developing world is to fall back into abject poverty, that will continue.

Contentious questions continue to surround some assumptions in the spectrum of socioeconomic projections and climate and economic models employed by the IPCC. Optimistically, there is a growing acceptance that the highest radiative forcing studied is implausible, and the real business-as-usual scenario lies in the moderate range. Under that assumption, the best policy would be to forgo emission suppression efforts and instead rely on adaptation measures where applicable when warming occurs.

Economic analyses still contain such a wide range of assumptions and findings that it's not yet possible for them to identify an optimal carbon tax strategy. While those analyses remain unsettled, the unprecedented international cooperation required to reduce emissions to "Net Zero" will be at odds with the interests of the developing world. Therefore, the best and perhaps only climate change response is adaptation.

Introduction

Many people consider climate change the greatest existential threat facing the planet today. The likelihood that someone will think this is true depends on whom you ask and where you live. But concern about a future climate "crisis" is essentially a rich-country phenomenon. The world's poor are more anxious about the negative effect that climate policy could have on economic growth than about climate change itself (Jayaraj 2022). Why? Because the policies aim to eliminate global use of ubiquitous coal, oil, and natural gas—fuels that are desperately needed to drive economic growth in developing countries. As a result, developing countries are willing to go along with the Western world's climate-mitigation efforts only if doing so does not inhibit economic growth. That is unlikely.

The number of people worldwide living in extreme poverty, defined as those living on less than US$1.90 per day, has declined in twenty-five years from more than 1.9 billion (36 percent of the world population)

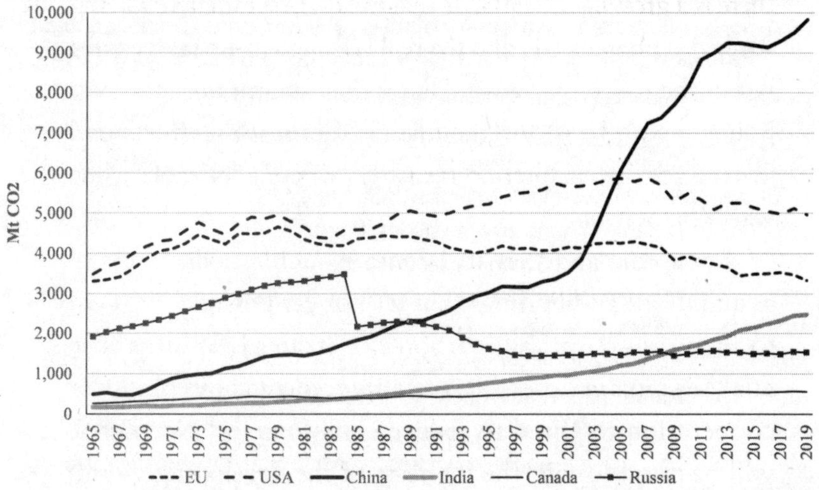

Figure 15.1. Global emissions of carbon dioxide (megatons per year) by selected regions/countries, 1965–2019. *Source: Author's construct based on data from the BP Statistical Review of World Energy, June 2020, online at http://www.bp.com/statisticalreview.*

in 1990 to 0.7 billion (9 percent) in 2015 (Roser and Ortiz-Ospina 2013). Economic growth in China and, to a lesser extent, India and elsewhere has accounted for the major advance in the well-being of the poor. This improvement in economic prospects is directly attributable to increased access to energy, especially abundant coal. This, in turn, led to large increases in carbon dioxide (CO_2) emissions (Figure 15.1). (Throughout this chapter, CO_2 is used to refer collectively to carbon dioxide plus other greenhouse gas emissions, where the latter are measured in CO_2-equivalent terms.)

Notice two trends in Figure 15.1: First, CO_2 emissions in developed countries have leveled off or even declined slightly. Second, emissions of the most populous developing countries, particularly China but increasingly India, are rising and overwhelming those of the developed countries. Even if the rich countries could curtail their CO_2 emissions, global emissions would continue to rise. Unless the developing countries

1st-Stage Integrated Assessment Models (IAMS): Shared Socioeconomic Pathways (SSP) & Representative Concentration Pathways (RCP)

CCCMA	Canadian Centre for Climate Modeling and Analysis
GISS	Goddard Institute of Space Studies (NASA), U.S.
CSIRO	Australian Commonwealth Scientific and Research Organization
GFDL	Geophysical Fluid Dynamics L aboratory, U.S .
IAP	Institute of Atmospheric Physics, China
IPSL	Institut Pierre Simon L aplace, France
MPI	Max-Planck Institute for Meteorology, Germany
MiniCAM	Mini Climate Assessment Model, U.S.
AIM	Asian Pacific Integrated Model, Japan
ASF	Atmospheric Stabilization Framework Model, U.S.
IMAGE	Integrated Model to Assess the Greenhouse E ect , Netherlands
MARIA	Multiregional Approach for Resource and Industry Allocatoin, Japan
MESSAGE	Model for Energy Supply Strategy Alternatives & General Environmental Impact, IIASA, Austria

↓

2nd-Stage Global Climate Models (GCM)

CCCMA	Canadian Centre for Climate Modeling and Analysis
GISS	Goddard Institute of Space Studies (NASA), U.S.
CSIRO	Australian Commonwealth Scientific and Research Organization
GFDL	Geophysical Fluid Dynamics L aboratory, U.S .
IAP	Institute of Atmospheric Physics, China
IPSL	Institut Pierre Simon L aplace, France
MPI	Max-Planck Institute for Meteorology, Germany

↓

3rd-Stage Integrated Assessment Models (IAMS)

DICE	Dynamic Integrated Climate and Economics, William Nordhaus
FUND	Framework for Uncertainty, Negotiation and Distribution, Richard Tol
PAGE	Policy Analysis of the Greenhouse Effect, Chris Hope

Figure 15.2. Climate-economic modeling at various stages and examples of models in each stage. *Source: G. C. van Kooten.*

were to stop growing and fall back into abject poverty, it would be nigh impossible to prevent global warming.

Regarding the need to reduce greenhouse gas emissions, the principal (moral or religious) issue pertains to the impact mitigation policies might have on the poorest in global society. Because poverty poses risks to health and life that far exceed those posed by climate change, any climate policies that result in a reduction in the prospects of the poorest should be avoided, even if that means the rest of the world needs to adapt to climate change rather than try to mitigate it. This suggests that the ultimate question is whether mitigation or adaptation is the better option. Here is where economics has a role to play.

It is important to realize that perceptions of climate change are driven solely by computer modeling that ignores or downplays actual data and that economic models drive the climate policy process. Economic models are referred to as integrated assessment models (IAMs) because they integrate economics with biophysical, climate, and other aspects (Nordhaus 2013; Wang et al. 2017). Economic models (IAMs) used by the United Nations' Intergovernmental Panel on Climate Change (IPCC) provide inputs to (2nd-stage) climate models (which are not IAMs) (Figure 15.2).

The 1st-stage economic models develop potential paths of future CO_2 emissions based on storylines concerning future economic developments, technological changes, and implementation of assumed mitigation strategies. For the third stage, economists have developed growth models that determine the optimal path of investment in climate change mitigation—spending on mitigation is a choice variable in these models, unlike in the case of 1st-stage models. It is these 3rd-stage IAMs that provide estimates of the social cost of carbon (SCC—the calculated value of net harm done per unit of CO_2 emitted) that inform policymakers regarding an appropriate carbon price or tax. Since the 3rd-stage IAMs include a climate emulator that translates CO_2 emissions into temperatures, the models are independent of the 1st-stage IAMs and

Table 15.1. Population, Income, CO_2 Emissions, and Energy Projections for Base SSPs

Year	Population (10^6)	PPP GDP per person (US$ 2005)	Emissions from fossil fuels & industry (Mt CO_2)	Total energy (EJ)[a]	Energy from coal (EJ)[a]
	Baseline				
2005	6,530.5	8,791	29,394.2	340.8	31.6
	SSP1 (RCP2.6, 4.5)[b]				
2050	8,530.5	34,148	42,668.6	547.6	22.3
2100	6,958.0	81,258	27,049.0	528.3	6.3
	SSP2 (RCP2.6, 4.5, 6.0)[b]				
2050	9,242.5	25,341	50,944.3	602.0	40.3
2100	9,103.2	59,127	73,019.3	831.8	64.9
	SSP3 (RCP4.5, 6.0)[b]				
2050	10,038.4	17,991	53,999.0	591.9	57.6
2100	12,793.2	21,849	75,119.4	797.6	99.5
	SSP4 (RCP2.6, 4.5, 6.0)[b]				
2050	9,213.0	24,886	44,829.1	587.4	30.6
2100	9,456.3	38,121	45,152.0	652.4	29.4
	SSP5 (RCP2.6, 4.5, 6.0, 8.5)[b]				
2050	8,629.5	43,855	80,325.7	856.4	56.8
2100	7,447.2	138,868	114,164.6	1,056.2	60.7

[a] 1 EJ (exajoule) = 277,777.778 gigawatt-hours (GWh); 1GWh = 1 million kilowatt-hours (kWh); 1 kWh = 1,000 watts delivered for an hour. [b] Depending on assumptions, any SSP can lead to more than one RCP but, as indicated, not to all, except SSP5 (Russell et al. 2022). *Source: This table is based on the SSP database hosted by the IIASA Energy Program at https://tntcat.iiasa.ac.at/SspDb.*

2nd-stage climate models. Indeed, models across and within stages essentially stand alone in the sense that they might inform or even provide inputs used in other models (for example, CO_2-emission pathways from 1st-stage IAMs are used in 2nd-stage climate models), but models are not in any other sense connected.

Modeling Climate Change: Physical and Economic Aspects

The IPCC relies on a variety of storylines to develop Shared Socioeconomic Pathways (SSPs) that provide information on future growth in population and global and regional gross domestic product (GDP); the rate at which per capita incomes in poor countries catch up with those in rich countries; expected technological changes and, thereby, the carbon intensity of future energy sources; and so on. The storylines underpinning the SSPs are indicated in Table 15.1, although often neglected in policy discussions.

SSP3 might be considered the *worst-case* scenario in terms of comparing what a person could buy in 2050 or 2100 compared with 2005. In this scenario, average global per capita GDP is projected to increase from $8,791 to only about $18,000 (double current income) by 2050 and $22,000 (250 percent increase) by 2100. The SSP3 storyline forecasts world population to rise to 10.0 billion by 2050 and to 12.8 billion by 2100, while coal continues to be a dominant source of fuel; energy requirements will be high, with coal expected to account for 9.7 percent of total energy use in 2050, rising to 12.5 percent by 2100. The determinants in this scenario are a rapidly expanding population constraining GDP per capita and failure to adopt low-carbon energy technologies driving CO_2 emissions.

The *best-case* scenario in terms of GDP per capita is SSP5; under this scenario, population is assumed to increase to 8.6 billion in 2050 but to fall to 7.4 billion by 2100. The average global per capita income rises to nearly $44,000 (five times current income) by 2050 and $139,000 (sixteen times) in 2100—absurdly large increases accompanied by high energy requirements and CO_2 emissions.

Clearly, SSP5 and SSP3 would result in the highest concentrations of atmospheric CO_2. In contrast, SSP1 has the lowest projected population in both 2050 and 2100 and the least emissions compared to other scenarios. SSP1 assumes a high rate of technical improvements in the provision of low-carbon energy, while real per capita incomes increase to nearly four times current income by 2050 and to over nine times by 2100.

Each SSP scenario also assumes that the gap between the per capita incomes of rich and poor countries shrinks; the poor get richer faster than the rich. In the worst scenario, SSP3, the average *real* incomes of Middle East and African countries are assumed to increase nearly fourfold by 2100; under SSP5, they rise to almost thirty-three times current income. Per capita incomes in low-income countries are projected to increase by 3.1 percent, 2.7 percent, 1.4 percent, 1.5 percent, and 3.7 percent annually, respectively, across the five SSP scenarios.

Given these projections, it would be better to let economic development proceed, as this provides all countries with sufficient incomes to adapt to climate change—that is, to protect themselves and their possessions from whatever changes to weather and climate result from whatever changes to global-average temperature result from the CO_2 emissions associated with that development.

The SSPs are used by 1st-stage IAMs to create Representative Concentration Pathways (RCP)—the trajectory of future CO_2 and other greenhouse gas emissions (Riahi et al. 2017; van Vuuren et al. 2011). This then gives the future path of atmospheric CO_2, which is used in climate models to project future global temperatures (Figure 15.3). Notice that, as indicated in Table 15.1, more than one SSP can lead to a particular RCP.

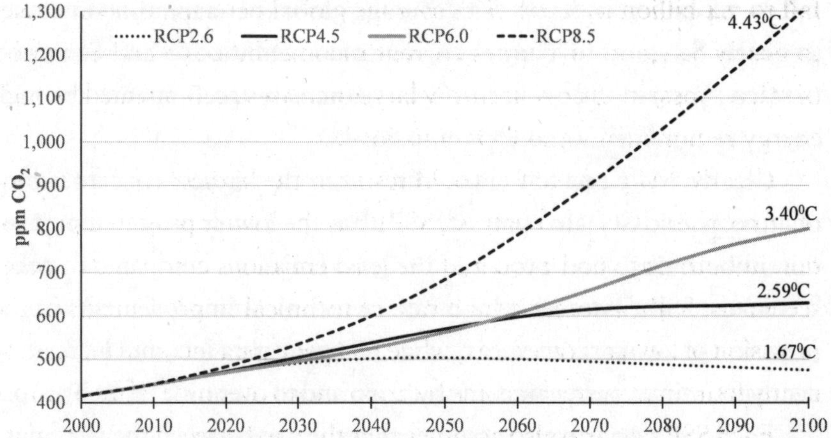

Figure 15.3. Four Representative Concentration Pathways (RCPs) of CO_2 used by climate models to derive IPCC projections of future atmospheric concentrations of CO_2 with potential 2100 temperatures provided on the right. *Data source: Russell et al. 2022. Graph source: G. C. van Kooten.*

The RCP scenarios are designated with a number (2.6, 4.5, and so forth) that represents the additional radiative forcing (heating) in watts per square meter (W/m^2) due to CO_2 in 2100 relative to pre-industrial times. As of 2019, the additional forcing from CO_2 was estimated to be 2.08 W/m^2, with the total forcing from all greenhouse gases equal to 3.14 W/m^2. In 1979, the CO_2 forcing was 1.03 W/m^2 and the total forcing was 1.70 W/m^2, implying an annual rate of increase over the forty-year period in overall CO_2 forcing of 1.5 percent. If this exponential trend continues, the overall forcing from all greenhouse gases in 2100 would be 7.88 W/m^2, although most scientists believe that the upward trend would slow over time as absorption bands become increasingly saturated (Schildknecht 2020; van Wijngaarden and Happer 2019, 2020; see chapter 9).

It is important to recognize that any SSP or RCP is based on storylines. In the past, none was considered more likely than any other. That is changing. Although RCP8.5 is often considered by climate researchers (and the media), erroneously, as the business-as-usual scenario, it has never been considered more likely than any other scenario. Other scenarios considered just as valid by the IPCC, but ignored by many researchers and the media, are RCP6.0, RCP4.5, and RCP2.6. Indeed, RCP8.5 has been criticized for relying on too optimistic assumptions regarding future per capita incomes associated with SSP5 (Table 15.1), while exaggerating the actual warming experienced since 1979 (Hausfather and Peters 2020; Zhu, Poulsen, and Otto-Bliesner 2020). Hence, according to Curry (2022), "[T]here is growing acceptance that RCP8.5 is implausible, and RCP4.5 is arguably the current business-as-usual emissions scenario." If RCP4.5 or RCP2.6 were to occur, the best strategy for dealing with climate change would be to forgo mitigation (trying to curb global warming) and rely on adaptation when and if the warmer temperatures are realized (Russell et al. 2022).

Economic Modeling and the Social Cost of Carbon

Policymakers need estimates of marginal damages—also known as the social cost of carbon (SCC)—to guide decisions about carbon taxes and for determining the benefits (damages avoided) of mitigation strategies. Estimates of SCC are currently available from a suite of 3rd-stage IAMs, the best known of which is the Dynamic Integrated Climate and Economics (DICE) model (Nordhaus 2013, 2018). IAMs have been criticized by economists and climate scientists as too ad hoc, with outcomes highly sensitive to assumed parameter values (Pindyck 2013, 2017; Lewis 2018). Three of the most contentious parameters are the equilibrium climate sensitivity (ECS)—the temperature increase associated with a doubling of the atmospheric concentration of CO_2— (see chapter 9); the discount rate employed; and the projections of future damages from climate change (van Kooten et al. 2021). For example, Figure 15.3 employs an ECS value of 3.1. Empirical studies have estimated ECS to be around 2.0°C. Chapter 9 above concludes that it is between 1 and 2°C, while computer models provide estimates over 3.0°C, some even exceeding 4.5°C (van Kooten et al. 2021, 16–18). Yet IAMs offer one of the only ways that economists can provide policy advice informed by the findings of the climate models.

The 3rd-stage models provide estimates of the SCC. Surprisingly, the models do not use any of the outputs from the climate models or the 1st-stage IAMs. DICE is a standard economic growth model that allows for investment in climate change mitigation if such investment leads to an increase in future income—a reduction in future damages. Damages are a function of temperature and investments that reduce atmospheric CO_2. The damages in question are the result of sea level rise, increased chance of malaria and other tropical diseases, lost biodiversity, increased damage from adverse weather events, and so forth (van Kooten 2021, 250–52; van Kooten 2013, 221–52). Given that little is known about how damages are affected by changes in the mean global temperature, the damage function is ad hoc—a guess at best (Russell et al. 2022).

But there are other issues with the models. There is disagreement among economists concerning the social rate of discount (the difference between the value today of $1 possessed today and the value of of $1 possessed in the future—for example, in 2050 or 2100) used to make comparisons across generations, which is important when models project incomes fifty to one hundred or more years into the future. Assumptions need to be made about how to measure the intrinsic value of per capita consumption, because this affects how the discount rate changes over time—a technical issue of great importance because projected future temperatures are as sensitive to this assumption as to assumptions of ECS. As noted earlier, the models include a climate component that is unrelated to any 2nd-stage climate model, except that these 3rd-stage models are informed by the underlying physics and temperatures predicted by the climate models (van Kooten et al. 2021). Thus, the economic models rely on ECS values from the IPCC's climate models, even though such values remain contentious. (See chapter 9.)

An indication of how sensitive the social cost of carbon is to these assumptions is provided in Table 15.2. Based on the table, different assumptions concerning the three parameters discussed in the previous paragraph result in values of the SCC in 2020 that vary from about \$15/tCO_2 (metric ton of carbon dioxide equivalent) to nearly \$300/tCO_2; by 2050, the price of carbon can vary from \$45/tCO_2 to \$555/tCO_2. While policymakers likely assume that a carbon tax should be set to the marginal damages (SCC), economists recognize that the SCC would need to be divided by the marginal cost of public funds—the cost associated with the distortion in resource allocation that results when governments raise revenue and that varies across jurisdictions and by tax instrument (Sandmo 1975, 1998; Dahlby 2008). A good rule of thumb is to divide it by 2.0, which implies that, based on Table 15.2, the current carbon tax should be set between \$8/tCO_2 and \$150/tCO_2. Since the base case scenario in the DICE model assumes an ECS close to 3.0°C, an elasticity of marginal utility of consumption of 1.45, and a social rate of time preference of 1.5 percent, the appropriate tax would be about \$18/tCO_2 in 2020.

Economic analyses based on 3rd-stage IAMs are problematic. First, given the wide range of potentially optimal SCCs and differing marginal costs of public funds, it is impossible to settle on any path of optimal carbon taxes—a policymaker could justify almost any level of a carbon tax. Second, based on recent results from the DICE model, the optimal tax is a lot lower than that being implemented in some jurisdictions. For example, the Canadian government plans to increase the price of (that is, the tax on) carbon to C\$170/tCO_2 (about US\$135/tCO_2) by 2030. However, most 3rd-stage IAMs find that the SCC should be no more than about US\$120/tCO_2, implying a tax of some US\$60/tCO_2,

Table 15.2. Estimated Optimal Social Cost of Carbon ($/tCO$_2$), Various Scenarios and Selected Years, 2015–2100[a]

	ECS = 3.0°C				ECS = 2.0°C	
	Elasticity of the marginal utility of consumption					
	1.45	3.0	1.45	1.0	1.0	1.45
	Social rate of time preference (intergenerational rate of discount)					
Year	1.50%	0.10%	0.10%	0.10%	0.10%	1.50%
2015	29.48	12.99	113.48	252.62	144.33	17.14
2020	35.25	15.35	136.66	295.15	170.67	20.41
2030	49.10	22.03	187.36	376.15	220.71	28.19
2040	66.32	31.76	245.65	460.25	271.95	37.75
2050	87.25	45.14	312.98	554.77	326.91	49.27
2060	112.25	62.84	390.75	659.72	386.64	62.90
2070	141.66	85.56	481.92	772.46	452.37	78.80
2080	175.79	114.03	587.60	890.71	524.19	97.14
2090	214.94	148.92	706.04	1,012.09	600.09	118.08
2100	259.38	190.85	835.73	1,134.03	678.50	141.76

[a] *Source: Van Kooten et al. (2021), 44.*

a little over a third of what is planned. Third, the optimal tax cannot be applied equally across all jurisdictions because the marginal cost of public funds varies greatly across jurisdictions.

In contrast, McKitrick (2011) provides a simple pricing rule for addressing global warming, namely, a carbon tax {XE "tax:carbon"} that is contingent on the global mean temperature (GMT) and its rate of change. The tax would rise or fall with increases or decreases in GMT and would be modified more or less frequently depending on how fast GMT changes. This would make the carbon tax dependent on actual rather than on hypothetical changes in GMT. Unfortunately, few climate lobbyists and policymakers appear willing to adopt such a rule.

International Policy Formation

The preceding discussion suggests that it is not yet possible to settle on a strategy for addressing climate change, because it is not clear whether adaptation or mitigation would be preferred. Nor is it obvious which storyline will evolve, though few if any would result in catastrophic warming (Koonin 2021). Reducing global emissions of CO_2 will require an unprecedented level of international cooperation that would be extremely difficult and likely unachievable. At the very least, if that reduction is to be achieved, the major emitters need to fall in line, or else anything the United States and Europe do to reduce emissions is undone within a few years by increases in China, India, and other developing countries (as evident in Figure 15.1).

The current U.S. administration is focused on eliminating fossil fuels as an energy source and achieving "Net Zero" by 2050—the agenda currently pursued by developed countries to halt further increases in the atmospheric concentration of CO_2. Thus, President Joe Biden convened a climate summit in April 2021 to lobby thirty heads of state to increase their climate-mitigation efforts ahead of the November COP26 meeting in Glasgow. The president committed the United States to reduce CO_2 emissions by 50 percent by 2030 from base year 2005 and make the electricity grid carbon neutral by 2035 (White House 2021). Several nations also pledged to reduce their domestic CO_2 emissions by more than originally indicated in their Nationally Determined Contributions (NDC) to the Paris climate agreement. Japan committed to reducing its CO_2 emissions by 46 percent by 2030 compared to 2013 emissions but has since appeared to renege on this promise due to energy security concerns. The European Union had already committed to reduce emissions by 55 percent by 2030, while the United Kingdom would reduce them by 78 percent by 2035 (BBC 2021; European Commission 2021), although these targets are likely to change following the Russian invasion of Ukraine. (See chapter 14.)

India, China, Russia, Brazil, and many other developing nations refuse to commit to reducing their emissions beyond what they had declared in their original NDCs. China and India are leaders in adopting renewable energy, but at the same time they are also greatly expanding their coal-fired generation capacity (Reuters 2021; Doshi and Krishnadev 2021). Developing countries are demanding more than a trillion dollars from rich countries to help them protect tropical forests and develop wind and solar facilities (Harvey 2022; Newburger 2021); this is unlikely given that developed countries have yet to meet their commitment, made in 2009 at Copenhagen's fifteenth Conference of the Parties (COP15) to the United Nations Framework Convention on Climate Change, to establish an international fund that would provide developing countries $100 billion per year to address climate change.

An indication of the problem is provided in Table 15.3. Unless countries adhering to the rule of law pass legislation to achieve emission-reduction targets, politicians have no incentive to adhere to targets—targets are not mandatory, and there is no supra-authority to enforce them (van Kooten 2004).

The electricity sector has been targeted because it is assumed that, in the future, almost all forms of energy can somehow be electrified. Fossil fuel generation of electricity will almost need to be eliminated, with any such remaining generation offset through forestry activities and carbon capture and storage (CCS). While forests can indeed remove CO_2 from the atmosphere, there is a limit on how much can be removed and stored in terrestrial carbon sinks (van Kooten 2020). CCS remains

Table 15.3. Current (2019) CO_2 Emissions in Major Jurisdictions and Changes in Emissions from Base Years 1990 and 2005

Item	EU	USA	UK	China	India	Japan	Russia	World
2019 emissions (Mt CO_2)	3,330.4	4,964.7	387.1	9,825.8	2,480.4	1,123.1	1,532.6	34,169.0
% of global emissions	9.7%	14.5%	1.1%	28.8%	7.3%	3.3%	4.5%	100.0%
Change in 2019 emissions compared to those in:								
1990	−23%	0%	−35%	+323%	+312%	+3%	−31%	+60%
2005	−22%	−16%	−33%	+61%	+106%	−14%	+5%	+21%
Share of global income (2020)	17.0%	23.6%	3.5%	17.9%	3.1%	5.4%	1.7%	100.0%

Source: BP Statistical Review of World Energy (June 2020); World Bank, https://data.worldbank.org/indicator/NY.GDP.MKTP.KD.

a questionable option because it is still in the testing stage, while it is extremely expensive in parasitic energy terms—capturing carbon and storing it requires some 30 percent of the electricity generated by a power plant. It is also controversial. Activists in the United States are lobbying to remove CCS and nuclear energy from Biden's arsenal for achieving zero emissions for the electricity sector by 2035 (Smith 2021). Assuming there is no appetite for nuclear energy or the construction of hydroelectric dams on major rivers, the electricity sector will need to rely almost exclusively on non-hydro renewable sources of generation (that is, intermittent wind and solar power plus limited biomass). Economic issues related to the use of intermittent sources to generate electricity are discussed in more detail in chapter 14.

Concluding Discussion

It has been evident for years that huge and growing energy demands by China, India, and other emerging nations and the Net Zero agenda being pursued by the United States, the United Kingdom, the European Union, and other Western countries are incompatible when it comes to the mitigation of climate change. Regardless of how much the wealthy, developed world reduces its greenhouse gas emissions, the developing world's future emissions will overwhelm that reduction. As the outcome of the November 2021 COP26 meeting in Glasgow illustrates, it also appears that an agreement to resolve this incompatibility may be unachievable. However, if the price for an international compromise is the abandonment of the 1.5°C goal, the West's 2050 Net Zero agenda itself would become futile and self-destructive in the face of China's unrestrained expansion of cheap energy and its rise to global dominance. Clearly, all signs point to adaptation as opposed to mitigation as the best and perhaps only means for responding to climate change.

References

BBC (2021). "Climate Change: EU to Cut CO2 Emissions by 55% by 2030." BBC, April 21. Online at https://www.bbc.com/news/world-europe-56828383.

Curry, J. (2022). "The Climate 'Crisis' Isn't What It Used to Be." Climate Etc., November 2. Online at https://judithcurry.com/2022/11/02/the-climate-crisis-isnt-what-it-used-to-be.

Dahlby, B. (2008). *The Marginal Cost of Public Funds: Theory and Applications*. Cambridge, Massachusetts: The MIT Press.

Doshi, T. K. and C. S. Krishnadev (2021). "India's Energy Policies and the Paris Agreement Commitments: Economic Growth and Environmental Constraints." RealClear Energy, August 25. Online at https://www.realclearenergy.org/articles/2021/08/25/indias_energy_policies_and_the_paris_agreement_commitments_economic_growth_and_environmental_constraints_791590.html.

European Commission (2021). Climate Strategies & Targets. Online at https://ec.europa.eu/clima/policies/strategies_en.

Harvey, Fiona (2022). "Developing Countries 'Will Need $2tn a Year in Climate Funding by 2030.'" *The Guardian*, November 7. Online at https://www.theguardian.com/environment/2022/nov/08/developing-countries-climate-crisis-funding-2030-report-nicholas-stern.

Hausfather, Z. and G. P. Peters (2020). "Emissions—the 'Business as Usual' Story Is Misleading." *Nature* 577, no. 7792 (January): 618–20. Online at https://www.nature.com/articles/d41586-020-00177-3.

Jayaraj, V. (2022). "Op-Ed: The Rich Are Taking the Poor to the Cleaners on 'Green' Energy in Countries That Can Least Afford It." *The Western Journal*, March 30. Online at https://www.westernjournal.com/op-ed-rich-taking-poor-cleaners-green-energy-countries-can-least-afford.

Koonin, S. E. (2021). *Unsettled: What Climate Science Tells Us, What It Doesn't, and Why It Matters.* Dallas, Texas: BenBella Books.

Lewis, N. (2018). "Abnormal Climate Response of the DICE IAM—a Trillion Dollar Error?" NicholasLewis.org, April 22. Online at https://www.nicholaslewis.org/abnormal-climate-response-of-the-dice-iam-a-trillion-dollar-error.

McKitrick, R. R. (2011). "A Simple State-Contingent Pricing Rule for Complex Intertemporal Externalities." *Energy Economics* 33, no. 1 (January): 111–20.

Newburger, E. (2021). "Here's What Countries Pledged on Climate Change at Biden's Global Summit." CNBC, April 22. Online at https://www.cnbc.com/2021/04/22/biden-climate-summit-2021-what-brazil-japan-canada-others-pledged.html.

Nordhaus, W. D. (2013). "Integrated Economic and Climate Modeling." In *Handbook of Computable General Equilibrium Modeling*, Vol. 1A, edited by P. B. Dixon and D. W. Jorgenson, 1069–1131. Amsterdam: North Holland. Online at http://dx.doi.org/10.1016/B978-0-444-59568-3.00016-X.

———. (2018). "Evolution of Modeling of the Economics of Global Warming: Changes in the DICE Model, 1992–2017." *Climatic Change* 148, no. 4 (June): 623–40. Online at https://link.springer.com/article/10.1007/s10584-018-2218-y.

Pindyck, R. S. (2013). "Climate Change Policy: What Do the Models Tell Us?" *Journal of Economic Literature* 51, no. 3 (September): 860–72.

———. (2017). "The Use and Misuse of Models for Climate Policy." *Review of Environmental Economics and Policy* 11, no. 1 (Winter): 100–114. Online at https://www.journals.uchicago.edu/doi/abs/10.1093/reep/rew012?journalCode=reep.

Reuters (2021). "Energy: China's Provinces Still Planning over 100 GW of New Coal Projects—Greenpeace." Reuters, August 24. Online at https://www.reuters.com/business/energy/chinas-provinces-still-planning-over-100-gw-new-coal-projects-greenpeace-2021-08-25.

Riahi, K., et al. (2017). "The Shared Socioeconomic Pathways and Their Energy, Land Use, and Greenhouse Gas Emissions Implications: An Overview." *Global Environmental Change* 42 (January): 153–68.

Roser, M., and E. Ortiz-Ospina (2013). "Global Extreme Poverty." Our World In Data. Online at https://ourworldindata.org/extreme-poverty. Available via the WayBack Machine: https://web.archive.org/web/20211229072707/https://ourworldindata.org/extreme-poverty

Russell, A. R., et al. (2022). "Damage Functions and the Social Cost of Carbon: Addressing Uncertainty in Estimating the Economic Consequences of Mitigating Climate Change." *Environmental Management* 69, no. 5 (May): 919–36. Online at https://doi.org/10.1007/s00267-022-01608-9.

Sandmo, A. (1975). "Optimal Taxation in the Presence of Externalities." *Swedish Journal of Economics* 77, no. 1 (March): 86–98. Online at https://www.jstor.org/stable/3439329.

———. (1998). "Redistribution and the Marginal Cost of Public Funds." *Journal of Public Economics* 70, no. 3 (December): 365–82. Online at https://www.sciencedirect.com/science/article/abs/pii/S0047272798000401.

Schildknecht, D. (2020). "Saturation of the Infrared Absorption by Carbon Dioxide in the Atmosphere." *International Journal of Modern Physics B* 34, no. 30 (October): 2050293. Online at https://doi.org/10.1142/S0217979220502938.

Smith, A. (2021). "Left-Wing Activists Demand Democrats Exclude Nuclear and Carbon Capture from Climate Bill." *Washington Examiner*, May 12. Online at https://www.washingtonexaminer.com/policy/activists-demand-renewable-energy-standard.

Van Kooten, G. C. (2004). *Climate Change Economics: Why International Accords Fail.* Cheltenham, United Kingdom: Edward Elgar.

———. (2013). *Climate Change, Climate Science and Economics: Prospects for a Renewable Energy Future.* Dordrecht: Springer.

———. (2020). "How Effective Are Forests in Mitigating Climate Change?" *Forest Policy and Economics* 120 (November): 102295. Online at https://www.sciencedirect.com/science/article/abs/pii/S1389934120302914.

———. (2021). *Applied Welfare Economics, Trade and Agricultural Policy Analysis.* Toronto, Ontario: University of Toronto Press.

Van Kooten, G. C., et al. (2021). "Climate Change and the Social Cost of Carbon: DICE Explained and Expanded." REPA Working Paper #2021-01. June. Online at http://web.uvic.ca/~repa/publications.htm.

Van Vuuren, D. P., et al. (2011). "The Representative Concentration Pathways: An Overview." *Climatic Change* 109, no. 1 (August): 5–31.

Van Wijngaarden, W. A., and W. Happer (2019). *Methane and Climate.* Arlington, Virginia: CO2 Coalition. Online at https://wvanwijngaarden.info.yorku.ca/files/2020/09/Methane-PaperREV1-Jan.-17-2019.pdf?x45936.

———. (2020). "Dependence of Earth's Thermal Radiation on Five Most Abundant Greenhouse Gases." arXiv:2006.03098 [physics.ao-ph], June 8. Online at https://arxiv.org/abs/2006.03098.

Wang, Z., et al. (2017). *Integrated Assessment Models of Climate Change Economics.* Singapore: Springer Nature.

White House (2021). "FACT SHEET: President Biden Sets 2030 Greenhouse Gas Pollution Reduction Target Aimed at Creating Good-Paying Union Jobs and Securing U.S. Leadership on Clean Energy Technologies." April 22. Online at https://www.

whitehouse.gov/briefing-room/statements-releases/2021/04/22/fact-sheet-president-biden-sets-2030-greenhouse-gas-pollution-reduction-target-aimed-at-creating-good-paying-union-jobs-and-securing-u-s-leadership-on-clean-energy-technologies.

Zhu, J., C. J. Poulsen, and B. L. Otto-Bliesner (2020). "High Climate Sensitivity in CMIP6 Model Not Supported by Paleoclimate." *Nature Climate Change* 10, no. 5 (April): 378–79. Online at https://www.nature.com/articles/s41558-020-0764-6.

Chapter 16

Climate and Energy Policy in the Developing World

by Vijay Jayaraj

Chapter Summary

The developing world is nowhere close to having sufficient energy to eradicate extreme poverty, open education and employment opportunities, and elevate economic prospects. Leaders in the developing world realize the real climate threat lies in pro-renewable, anti–fossil fuel policies of Western governments and organizations seeking to impose restrictive conditions on the poorest people of the world. They've often had to subscribe to Western mandates when forced to choose between what will be funded (but fail), and alternatives to produce enough energy for their countrymen.

Leaders have noted self-inflicted fuel poverty in Western countries resulting in tens of thousands of excess winter deaths, driven by skyrocketing costs from drastic coal-to-wind energy transitions. They recognize wind and solar intermittency problems and the cost and scalability issues. With the passage of years, climate change impacts aren't as dangerous as predicted, fossil fuel benefits continue to accrue to those using them, and temperature trends remain far below IPCC climate model forecasts. Economic slowdowns driven by regressive energy policy will push hundreds of millions of people around the world into poverty for decades.

Western governments and agencies should be called upon to humanely support developing world goals without harmful energy policies pursued for unattainable climate targets. Otherwise, it should come as no surprise when the developing world seeks an alternative in abundant coal, which already provides electricity to billions of people in Asia.

While climate activists fret about possible tenth-of-a-degree changes in global-average temperature, billions of people across the developing world worry about how they will obtain food, water, health care, and other necessities that their wealthier neighbors take for granted. More importantly, officials in the developing world worry about producing enough electricity to meet the demands of growing economies. Their worry stems from the fact that fear of climate change dominates global politics and has ignited a war on fossil fuels.

As a citizen of a third world country, and a climate scientist, I offer a perspective on climate science and politics that differs from that held by many in wealthy countries. Academy Award–winning movies like *Slumdog Millionaire* give Westerners a glimpse of the poverty in India's most famous cities, but the reality is much worse, especially when it comes to energy poverty. Suffice it to say that India and other developing countries are nowhere close to making adequate energy available to their people and eradicating their poverty—nor even to reaching the living standards of the poorest in the West.

In comparison to pre–World War II Western societies, the developing economies of today have the additional burden of catering to a large population that is below the poverty line. For the many millions in poverty, disruption of economic growth could mean the difference between life and death. For example, around three hundred million people—equivalent to almost the entire U.S. population—in India alone live in poverty. Not "poverty" like that in America, defined in 2017 as income below $24,600 for a family of four, but Indian poverty, defined in 2017 as income below $2,920 (in purchasing power parity, equivalent to about $11,401 in the United States, less than half the U.S. poverty level) for a family of four. Just one year of the COVID-19 economic lockdown pushed 230 million people around the world into poverty (IANS 2021). An economic slowdown driven by regressive energy policy would have an equally damaging effect but would last not for a year or two but for decades.

In Nigeria, one of Africa's fastest-growing economies, 54 percent of the people are still without access to electricity. The situation is even worse in sub-Saharan Africa, with only 19 percent having access to electricity in the Democratic Republic of Congo and 7 percent in South Sudan. Africans are very nearly one-sixth of the world's people, but they consume just one-thirtieth of the world's primary energy. Thirteen of the world's twenty least electrified countries are in Africa. According to Our World in Data (2022), 940 million (that is, 13 percent of the world's population) do not have access to electricity, and that includes thousands of hospitals in Africa. Only one in four hospitals in Cambodia, Myanmar, Nepal, Kenya, Ethiopia, and Niger has access to electricity (World Bank et al. 2021). Lack of energy access hampers health care services, putting millions of people far from the reach of even basic medical facilities that people in the developed West take for granted. From performing surgeries to storing vaccines, the lack of electricity hampers all critical functions of hospitals. This situation in African states means that their economies and people's livelihoods will grow only slowly. Restricting them to unreliable, expensive, and smaller-scale renewables will not solve the problem. In the developing world, millions who do have electricity lack uninterrupted supply, suffering frequent blackouts and having power only a few unpredictable hours a day. How many in the developed world would put up with that?

Even in relatively advanced economies like China's, energy poverty has been a difficult issue to resolve. The Chinese economy, despite billions of dollars' worth of renewable tech, experienced continued energy instability in 2021. More than a dozen Chinese provinces experienced widespread power blackouts (Bradsher 2021) and sustained load shedding, leading to the collapse of small industries in numerous provinces. Some industries laid off their workers. Others sent them home on unpaid leave for a month. China's winter fuel crisis in 2017 was another classic example. The Chinese government, to please climate crusaders, had introduced various "green" reforms (Al Jazeera 2021). One was Beijing's decision to force millions of households to abandon coal for natural gas. The country imposed heavy restrictions on coal use in northern villages. When winter arrived, thousands of families were left without heat. Since then, Beijing has scrambled to make sure there is enough coal to avoid a repeat of 2017. China's fallback to coal is a reminder that any anti-coal solution is likely to be a short-lived fantasy, far detached from the reality of practical energy demand.

China has learnt a thing or two from Western economies, where anti–fossil fuel policies have led to deaths in winter. During the winter of 2014–2015, the United Kingdom experienced 40,000 excess winter deaths (EWD) because of "fuel poverty." This fuel poverty was driven by skyrocketing electric rates resulting from the United Kingdom's drastic switch from coal to wind energy. This was the deadliest year since 1999–2000 (48,440), exceeding even "the flu-induced spike" of 2008–2009 (36,450). In each of the five prior winters, "England and Wales recorded an average of about 27,860 EWDs. Research by the World Health Organization concludes that from 30 to 40 percent of EWDs in Europe and Great Britain over that period are attributable to fuel poverty. If that is so, then fuel poverty caused an average of 8,358 to 11,144 extra EWDs in each of those winters in England and Wales alone" (Beisner 2015).

How can we expect those in developing countries to go without power for days or weeks while people in developed countries consider even brief outages, lasting a few minutes to a few hours, apocalyptic crises? In the developed world, fossil fuels have been used to generate energy for over two centuries. In most developed countries, oil is reserved for transportation fuel and literally thousands of byproducts and is rarely used to generate electricity. Natural gas and especially coal are the primary inputs for electricity generation in all but a few major economies of the world. Some countries are blessed with other resources like rivers, from which they can generate electricity using turbines in dams. Since the 1950s, advances in science and technology have enabled us to generate electricity from nuclear materials. Canada and France are prime examples of countries that rely on hydroelectric and nuclear power. The United States, Japan, India, China, Russia, and major European countries also use nuclear energy extensively. Countries that don't have these resources or can't afford to import fossil fuels tend to lack electricity or have it only intermittently. Interruptions in imports of raw materials needed for energy generation make developing countries highly susceptible to blackouts (World Bank and Enterprise Surveys n.d.). Though abundant in nature, wind and solar are the most difficult resources to harness. Their low energy and power density, combined with their intermittency, make them costly, unreliable sources from which to generate electricity (see chapters 12 and 14).

Developing countries have come a long way, thanks largely to fossil fuels. In my own childhood, fossil fuels transformed my life from the powerless dark nights of the 1990s to the bright, reliable power supply of the 2010s. Coal and hydro provided most of the electricity in my area. A coal shortage meant electricity interruption and hours of darkness. Industries came to a halt. Power blackouts were nearly daily affairs. I never thought I would see a day with uninterrupted electricity. Two decades later, India has advanced by leaps and bounds. Nuclear plants have increased our generating capacity, but coal remains our primary energy source, providing more than 75 percent of our electricity. India achieved an energy surplus in 2018. How? It increased its use of coal. Nonetheless, while the situation has improved dramatically since my childhood, India's electric grid, like that of most developing countries, is still not nearly reliable enough.

The poor in the developing world need empowerment through education, employment, and economic development. An industrial revolution akin to that in the West is what is really needed. Energy—abundant, affordable, reliable, instant-on-demand, unintermittent—is critical in this economic revolution. Unfortunately, instead of supporting energy development, Western governments, persuaded by those who fear catastrophic man-made climate change, are intent on banning fossil fuels. In the developed West, blackouts are very rare and are almost always due to opposition to the expansion of fossil fuel–based energy plants, inefficient grid management practices, and the premature introduction of renewable energy technologies that cannot match the capacity of conventional technologies. Rare in occurrence, they are rarely due to lack of resources. But blackouts remain part of everyday life for hundreds of millions in Asia, Africa, and South America. To become blackout free, developing countries must steer clear of restrictive energy policies.

Climate Fears and the War on Fossil Fuels

But the onward march of developing economies has been met with significant resistance from a section of politicians who have championed the global climate movement. During the 2000s and 2010s, claims of dangerous climate change began gaining momentum. Political leaders in developing parts of the world have become integral members (either by choice or coercion) of the global pact to reduce carbon dioxide emissions. In 2015, 195 countries signed the Paris Agreement. Signatory countries (parties) of this global climate agreement were expected to curb carbon dioxide emissions to keep global-average temperature increase below 2°C above pre-industrial levels—the science behind which is extremely volatile, unsettled, and debatable (Kreutzer et al. 2016, and chapters 3–9 above).

As a result of relentless pressure from the climate lobby, fossil fuel access and use are now under serious threat. "Net Zero," "Climate Action," "Build Back Better," and "the Great Reset" are some of the names for policies at the national and global levels aimed at expediting the transition of the global energy sector from fossil fuel to renewable technology, primarily wind and solar. The goal? Saving the planet from climate apocalypse. But there is a huge hurdle to overcome before making this transition a reality. Most of the world's primary energy comes from coal, oil, and gas. These fuels dominate the global energy sector because they are reliable, abundant, and affordable, not subject to the vagaries of weather or the cyclical lack of sunlight. Further, with constant innovations, the amounts of pollutants emitted from burning them have fallen dramatically in recent times. For example, between 1970 and 2000, emissions of sulfur and nitrogen pollutants from an average U.S. coal-fired power plant declined by 70 percent and 45 percent respectively (Vega et al. 2019), thanks to cleaner coal-burning technology.

Today, developing countries find themselves forced to choose between policies that produce enough energy for their booming economies but are condemned by the West and policies that fail to produce adequate energy but are approved—and funded—by the West. The West developed economically during the nineteenth and twentieth centuries while relying heavily on fossil fuels. Families rose out of poverty. Only a reliable and affordable energy source could empower emerging economies that became increasingly industrialized. Socio-economic standards eventually rose when much of the population turned from farming to manufacturing, retail, and service occupations (Goklany 2007; Simon 1995, 1998). At the same time, those who continued farming greatly improved their productivity, substituting gasoline- and diesel-driven machinery for human and animal muscle and using petroleum- and natural gas–derived fertilizers and seeds that were hybrid and eventually genetically engineered. Developing countries need, like the West, to use fossil fuels to propel their own economies (see chapters 12 and 13 above).

Another important factor is that energy demand will grow faster in developing than developed countries as they replace human and animal muscle and primitive windmills and waterwheels with fossil fuels. India's energy demand will increase more than that of any other country between 2021 and 2040 (Verma 2021). There is also a significant difference in the percentage of dependence on fossil fuel reserves. British Petroleum (BP) says India's oil consumption growth will be the fastest among all major economies by 2035 (PTI 2017). More than 70 percent of the electricity consumed in China and India—for around 3 billion people—came from coal alone. Africa's energy demand is projected to multiply six times by 2040.

Fossil fuels will be the key to many such developing countries' meeting their growing energy demand. In India, the use of recently discovered gas-hydrate reserves (USGS 2020) could mean a monumental shift in the country's energy sector, just as the natural gas revolution revived the American energy sector in the 2010s. India has the second-largest gas-hydrate reserves in the world after the United States (Jacob 2018). But just like in the United States and the United Kingdom, India is plagued by environmental groups that oppose oil and gas exploration. Soon after the government of India announced a contract for gas extraction, protests broke out in several parts of the country. Although portrayed as a common man's protest, the local people involved appear to be convinced by foreign environmental groups to believe that the proposed hydrocarbon drilling would result in permanent environmental damage (Jayaraj 2021b).

Renewables as a Solution Are Impractical

The media routinely report that the need to choose between fossil fuel–powered economic growth and poverty can be avoided by using renewable energy (Heginbotham 2018), primarily wind and solar, resulting in a win-win situation for both economy and climate (Dawood 2021). But this argument lacks support from real-world examples—that is, instances in which large-scale industrial and commercial energy demand is met predominantly by renewable energy technologies. Seldom do the media inform the public about the limitations of renewables compared to fossil fuels, nuclear, and hydro, which provide over 90 percent of the world's energy (BP 2021). Many countries now face blackouts because, pressured by environmentalists, they rely on wind and solar instead of coal, oil, and natural gas. The intermittency of wind and solar destabilizes electric grids (van Kooten 2019, and chapters 12–14 above), and the effect grows with the percentage of electricity derived from them. Even when they work at their optimum levels, the power generated from them is expensive, unreliable, and insufficient to meet the demand of huge cities and industries. Developments in battery technology are nowhere near solving the problem, nor can batteries provide adequate backup when there is no power from renewables (Lomborg 2022).

Consequently, the more energy an electric grid gets from renewables, the more it must depend on backup from fossil fuels or nuclear. That means consumers must pay twice for electricity: once for generating it from wind and solar and again for running backup plants even when they're not needed. Scientific studies have shown that shifts to renewable energy can drive up energy poverty, not decrease it (McGee and Greiner 2019).

A failure of Australia's renewable resources led to widespread blackouts in 2016 (Harmsen 2017). Germany is likewise facing the pain of blackouts from its reliance on renewables (Pandey 2021). Parts of California, Texas, and other renewable-dependent states in America faced blackouts in recent times (Shellenberger 2021). Abandoning conventional energy sources is suicide. The top users of fossil fuels are still actively generating power from fossil fuels and are helping other countries to develop fossil fuel technology. Not one major city in the world is ready to rely solely on renewables.

Emerging Trend in Developing Countries Offers Hope

Though reluctant participants of the international climate agreements, fast-growing Asian economies are devising plans for sustained use of fossil fuels well into the second half of this century. With each passing year, more and more people are becoming sensitive to the fact that climate change is not as dangerous as it was believed to be. Crop yields continue to increase, life expectancy has risen dramatically, and, more importantly, global temperature levels fall well below model forecasts (see chapters 4, 5, and 9 above). As a result, and because of their responsibility to meet growing domestic energy demands, countries are finding new ways to bypass pressure from international institutions like the United Nations.

The biggest challenge is to fulfill the emission-reduction commitments made under the Paris Agreement. Pulling out of the Paris Agreement is not easy, especially for developing countries that depend on the support of international institutions and aid from developed countries. There is no guarantee against international political bodies (like the UN) pressuring those countries that are overly dependent on international funding. In response, the biggest consumers of fossil fuels have adopted a new strategy. They affirm allegiance to the Paris Agreement by promising emission reduction and installing large amounts of renewables (though they still generate only a tiny proportion of total energy consumed), but they simultaneously develop their fossil fuel sectors (PTI 2021). The main nations that appear to be living out this dual life—of illusory climate-mitigation promises and a determined domestic policy to enlarge fossil fuel use—are China, India, Japan, Indonesia, Russia, and Brazil, with a combined population nearly half the world's total. Among them, China, India, and Japan have displayed open defiance of emission-reduction commitments by announcing new policies that guarantee an increase in the production, consumption, and export of fossil fuel resources (Jayaraj 2021a). The international climate community has been powerless when it comes to stopping the development of the fossil fuel sector in these countries. The reason for this is the nature of the Paris Agreement. It has overarching targets to reduce emissions and control the warming rate, but it does not stipulate emission-reduction targets for individual countries. Instead, each country determines its own contribution, and there is no enforcement mechanism. Most of the fossil fuel powerhouses are determined to meet their commitments to install more renewables. However, they have been unable to reduce their fossil fuel consumption. This means that fossil fuel–dependent countries are keener on achieving domestic energy development goals.

Fiona Kobusingye, former chairwoman of the human rights and economic development group CORE Uganda, conveyed this well in her article "End Environmental Experiments on Africans!" She writes,

> China and India put up with immoral eco-colonialism for decades. Finally, they had enough. They refused to be the environmentalists' experimental pawns any longer. They took charge of their own destinies, charted their own future, financed their own projects, and refused to be stopped again by anti-development green policies, politicians and pressure groups. (Kobusingye 2010)

Countries in Africa, Eastern Europe, and South America should follow the example set by the better-off developing countries like India and China, both of which have achieved rapid GDP growth in the past two decades by prioritizing fossil fuels.

Conclusion

Fossil fuels, especially coal, pose little threat to our climate, as explained in other chapters of this book, and they have also almost singlehandedly pulled many people out of poverty (see chapters 12–14). No major economic superpower in the world became so by depending on renewable energy. Each of the current economic powerhouses was fostered and supported by a vibrant and fast-growing fossil fuel industry. Developing countries can't afford more expensive, lower-yield energy technologies. They, like developed nations, rely predominantly on conventional energy sources like coal, natural gas, and nuclear to power their growing industries and oil to power their transportation. Without the growth of these industries, improved livelihood in poor countries is highly unlikely.

The threat from the pro-renewable, anti–fossil fuel entities could prove to be the biggest hurdle for the development of the energy sector in developing economies—and consequently for their conquest of poverty. The cure for climate change (in renewables) proposed by those convinced that the use of fossil fuels will cause dangerous climate change is itself dangerous to economic growth and human welfare. Marrying bad science with inefficient technology is a recipe for disaster. In most parts of the world, policies made at the highest levels decide the fate of billions. There is little room for error, and any discrepancy will negatively impact the lives of millions. The danger posed by these policies is real and immediate. Shutting down the largest energy source—coal—on the basis of erroneous scientific predictions about global temperature and adopting energy systems that fail regularly will produce disasters that dwarf any damage threatened by changes in climate. If there is any real threat, it is not from climate change—natural or man-made—but from powerful people in the United Nations and national governments who remain out of touch and infatuated with the dangerous notion of renewable transition solutions and continue to impose dictatorial, restrictive climate change policies on people who cannot defend themselves.

Restrictive energy policies are destructive. The world should not remain silent on the potential harm that these policies are causing and will continue to cause for the poorest in the world. A measured rebuttal is necessary at both the institutional and the academic level, helping policymakers understand the real dangers posed by green energy policies.

References

Al Jazeera (2021). "'Unprecedented' Power Cuts in China Hits Homes, Factories." September 28. Online at https://www.aljazeera.com/news/2021/9/28/chinas-northeast-suffers-power-crunch.

Beisner, E. C. (2015). "Fuel Poverty: The Deadly Side of Renewable Energy." Cornwall Alliance for the Stewardship of Creation, July 16. Online at https://cornwallalliance.org/2015/07/fuel-poverty-the-deadly-side-of-renewable-energy.

BP (2021). *Statistical Review of World Energy: 2021*. 70th ed. London: British Petroleum. Online at https://www.bp.com/en/global/corporate/energy-economics/statistical-review-of-world-energy.html.

Bradsher, K. (2021). "Power Outages Hit China, Threatening the Economy and Christmas." *New York Times*, October 13. Online at https://www.nytimes.com/2021/09/27/business/economy/china-electricity.html.

Dawood, S. (2021). "The Role of Renewables in Tackling Poverty." *New Statesman*, November 2. Online at https://www.newstatesman.com/spotlight/energy/2021/11/renewable-energy-tackling-poverty-developing-countries.

Goklany, I. (2007). *The Improving State of the World: Why We're Living Longer, Healthier, More Comfortable Lives on a Cleaner Planet*. Washington, D.C.: Cato Institute.

Harmsen, N. (2017). "AEMO Releases Final Report into SA Blackout, Blames Wind Farm Settings for State-Wide Power Failure." ABC (Australia), March 28. Online at https://www.abc.net.au/news/2017-03-28/wind-farm-settings-to-blame-for-sa-blackout-aemo-says/8389920.

Heginbotham, C. (2018). "Renewable Energy Can Help Solve Poverty." WindSoleil, April 21. Online at https://www.windsoleil.com/blog/2018/4/21/renewable-energy-can-help-solve-poverty.

IANS (2021). "230 Million Indians Pushed into Poverty amid Covid-19 Pandemic: Report." *Business Standard*, May 6. Online at https://www.business-standard.com/article/economy-policy/230-million-indians-pushed-into-poverty-amid-covid-19-pandemic-report-121050600751_1.html.

Jacob, S. (2018). "India Might Hold World's Second Largest Gas Hydrate Reserves." *Business Standard*, June 5. Online at https://www.business-standard.com/article/economy-policy/india-might-hold-world-s-second-largest-gas-hydrate-reserves-118060501430_1.html.

Jayaraj, V. (2021a). "Asia's Fossil Fuel Plans Oblivious to UN's Climate Scare." BizPac Review, August 12. Online at https://www.bizpacreview.com/2021/08/12/asias-fossil-fuel-plans-oblivious-to-uns-climate-scare-1117819.

———. (2021b). "Environmental Activism as Carbon Imperialism: Nightmare for the Poor." MasterResource, February 1. Online at https://www.masterresource.org/vjayaraj/environmental-activism-carbon-imperialism.

Kaze, O. (2022). "EIA Expects U.S. Fossil Fuel Production to Reach New Highs in 2023." U.S. Energy Information Administration, January 21. Online at https://www.eia.gov/todayinenergy/detail.php?id=50978.

Kobusingye, F. (2010). "End Environmental Experiments on Africans!" Canada Free Press, August 23. Online at https://canadafreepress.com/article/end-environmental-experiments-on-africans.

Kreutzer, D., et al. (2016). *The State of Climate Science: No Justification for Extreme Policies*. Washington, D.C.: The Heritage Foundation. Online at http://www.heritage.org/research/reports/2016/04/the-state-of-climate-science-no-justification-for-extreme-policies.

Lomborg, B. (@BjornLomborg) (2022). "Batteries won't save Europe....," Twitter, January 21, 6:32 a.m. Online at Twitter, https://twitter.com/BjornLomborg/status/1484489059435229193.

McGee, J. A., and P. T. Greiner (2019). "Renewable Energy Injustice: The Socio-Environmental Implications of Renewable Energy Consumption." *Energy Research & Social Science* 56 (October): 101214. Online at https://www.sciencedirect.com/science/article/abs/pii/S2214629618310971.

Pandey, A. (2021). "Spare Germany the Blackouts." DW (Deutsche Welle), September 23. Online at https://www.dw.com/en/climate-change-germany-renewable-energy/a-59237757.

PTI (2017). "India to Become the Fastest Oil Consumer by 2035." *Economic Times*, January 26. Online at https://economictimes.indiatimes.com/industry/energy/oil-gas/india-to-become-the-fastest-oil-consumer-by-2035/articleshow/56793984.cms.

———. (2021). "India's Coal Ambition Negating Its Climate Action, Feel Experts." *Economic Times*, August 15. Online at https://economictimes.indiatimes.com/industry/renewables/indias-coal-ambition-negating-its-climate-action-feel-experts/articleshow/85331754.cms.

Ritchie, H., and M. Roser (2022). "Access to Energy." Our World in Data. Online at https://ourworldindata.org/energy-access.

Shellenberger, M. (2021). "Renewable Energy Boom Risks More Blackouts without Adequate Investment in Grid Reliability." *Forbes*, April 20. Online at https://www.forbes.com/sites/michaelshellenberger/2021/04/20/why-renewables-cause-blackouts-and-increase-vulnerability-to-extreme-weather/?sh=2267d0d74e75.

Simon, J. L. (ed.) (1995). *The State of Humanity*. Cambridge, Massachusetts: Wiley-Blackwell.

———. (1998). *The Ultimate Resource 2*. Princeton: Princeton University Press.

USGS (United States Geological Survey) (2020). "Special Issue of Indian Ocean Gas Hydrate Expedition." News release, January 27. Online at https://www.usgs.gov/news/national-news-release/special-issue-highlights-one-most-extensive-gas-hydrate-datasets-ever.

Van Kooten, G. C. (2019). "The Problem of Renewable Energy and Intermittency." MasterResource, May 14. Online at https://www.masterresource.org/renewable-energy-fallacies/the-problem-of-renewable-energy.

Vega, F., et al. (2019). "Technologies for Control of Sulfur and Nitrogen Compounds and Particulates in Coal Combustion and Gasification." In *New Trends in Coal Conversion: Combustion, Gasification, Emissions, and Coking*, edited by I. Suárez-Ruiz, M. A. Diez, and F. Rubiera, 141–73. Amsterdam: Woodhead Publishing. Online at https://www.sciencedirect.com/science/article/pii/B9780081022016000066.

Verma, N. (2021). "India to Be Biggest Driver of Global Energy Demand Growth in Next Two Decades—IEA." Reuters, February 9. Online at https://www.reuters.com/world/india/india-be-biggest-driver-global-energy-demand-growth-next-two-decades-iea-2021-02-09.

World Bank and Enterprise Surveys (n.d.). "Power Outages in Firms in a Typical Month (Number)." Online at https://data.worldbank.org/indicator/IC.ELC.OUTG.

World Bank et al. (2021). *Tracking SDG7: The Energy Progress Report 2021*. Washington, D.C.: International Bank for Reconstruction and Development. Online at https://trackingsdg7.esmap.org/data/files/download-documents/2021_tracking_sdg7_chapter_1_access_to_electricity.pdf.

Appendix

Climate Change Papers You Should Read

by David R. Legates

This is an annotated compilation of published, refereed papers that, in my view, are fundamental to an understanding of the science of climate change. Millions of papers are published each year, and thus it is difficult to reduce the myriad of articles to just forty-four fundamental papers. Moreover, this annotated anthology is compiled from a climate change realist perspective, rather than an alarmist one. Its purpose is to present a list of the cadre of articles that convey the current understanding of climate change and to provide an interpretation of their significance from a layman's perspective. To be included, these papers must have been published in reputable refereed journals.

Although the papers span 128 years (from 1896 to 2023), most of the articles were published in the last fifteen years. In part, this is because the science is developing and more papers are written each year than the year before. Moreover, it takes several years before the full importance of a paper becomes apparent and it is vetted by the larger scientific community. But also contributing has been the nature of the development of the field of climatology over the past seventy-five years.

Originally, the study of climate, or climatology, was largely an actuarial science. Research usually focused on climate classification (identification of the various climates of the Earth) by examining the average and variability of weather conditions for a given region. In addition, much research was focused on applied climatology—the description, definition, interpretation, and explanation of the relationship between climate and a wide variety of weather-sensitive activities. Since it overlapped with many disciplines, applied climatology is very broad and eclectic, and thus the climatologist had to be conversant not just in climatology, but also in studies affected by weather and climate, such as agriculture, business, and engineering.

Climate change was not usually a topic of discussion since climate was described as "average weather." But in the middle of the last century, it became clear that climate itself was variable and subject to changes caused by natural variability and human-induced effects. This led to a new area of inquiry related to the study of climate dynamics, which fostered a plethora of questions related to climate change. Although recent research exhibits an inordinate focus on the impact of greenhouse gases and the behavior of climate models, climatology has emerged as a complex and sophisticated area of research, far removed from its roots as the simple study of the statistics of local climates.

Selection of these forty-four papers was a very difficult task and reflects my biases on what constitutes the cadre of important papers on climate change. I have tried to provide a viable cross-section of papers that addressed important questions as well as those which have provided breakthrough research that changed the course of climate change research. If I have omitted or missed a paper that you feel would be a better choice, you have my apologies.

Putting this list together has been enjoyable; I hope you find the articles and their layman's abstracts interesting as well.

1896, Arrhenius, S. "On the Influence of Carbonic Acid in the Air upon the Temperature of the Ground," *Philosophical Magazine and Journal of Science* 41, no. 251 (April): 237–76.

Svante August Arrhenius is largely viewed as the father of the "greenhouse effect" based on his work in this 1896 paper. It is often argued that this paper first quantified the contribution of carbon dioxide (or "carbonic acid," as carbon dioxide was called at the time) to the greenhouse effect and made significant speculations about whether long-term climate variability could be influenced by changes in atmospheric carbon dioxide. Although Arrhenius does not suggest that global warming will result from burning fossil fuels, he is aware that burning them will increase the amount of carbon dioxide in the atmosphere and explicitly suggested this in his later writings.

Although earlier important papers on this topic do exist (for example, J. Fourier in 1822 and J. Tyndall in 1859), this paper is more important because, unlike these other works that were largely chemistry experiments, Arrhenius tried to connect carbon dioxide effects to nebulosity (that is, obstruction of the atmosphere energy transmission by changes in carbon dioxide concentrations) by latitude and land versus oceans. Thus, this paper transformed the influence of carbon dioxide from a mere evaluation of atmospheric chemistry to a forcing of climate change within environmental science.

The latter portion of this paper argues strongly that proof must be found for the argument that carbon dioxide is largely responsible for the variation in ice ages. The paper dedicates much discussion to rejecting the hypothesis of James Croll regarding the importance of orbital parameters, which was generally discredited at the time but later modified by Milankovitch, and subsequently Milankovitch Cycles prevailed in 1976.

1920, Gradenwitz, A. "Carbonic Acid Gas to Fertilize the Air," *Scientific American* 123, no. 22 (November): 549, 557.

Gradenwitz's paper is a bit obscure, but I included it here because it is one of the first papers to note that carbon dioxide ("carbonic acid") provides a beneficial effect to plant life. By the time this paper was published, the utility of carbon dioxide in photosynthesis from intake through the stomata of leaves had long been known, and the assumption that carbon was acquired through the root system had been abandoned.

But Gradenwitz noted that the carbon dioxide concentration of the atmosphere was relatively low in 1920 (~0.03 percent) but had been much higher in earlier periods when lush vegetation was prevalent. He "suggested the idea of heightening the fertility of the soil by increasing [the carbon dioxide content] and thus producing conditions resembling those of antediluvian ages."

To validate his claim, Gradenwitz cites research from Germany, where combustion gases from blast furnaces were purified (to remove sulfur compounds) and then pumped into test greenhouses (with two others as a control group). Cucumbers and tomatoes within the enhanced–carbon dioxide greenhouse grew to almost twice the size of those in the control group. He concludes that "careful analysis has shown the increase in the percentage of carbonic acid in the air to remain far below the limit where the gas becomes liable to endanger the health of man."

1967, Manabe, S., and R. T. Wetherald. "Thermal Equilibrium of the Atmosphere with a Given Distribution of Relative Humidity," *Journal of the Atmospheric Sciences* 24, no. 3 (May): 241–59. The importance of this paper by Manabe and Wetherald is that it began the era of four-dimensional (three spatial dimensions and time) climate modeling. The paper discussed the development of the climate model using the current knowledge of climate at the time and explored the impact of a doubling of carbon dioxide on the global climate.

Crude by today's standards, the model focused primarily on the radiative convective equilibrium of the atmosphere using its moisture content as an initial boundary condition. The model illustrated that it was highly dependent on the moisture content of the atmosphere and how it was specified, as this early model used prescribed initial conditions of moisture content. The model also suggested that the surface equilibrium temperature was sensitive to forcings such as the solar constant, the concentration of ozone and carbon dioxide, and cloudiness.

Nevertheless, this early model suggested that "a doubling of the carbon dioxide content in the atmosphere has the effect of raising the temperature of the atmosphere (whose relative humidity is fixed) by about 2°C" (3.6°F). The authors also noted that the model lacked the extreme sensitivity to changes in carbon dioxide concentrations that others had suggested at the time.

1974, Bryson, R. A. "A Perspective on Climatic Change," *Science* 184, no. 4138 (May): 753–60. Bryson was an early climatologist who focused on climate change. This article appears during the height of the global cooling discussion but nevertheless provides a prescient evaluation of the processes that drive climate change.

Bryson argues that all climate forcings pale in comparison to the effect of the Sun. He notes that climate is thermodynamically forced; therefore, the overall response of the atmosphere "is an internal response to this forcing." Nevertheless, he shows that even small changes in climatic variables can produce significant changes in the environment. In particular, he argues that past climates can result from slight modifications to the general atmospheric circulation. He also notes that human activity can affect several of these so-called "control variables"; he cites atmospheric turbidity (for example, haze or volcanic activity) and carbon dioxide concentration as examples.

Moreover, Bryson further suggests that climate can change very rapidly. Although some parameters vary on long timescales (for example, orbital forcings), others (for example, volcanic activity) may change the atmosphere both rapidly and sporadically. Indeed, he argues that the speed of climatic change is dictated by "the time constant of the active layer at the surface of the Earth and the time constant of glaciers."

Overall, this is an excellent overview of climate change, even though it was written almost fifty years ago.

1976, Keeling, C. D., R. B. Bacastow, A. E. Bainbridge, et al. "Atmospheric Carbon Dioxide Variations at Mauna Loa Observatory, Hawaii," *Tellus* 28, no. 6 (December): 538–51. This paper touted the continuation of a long-term project to measure atmospheric carbon dioxide concentrations from a continuously recording, nondispersive infrared gas analyzer. The site—the Mauna Loa high-altitude observatory on the island of Hawaii—is situated 3,400 meters (~11,155 ft) above sea level on the north slope of the active volcano. The purpose is "to document the effects of the combustion of coal, petroleum, and natural gas on the distribution of carbon dioxide in the atmosphere."

This paper established (along with a companion paper documenting an observatory on Antarctica) an ongoing program that continues to this day. The existing record was extended by eight years (thus, analyzed in the paper from 1959 to 1971) and suggested the rise in carbon dioxide was about 1 ppm per year with a significant seasonal cycle, owing to the use and release of carbon dioxide by land plants and the soil.

The importance of this paper is its argument for a significant secular increase in carbon dioxide concentrations, in addition to its diurnal and annual oscillations. This analysis of the long-term increase in carbon dioxide set the stage for carbon dioxide to become a variable worthy of further study and research. The authors conclude that "the air... may be slightly influenced by local processes which cannot be expunged from the record, but the observed long term trend of rising carbon dioxide appears clearly to be in response to increasing amounts of industrial carbon dioxide in the air on a global scale."

1981, Namias, J., and D. R. Cayan. "Large-Scale Air-Sea Interactions and Short-Period Climatic Fluctuations," *Science* 214, no. 4523 (November): 869–76. Namias was a pioneer in the study of interactions between the atmosphere and the ocean. Beginning in the late 1950s, he began to realize that long-range weather forecasting required a "memory" of events beyond the time frame that the atmosphere could provide. While listening to a series of presentations on recent oceanic oscillations at a conference, he concluded that long-range weather forecasting might be driven by the coupled air-sea system. He noted the disparate timescales between the ocean and the atmosphere and that the "memory" could be imparted to the atmosphere by the longer timescale of the oceans. This paper is an overview of the research that followed that observation.

Coupling between the atmosphere and the ocean can provide keys to observed patterns present in both, individually and together. Anomalies in sea surface temperature "are about an order of magnitude more persistent than those of atmospheric circulations," and the article describes the process of including sea surface temperature patterns in long-range weather prediction. Despite these advances, however, the authors conclude that "our understanding is woefully inadequate to achieve reliability in prediction." Describing the phenomena is one thing; determining a dependence of the atmosphere on the oceans (or vice versa) is a level to which the authors believe science has not yet advanced. Nevertheless, we have seen some success in prediction on seasonal timescales due to the scientific advances in explaining climatic fluctuations. The authors conclude that "the present rapid pace of research implies that much better understanding will be achieved in the years to come." It has been.

1983, Philander, S. G. H. "El Niño Southern Oscillation Phenomena," *Nature* 302, no. 5906 (December): 295–301. Initial realization of the conclusion of Namias and Cayan (1981) came quickly. Much research had been focused on explaining the periodic warming of the central and western Equatorial Pacific Ocean, the concomitant relaxation of the Walker Circulation in the Equatorial Pacific, and associated global teleconnections that arise from it. Although the seeds of what is known as the El Niño and Southern Oscillation (ENSO) had been sown in the early years of the twentieth century, Philander's paper codified the extensive research in this seminal paper.

Philander presents the combined El Niño (the ocean) and Southern Oscillation of the Walker cell circulation (the atmosphere) phenomenon. An ENSO event occurs at a timescale that varies from two to ten years. During El Niño, both sea surface temperatures and rainfall in the tropical Pacific Ocean are anomalously high with weakened trade winds (east-west). This warming of the tropical Pacific waters leads to changes in atmospheric circulation which can cause severe winters over North America or create heavy rainfall in western South America, for example. Interestingly, these teleconnection patterns tend to develop in a remarkably predictable manner.

The paper discusses the 1982–1983 ENSO event which developed in a manner far different from the canonical ENSO events that had preceded it. This began research as to whether the oceans drive the atmosphere (more likely the usual pattern since the oceans have far more mass and momentum) or whether the atmosphere may, at times, drive the oceans (in this particular case, due to the eruption of the El Chichón volcano in Mexico in 1982).

1990, Lindzen, R. S. "Some Coolness concerning Global Warming," *Bulletin of the American Meteorological Society* 71, no. 3 (March): 288–99. By the end of the 1980s, global warming had taken hold in the climate community and many scientists were getting in on the research and funding bandwagon. Lindzen was one of the first scientists to raise concern publicly that a consensus on global warming may be unhealthy for climate science. Self-identifying as a skeptic, Lindzen presented his arguments as to why some issues left him unconvinced.

In particular, Lindzen noted that our considerable lack of understanding of climate processes does not justify a consensus. He cast doubt on whether the models would ever be capable of modeling the climate to the degree necessary to determine accurately the small increase in energy storage arising from a doubling of CO_2 granted that the inability to model the oceans at sufficient resolution was a formidable stumbling block.

The conclusion alludes to research on the Earth's "adaptive infrared iris" that Lindzen would expand upon more than a decade later. He suggested that model developments and observations over the next decade or two (that is, through 2010) should provide insight as to whether we would ever have a definitive answer to the question of the impacts of global warming, short of experiencing it directly. He concludes by stating that "there is one thing that is surprisingly clear right now; it is difficult to envision any practical action that will make much difference to the final outcome."

1990, Spencer, R. W., and J. R. Christy. "Precise Monitoring of Global Temperature Trends from Satellites," *Science* 247, no. 4950 (March): 1558–62. Global air temperature reconstructions were usually based on surface observations, which are limited, for example, by changes in station location, instrumentation, and observers and their practices, and by the fact that weather stations are most often located where people live—in mid-latitudes, at lower elevations, and along the coasts. This paper presents a summary of one of the major efforts to measure air temperature from satellite data.

The authors demonstrate that problems associated with air temperature measurements from surface-based thermometers can be alleviated by using passive microwaves from satellites. Satellites provide a near complete coverage of the Earth's surface (except for the extreme polar regions) in both space and time and are devoid of biases resulting from the local environment surrounding the thermometer. The authors conclude that "because of their demonstrated stability and the global coverage they provide, these radiometers should be made the standard for the monitoring of global atmospheric temperature anomalies since 1979."

Their methodology relies on passive microwave radiometers aboard NOAA satellites. These instruments measure the emitted energy from atmospheric ozone at frequencies between 50 and 70 GHz. Specific frequencies can be related to different levels in the atmosphere so that a vertical temperature profile can be estimated. Instruments are continually calibrated in orbit and new satellites overlap in time with old satellites to provide intra-satellite consistency. In sum, this methodology has allowed the development of the best time series of atmospheric temperatures dating back to 1979.

1996, Michaels, P. J., and P. C. Knappenberger. "Human Effect on Global Climate?" *Nature* 384, no. 6609 (December): 522–23. In the second IPCC report, the text "[T]he balance of evidence suggests that there is a discernible human influence on global climate" was inserted. This text was supported by a pattern-correlation-based paper written by

Santer et al. Michaels and Knappenberger's comment was one of the first to expose the convolutions behind the results of the Santer et al. research and, as a result, raise considerable doubt about the major message provided by the second IPCC report.

Santer et al.'s research focused on correlating the observed spatial patterns of atmospheric temperature change with those predicted by climate models driven by carbon dioxide, aerosols, and ozone. They found that since the correlation between the models and the observations increased during the period from 1963 to 1987, it was likely that the observations were driven by the changing conditions represented by the climate models.

The authors demonstrated that Santer et al.'s research conclusions were based on their cherry-picked selection of data only from 1963 to 1987. By extending the time period to include all the data—from 1958 through 1995—the authors were able to show that the correlation was valid only for the time period chosen by Santer et al. Outside of this time period, the correlation did not suggest a causal relationship between the observations and the model simulations.

1997, Legates, D. R., and R. E. Davis. "The Continuing Search for an Anthropogenic Climate Change Signal: Limitations of Correlation-Based Approaches," *Geophysical Research Letters* 24, no. 18 (September): 2319–22. To address the inserted phrase in the second IPCC report, these authors focused on the statistics associated with the centered-pattern-correlation-based paper written by Santer et al. While Michaels and Knappenberger focused on cherry-picking of the time period, Legates and Davis demonstrated that the centered pattern correlation coefficient is a limited and biased statistic in that it does not represent what Santer et al. purport that it does.

Legates and Davis's demonstration used a simple example to illustrate these problems. The authors took two spatial fields that change over time—one called "the observations" and the other called "the model." The two fields were identical at the beginning but diverged over time. Surprisingly, the centered pattern correlation coefficient increased over time, suggesting that the correlation between the two fields was increasing when, in fact, it was decreasing.

This example shows that the statistic "does not fundamentally indicate cases where a strong agreement exists between the model and observations" due to a number of well-known issues associated with simple linear correlation. The authors suggest an alternative approach to assessing pattern correlation that alleviates these problems.

2001, Lindzen, R. S., M.-D. Chou, and A. Y. Hou. "Does the Earth Have an Adaptive Infrared Iris?" *Bulletin of the American Meteorological Society* 82, no. 3 (March): 417–32. This paper describes the interaction between water vapor and clouds in the tropics, thereby suggesting that high cirrus clouds (due to their absorption of heat energy and limited impact on reflected sunlight) modulate changes in temperature. This provides strong negative feedback where changes in temperature are mitigated by changes in high cloud cover (~ −22% $°C^{-1}$).

Using high-resolution satellite data and a two-dimensional radiative convective model, the authors documented changes in cloud coverage concomitant with changes in sea surface temperatures, which were mimicked within the model. The loss of infrared radiation to space as sea surface temperature increased was facilitated by the shrinkage of the area covered by cirrus clouds in the vicinity of cumulus towers.

Reasons for this are quite detailed but are based largely on the fact that detrainment (that is, the transfer of air from rising motions to the surrounding atmosphere) of cirrus clouds decreases as a result of convection arising from increasing temperature. Calculations by the authors show that this negative feedback potentially cancels all positive feedbacks in overly sensitive climate models, or at least model water-vapor feedbacks. Calling this an "adaptive infrared iris," the authors demonstrate that this process controls outgoing long-wave radiation in response to surface temperature changes much as the iris of one's eye controls light on the optic nerve. Although the paper was initially met with strong criticism, a number of papers have since been published that confirm the existence of an adaptive infrared iris.

2003, Kalnay, E., and M. Cai. "Impact of Urbanization and Land-Use Change on Climate," *Nature* 423, no. 6939 (May): 528–31. Urban effects are one of the major influences on surface air temperature records. But since the early work of Landsberg and others, urbanization and land-use changes have been known to have a significant effect on the local climate. This article serves to highlight the impact of these important influences.

The authors note that both the increase in greenhouse gases and land-use changes, including the effects of urbanization and agriculture, are more likely to increase global temperatures. To assess the impact of land use, the authors compare the difference between observed air temperatures in the United States and surface temperatures derived from a fifty-year reanalysis (a combination of weather forecasts and data assimilation) that does not use observations of air temperature, moisture, and winds. These data were omitted from the reanalysis to guarantee that the reanalysis product was insensitive to land-use changes but reflected larger-scale climate changes (due to observations above the surface).

Results indicate that land-use changes skew apparent global temperature rise by about 0.27°C per century, or about a third of total warming since the 1880s; that is, *actual* global temperature rise over the period was about two-thirds of *apparent* global temperature rise.

Moreover, land-use changes are responsible for about half of the observed decrease in the diurnal (that is, day versus night) temperature range.

2003, Soon, W., S. L. Baliunas, C. D. Idso, et al. "Reconstructing Climatic and Environmental Changes of the Past 1000 Years: A Reappraisal," *Energy & Environment* 14, no. 2–3 (May): 233–96. Following the advent of the Mann et al. Hockey Stick, the existence of the Medieval Warm Period and the Little Ice Age was called into question. To assess whether the extensive research on site-specific paleoclimatic reconstructions over the last millennium indicates the presence of these warm and cold periods, respectively, the authors posed three questions to numerous individual climate proxies: Is there an objectively discernible climatic anomaly occurring (1) during the Medieval Warm Period (800–1300 AD), (2) during the Little Ice Age (1300–1900 AD), and (3) within the twentieth century (putatively the warmest period in the record)? The disparate nature of proxy indicators means that the results cannot be summarized as a hemispheric or global composite value.

The preponderance of the evidence from this extensive compendium of climate proxies "establishes the reality of both the Little Ice Age and the Medieval Warm Period as climatic anomalies with world-wide imprints" and corroborates the viewpoints held by Bryson, Lamb, and numerous other researchers over the preceding forty years. Moreover, many of the existing proxy records do not suggest that the twentieth century is the warmest period over the last thousand-plus years, thereby indicating that the temperature during the Medieval Warm Period was higher than it is today.

The authors conclude that Mann et al. misrepresent key sources on the temperature reconstruction of the Medieval Warm Period. Specifically, they state, "Many records reveal that the 20th century is likely *not* the warmest nor a uniquely extreme climatic period of the last millennium, although it is clear that human activity has significantly impacted some local environments" (p. 233).

2005, McIntyre, S., and R. R. McKitrick. "Hockey Sticks, Principal Components, and Spurious Significance," *Geophysical Research Letters*, 32, no. 3 (February). McIntyre and McKitrick also evaluated the Mann et al. Hockey Stick representation of Northern Hemisphere air temperatures. Through their research, the authors had uncovered that although undocumented, Mann et al. had employed a data transformation that had strongly adversely affected the results, which the authors characterized as "unusual."

Principal components analysis (PCA), used by Mann et al. to develop their global air temperature reconstruction, is a linear decomposition of the data; thus, derived components can be affected if the raw data are subjected to linear transformations prior to the application of PCA. Mann et al. subtracted the 1902–1980 mean from the raw data (a linear transformation), and since that mean is likely different from the mean of the entire time series (that is, from 1400–1980), the residuals are increased, which, in turn, inflates the series variance (a function of the square of the residuals). As principal components are calculated using a maximum-variance-explained criterion, hockey-stick-shaped patterns are likely to be selected. That methodology downplayed or removed the presence of the Medieval Warm Period and the Little Ice Age in the data.

The authors tested the Mann et al. method on red noise (data with no long-term signal) and found that the method "nearly always produces a hockey stick shaped first principal component." It also inflates the variance explained by that component as well (thereby increasing its apparent influence). In particular, the authors concluded that the reconstruction during the fifteenth century is not statistically significant.

2007, McKitrick, R. R., and P. J. Michaels. "Quantifying the Influence of Anthropogenic Surface Processes and Inhomogeneities on Gridded Global Climate Data," *Journal of Geophysical Research* 112, no. D24 (December). Trends in observed air temperature data are affected by changes in local land use, but these effects are not induced by global climate change and must be filtered out of the data. The authors argue that if such effects are properly removed, the filtered time series should be uncorrelated with socioeconomic variables since they effectively determine these extraneous trends. This article tests that hypothesis.

The authors' premise is that trends in a linear regression using lower tropospheric temperatures, atmospheric pressure, humidity, and coastal and latitude locations should be uncorrelated with population and gross domestic product. Results indicate that this premise is rejected with a high degree of statistical significance, thereby leading to the conclusion that non-climatic signals contaminate the gridded climate data. In addition, the contamination exists in countries regardless of their financial status but tends to be greater for countries where a growth in real income exists. After assessing for spurious correlations and intra-variable dependencies, the authors conclude that the influence of anthropogenic surface processes and inhomogeneities "leads to an overstatement of actual trends over land" and that "nonclimatic effects [reduce] the estimated 1980–2002 global average temperature trend over land by about half."

2007, Wunsch, C., R. M. Ponte, and P. Heimbach. "Decadal Trends in Sea Level Patterns: 1993–2004," *Journal of Climate* 20, no. 24 (December): 5889–5911. Combining oceanographic and meteorological observations with a general circulation model, sea level rise is addressed over the twelve-year period from 1993 to 2004. This database contains an extensive number of observations to provide the most detailed decadal assessment of sea level trends and factors that influence sea levels—including "about 100 million ocean observations and many more meteorological estimates." The data includes all types of observations including altimetric variability, profiles taken from Argo floats, measurements of sea surface temperature, and current hydrography.

Results indicate that although few locations exhibit statistically significant trends, some regions show spatially correlated signals with regional sea level change being driven directly by the general oceanic circulation. The authors' assessment is that estimates of global sea level rise are about 1.6 mm yr^{-1} (6.3 in. $century^{-1}$), of which about 70 percent results largely from melting ice. Their conclusion is that thermal expansion of sea water through warming of ocean waters is dominated by meltwater, even for interannual global variations. This estimate of 1.6 mm yr^{-1} is only about 60 percent of the pure altimetric estimate (that is, pure measurement of height) but, as the authors conclude, "the widely quoted altimetric global average values may well be correct, but the accuracies being inferred in the literature are not testable by existing *in situ* observations." Moreover, "systematic errors are likely to dominate most estimates of global average change: published values and error bars should be used very cautiously."

The telling quote from this extensive assessment by a well-recognized expert in sea level trends is that "it remains possible that the database is insufficient to compute mean sea level trends with the accuracy necessary to discuss the impact of global warming—as disappointing as this conclusion may be."

2010, Koutsoyiannis, D. "A Random Walk on Water," *Hydrology and Earth System Sciences* 14, no. 3 (March): 585–601. The usual scientific viewpoint is that natural phenomena (for example, air temperature, precipitation, streamflow) can be decomposed into deterministic (cause-and-effect) and stochastic (random) components. Science usually pursues identifying and explaining the deterministic component while the stochastic component is little more than "noise" that must be removed or otherwise dealt with.

Koutsoyiannis argues that uncertainty is an intrinsic property of all natural phenomena and is not simply noise in the system. Consequently, causality implies predictability, but uncertainty can grow over time to degrade predictability. This is a statement of how the uncertainties in initial conditions propagate to make predictability virtually impossible after some time period—like the chaos found by Lorenz. Koutsoyiannis goes further, suggesting that the deterministic and stochastic components are neither independent nor separable, but which one is dominant depends on the timescale of the prediction. He concludes that "long horizons of prediction are inevitably associated with high uncertainty, whose quantification relies on the long-term stochastic properties."

2011, Curry, J. A. "Reasoning about Climate Uncertainty," *Climatic Change* 108, no. 4 (October): 723–32. Regarding the concept of uncertainty, Curry suggests that climatologists in general, and the IPCC in particular, have underestimated uncertainty through oversimplification of processes and conclusions. This has resulted in "misleading overconfidence" as to assertions of climate processes and their conclusions within the IPCC assessments.

To improve the representation of our uncertainty about the climate system within the IPCC reports, Curry argues that a better characterization of it is required—confidence levels must be portrayed in a more realistic manner. Doing so would reduce the "'noise' and animosity portrayed in the media that fuels the public distrust of climate science that is clouding the policy process." In her view, the challenge of communicating uncertainty will reap benefits in the development of policy options and with policymakers and communicators. Moreover, she argues that a consensus approach, such as that used by the IPCC, enforces "overconfidence, marginalization of skeptical arguments, and belief polarization."

Curry concludes that "a concerted effort by the IPCC is needed to identify better ways of framing the climate change problem, explore and characterize uncertainty, reason about uncertainty in the context of evidence-based logical hierarchies, and eliminate bias from the consensus building process itself."

2011, Spencer, R. W., and W. D. Braswell. "On the Misdiagnosis of Surface Temperature Feedbacks from Variations in Earth's Radiant Energy Balance," *Remote Sensing* 3, no. 8 (July): 1603–13. The authors focus on the climate system and its sensitivity to radiative forcing, which, they assert, is the "largest source of uncertainty in projections of future anthropogenic climate change." From an observational perspective, they argue that this uncertainty arises largely from internal climate variability, most likely due to natural variations in cloud cover.

Daily estimates of reflected solar radiation and outgoing thermal longwave were obtained from NASA's Terra satellite. Selected climate model data from CMIP3 for 1900–1999 also were used to provide radiative fluxes as well as surface temperatures. Lagged regression analysis between the surface temperature and the time series of the net radiative flux (incoming shortwave minus the sum of the outgoing longwave and reflected shortwave) then was used to assess the magnitude of the internal radiative forcings and how (or whether) they corrupt estimates of feedbacks.

Results indicate that satellite observations and climate models differ widely on the response of temperature versus variations in net radiation. This difference was even greater over the oceans. Moreover, the discrepancy points mildly toward a lower climate sensitivity of the real climate system. The authors conclude that "atmospheric feedback diagnosis of the climate system remains an unsolved problem, due primarily to the inability to distinguish between radiative forcing and radiative feedback in satellite radiative budget observations."

2012, Lindzen, R. S. "Climate Science: Is It Currently Designed to Answer Questions?" *Euresis Journal* 2:161–92. Here, Lindzen addresses the fundamental question of whether we are capable of actually solving problems of climate science. He laments that progress in climatology has moved at a much slower rate than should be expected, caused to a large degree by the overbearing influence of politics. A change in the scientific paradigm of theory versus observation to an overt emphasis on model simulation and large observational programs is partly responsible.

This change, Lindzen argues, has obscured the potential for the convergence of ideas and thoughts through scientific testing and analysis by replacing it with a much less effective emphasis on institutional expansion. A growing university administration and the quest for grant monies have fostered a scenario of perpetual programs that grow larger each year. Scientific organizations become empowered where a small executive council can declare the intent of thousands of scientists and punish scientists who dissent.

Facilitating this change is extensive financial support from the federal government, which dictates scientific results through the establishment of the political agenda, and not the other way around. Throughout the paper, Lindzen discusses the origin of these changes and provides insight into the actions of both scientific institutions and scientists to bend data and theory to support the political narrative. He also discusses how dissension from the political agenda is dealt with.

2013, Essex, C. "Does Laboratory-Scale Physics Obstruct the Development of a Theory for Climate?" *Journal of Geophysical Research: Atmospheres* 118, no. 3 (January): 1218–25. Physical processes, including those that drive the climate, occur at a variety of temporal and spatial scales. Essex argues that climate modeling is akin to studying kinetic theory using laboratory-scale calculations—just like climate and weather, these processes operate at quite disparate space and time scales.

The article suggests how climate science should proceed. Despite much work to the contrary, no physical theory of climate currently exists. Climate processes are not simply averages of weather events; therefore, any solution must address this fundamental issue. Climate-scale observations are quite disparate from our everyday world. Weather events are invisible at the scale of climate processes, but climate processes are, in turn, invisible at the weather scale. Just as long-exposure (or slow-shutter) photography ignores high-speed motion and focuses on slow, deliberate changes, Essex calls for a change in the paradigm from classical physics to equations that describe, for example, "generalized wind," which he defines as internal energy flows divided by the entropy density (entropy measures the degree of disorder while density is the closeness of the atoms) and is measured in ms^{-1}.

Essex notes that this concept is still in its infancy since the equations are not closed, although the prospect of closing the system is possible—or maybe not. However, the article purports to study the climate from a more fundamentally appropriate perspective and freshen and revolutionize climate science.

2013, Ridd, P. V., E. T. da Silva, and T. Stieglitz. "Have Coral Calcification Rates Slowed in the Last Twenty Years?" *Marine Geology* 346 (December): 392–99. The authors reexamine calcification rates of 328 *Porites* corals (a genus of stony coral) from the Great Barrier Reef. Previous researchers had concluded that between 1990 and 2005, a dramatic decline in coral calcification of 14 percent had occurred. This decline was attributed to a consequence of rising carbon dioxide concentrations and a subsequent decrease in ocean pH due to the absorption of carbon dioxide (that is, carbonic acid) which causes the degradation of calcareous marine organisms. This previous analysis suggested that 1990 represented a tipping point in coral decalcification.

The authors note that this result is surprising in that a previous comprehensive study that utilized a subset of the data demonstrated that the corals had grown by 4 percent over the twentieth century. Research by the authors indicates that the apparent reduction in the calcification rates since 1990 was due to a combination of two factors. First, ontogenetic effects (that is, the development of an organism through tissue growth and cellular differentiation), coupled with the variable width of coral growth bands with age, were ignored. Second, "a systematic data bias [was] clearly evident in the last growth band of each core." In particular, the dramatic fall in calcification post-1990 disappeared when bands with a coral age of less than twenty years were excluded.

The authors caution that care must be taken to ensure that coral age is held constant. Young corals are more susceptible to changes in their environment, and thus future research must focus on sampling small colonies where early growth rates can be successfully measured. They conclude that "whilst large data sets of calcification rates of massive corals are an excellent archive of environmental effects on reef-building organisms, currently available data of coral calcification in the GBR cannot reliably resolve a systematic dramatic reduction in calcification in recent years."

2014, Happer, W. "Why Has Global Warming Paused?" *International Journal of Modern Physics* A 29, no. 7 (March): 1460003. Happer has written extensively on the absorption of electromagnetic radiation by the various molecules in the atmosphere, most notably carbon dioxide and water. This article, however, discusses these processes in less technical but scientifically correct prose.

The question posed in the title of the article addresses the so-called global pause in the increase in air temperature that had been observed since 1999. Happer notes that both the popular press and scientific journals noted this pause and pondered its cause. Rather than address it from a statistical perspective, as was the case in many other articles, Happer focused on a comprehensive assessment of climate forcings, with particular attention to the absorption of radiation by gases in the atmosphere. Although scientifically complete, this presentation is much easier for lay people to understand.

Happer answers the question "Why has global warming paused?" by showing that the popular notion that carbon dioxide is the climate control knob is a fallacy—carbon dioxide is a minor player in climate change.

2015, Legates, D. R., W. W.-H. Soon, W. M. Briggs, and C. o. B. Monckton. "Climate Consensus and 'Misinformation': A Rejoinder to *Agnotology, Scientific Consensus, and the Teaching and Learning of Climate Change*," *Science & Education* 24, no. 3 (April): 299–318. This is a follow-up to an article written two years earlier that had questioned the application of agnotology to politically charged debates. Agnotology is defined as "the study of how ignorance arises via circulation of misinformation calculated to mislead." A charge leveled against the first article was that the "overwhelming" climate consensus was being undermined by the fossil fuel industry and its allies through their "campaign of obfuscation." This so-called "climate misinformation" was based on postmodernist assertions that truth is determined solely by expert consensus and that near unanimous agreement on climate alarmism exists.

The authors evaluated this so-called consensus—that most warming since 1950 is anthropogenic in origin—determined by research from the authors' detractors and found that their claim of a 97.1 percent consensus was attained only by asserting that all research that did not explicitly state opposition to the consensus was, in fact, in agreement with it. Using data provided by the detractors in developing the consensus, the authors showed that just 0.3 percent of their sampled articles explicitly agreed with their consensus.

The authors concluded that agnotology and the definition of "misinformation" is a bogus claim since either side can accuse the other that its dissenting views are misleading. Nevertheless, the authors suggest that all sides should be presented in any scientific debate and silencing opposing views has no place in educating the public.

2016, Parker, A., and C. D. Ollier. "Coastal Planning Should Be Based on Proven Sea Level Data," *Ocean & Coastal Management* 124 (May): 1–9. Absolute sea level is the average height of the ocean above a fixed reference height whereas relative sea level is the sea level recorded by gauges. Absolute sea level is much more difficult to measure, since the land elevation may also be changing due to land subsidence or uplift, groundwater depletion, or sediment compaction. The authors argue that relative sea level is a better measure for proper coastal management as the computations of absolute levels are fraught with substantial errors that are greater than the observed rise.

Using data from 570 tide gauges of varying length, the authors show that the global relative sea level rise is +1.04 mm yr^{-1}, but if the analysis is limited to gauges with more than eighty years of data (100 gauges), the rise is only +0.25 mm yr^{-1}. Thus, sea levels are slowly rising, but they are not accelerating. Moreover, the authors show that larger trends in sea level rise using satellite altimetry can only be achieved by arbitrary adjustments to the raw data.

They conclude that "the effects of climate change are negligible" and "local patterns may be used for local coastal planning without any need of purely speculative global trends." Relative sea level rise is stable worldwide, such that coastal planning should focus on tangible short-term threats.

2016, Zhu, Z., S. Piao, R. B. Myneni, et al. "Greening of the Earth and Its Drivers," *Nature Climate Change* 6, no. 8 (April): 791–95. If carbon dioxide is indeed plant food, then one would expect that the Earth would exhibit significant greening. Using three long-term satellite records of leaf area index (LAI), the authors examined changes in vegetation greenness between 1982 and 2009. Results demonstrate "a persistent and widespread increase of growing season integrated LAI (greening) over 25% to 50% of the global vegetated area, whereas less than 4% of the globe shows decreasing LAI (browning)."

In an attempt to explain the reason for the relative greening of the Earth, the authors employed factorial simulations from ten global ecosystem models. The results indicated that fertilization from carbon dioxide increases explain 70 percent of the observed greening trend, while nitrogen deposition, climate change (that is, temperature increase), and land-use changes accounted for 9 percent, 8 percent, and 4 percent, respectively. Latitudinally, increases in carbon dioxide provided the dominant effect in the tropics, while climate change was most responsible for greening in high latitudes and over the Tibetan Plateau. In the eastern United States and southeast China, the dominant reason for greening was land-use and land-cover changes.

Further results of this paper included that future ecosystem models must include "the impacts of forest demography, differences in regional management intensities for cropland and pastures, and other emerging productivity constraints such as phosphorus availability."

2017, Ahlström, A., G. Schurgers, and B. E. Smith. "The Large Influence of Climate Model Bias on Terrestrial Carbon Cycle Simulations," *Environmental Research Letters* 12, no. 1 (January): 014004. In the quest to make climate models more realistic, detailed models of global vegetation and the terrestrial carbon cycle are being developed and used to study the carbon balance of terrestrial ecosystems. Unfortunately, the disparate models that have been developed exhibit large discrepancies in their predictions of changes in the carbon balance. This is because the large magnitude of carbon flows within the terrestrial biosphere affects the model-simulated feedbacks associated with changing atmospheric concentrations of carbon dioxide.

The authors suggest that the reasons for model biases and uncertainties include the implicit structure of ecosystem models as well as errors in specification of parameters and the concomitant forcing from the atmospheric component of climate models. They conclude that "the relative importance of these contributing factors to the overall uncertainty in carbon cycle projections is not well characterised." From model diagnostics, the authors show that biases and uncertainties in the parameterization of the carbon cycle bias the annual means of air temperature, precipitation, and solar radiation receipt. Consequently, changes in carbon sinks are affected by climate biases which could be responsible for up to 40 percent of the uncertainties in model simulations of carbon flows and sinks. As a result, the authors suggest "that climate bias-induced uncertainties must be decreased to make accurate coupled atmosphere-carbon cycle projections."

2017, Christy, J. R., and R. T. McNider. "Satellite Bulk Tropospheric Temperatures as a Metric for Climate Sensitivity," *Asia-Pacific Journal of Atmospheric Science* 53, no. 4 (November): 511–18. Climate sensitivity is how much the Earth's temperature will change following a specified change in the climate system, usually a doubling of atmospheric carbon dioxide. To estimate the climate sensitivity to human-induced forcings, the authors removed natural variability (caused by, for example, volcanism and El Niño) from the global mean lower tropospheric air temperatures from January 1979 through June 2017 and used the resulting time series to estimate the anthropogenic component.

After natural variability was removed (primarily affected by volcanic cooling in the early years), the estimated trend was +0.096°C per decade—a reduction of 0.059°C per decade over the raw trend. This updated value is essentially the same rate that the authors had calculated twenty-three years earlier using less than half the current time series. From this value, the authors estimated the transient climate sensitivity (that is, the change in temperature when carbon dioxide doubles) for the lower troposphere to be +1.10 ± 0.26°C, or about half the sensitivity obtained from climate models used in the *Fifth Assessment Report* of the IPCC.

Results indicate that climate models considerably overestimate the radiative forcing. Additional analysis shows that the enhanced sensitivity arises in the tropics, most likely due to the way models parameterize deep tropical convection or the partitioning of heat between the ocean and the atmosphere. Additional unknown natural variability in the models also could account for this enhanced sensitivity.

2017, Dayaratna, K. D., R. R. McKitrick, and D. Kreutzer. "Empirically Constrained Climate Sensitivity and the Social Cost of Carbon," *Climate Change Economics* 8, no. 2 (April): 1750006. This article focuses on assessment models that integrate the projected effects of climate change (including ocean heat uptake and equilibrium climate sensitivity—the effect that a doubling of carbon dioxide will ultimately have on air temperature) and socioeconomic projections (for example, population changes) with the economic response. The purpose of these models is to determine how much the adaptation to prognostications of climate change will cost and the discount rate (that is, the rate at which society will trade present benefits for future ones).

Traditionally, the equilibrium climate sensitivity has been taken from climate model simulations, but these authors used empirically derived estimates in these integrated assessment models. Their resulting estimates of the resulting social cost of carbon are much lower—by 40–50 percent in one integrated assessment model and more than 80 percent in another. The reason for the much lower estimates in the latter model is that it takes into account the potential regional benefits from carbon dioxide fertilization and increased agricultural productivity. This leads the authors to question whether carbon dioxide emissions are even a social cost. The authors conclude that the "use of empirically constrained parameters reduces uncertainty [in] the shrinking of the social cost of carbon range across discount rates."

2017, Harde, H. "Scrutinizing the Carbon Cycle and CO_2 Residence Time in the Atmosphere," *Global and Planetary Change* 152 (May): 19–26. Traditional assessments of climate change purport that the Earth's carbon cycle has been adversely affected by anthropogenic combustion of fossil fuels and changes in land use. This has rapidly and dramatically increased atmospheric carbon dioxide concentrations, which will remain resident for millennia. However, Harde argues that the classic representation of the carbon cycle is incorrect, and he proposes an alternative concept.

Harde suggests that the rate of uptakes by the natural sinks of carbon dioxide is proportional to the concentration of carbon dioxide. Moreover, paleoclimatic variations in carbon dioxide and the actual growth rate of carbon dioxide are strongly temperature dependent, driven by the vegetative response to enhanced carbon dioxide. Harde concludes that the anthropogenic contribution to the concentration of carbon dioxide in the atmosphere is only 4.3 percent and the increase in carbon dioxide for the Industrial Age is only 15 percent with an average residence time of four years.

Although the results of this paper may be controversial, the article is nevertheless useful for its overview of the IPCC representation of the carbon cycle and for Harde's discussion of the uncertainties associated with it. His assumption for a temperature dependency on carbon dioxide which is proportional to the actual carbon dioxide concentration is food for thought.

2017, Hourdin, F., T. Mauritsen, A. Gettelman, et al. "The Art and Science of Climate Model Tuning," *Bulletin of the American Meteorological Society* 98, no. 3 (March): 589–602. Most of the general population (and many climate scientists) assume that climate models take our current understanding of climate physics, parameterize that into a computer code model, and then run the model and present the results. What some knew and many others suspected was that climate models are tuned to provide certain preferred results, and the outcome of model simulations may, to some degree, be predetermined.

Most modeling centers tune the global net radiation at the top of the atmosphere as well as global mean surface temperature, focusing primarily on cloud parameterizations and their optical properties and fraction, convective processes, the reflectivity of ice, and the treatment of ocean-atmosphere interactions. This is a rather extensive list of components, most of which are the main uncertainties in our understanding of climate processes.

The authors conclude that "some diversity and subjectivity [exist] in the tuning process because of the complexity of the climate system and because of the choices made among the equally possible representations of the system." Moreover, the conclusion indicates that higher-order estimates made by the model—the equilibrium climate sensitivity, for example—also are tuned to keep it within the "anticipated acceptable range."

2017, Lindzen, R. S. "Straight Talk about Climate Change," *Academic Questions* 30, no. 4 (November): 419–32. Rather than focus on a technical issue regarding climate change, Lindzen departs from a scientific discussion to engage in a presentation of why, despite an overwhelming lack of evidence for terrestrial warming, alarmists succeed with their illogical arguments and, at times, blatant dishonesty. He is amazed that much of the general public believes the alarmist claims and attempts to explain why they are evidence of willful dishonesty.

Lindzen identifies a number of examples of how the alarmist claims are accepted without proof. They include what amount to no more than memes: the 97 percent consensus, the "Warmest Years on Record," extreme weather, sea level rise, Arctic sea ice, polar bear depletion, ocean acidification, and death of coral reefs. Despite evidence to the contrary, and even defying the logic of physics at times, these memes dominate the public discourse and are taken as proven fact. Recently, almost everything imaginable has been attributed to global warming. Spurious correlations aside, the EPA has made a considerable number of specious claims that global warming is responsible for numerous health issues and air quality deterioration.

Lindzen points out that the climate system is a highly complex system with lots of flows and variability—and yet we are supposed to believe that a 2 percent perturbation of just one variable (carbon dioxide) can wreak havoc on the climate system. He concludes that believing in this is akin to believing in magic, not science, and that "science is a mode of inquiry rather than a belief structure."

2018, Christy, J. R., R. W. Spencer, W. D. Braswell, and R. Junod. "Examination of Space-Based Bulk Atmospheric Temperatures Used in Climate Research," *International Journal of Remote Sensing* 39, no. 11 (June): 3580–3607. In the IPCC *Fifth Assessment Report*, tropospheric temperatures were identified as key variables in climate change since they are an indicator of heat accumulation, and thereby an indicator of the impact of additional greenhouse gases on the Earth's climate. The authors examine four satellite data records that estimate bulk temperature of the tropics; all have been updated since the *Fifth Assessment Report.* While all four datasets are highly correlated, as expected, they provide different estimates of the linear trend—the most important consideration.

Satellite assessments show that global trends range from +0.07 to +0.13°C per decade, with the rates being slightly greater in the tropics (+0.08 to +0.17°C per decade). This latter range is considerably less than the IPCC model simulations for the same period, where the rate is about twice the satellite estimate. In the tropics, the satellite estimates are less than those obtained from the models in the *Fifth Assessment.*

The authors conclude that satellites in the 1990s exhibited spurious warming, although this influence is minimized by the UAH estimates due to its merging process. Climate model simulations likely overstate the rate of warming due largely to "a misrepresentation of the basic model physics of the tropical hydrologic cycle (that is, water vapor, precipitation physics, and cloud feedbacks)."

2018, Lewis, N., and J. A. Curry. "The Impact of Recent Forcing and Ocean Heat Uptake Data on Estimates of Climate Sensitivity," *Journal of Climate* 31, no. 15 (August): 6051–71. Best assessments of climate forcings and estimates of their uncertainty are used to evaluate the equilibrium climate sensitivity (ultimate temperature increase due to a doubling of greenhouse gases) and the transient climate response (the temperature increase as of the time when greenhouse gas concentrations double). Such evaluations include the contribution from aerosol forcing and ozone, including contributions from volcanic activity and internal variability.

Results show that the range of equilibrium climate sensitivity (at a 90 percent level of confidence) lies between 1.05 and 2.34°C with a median value of 1.50°C. The transient climate response is between 0.9 and 1.7°C with a median value of 1.20°C. Although the lower bounds are increased slightly over a previous study ending in 2011, the upper bounds have been greatly reduced. When time-varying climate feedbacks are assumed, the equilibrium climate sensitivity lies between 1.2 and 3.1°C with a median value of 1.76°C. Biases arise from the estimation of future air temperatures, the variability in sea surface temperatures, and non-unit forcing efficacy. Thus, models are almost twice as warm as these observationally derived values.

The authors conclude that high values of the equilibrium climate sensitivity and the transient climate response from IPCC models "are inconsistent with observed warming during the historical period." In addition, these estimates suggest that warming will be only 55–70 percent of the warming proffered by the IPCC models.

2018, Zeng, Z., S. Piao, L. Z. X. Li, et al. "Impact of Earth Greening on the Terrestrial Water Cycle," *Journal of Climate* 31, no. 7 (April): 2633–50. This article opens with the statement that "leaf area index is increasing throughout the globe, implying Earth greening." It then proceeds to evaluate this statement by comparing satellite observations of Earth greening with climate model projections. Using a coupled land-climate model, model simulations are evaluated with satellite observations to determine the impact of greening on the terrestrial water cycle.

Results show that the increase in leaf area index over a thirty-year period (early 1980s to early 2010s) has caused increases in both land evapotranspiration (water put into the atmosphere through the transpiration of plants) and precipitation (because what goes up must come down). In areas where moisture was prevalent, this greening did not lead to decreased streamflow and soil moisture content because of the increase in both evapotranspiration and precipitation. In dry areas, soil moisture content was simulated to decrease, but the authors note that model biases may have played a role since precipitation is badly simulated, particularly in areas where precipitation is low.

This article suggests that increasing leaf area index has an unexpected contribution to hydrological enhancement (that is, more water fluxes), although some would argue this fact was expected. The authors conclude that a proper assessment of the hydrological cycle in land surface models demands an accurate representation of precipitation, which models do not simulate well.

2020, Koutsoyiannis, D. "Revisiting the Global Hydrological Cycle: Is It Intensifying?" *Hydrology and Earth System Sciences* 24, no. 8 (August): 3899–3932. One of the persistent claims associated with globally warming air temperatures is the intensification of the hydrologic cycle. With the proliferation of databases and advances in monitoring environmental processes, Koutsoyiannis revisited the global hydrological cycle to better quantify it and to test climatological hypotheses. He concludes that the data do not confirm established hypotheses.

Expected trends of most hydrologic variables, based on increasing carbon dioxide concentrations, should be monotonic; that is, a distinct trend should be present. By contrast, virtually all hydrological variables exhibit fluctuations from intensification to de-intensification with less variability dominating since 2000. Koutsoyiannis notes that both the terrestrial water balance and the oceans exhibit less variability today but much greater variability in the climatic past. He points out that the largest effect on the hydrological cycle is both exploitation of groundwater reserves and the melting of glaciers. Although groundwater use is anthropogenic and has a noted effect on sea level rise, the impact of human activity on glacier melt is more difficult to assess as research on ice loss at the poles attributes mass loss to changes in ice dynamics.

Koutsoyiannis concludes by suggesting that hydrologists should play a more active role in assessing climate change. In the last century, hydrologists supported hydro technology, water management, and risk assessment/reduction. They need to do the same in the arena of climate change, rather than taking a passive role by using questionable climate model simulations to assess hydrological impacts.

2020, Koutsoyiannis, D., and Z. W. Kundzewicz. "Atmospheric Temperature and CO_2: Hen-or-Egg Causality?" *Sci* 2, no. 4 (November): 83. In this article, Koutsoyiannis and Kundzewicz investigate the conventional assessment that an increase in greenhouse gases leads to global warming by evaluating the opposite: that global warming leads to an increase in greenhouse gases. They note that since an increase in air temperature leads to an increase in carbon dioxide concentrations, the relationship between carbon dioxide and air temperature is a "chicken or egg" question and thus separating cause from effect is difficult.

Examining the relationship between the two variables from the instrumental record (that is, 1980 through 2019) using time lags and reducing the possibility that results are merely statistical artifacts, they determined that soil respiration (plant respired carbon dioxide) and sea respiration both increase with air temperature. Moreover, chemical reactions, metabolic rate, and microorganism activity also increase with air temperature.

Noting that both directions of causality exist, the results show that the dominant direction is that increasing air temperature leads to enhanced carbon dioxide concentrations. Over the last thirty years, changes in carbon dioxide have lagged changes in air temperature by about six months to a year. The authors argue that due to the rise in air temperature, biochemical reactions through soil and sea respiration are largely responsible for increasing carbon dioxide emissions.

2021, Connolly, R., W. Soon, M. Connolly, et al. "How Much Has the Sun Influenced Northern Hemisphere Temperature Trends?

An Ongoing Debate," *Research in Astronomy and Astrophysics* 21, no. 6 (May): 68. Solar forcing of the surface temperature of the Earth has been of considerable interest since before climate change became a political issue. Here, the authors evaluate the effect of total solar irradiance on the surface air temperature trends in the Northern Hemisphere. The sixteen different measures of total solar irradiance fall into two distinct groups—those with low solar variability and those with high solar variability. Northern Hemisphere temperature trends were obtained from all available station data, rural-only stations, sea surface temperatures, and air temperature proxies obtained from tree rings and glaciers. Although the estimates that include urban stations exhibit greater warming than other estimates, all sources indicate warming since the late nineteenth century.

Linear least-squares were used to remove the solar influence from the air temperature estimates; the residuals then were correlated with the time series of anthropogenic forcings recommended by the IPCC. The disparate estimates of total solar irradiance suggest a range of conclusions from recent warming being mostly human-induced to recent warming being mostly solar-induced. The authors conclude that previous studies have simply assumed humans were the cause of recent warming without considering all estimates of solar forcing.

The authors conclude that studies must consider all estimates of total solar irradiance, not just those that underestimate solar influence. Moreover, researchers must consider differences between and uncertainties in estimates of Northern Hemisphere air temperatures.

2023, Lewis, N. "Objectively Combining Climate Sensitivity Evidence," *Climate Dynamics* 60, no. 9–10 (May): 3139–65. Assessments of climate sensitivity to a doubling of atmospheric carbon dioxide utilize many sources; the IPCC *Sixth Assessment Report* raised the lower limit from a likely value of 1.5°C to 2.5°C. Lewis evaluates the methods used to derive climate sensitivity and calls into question the use of a subjective statistical method where the researcher specifies an a priori distribution. Here, Lewis uses an objective method in which computed prior distributions are considered.

Results show that the resulting estimates of long-term climate sensitivity are much lower and with a tighter range of values than has been obtained with subjective a priori methods (that is, 1.55 to 3.2°C for a 90 percent confidence interval with a median estimate of 2.16°C). Lewis suggests that "this sensitivity to the assumptions employed implies that climate sensitivity remains difficult to ascertain, and that values [for climate sensitivity] between 1.5°C and 2°C are quite plausible."

This paper updates previous estimates of climate sensitivity by the author and others using more representative carbon dioxide forcings, employing a more realistic carbon dioxide–radiative forcing relationship, and using better justified and more recent information. Although values are higher than an earlier estimate by the author, differences are largely attributable to the base period used by the two articles.

About the Authors

E. Calvin Beisner is founder, president, and chairman of the Cornwall Alliance for the Stewardship of Creation, a network of Christian theologians, natural scientists, economists, and other scholars educating for Biblical Earth stewardship, economic development for the poor, and the proclamation and defense of the gospel of Jesus Christ. Dr. Beisner was associate professor of historical theology and social ethics at Knox Theological Seminary from 2000 to 2008 and of interdisciplinary studies at Covenant College from 1992 to 2000. He holds a B.A. in Interdisciplinary Studies with concentrations in Religion and Philosophy (University of Southern California, 1978), an M.A. in Society with Specialization in Economic Ethics (International College†, 1983), and a Ph.D. in Scottish History focused on the History of Political Thought (University of St. Andrews, 2003). His early childhood in Calcutta, India, where he observed both the beauties of creation and the tragedies of poverty, stimulated his later concerns for caring for both the natural world and the poor. He is the author of *Prosperity and Poverty: The Compassionate Use of Resources in a World of Scarcity* (1988); *Prospects for Growth: A Biblical View of Population, Resources, and the Future* (1990); *Where Garden Meets Wilderness: Evangelical Entry into the Environmental Debate* (1997); and more than a dozen other books. In 1999, he composed *The Cornwall Declaration on Environmental Stewardship*, endorsed by over fifteen hundred leaders from around the world and the founding document of the Cornwall Alliance. His work emphasizes the importance of responsible stewardship of the Earth and rigorous scientific inquiry, recognizing the complexity of climate systems, and evidence-based decision-making. He has published hundreds of articles, popular and scholarly; lectured at universities, seminaries, conferences, and churches in North America, Europe, Africa, and Asia; testified as an expert witness before committees of the U.S. Senate and House of Representatives; briefed the White House Council on Environmental Policy; presented an invited paper at a colloquium on climate change at the Vatican's Pontifical Institute for Justice and Peace; and spoken for multiple meetings of the International Conference on Climate Change. In 2014, the Heritage Foundation honored him with the Outstanding Spokesman for Faith, Science, and Stewardship Award.

John R. Christy (who made final edits to chapter 4 after its author's death) is the Distinguished Professor of Atmospheric Science and director of the Earth System Science Center at the University of Alabama in Huntsville, where he began studying global climate issues in 1987. Since November 2000, he has been Alabama's state climatologist. In 1989, Dr. Roy W. Spencer (then a NASA/Marshall scientist and now a principal research scientist at UAH) and Christy developed a global temperature data set from microwave data observed from satellites beginning in 1979. For this achievement, the Spencer-Christy team was awarded NASA's Exceptional Scientific Achievement Medal in 1991. In 1996, they were selected to receive a Special Award by the American Meteorological Society "for developing a global, precise record of earth's temperature from operational polar-orbiting satellites, fundamentally advancing our ability to monitor climate." In January 2002, Christy was inducted as a fellow of the American Meteorological Society. He earned a B.A. in Mathematics at California State University in Fresno in 1973; an M.Div. at Golden State Baptist Theological Seminary in Mill Valley, California, in 1978; an M.S. in Atmospheric Sciences at the University of Illinois in 1984; and a Ph.D. in Atmospheric Sciences at the University of Illinois in 1987. In 1973–1975, he served as a missionary teaching science in Nyeri, Kenya. He has testified as an expert witness on climate change over twenty times before committees of the U.S. Senate and House of Representatives. He has been an author or co-author of over one hundred peer reviewed publications in *Nature*, *Science*, *Journal of Climate*, *Journal of Applied Meteorology*, *Geophysical Research Letters*, and many other journals. He has been an expert contributor to the Intergovernmental Panel on Climate Change (1992, 1994, 1995, 2001, 2007, and 2013), the National Research Council Panel on Reconciling Observations of Global Temperature Change, and other governmental reports.

Michael Connolly is an independent scientist based in Ireland. He obtained a B.Sc. (Hons.) in Chemistry with a minor in Mathematics (University College Dublin, Ireland, 1971); an H.D.E. (University College Dublin, Ireland, 1972); an M.Sc. in Catalysis (Lakehead University, Ontario, Canada, 1974); a D.E.E. in Electronic Engineering (University College Dublin, Ireland, 1980) and a Ph.D. in Spectroscopy (Trinity College Dublin, Ireland, 1989). He taught mathematics and science in high school from 1971 until 1980 in Ottawa, Ontario, Canada, and Dublin, Ireland. He has worked as a lecturer and tutor in physics and chemistry (Lakehead University, Ontario, Canada), electronic engineering (at what is now Dublin City University, Ireland), computer science (at what is now Technical University Dublin, Ireland), and mathematics and statistics (at Trinity College Dublin). He also has considerable expertise in construction, qualifying as a plasterer in 1969 and an electrician in 1970 and building his first house on his own in 1975. Since then, he has designed and built hundreds of buildings and houses. He has been passionate about the environment since an early age. In 1975, he was a founding member of the Irish Solar Energy Society. From 1989 to 1996, together with his wife, Dr. Imelda Connolly, he built, operated, and owned the National Aquarium, which became the top privately owned tourist attraction in Ireland, where they succeeded in breeding over eight hundred species of fish—more, at the time, than all other aquariums in the world combined—and received international acclaim for rescuing, reviving, and rereleasing many distressed marine creatures. From 1991 to 1999, he was an expert participant in hundreds of nature and environmental radio and television programs and acted as an environmental consultant to several multinational corporations and on several large redevelopment projects. From 2000 to 2010, together with his family, he owned and operated three research farms, carrying out research in wastewater treatment and sustainable aquaculture in Union, Missouri, United States; Rathfarnham, Dublin, Ireland; and Offaly, Ireland. During this period, he was awarded several patents in sustainable aquaculture, wastewater treatment, and heat exchangers. Currently, he is continuing this research at the facility in Offaly, Ireland. Since 2018, he has also been actively researching climate change and other environmental issues at the Center for Environmental Research and Earth Sciences (CERES-science.com).

Ronan Connolly is an independent scientist, environmentalist, and writer based in Dublin, Ireland. He has been actively researching climate change since 2009. In 2018, he began working full-time on his climate change and environmental research through the international research group the Center for Environmental Research and Earth Sciences (CERES-Science.com). He has been interested in science since he was a teenager and received several awards in the Aer Lingus Young Scientists Exhibition for research into chloroplast migration in the *Caulerpa floridana* marine algae. He also was interested in mathematics (and competed in the Irish Mathematical Olympiad) and an avid computer programmer—in 1996, he came in fourth in the under-eighteen category of the IBM/DCU All Ireland Schools Programming Competition and was awarded the Professor Rykov Trophy for computer programming in 1994. His primary university degree was a B.Sc. in Chemistry with a minor in Mathematics

(University College Dublin, 2000), and his Ph.D. (University College Dublin, 2003) was in Computational Chemistry/Polymer Physics. His Ph.D. thesis was "Conformations of Branched Polymers," for which he was awarded the BOC Gases Award for best Ph.D. research in the department in 2003. In 2004, he shifted his primary research interests to environmentalism and began working with Dr. Michael Connolly (his father) developing sustainable methods of fish farming, aquaponics, and wastewater treatment. Together they also carried out research into developing low-cost heat-exchanger systems and new energy-efficient building materials and techniques. In 2009, they began systematically investigating climate change. After five years, they set up a website, OpenPeerReviewJournal.com, where they published their initial findings in eight scientific papers. Realizing that their findings could be of interest to the general public, they set up a separate website, GlobalWarmingSolved.com, in which, with Dr. Imelda Connolly, they summarized their findings in a less technical format. Since then, they have met and discussed their findings with hundreds of scientists around the world. They have sought and received useful feedback on their research, and this has led to several useful scientific collaborations with other scientists, including Dr. Willie Soon. They have published the results of several of these collaborations in peer reviewed journals.

Robert A. Hefner V is an entrepreneur, author, and speaker specializing in the global energy sector. His leadership, foresight, and innovative pursuits have profoundly impacted the fields of energy and technology. He has made significant strides toward the sustainable and responsible development of energy resources, ultimately aiming to alleviate poverty and contribute to global economic stability. In 2021, Hefner founded Hefner.Energy, which addresses the frequently destructive mischaracterizations of climate change while offering expert guidance on energy policy. The organization's mission reflects Hefner's commitment to balanced perspectives and recognizing the intricate link between environmental sustainability and global development. His nuanced understanding of the global climate extends beyond rhetoric, as evidenced by his accurate prediction of the global energy crisis in 2019 and his current insights into natural gas prices. Over his career, Hefner has committed more than $100 million to energy and technology businesses, including investments in minerals and royalties, privatizing water technology patents out of public companies, infrastructure, software, and bitcoin mining. This wide range of investments demonstrates his knack for identifying promising opportunities and aligning technology and energy toward a sustainable future. Hefner has been published across the ideological spectrum, transcending partisan boundaries and influencing energy politics at large. His influence has earned him the attention and respect of prominent figures in the energy field such as Marc Andreessen, Meredith Angwin, Alex Epstein, and Mark P. Mills. Above all, Hefner's work is driven by a sense of adventure, with his passion for innovation and exploration propelling his efforts to shape the energy sector positively. His contributions have highlighted the nuanced complexities of global energy issues, providing both a realistic perspective and offering innovative solutions. He earned a B.B.A from the University of Oklahoma in Entrepreneurship and Venture Management, where he also did extensive studies in aviation, religion, philosophy, and meteorology. Hefner is a contributing writer for the Cornwall Alliance.

Vijay Jayaraj is a multifaceted professional with an interdisciplinary background, bringing the Renaissance era back to the professional marketplace in order to deliver beneficial contributions to global society. His expertise spans across multiple schools of thought, particularly climate science, philosophy of science, philosophy of religion, and engineering. He earned his M.Sci. in Environmental Science from the University of East Anglia and a B.S. in Engineering from Anna University in India. A prolific writer about CO_2 benefits, energy, and climate science, most often from the viewpoint of the developing world, he is an environmental researcher currently serving as a research associate for the CO_2 Coalition. Before joining the CO_2 Coalition, he served as a research contributor for developing countries with the Cornwall Alliance. A former research assistant at the University of British Columbia, Canada, he has worked with nonprofits, policy think tanks, and consultancies in the spheres of climate change, energy, wildlife conservation, and public policy. His columns appear on RealClearEnergy, Townhall, *Washington Times*, Daily Caller, Patriot Post, The Stream, and many others. Jayaraj is a third-world-culture millennial who has lived and experienced social life in India, the United Kingdom, Canada, and Portugal. He currently resides in Scotland.

David R. Legates received a B.A. in Mathematics and Geography (double major) in 1982, an M.S. in Geography-Climatology in 1985, and a Ph.D. in Climatology in 1988, all from the University of Delaware. His expertise lies in hydroclimatology/surface water hydrology, precipitation and climate change, spatial analysis and spatial statistics, and statistical/numerical methods. Legates's dissertation was entitled "A Climatology of Global Precipitation" and focused on obtaining a better picture of global precipitation by incorporating a high-resolution precipitation gauge database that was adjusted for changes in instrumentation and biases associated with the precipitation gauge measurement process. His climatology of precipitation continues to be widely used, as it is the only global climatology available that addresses the gauge measurement bias problem. Upon receiving his Ph.D., Legates became an assistant professor in the School of Geosciences at the University of Oklahoma. He was granted tenure and promoted to associate professor in 1994. He became the chief research scientist for the Center for Computational Geosciences at the University of Oklahoma in 1995. In 1998, Legates moved to Louisiana State University and became an associate professor in the Department of Geography and Anthropology as well as a research scientist with the Southern Regional Climate Center. Legates returned to the University of Delaware in 1999 as an associate professor and was promoted to full professor in 2010. While at Delaware, Legates served as the Delaware state climatologist (2005–2011), director of the Center for Climatic Research (2001–2007), founder and co-director of the Delaware Environmental Observing System (2003–2011), and coordinator of the Delaware Geographical Alliance, now known as the Delaware Center for Geographic Education (2005–2022). For the National Oceanic and Atmospheric Administration, he was Assistant Deputy Secretary of Commerce for Environmental Observation and Prediction, detailed to the White House Office of Science and Technology Policy as executive director of the U.S. Global Change Research Program. Legates has testified three times as an expert witness before the U.S. Senate Committee on the Environment and Public Works and before both Pennsylvania House and Senate committee meetings on climate change. He participated in the historic joint USA-USSR protocol for the exchange of climate information in 1990, won the 2002 Boeing Autometric Award for the Best Paper in Image Analysis and Interpretation by the American Society of Photogrammetry and Remote Sensing, won first place in the International Statistical Institute (ISI) and Esri Paper Competition in Kuala Lumpur, Malaysia, and was awarded the Courage in Defense of Science Award in 2015. In 2021, he was awarded the Frederick Seitz Memorial Award and the Petr Beckmann Award. He has received over $7 million in grants over his career and has published more than eighty refereed articles. He has made more than 250 professional presentations. He is a senior fellow of the Cornwall Alliance and since early 2022 has served as its Director of Research and Education.

Anthony R. Lupo is Professor of Atmospheric Sciences in the Atmospheric Science Program at the University of Missouri. He earned his B.S. in Meteorology from the State University of New York at Oswego in 1988, and his M.S. and Ph.D. degrees from Purdue University in 1991 and 1995, respectively. His research has been in the areas of large-scale atmospheric dynamics, climate dynamics, tropical meteorology, and climate change, including modeling, and he has more than 160 peer reviewed publications across these areas. Additionally, he edited and contributed to three books on hurricanes, including *Recent Hurricane Research: Climate, Dynamics, and Societal Impacts* (published in 2011), and was the lead guest editor of the publication *Advances in Meteorology* for the special issue "Large-Scale Dynamics, Anomalous Flows, and Teleconnections" (2014, 2015, 2018). He has been a member of the American Meteorological Society since 1987 (Certified Consulting Meteorologist #660) and the National Weather Association since 1998. He was a Fulbright Scholar for the first time during the summer of 2004, studying atmospheric blocking at the Russian Academy of Sciences in Moscow. Additionally, he has served as an expert reviewer and/or contributing author to the Intergovernmental Panel on Climate Change (IPCC) (sponsored by the United Nations—World Meteorological Organization) and *The Report* of the Nongovernmental International Panel on Climate Change (NIPCC) (sponsored by the Heartland Institute) Assessment Reports. His other professional associations include the Royal Meteorological Society (Fellow), American Geophysical Union, Sigma Xi, Gamma Sigma Delta, Phi Kappa Phi, and the Missouri Academy of Science (fellow). He has won awards for teaching and advising at the University of Missouri, including the College of Agriculture, Food, and Natural Resources Senior Teaching Award (2006), the Outstanding Undergraduate Advisor Award (April 2008), and the University of Missouri Kemper Foundation Award for Excellence in Teaching (April 2008). He was awarded the Most Distinguished Scientific Achievement Award by the Missouri Academy of Science (2009). He was the University of

Missouri Professor of the Year (2010) and the University of Missouri submission for the SEC Professor of the Year (2020). In 2013, he was awarded by the Earth and Atmospheric Science Department at Purdue the outstanding alumnus for the year. He won a second Fulbright to teach and research at Belgorod State National Research University in Russia for 2014–2015 and fall 2017 and was selected to be part of the Fulbright Specialist Roster (2016–2023). Professor Lupo was part of the scientific committee for the First Conference on Atmospheric Blocking in Reading England (2014–2016). He was the third author of the book *Hot Talk, Cold Science*, 3rd edition, along with Professors Fred Singer and David Legates. Dr. Lupo is a contributing writer for the Cornwall Alliance.

Patrick J. Michaels was best known for his work in climatology, where he shared his knowledge and expertise as a scientist, author, speaker, educator, expert witness, and public policy influencer. He held A.B. and S.M. degrees in Biological Sciences and Plant Ecology from the University of Chicago and a Ph.D. in Ecological Climatology from the University of Wisconsin at Madison. He was a research professor of Environmental Sciences at the University of Virginia for thirty years, actively engaging in groundbreaking research, focusing on the analysis of climate data and studying the natural and anthropogenic factors influencing global temperature trends. He was the author or editor of seven books and of articles published in leading scientific journals including *Nature*, *Science*, and *Geophysical Research Letters*, as well as more popular outlets such as the *Washington Post*, *Los Angeles Times*, and *USA Today*. He was state climatologist for Virginia from 1980 to 2007, monitoring and analyzing climate patterns within the state and contributing to the development of local climate policies and initiatives. He served as president of the American Association of State Climatologists in 1987–1988, program chair for the Committee on Applied Climatology of the American Meteorological Society, director of the Center for the Study of Science at the Cato Institute, and contributing author and reviewer of the United Nations Intergovernmental Panel on Climate Change. His charisma and dynamic personality, coupled with his skills as a communicator and advocate for scientific accuracy, led to frequent appearances on television and radio news programs and as a speaker at science and policy conferences worldwide, in all of which he distilled complex scientific concepts into terms understandable to the general public. Michaels's lifelong contributions made a lasting effect on the intersection of climate science and policy. He popularized the concept of "lukewarming"—a term he coined to illustrate his understanding that the climate was warming, humans had something to do with it, but public policy shouldn't be led by climate models that tended to significantly exaggerate expected future warming. His dedication to scientific rigor made him a respected authority in the field of climate science, where he played a vital role in advancing the understanding of climate change and its implications. His dedication to scientific rigor made him a respected authority in the field. At the time of his death shortly after writing his chapter for this book, Michaels was a senior fellow at the Competitive Enterprise Institute and the CO_2 Coalition.

Bill Peacock has spent the last thirty-plus years working in and around the Texas legislature fighting for liberty by combining his love for theology, economics, and public policy. He is the policy director for the Huffines Liberty Foundation and the Energy Alliance. He teaches high school government and economics and hosts ExcellentThought.net, where he writes about the intersection of faith, culture, and public policy. He also hosts the *Liberty Cafe*, a podcast on TexasScorecard.com. Bill engages in research on a variety of issues, including energy, economics, regulatory, and fiscal policy, property rights, natural resources, public education, and the relationship between faith, free markets, and economic prosperity. One of his primary areas of research is energy. Since 2005, Bill has written and edited dozens of research papers related to the electric grid. The papers have covered competition in the generation, transmission, and sale of electricity, the cost of renewable energy subsidies, the effects of renewable energy generation on grid reliability, emissions related to generation of electricity, and how the growth of capital and its deployment through capital markets has led to the development of modern energy sources (for example, coal, oil, natural gas, and nuclear fuel), and great prosperity in countries that have allowed this to take place. His research has shown that recent efforts to turn away from capital-driven energy markets to government mandates and subsidies are leading to reduced economic growth in developed countries that will eventually result in energy poverty as is currently being experienced in most third world countries. He has appeared and been quoted and published in numerous media outlets, including the *Wall Street Journal*, *New York Times*, *Dallas Morning News*, *Houston Chronicle*, RealClearEnergy, Al Jazeera, *The Hill*, and the *Power Hungry Podcast*. He has a B.A. in History from the University of Northern Colorado and an M.B.A. with an emphasis in Public Finance from the University of Houston. Mr. Peacock is a contributing writer for the Cornwall Alliance.

Nicola Scafetta graduated in Physics at the University of Pisa and, in 2001, earned his Ph.D. in Physics at the University of North Texas. From 2002 to 2014 he worked as a research scientist at Duke University and taught astronomy and physics courses at the University of North Texas, Duke University, University of North Carolina at Chapel Hill, Elon University, and the University of North Carolina at Greensboro. From 2010 to 2014 he also worked with the Active Cavity Radiometer Irradiance Monitor (ACRIM) Laboratory (linked to NASA's Jet Propulsion Laboratory) on total solar irradiance satellite monitoring data. He is currently Professor of Atmospheric Physics and Oceanography at the University of Naples Federico II, Italy, where he teaches courses in Meteorology, Climatology, and Oceanography. In

2019, 2020, 2021, and 2022, he was named in the Stanford University global list of the World's Top 2% Scientists in various disciplines. Scafetta conducted interdisciplinary research in the areas of complex systems, astronomy and solar physics, solar-climate interactions, and climate change and addressed a variety of issues related to climate prediction and weather-related environmental hazards. He developed novel statistical methodologies for the analysis of complex multifractal signals, with applications primarily in astrophysics, geophysics, and biophysics. His research primarily advanced the understanding of changes in solar activity and climate variability driven by natural (primarily solar and astronomical) and anthropogenic factors. In particular, he studied and identified several natural climate oscillations over timescales ranging from interannual to several thousands of years and used them to develop empirical climate prediction models. These oscillations appear to be synchronized with solar activity oscillations and are also found to be associated with major gravitational resonances in the solar system. Thus, both changes in solar activity and climate variability appear to be synchronized by astronomical oscillations and could theoretically be forecast by them. Climate models were found to contradict each other and to fail to reproduce the identified natural climate oscillations, resulting in a significant overestimation of anthropogenic global warming while underestimating the solar and astronomical climate components. Dr. Scafetta has published several books and 153 papers in major peer reviewed scientific journals. He has also presented his research at more than 170 international conferences, workshops, and seminars.

Willie Soon, an astrophysicist and geoscientist, is a leading authority on the relationship between solar phenomena and global climate. In his thirty-two-plus years of singular pursuit, he seeks to understand the Sun-Earth relations in terms not only of meteorology and climate but also orbital dynamics of Sun-Earth–other planets interactions, as well as magmatic (volcanoes) and tectonic (earthquakes) activities. His discoveries challenge computer modelers and advocates who consistently underestimate solar influences on cloud formation, ocean currents, and wind that cause climate to change. Though a target of unethical attacks on his research and character, he has become one of the world's most respected and influential voices for climate realism. Dr. Soon was an astrophysicist at the Solar, Stellar and Planetary Sciences Division of the Harvard-Smithsonian Center for Astrophysics from 1991 to 2022. He served as receiving editor for *New Astronomy* from 2002 to 2016 and astronomer at the Mount Wilson Observatory from 1992 to 2009. He is on the editorial board of *Geoscience*, an MDPI publication, since 2020, and has served as review editor of *Frontiers in Earth Science* since 2022. Dr. Soon has been a visiting professor at the University of Putra, Malaysia; the Institute of Earth Environment of Xian, China; the State Key Laboratory of Marine Environmental Science at Xiamen University; and other institutions. Since September 2021, Dr. Soon has been affiliated with Hungary's Institute of Earth Physics and Space Science. Dr. Soon earned bachelor's and master's degrees in science and a Ph.D. in Aerospace Engineering from the University of Southern California. His honors include a 1989 IEEE Nuclear and Plasma Sciences Society Graduate Scholarship Award and a Rockwell Dennis Hunt Scholastic Award from the University of Southern California for the most representative Ph.D. research thesis of 1991. In 2003, Dr. Soon received the Smithsonian Institution (Smithsonian Astrophysical Observatory) Award in official recognition of his high standard of accomplishment. In 2004, Doctors for Disaster Preparedness honored him with the Petr Beckmann Award for courage and achievement in defense of scientific truth and freedom. In 2014, Dr. Soon received the Courage in Defense of Science Award from the George C. Marshall Institute, and in 2017 the Frederick Seitz Memorial Award from the Science and Environmental Policy Project. Dr. Soon is the author of *The*

Maunder Minimum and the Variable Sun-Earth Connection (2004). He is the co-author, with Sebastian Lüning, of "Chapter 3: Solar Forcing of Climate" in *Climate Change Reconsidered II: Physical Science* (Heartland Institute, 2013); the author of "Sun Shunned" in *Climate Change: The Facts 2014* (Melbourne, Australia: Institute of Public Affairs); and co-author, with Sallie Baliunas, of "A Brief Review of the Sun-Climate Connection, with a New Insight concerning Water Vapour" in *Climate Change: The Facts 2017* (Melbourne, Australia: Institute of Public Affairs). Dr. Soon has published 125 refereed papers and at least 37 book chapters and magazine articles and has given over one hundred invited presentations at universities and international and national meetings.

Roy W. Spencer is a principal research scientist at the University of Alabama in Huntsville, where he performs weather and climate research sponsored by the U.S. government and the state of Alabama. Previously he was a senior scientist for climate studies at NASA's Marshall Space Flight Center, where he worked on Earth observation missions for the Space Shuttle and International Space Station. Dr. Spencer has published numerous peer reviewed articles on weather, climate, and satellite remote-sensing techniques. Along with Dr. John Christy, he is co-developer of the original method for monitoring global temperatures from satellites, is a recipient of NASA's Exceptional Scientific Achievement Medal, and has provided congressional testimony on climate issues. Dr. Spencer has served as the U.S. Science Team Leader for NASA's Advanced Microwave Scanning Radiometer for the Earth Observing System. He is the author of the *New York Times* best-selling books *Climate Confusion: How Global Warming Hysteria Leads to Bad Science, Pandering Politicians and Misguided Policies that Hurt the Poor* (2008), *The Great Global Warming Blunder: How Mother Nature Fooled the World's Top Climate Scientists* (2010), and more recently *A Guide to Understanding Global Temperature*

Data (2016) and *Global Warming Skepticism for Busy People* (2018). Spencer's current research includes analysis of satellite data and climate models to explore climate sensitivity and developing a new technique for determining the extent to which global temperature trends have been spuriously inflated from the urban heat island effect. He has been a member of the board of advisors and a senior fellow of the Cornwall Alliance since its beginning in 2005 and currently serves on its board of directors.

Timothy D. Terrell is T. B. Stackhouse Professor of Economics at Wofford College, a liberal arts college in South Carolina, where he has taught courses on Regulation, Public Finance, American Economic History, and other subjects since 2000. Dr. Terrell completed his B.S. and M.A. in Economics at Clemson University, going on to finish a Ph.D. in Economics at Auburn University in 1998 with a focus on Environmental Regulation. He is senior fellow at the Mises Institute and serves as senior associate editor of the Institute's *Quarterly Journal of Austrian Economics* and associate editor of the *Journal of Libertarian Studies*. His research includes work on environmental regulation, property rights, and the ethics of market systems, which has led to dozens of publications in academic journals, edited books, and policy papers on environmental economics and other public policy issues, and testimony on Capitol Hill on environmental regulation. Additionally, he is author of numerous op-eds on economics and environmental issues. Recent work includes a paper in the *Journal of Environmental Economics and Policy*, "Carbon Flux and N- and M-Shaped Environmental Kuznets Curves: Evidence from International Land Use Change." He has given invited talks across the United States and at several universities in Europe and is a regular lecturer at the annual "Mises University" summer conference on Austrian economics. Dr. Terrell has also led several international study trips for students, including two to New Zealand that focused on environmental concerns such as invasive species and the littoral property rights of indigenous people. He blogs at MarketsWork (marketswork.com) and The Machen Seminar (jgmachen.org) and maintains a personal site at timothyterrell.net. A native of South Carolina, he spends his spare time hiking and camping in the nearby Blue Ridge Mountains and elsewhere in the United States. Dr. Terrell is a senior fellow, contributing writer, and member of the board of advisors of the Cornwall Alliance.

G. Cornelis van Kooten received his Ph.D. in Agricultural and Resource Economics from the University of Oregon. He has more than thirty-five years of experience in natural resource economics, including agricultural and forest economics, land-use management, mathematical programming, and the economics of renewable energy and climate. His interests range from agricultural and forest economics to development economics and computational economics. He has published more than 230 peer reviewed journal articles and 50 book chapters. Former Professor of Economics and Research Chair in Environmental Studies and Climate at the University of Victoria, British Columbia, he is the author or co-author of *Climate Change, Climate Science and Economics: Prospects for an Alternative Energy Future* (Springer, 2013), *Climate Change Economics: Why International Accords Fail* (Edward Elgar, 2004), four books on natural resource economics, and two books on agricultural policy. He is also the co-editor of four books. His book with Erwin H. Bulte entitled *The Economics of Nature* (Blackwell, 2000) is considered a classic reference book for researchers in the field of wildlife and public land economics, and his 1995 paper in the *American Journal of Agricultural Economics* on the uptake of carbon in forest ecosystems is the standard reference for work in the field of terrestrial carbon offsets. Professor van Kooten has been a consultant to industry, various governments and government agencies, the United Nations, the World Bank, the European Union, and a variety of nongovernmental organizations, including the International Fund for

Animal Welfare and the WWF (World Wildlife Fund). His numerous graduate students have gone on to work in the private sector, academia, and government. He earned the Canadian Agricultural Economics Society's Publication of Enduring Quality Award in 2011 and the Faculty of Social Sciences' Research Excellence Award in 2014. He is a fellow of the Canadian Agricultural Economics Society, former editor of the *Canadian Journal of Agricultural Economics*, a senior fellow of the Fraser Institute, and a senior fellow of the Cornwall Alliance.

Index

N

T